IMAGERY
Volume 2
Concepts, Results, and Applications

IMAGERY

IMAGERY

Volume 2

Concepts, Results, and Applications

Edited by

Eric Klinger

University of Minnesota
Morris, Minnesota

Plenum Press · New York and London

Library of Congress Cataloging in Publication Data

Main entry under title:

Imagery: concepts, results, and applications.

"Vol. 2."
"A selection of papers delivered at the 1980 annual conference of the American Association for the Study of Mental Imagery (AASMI)"
Bibliography: p.
Includes index.
1. Imagery (Psychology)–Congresses. I. Klinger, Eric, 1933- . II. American Association for the Study of Mental Imagery.
BF367.I458 153.3'2 81-8680
ISBN 978-1-4684-3976-2 ISBN 978-1-4684-3974-8 (eBook) AACR2
DOI 10.1007/978-1-4684-3974-8

Proceedings of the Second Annual Conference of the American Association for the Study of Mental Imagery, held June 20-22, 1980, Minneapolis, Minnesota

A Division of Plenum Publishing Corporation
233 Spring Street, New York, N.Y. 10013

Softcover reprint of the hardcover 1st edition 1981

PREFACE

The stream of our consciousness contains an almost unceasing parade of sensation-like experiences, even in the absence of any external stimulation to produce them. We experience picture-like things, sound-like things, and more; our experiences can resemble any of our sense modalities. These experiences are what we refer to by the phrase "mental imagery." The images need not be vivid. People who doubt that they experience visual imagery are often persuaded by a simple exercise: count the windows of the house in which you live. Nearly everyone performs this task by walking around the house in imagination while counting windows, or by walking through the house counting them from the inside. The imaginary windows seem to be set in visual space. There is a temptation to point at them with an index finger while one counts, even though the images may never become vivid enough to seem like an actual visual experience. But if they seem set in visual space, if they can be pointed at, they clearly constitute a sensory-like experience in some meaningful way.

The study of mental imagery was very much a central part of psychology until about 1920, when it went largely underground and nearly disappeared, especially in the United States, before reemerging in the 1960's. In the past two decades, work on imagery has steadily accelerated; and as the data have piled up it has become plain not only that imagery is an attractive research area but that the imagery itself constitutes a process quite central to human functioning. It follows that knowledge of imaginal processes provides a powerful tool, both for the theoretician of human nature and for the practitioner who seeks to bring about behavioral change.

This book presents a selection of papers delivered at the 1980 annual conference of the American Association for the Study of Mental Imagery (AASMI), in Minneapolis. It is a selective proceedings volume in the sense that the papers were resubmitted in their complete form for rescreening. The criteria for inclusion were chosen to be appropriate to the varied disciplines and professions represented and to preserve the character of the conference, but, in general, those papers that seemed both sound and instructive were retained. Inevitably, the selection reflects the diversity of the conference, an impressive diversity that runs the gamut from theoretical constructions to philosophical critiques to reports of experiments to descriptions of innovative treatment methods. In its diversity, it samples rather well the diverse field of imagery. It is not a handbook--not truly comprehensive--but in it the reader will find major expositions of theory, a survey of methods for assessing imagery, ground-breaking empirical work on synesthesia, fundamentally important work on imagery and hypnosis, empirical analyses of imagery in cognition that introduce the reader to a wide sampling of methods and results in that field, conceptual analyses of imagery techniques in psychotherapy and behavior therapy, and applications of imagery-based techniques to improving the memory of the older adult, training spatial ability, sexual adjustment, interpersonal conflict, grieving, drug abuse, and psychological problems in general.

The empirical results include some real plums. Perhaps most startling are the findings that excellent hypnotic subjects are remarkably prodigious fantasizers--have been since childhood--and yet are also well-adapted adults (Wilson and Barber); and that the much-publicized phenomenon of "divided consciousness" supposedly produced by automatic dissociation under hypnosis can be explained by experimental artifact (Spanos).

The book begins with some important theoretical contributions. The opening chapter brings together evidence from experimental and clinical research to support the argument that imagery is a conscious facet of processes that constitute most of a person's total psychological apparatus. Knowledge of the laws that govern imagery is therefore fundamental to a psychological science and provides powerful tools for changing behavior. In the next chapter, Jerome Singer, AASMI President-Elect and leading researcher in the areas of daydreaming and play, traces out the origins of adult imagery and fantasy in play and discusses ways to enhance play, family and television influences on play, and the implications of all this for adult inner experience. Tomasulo presents a developmental theory concerning the role of imagery in cognitive development, with the conclusion that "imaginal processing facilitates and precedes cognitive developmental stages." Gilgen's chapter deduces the information-processing capabilities necessary for survival of free-moving organisms and places human consciousness in the context of those requirements. Senchuk performs a philosophical analysis of Piaget's concept of images as interiorized actions, spelling out the theoretical ramifications of so considering them. List shows that images cannot be considered natural signs and therefore cannot, as Russell thought, form the basis for the meaning of words.

Part II of the book brings together work on measurement of imagery. Tower surveys existing measures and lists them by type of measure and by what it is that they primarily measure--state or trait, modality, and principal dimensions. This is likely to be the handiest quick-reference tool on the subject now available. Anderson describes a content-analytic approach to imagery measurement for variables not readily tapped by existing measures of formal imaginal properties.

Increasing evidence suggests that the "effective ingredient" in hypnosis is the subject's voluntary manipulation of his or her imagery. This evidence sheds light on the nature of hypnosis at the same time as it attests to the centrality and power of imaginal processes. The hypnosis section of the book, Part III, brings together three of the investigators who have done most to advance our understanding of these areas. Spanos offers an acute analysis of hypnotic effects on pain perception and an experimental analysis that reduces the apparent dissociation of "divided consciousness" to subjects' reporting practices under the demand characteristics of instructions and setting. Wilson and Barber describe for the first time the extremely vivid fantasy lives of excellent hypnotic subjects, thereby lending further support to experimentally based conclusions regarding the role of fantasy in hypnosis and expanding our knowledge of the relation of both of these to adaptation.

Part IV presents empirical work on synesthesia. Rader and Tellegen show that people who experience vivid synesthetic imagery score higher than others on absorption and are otherwise little different in personality, intelligence, and synesthetic translation processes, contrary to presuppositions in the field. Polzella and Kuna report that in Handel's music excerpts written in major keys tend to evoke yellow photisms and excerpts in minor keys blue photisms.

Part V presents a series of cognitive studies, showing relationships between conjugate lateral eye movements and daydreaming (Bakan & Glackman), relationships between properties of imagery, learning style, and divergent thinking (Sarnoff), an interaction between the originality of a learner and the effectiveness of experimenter-provided versus self-generated imagery in facilitating learning (Horng), factors that influence the creative use of imagery by children (Greeson), the relationship of self-consciousness to focusing ability (Kuiken), the use of mental imagery as a memory aid for the older adult (Mason), and the trainability of spatial ability (Rhoades).

Finally, Part VI provides an array of material for the clinical application of imgery. There is the elaboration of a general model (Strohsahl & Ascough), a review of imagery in behavior therapy (House & Campbell), a description of advances in psycho-imagination therapy (AASMI founder and Past President Joseph Shorr), the application of imagery techniques to interpersonal conflict (Mallouk) and grieving (Morrison), and the development of clinical applications of humor (Prerost), storytelling as a form of modeling (Van Wyke), movement (Dosamantes-Alperson), and art therapy (Spring), including art therapy with drug abusers (Virshup & Virshup).

The production of the book was an effort shared by a number of people. We are especially indebted for the typing and proofreading to Brenda Hayunga and Kelly Knutson, who worked with the assistance of Shelly Reese, Dana Meneghel, and other fellow students at the University of Minnesota, Morris. The Plenum staff, and especially Pat Vann, have been most helpful with the technical aspects of production. The conference itself could not have been the success it was without the superb efforts of Anne Dickason and Mary Walde of the University of Minnesota Department of Conferences in organizing the conference. Finally, of course, the support of AASMI's more than 350 members has made all of this possible.

Eric Klinger
President, American Association for the Study of Mental Imagery
Morris, Minnesota
February, 1981

CONTENTS

I. CONCEPTS OF IMAGERY

II. MEASUREMENT OF IMAGERY

III. HYPNOSIS AND IMAGERY

I. CONCEPTS OF IMAGERY

THE CENTRAL PLACE OF IMAGERY IN HUMAN FUNCTIONING

Eric Klinger

University of Minnesota

Morris, Minnesota

This paper presents three broad propositions regarding imagery. First, imagery partakes of processes central to human functioning. Second, control over imagery constitutes control over a large part of a person's total psychic apparatus. Third, intervention methods based on imagery therefore have great power. The paper is not intended as a comprehensive or critical review but rather as a broad overview intended to highlight the argument.

THE CENTRALITY OF IMAGERY

I would like to begin with a fact so fundamental and pervasive that we too often lose sight of it, as we do of the air we breathe. This fact is that humans are subsystems in a larger cosmic system--that people and their environments form a single system of interacting variables. As a result of their interactions, and especially as a result of natural selection, we human subsystems are designed around our environments, with a number of interfaces that differ according to the variables we are talking about.

For some purposes people's interfaces with the world are sensory and behavioral--our sense organs act as transducers to convert physical events into biological information, and our physical movements alter the world. For other purposes, however, including the psychologically most central purposes, the interfaces cannot be so peripheral. I shall argue that the most pertinent psychological interfaces must be located in the brain.

What happens in the brain to provide these interfaces? First, we must recognize that raw sensory information as it arrives at our end-organs cannot by itself constitute more than part of the total interface. We cannot see without a retina or hear without a cochlea, but neither can we see or hear with just retinal or cochlear patterns of stimulation. These can represent world events as they affect our end-organs, but however veridically end-organ sensations represent the world, they cannot interpret them. That kind of sensory information is too changeable and too complex to be usable as is. Actually, these end-organs are only a small part of the perceptual process and even, perhaps, of the sensory process more broadly conceived. As Eleanor Gibson (1969) and James Gibson (1966) have put it, our sensory apparatus is really a set of systems for picking up information--a highly active set of systems that make sensation an active process of coming to grips with the environment. That is, picking up information is a matter of focusing and distinguishing, searching and comparing. It is a process that we have in large part learned to do, rather than something that happens to us as we passively receive.

Perception is the larger process of making meaningful sense out of sensation. Perception arises out of the give and take--this constant interplay--between an active sensing organism and its physical environment. In what follows, "sensation" refers to the information-pickup aspect of this process and "perception" to the construction of meaningful sense out of the information. That one can talk about them separately does not, of course, mean that they are ordinarily separable in nature or that they take place in discrete phases--first all the sensation, then all the perception. The distinction is worth making, however, first because raw information remains meaningless if it cannot be referred to something inside the organism that gives it meaning, and second because sensation cannot be an active process without something to guide the activity. It is clear, then, that perception and even sensation depend on central brain processes. What might these be?

A great variety of theorists, in an equally great variety of ways, suggest that in order for perception to occur the brain must construct models. For some theorists these are models of the sensory input, for others they are models of the organism's own overall activity as it interacts with the environment. In any case, the brain must construct and store models so that it can later compare them with new receptor activity. Tomkins (1962), Sokolov (1969), Neisser (1967), Piaget (1945/1962), Leuner (1980)--even, in a way, Freud (1895/1960)--have posited nervous systems that model stimulation or the coping with stimulation. It is these models that complete people's interfaces with their environments.

What I here call "models" have been called by other names, especially by the name "schema." Neisser provides the following description of a schema:

> A schema is that portion of the entire perceptual cycle which is internal to the perceiver, modifiable by experience, and somehow specific to what is being perceived. The schema accepts information as it becomes available at sensory surfaces and is changed by that information; it directs movements and exploratory activities that make more information available, by which it is further modified. (Neisser, 1976, p. 54)

The idea here is that we may <u>sense</u> the world more or less directly, but we perceive in a meaningful way our own models or schemata of the things we sense. Whether or not there is an object out there, what we perceive is not precisely what out end-organs sense. What we perceive is our own model. This, incidentally, is in essence the view advanced so cogently by Silvan Tomkins in 1962.

To illustrate this view, consider two examples. When we look as something we seem to see it as it exists, in its essential entirety; but we really see in a psychologically usable way that which we expect, or (with somewhat greater delay) one of the expectable alternatives. We walk into a lecture hall, marvel at a large chandelier, and look at it admiringly. When we look away, we have little idea how many bulbs are burned out. If we look back to count those bulbs we will really see them, in a psychologically meaningful sense. Or consider another situation. You are looking at a list of graduating seniors in alphabetical order, each name followed by the person's major. If you wish to look for psychology majors, it is an easy task to let your eye run down the list and pick them out. But if you wish to look for majors in either of two fields--say psychology or human services--the task is much harder. It is as if one can maintain a set to find only one category at a time expeditiously. To use an ethological term, it is as if we can efficiently use only one "search image" at a time. Whether looking for members of one class or two we "see" the same list but we cannot reliably "notice" everything on it, even during a deliberate scan, without interposing some additional, very cumbersome processing steps.

The neural models that underlie perception do not appear in their final form instantaneously. A few of them we are probably born with. But for the rest, they come harder. Anyone who can remember seeing an altogether unfamiliar type of landscape or a completely unfamiliar object or figure knows that developing visual perception is in part a process of differentiation and of integration. Anyone who has learned a foreign language and recalls how hard it was at first to <u>hear</u> the sounds of the language--to make figure out of the blur of sensations--knows that developing auditory perception is a differentiating and an integrative process. And later, when we have overlearned the seeing and the hearing, we often perceive things differently from the way we sense them, as much research, such as that with eyewitness reports, has repeatedly shown. The neural models have become the more immediate, the more powerful determiners of behavior.

The neural models that make perception possible are not the only ones that exist. We also construct motoric models. Constructing the models that underlie smooth motor acts is also an integrative process. Furthermore, our motoric models are virtually always models of action in relation to sensory feedback. Perceptual and motor models in our head are not separate but intimately linked. They are themselves integrated, one with the other. To recognize the truth of these statements intuitively, recall the process you went through when you learned to drive a car or play an instrument. Learning to match up the right movements to your perceptions of what is going on was a large part of the learning process. It is also plain in our studies of stimulus effects on thought content that stimuli evoke not simply memories of scenes associated with the stimuli but often imagery of present, past, or future situations linked to actions, reflections, expectations, mental note-taking, etc. on the part of the subject. Thus, it seems likely that stimuli evoke both representations of stimulus input and representations of those operant acts that might get us to the goals of our concerns. These representations may, to be sure, occur under various transformations that give fantasy its fanciful or fused character. Finally, the fact that neonates can imitate facial expressions (Meltzoff & Moore, 1977) at an age so early as to rule out learning and other environmental explanations strongly points to at least one type of instance in which perceptual and motor schemata are innately linked. Thus, perceptual and motor schemata are not generally separate but are integrated, and they provide parts of one anothers' apperceptive mass.

The argument has so far focused on perceptual and motor models. It would be easy to extend it to all cognitive responses as well. Furthermore, since all that we perceive and intend we do in terms of these neural models, it is clear that our affective responses are also ultimately responses to the activation of these models. In short, when neural models are activated they constitute "implicit" or "covert" response complexes that include all of the elements necessary for psychological functioning--perceptual, cognitive, motor, affective--except sensory and effector elements.

Earlier in this paper I couched the argument in terms of an interface between world and psyche. What happens when the interface is broken, when we have only one side? It is not too hard to imagine what life must be like without the ability to apply our models to the sensory input or to our effector organs. The agnosias and apraxias would seem to fit this condition. It is even easier to imagine what life is like without sensory input and effector activity because these are to a degree controllable; and the act of imagining itself constitutes an instance of what then goes on. To the extent that sensory input and effector activity are reduced in consciousness, mental imagery takes over. We continue to perceive and we continue to act, psychologically speaking, even as we cease to sense or move.

We come now to a crucial proposition. It is that images and affects are conscious aspects of our neural models (or of integrated response complexes) when they become activated. In this sense, imagery is at the center of the organism's capacity for adaptive action in relation to the world. In Neisser's words, "Perception is a cyclic activity that includes an anticipatory phase; imagery is anticipation occurring alone" (1976, p. 147). But imagery anticipates action as well.

This is not to understate the problems of a theoretical model such as the one presented above. To mention two towering sets of problems: first, there is the problem of relating neural models to external stimulation--that is, how does the fitting of models to stimulation or the comparison of models with input take place? Second, how can models be constructed flexibly in accordance with highly variable conditions of sensory input and yet maintain the invariance necessary for retention and reuse?

Regarding the first of these problems, we have not moved much beyond Johann Friedrich Herbart 150 years ago. Perhaps the best that can be said at this point--metaphorically rather than directly--is that when our neural models (our images) are activated by sensory input, they are taken in tow, constrained by environmental realities. It is as if the availability of raw receptor information, or perhaps the activity involved in "picking up" this information, overrides the other factors that determine the flow of images. Similarly, neural models are constrained when activated in relation to effector activity. But in the absence of sensory or effector activity, they are still active, a flow of our inner human activity, without the constraints. This notion is consistent with the common clinical observation that mental images come most freely and interestingly with eyes closed and musculature relaxed.

Regarding the second problem, the dilemma of giving neural models flexibility and at the same time certain constancies, we may be able to find a solution by supposing that the neural models we construct are not static templates but are rather structures capable of representing motion, rotation, and transformations in form and amplitude, both cross-sectionally and longitudinally in time. Just as we might turn a picture until it seems "right side up," so perhaps we can transform our images until we find a "fit" between them and the world. Yet, the transformations do not violate the continuing unity of the neural model being transformed. Thus, it remains recognizably the same entity throughout the transformations in a kind of semantic constancy.

To summarize, then, the implications of the view being presented here: imagery represents some of the most central processes in psychological functioning. Whoever harnesses imagery holds a most powerful tool for controlling and altering human functioning.

SOURCES OF EXPERIMENTAL EVIDENCE REGARDING THE CENTRALITY OF MENTAL IMAGERY

I have quite deliberately presented the basic ideas of this paper in a rather general way that I hope has not seemed unduly ex cathedra. The theoretical view incorporates a sweep of territory that clearly exceeds the available evidence in scope. But this is not to say that its most basic premises are completely unsupported. We have clusters of experimental data here and there to shore the theory up at a number of critical points. I shall quickly indicate some of these.

First, we have a growing body of evidence showing that mental images are functionally equivalent in certain ways to physical sensations in activating visual information processing. This evidence has been brought together recently by Finke (1980). There are data here to indicate that imagery is governed by psychophysical functions similar to those of perception. At least in the area of size estimation, the psychophysical function for imagined objects is a power function that is the square of the function for perceived objects. It is as if, when we ask subjects to imagine something and to report on its size, they are perceiving a perception. When we ask people to imagine objects at different distances or of different sizes, they take longer to recognize or distinguish the imagined objects that are smaller or farther away, just as they do with actual objects of different sizes or at different distances. Then there is the "McCollough effect" (Shute, 1979), the color after-effect of looking alternately at black horizontal and vertical gratings on, respectively, blue and orange fields of color. When people are asked to imagine seeing the black horizontal and vertical bars while looking at actual fields of unbroken color, they subsequently report the after-effects of complementary colors. Thus, the McCollough effect obtains in imagery as it does in perception. It is well known that if people wear distorting lenses, so that, for instance, all objects seem shifted to one side, their perception gradually changes to compensate for the distortion. Whereas such subjects have great difficulty in walking around or grasping objects correctly just after putting on the lenses, their accuracy improves with time, and after removing the lenses they are left with a compensatory error that it takes time to unlearn. These after effects have been found, through more weakly, with subjects who were asked just to imagine making the kinds of errors produced by distroting prisms.

These are remarkable results, and they invite the criticisms that they must arise simply from subjects trying to be "good subjects," that is, from subjects who are role-playing their responses so as to conform with experimental demand characteristics. But Finke shows convincingly that deliberate simulation by subjects is a most improbable explanation. For one thing, these effects in imagery occur only with some kinds of perceptual variables. For instance, where the perceptual effects are produced at the retina rather than centrally, the corresponding effects are not found with imagery. Deliberately simulating subjects would be unlikely to make this distinction. Furthermore, with all classes of these effects that do occur in imagery, the effects are stronger for subjects who are vivid imagers than for subjects who are not. It appears that the reported effects are real and that visual perception and imagery share a common pathway.

It is nevertheless likely that neither the phenomena described above nor the conclusions that can be drawn from them are quite as straight forward as they appear. Some findings are perhaps conditioned on certain kinds of cognitive sets and might be subject to being overridden by cognitive manipulations. But in the main the evidence is persuasive.

A second cluster of data shows that mental images produce low-level motor effects, too weak to move effector organs but strong enough to be picked up electromyographically, and in patterns of muscle activation that correspond to the patterns of the imagined activity. Edmund Jacobson (1932) had already shown this to occur in the 1920s. Subsequent work--much of it by McGuigan (1970) and colleagues--has focused heavily on activity of the mouth and larynx. Reading silently produces motor activity in the speech muscles. Schizophrenics produce activity in the larynz as they hallucinate. These findings are consistent with ideomotor theories that have enjoyed prominence from Aristotle to James (McMahon, 1973). It is hard not to conclude that mental imagery can be partly uncoupled from effector organs but that it nevertheless represents the ordinary functioning of the psychological processes underlying action.

A third body of evidence confirms with increasing clarity that images arouse--or perhaps it would be better to say carry with them--emotional activity. When people are asked to imagine scenes that are happy or enraging or sad, they are left <u>feeling</u> happier, angrier, or sadder (Schwartz et al., 1976; Strickland, Hale & Anderson, 1975). When subjects are asked to imagine being shocked electrically every time they hear a certain tone, the skin conduction responses to the tone habituate more slowly for the vivid imagers than for the nonvivid imagers (Drummond, White, & Ashton, 1978). But apart from these kinds of experimetal evidence, it has long been plain subjectively that people can arouse, please, anger, frighten, and disgust themselves by conjuring up the appropriate images.

Finally, my own thought-sampling work shows that imagery shifts in accordance with cues related to people's current concerns during both waking states (Klinger, 1978) and sleep (Hoelscher, Klinger, & Barta, in press). That is, in the absence of actual steps that people can take in a particular situation to advance toward their various goals, their imagery still responds in a goal-oriented way, spontaneous and unbidden. This is obviously a highly effecient use of time and of one's biological machinery: When one's mind is not completely occupied with an immediate task at hand, it spontaneously shifts to other pressing concerns to work them over. In doing this, imagery responds to the same motivational principles that govern overt behavior, only without the constraints imposed by external reality.

To summarize the argument up to this point, I have tried to show that imagery represents anticipatory perception and anticipatory action, that it carries with itself emotion and that it obeys motivational principles similar to those that govern overt behavior, and that, indeed, it represents the bulk of human functioning save only for end-organ sensation and motor action. What we experience as imagery may be merely a conscious facet of the larger process, but it is a conscious facet of central human functioning.

IMAGERY AND INTERVENTION

I have spoken of imagery as "representing" central processes or as a conscious "facet" of central functioning. Is imagery perhaps really just an epiphenomenon, an indicator of what goes on inside that, like the movie on a screen, does not affect the events it represents? Clinical evidence indicates strongly that this is not the case, that modifying imagery modifies the models or schemata that underlie subsequent behavior. Hanscarl Leuner, who has contributed much of this evidence, writes of the "unity of symbol and dynamic intrapsychic structure" (Leuner, 1980, P. 44 [my translation]). Supposing that this is true, working on a person's imagery gives us direct access to the processes necessary for change. It would make imagery techniques among our most powerful techniques for intervening in people's lives. Through working with imagery, we can examine the models or schemata with which people meet their worlds and, with the collaboration of our clients, revise these models directly. What is the evidence that such methods work?

We have over the past two decades had a rapidly growing literature of case descriptions--articles by excited clinicians describing favorable outcomes with particular clients. The case literature has become so rich as to be increasingly persuasive in its own right. However, case studies can never be conclusive, given the selective nature of the decision to publish them and the selective nature of the clinician's observations in reporting them. Control groups are indispensable to judging the validity of particular therapeutic techniques.

Fortunately, controlled studies of imagery techniques in psychotherapy have begun to appear. Thus, Wachter and Pudel (1980; also summarized by Leuner, 1978) have shown that Leuner's guided affective imagery (GAI) method reduces the negative affect and somatic complaints reported by patients in comparison with a waiting-list control group. Clinicians other then the therapists, working from case notations and descriptions of symptoms, also judged the GAI group to have improved more than the control group. The treatment was limited for pragmatic reasons and for purposes of experimental design to diagnostic and orienting sessions plus 15 GAI sessions, and the latter were restricted to the more elementary motifs and techniques of the GAI system, thereby artificially limiting the effectiveness of the technique. The strength of the results obtained with this small sample is therefore particularly impressive. A two-year follow-up of the GAI group showed substantial maintenance of gains. In another outcome study of GAI methods, Wilke (1980) compared the process of two groups of ulcerative colitis patients, one treated by GAI and the other by psychoanalytically oriented psychotherapy combined with hypnoid relaxation. Both groups improved in self-ratings of well-being and somatic complaints as well as on measures of neuroticism ("Nervösität"), depression, and certain other self-report scales, and they tended to maintain their gains on two-year follow-up. The GAI group appeared to do somewhat better than the psychoanalytically-oriented comparison group but significance levels for the differences between groups were not reported. Duration of therapy was not systematically equalized for these groups, the GAI group averaging 21 sessions in 39 days versus 25 sessions in 50 days for the controls.

Outside the realm of GAI methods, Connella (1980) has reported a comparison of group psychoimagination therapy (Shorr, 1974; in press) with "traditional verbal group psychotherapy" and an unspecified type of control group, all patients being inpatients in a "multidisciplinary" treatment program for intractable benign pain. The treatment included 70 hours of group psychotherapy. With eight patients per group, all patient groups reported significantly reduced depression and pain after treatment with no significant differences among groups. Another recent investigation has explored the therapeutic contribution of guided imagery in rational-emotive therapy (RET) with outpatient neurotics (Lipsky, Kassinove, & Miller, 1980). There were four groups: RET with imagery was superior on all variables to both an untreated waiting-list control group and a group who received relaxation training and support. That is, patients treated with RET plus imagery scenes improved significantly more on measures of state and trait anxiety, depression, neuroticism, and irrational ideas. On two anxiety measures, RET plus imagery was significantly more effective than RET alone. RET with imagery was about equally as effective as a treatment condition that used RET plus role reversal. Since there were only ten subjects per treatment condition, significance here represents large absolute differences.

The controlled outcome studies of imagery therapy that have been completed to date thus indicate that imagery techniques indeed make a therapeutic contribution and fare at least as well as the alternatives with which they have been compared, if not better at a cost that also compare's favorably. Furthermore, there are encouraging indications that the therapeutic gains are enduring. Obviously, the outcome studies that have appeared constitute only a beginning. They need to be replicated with varying populations of patients and therapists and focused on particular techniques. It is therefore too early to say with assurance that particular imaginal components in these therapies are responsible for their effectiveness. However, when viewed in combination with the accumulating laboratory evidence regarding imagery and with the evidence for the efficacy of mentally practicing motor skills, it seems reasonable to conclude provisionally that imagery techniques offer tools as powerful for psychological intervention as the view sketched earlier in this paper promises; and the evidence that they are effective supports the theroy that imagery constitutes a set of processes at the center of human psychological functioning.

Because of the dramatic personal transformations Leuner and his coworkers have observed in their patients, he speaks of his imagery methods as tantamount to "experimental psychoanalysis." In a very different vein, experimental investigators have repeatedly demonstrated that when people mentally practice motor skills that they have already partly learned, the mental practice improves their motor performance (Beasley, 1979; Jeffrey, 1976; Rawlings & Rawlings, 1974; Rawlings, Rawlings, Chen & Yilk, 1972; Richardson, 1967 a & b; Smyth, 1975; Start & Richardson, 1964; Summers, 1977; Ulich, 1967), the moreso as their imagery is vivid and appropriate to the modality being practiced (Rawlings & Rawlings, 1972; Start & Richardson, 1964; White, Ashton, & Lewis, 1979). (Weakness in some of Smyth's results is probably attributable to design factors such as complete lack of experience with the task before beginning mental practice. The implication is clear: manipulating imagery constitutes a manipulation of the processes the imagery represents. It is not necessary to suppose that the imagery represents the entirety of those processes--not necessary to revive the debate about the existence of imageless thought--to recognize that manipulating a conscious facet of a larger process forces changes on the larger process as well. The laws that govern those relationships still remain to be worked out.

SUMMARY

Imagery is a part of the human organism's psychological interface with the surrounding environment. It is a conscious aspect of the neural modeling that underlies both perception and motor activity. The flow of imagery encompasses perceptual, cognitive, motor, and affective elements. Imagery is not simply an epiphenomenal reflection of these processes but is rather an integral part of them. Therefore, imagery represents some of the most central processes in psychological functioning--indeed, most of our psychological being, save chiefly receptor and effector activity. Although it continues to be true that much psychological processing goes on outside of conscious awareness, imagery provides access to larger psychological processes. It follows that manipulation of imagery, as in fantasy, provides a powerful tool for psychological intervention. The beginning flow of controlled studies of imagery methods in psychotherapy support this expectation in showing positive therapeutic results that endure after the end of therapy and are achieved at economical cost.

REFERENCES

Beasley, W. F. The effect of physical and mental practice of psychomotor skills on chemistry student laboratory performance. (Unpublished doctoral dissertation, University of Maryland, 1978.) Dissertation Abstracts International, 1979, 39 (9-A), 5428.

Connella, J. The effects of psycho-imagination therapy on the treatment outcome of chronic benign pain patients. Imagery: Bulletin of the American Association for the Study of Mental Imagery, 1980, 3, (3), 6-7.

Drummond, P., White, K. and Ashton, R. Imagery vividness affects habituation rate. Psychophysiology, 1978, 15, 193-195.

Finke, R. A. Levels of equivalence in imagery and perception. Psychological Review, 1980, 87, 113-132.

Freud, S. Project for a scientific psychology. In J. Strachey (Ed.), The standard edition of the complete psychological works of Sigmund Freud (Vol. 1). London: Hogarth, 1960. (First published in 1895..)

Gibson, E. J. Principles of perceptual learning and development. New York: Appleton-Century-Crofts, 1969.

Gibson, J. J. The senses considered as perceptual systems. Boston: Houghton-Mifflin, 1966.

Hoelscher, T. J., Klinger, E., and Barta, S. G. Incorporation of concern- and nonconcern-related verbal stimuli into dream content. Journal of Abnormal Psychology, in press.

Jacobson, E. The electrophysiology of mental activities. American Journal of Psychology, 1932, 44, 677-694.

Jeffrey, R. W. The influence of symbolic and motor rehearsal in observational learning. Journal of Research Personality, 1976, 10, 116-127.

Klinger, E. Modes of normal conscious flow. In K. S. Pope and J. L. Singer (Eds.) The stream of consciousness: Scientific investigations into the flow of human experience. New York: Plenum, 1978.

Leuner, H. Basic principles and therapeutic efficacy of guided affective imagery (GAI). In J. L. Singer and K. S. Pope (Eds.), The power of human imagination: New methods in psychotherapy. New York: Plenum, 1978.

Leuner, H. Grundlinien des Katathymen Bilderleben aus neuerer Sicht. In H. Leuner (Ed.), Kathathymes Bilderleben: Ergebnisse in Theorie und Praxis. Bern: Huber, 1980.

Lipsky, M. J., Kassinove, H., & Miller, N.J. Effects of rational-emotive therapy, rational role reversal, and rational-emotive imagery on the emotional adjustment of community mental health center patients. Journal of Consulting and Clinical Psychology, 1980, 48, 366-374.

McGuigan, F. J. Covert oral behavior during the silent performance of language tasks. Psychological Bulletin, 1970, 74, 309-326.

McMahon, C. Images as motives and motivators: A historical perspective. American Journal of Psychology, 1973, 86, 465-490.

Meltzoff, A. N., and Moore, M. K. Imitation of facial and manual gestures by human neonates. Science, 1977, 198, 75-78.

Neisser, U. Cognitive psychology. New York: Appleton-Century-Crofts, 1967.

Neisser, U. Cognition and reality. San Francisco: Freeman, 1976.

Piaget, J. Play, dreams, and imitation in childhood. New York: Norton, 1962. (First published in 1945.)

Rawlings, E. I., and Rawlings, I. L. Rotary pursuit tracking following mental rehearsal as a function of voluntary control of visual imagery. Perceptual and Motor Skills, 1974, 38, 302.

Rawlings, E. I., Rawlings, I. L., Chen, S. S., and Yilk, M. D. The facilitating effects of mental rehearsal in the acquisition of rotary pursuit tracking. Psychonomic Science, 1972, 26, 71-73.

Richardson, A. Mental practice: A review and discussion. I. Research Quartly, 1967, 38, 95-107. (a)

Richardson, A. Mental practice: A review and discussion. II. Research Quartly, 1967, 38, 263-273. (b)

Schwartz, G. E., Fair, P. L., Salt, P., Mandel, M. R., & Klerman, G. L. Facial muscle patterning to affective imagery in depressed and nondepressed subjects. Science, 1976, 192, 489-491.

Shorr, J. E. Psychotherapy through imagery. New York: Intercontinental Medical Book Corporation, 1974.

Shorr, J. E. An overview of psycho-imagination therapy. In R. Corsini (Ed.), Innovative psychotherapies. New York: Wiley, in press.

Shute, C. C. D. The McCollough effect: An indicator of central neurotransmitter activity. Cambridge: Cambridge University Press, 1979.

Smyth, M. M. The role of mental practice in skill acquisition. Journal of Motor Behavior, 1975, 7, 199-206.

Sokolov, E. N. The modeling properties of the nervous system. In M. Cole and I. Maltzman (Eds.), A handbook of contemporary Soviet psychology. New York: Basic Books, 1969.

Start, K. B., and Richardson, A. Imagery and mental practice. British Journal of Educational Psychology, 1964, 34, 280-284.

Strickland, B. R., Hale, W. D., and Anderson, L. K. Effect of induced mood states on activity and self-reported affect. Journal of Consulting and Clinical Psychology, 1975, 43, 587.

Summers, J. J. Adjustment to redundance in reaction time: A comparison of three learning methods. Acta Psychologica, 1977, 41, 205-223.

Tomkins, S. S. Affect, imagery, consciousness. Vol. 1: The positive affects. New York: Springer, 1962.

Ulich, E. Some experiments on the function of mental training in the acquisition of motor skills. Ergonomics, 1967, 10, 411-419.

Wachter, H.-M., and Pudel, V. Kurztherapie von 15 Sitzungen mit dem Katathymen Bilderleben. In H. Leuner (Ed.), Katathymos Bilderleben: Ergebnisse in Theorie und Praxis. Bern: Huber, 1980.

White, K. D., Ashton, R., and Lewis, S. Learning a complex skill: Effects of mental practice, physical practice, and imagery ability. International Journal of Sport Psychology, 1979, 10, 71-78.

Wilke, E. Das Katathyme Bilderleben bei der konservativen Behandlung der Colitis ulcerosa. In H. Leuner (Ed.), Katathymes Bilderleben: Ergebnisse in Theorie und Praxis. Bern: Huber, 1980.

IMAGINATIVE PLAY AS THE PRECURSOR OF ADULT IMAGERY AND FANTASY

Jerome L. Singer

Yale University

New Haven, CT

THE ORIGINS OF ADULT FANTASY

When clinicians refer to adult imagery or fantasies they are generally somewhat imprecise in terminology. Probably for scientific purposes it is best to view imagery as a function closely allied to perceptual processes, a basic capacity to reduplicate information gathered through specific sensory modalities. Thus, we can have auditory images or tactile images which roughly repeat information originally presented through the appropriate senses. Naturally-occurring fantasies and daydreams and many of the "imagery" procedures employed clinically or in self-development programs are more complex. They include <u>sequences</u> of images in various modalities as well as self-instructions and related forms of interior monologue. Perhaps what these functions have in common is an overriding attitudinal set of pretending or, as the neurologist Kurt Goldstein used to say, "taking an attitude toward the <u>possible</u>".

In looking for the origins of our adult imagery and fantasy processes it seems reasonable to go back to the make-believe play of early childhood. No one has yet carried out the necessary longitudinal studies to demonstrate that children who engage in a good deal of pretend or sociodramatic play eventually internalize these activities into silent, private and elaborate fantasy lives. Observers of children such as Piaget, Lewin, Vigotsky and Luria have generally all proposed that adult inner life grows out of children's make believe and this remains a likely possibility (Singer, 1973).

Some of the research by Dorothy and Jerome L. Singer described herein was supported by grants from the National Science Foundation and the Spencer Foundation.

The origins of the child's capacity for generating specific imagery is as yet rather obscure. Much of the psychoanalytic speculation from Freud's emphasis on thought being linked to the infant's "hallucination" of the absent mother's breast through the more recent object-representation theorists' emphasis on imagery in the first year of life seems based chiefly on adult patients' reports rather than systematic evidence obtainable from infants. The burgeoning field of infancy research is making it clear that there is little evidence of imagery or the capacity for anticipation until the period between nine months and eighteen months when children first manifest separation fears and stranger anxiety, or when they first show signs they can separate self from mother or from a mirror image by touching their face to rub a spot there when it is seen in a mirror reflection. By eighteen months we also see the beginnings of pretend play; the child's first playful "drinking" from an empty cup comes only after this age (Fein, 1975). By about two years of age some children move to "transformations" of an even more complex nature, pretending to "feed" a plastic toy identified as "baby" from an empty glass or bottle. Within the next year such often isolated pretend behaviors become increasingly crystallized into make-believe games and the period of imaginative play is initiated.

PIAGET'S DELINEATION OF PLAY FORMS

With the combination of his epistomological curiosity and his direct observation of the spontaneous activity of young children it was inevitable that Jean Piaget would confront the issue of children's play. Was play the exercise of inherent energies as Schiller proposed, the preparation for the development of adult capacities as Groos suggested, the attempted resolution of the conflict between instinctual needs versus reality as Freud and the psychoanalysts argued (Singer, 1973)? Piaget took a tremendous step by incorporating play into the broad system of the emerging cognitive capacities of the child. Play evolved as the child's efforts at imitation and accommodation to adult actions or words needed to be assimilated into the limited range of cognitive schemata already formed. For Piaget play occurred when assimilation was dissociated from accommodation prior to the eventual integration of these two basic processes into the equilibrium that characterizes operational and rational thought. He wrote ". . . Play constitutes the extreme pole of assimilation of reality to the ego, while at the same time it has something of the creative imagination which will be the motor of all future thought and even of reason" (Piaget, 1962, P. 161).

Piaget was able to delineate at least three major developmental sequences in play during the preoperational period. The infant and toddler are characterized by <u>sensory-motor play</u>, touching for the sheer joy of sensation, repetitive banging of a stick against a metal surface to produce a ringing sound. This type of play subtly becomes <u>mastery</u> play, the pleasure of expressing one's emerging motor competences, of being able to delineate details of the environment. The toddler climbing again and again up a small flight of stairs or repeating the joys of the sliding pond demonstrates what Karl Buhler had called funktionslust.

Somewhere after the second year as representional and language skills have evolved the child develops symbolic or make-believe play. Here Piaget proposed that "Symbolic play is to practice play as representational intelligence is to sensory-motor intelligence" (Piaget, 1962, P. 162). This is an important divergence from the psychoanalytic emphasis on infantile imagery. For Piaget, as the supreme developmentalist, pretending and make-believe must come only after the child's cognitive capacities have evolved to the level of maintaining symbolic or imagery representation.

Eventually make-believe play, which initially is directly observable because the child verbalizes most thought, becomes interiorized. Organizational and operational capacities of the child are expressed in games with rules and fantasy play "goes underground," becoming daydreaming or imagination. Here Piaget's observations, limited to a small segment of children from a limited cultural range, may have misled him. Studies of other cultures and also of older children suggest that make-believe games and rules games exist side by side--indeed all types of play never really fade although the necessities of conformity to school discipline or attention to household chores may mask their emergence (D. Singer & Revenson, 1978). In the following paper we will look more closely at the increasing body of evidence emerging from studies of imaginative or make-believe play in the preschool child and examine some recent data on studies of the play themes expressed by fairly large samples of children observed systematically over a year's time.

MAKE-BELIEVE PLAY AND PRETENDING

In a sense all play involves a kind of power transformation by which the child (and, ultimately, the adult as well) reconstitutes a miniature world which follows his or her rules.

> Play is what a person does when he can choose the arbitrariness of the constraints within which he will act or imagine. . . It may be, therefore, the ultimate source of all voluntary behavior on the levels of thought and action. The player substitutes his own conventions and his own urgencies for those of society and nature.
>
> (Sutton-Smith, 1972, P. xiii)

A miracle of our evolution as humans involves the early capacity for imaginative play, for transforming an empty paper cup into a pretend full one or into a car whose engine sounds can be mimicked by a "brrr" or horn by a "beep". The symbolic realm of make-believe is the most liberating transformation or miniaturization of power, which all play exemplifies. Once the child has developed the capacity for pretending, a tremendous range of games and possible self-controlled environments are subject to nearly arbitrary rules. In make-believe play a child who might be overwhelmed by the vastness and complexity of a real airplane or a locomotive or by the observation of violence in the home or on television can, by reducing size and using imagery, provide itself with more moderate levels of stimulation. It will then experience the affects of interest and joy rather than terror and distress (Singer, 1973).

Make-believe play, while hard to identify among primates, if it exists at all, is widespread across many diverse human societies (Schwartzman, 1978). In some cultures it is closely related to the major activities of the adults and involves a strong element of child imitation. In others where children are assigned home or field chores at early ages, e.g., care for younger siblings or animal herding, most anthropological studies report less of such pretending. Often this seems to be the case because there was insufficient observation of the children during spontaneous activity. In cultures where children are left to their own devices while adults work one sees a good deal of imaginative play even when there are no toys or active stimulants for such games. A study of children in the Okinawa town of Taira found ample evidence that children show considerable "inventiveness and enthusiasm" turning stones, seeds, or vegetables into marbles, cartons into boats, and foliage into uniforms, as well as relying on imagery to create novel characters or settings (Maretzki and Maretzki, 1963, P. 536).

Pretend and make-believe play emerges somewhere in the second and third year of life and reaches its peak (at least as publically observable) in the fifth year (Singer, 1973; Singer and Singer, 1980). It can be seen as a solitary game, the child alone in bed manipulating dolls or sticks or in small groups, becoming very elaborate at times when several children enact different roles.

Make-believe games and mastery play can become intertwined. A child may be swinging and enjoying the sheer sensuality or mastery of going higher and higher but then she may also suddenly pretend she's in a rocket ship, a Space Princess zooming off to another planet. The combination of symbolic play and mastery undoubtedly persists into adult life whether expressed in games or charades, amateur theatricals, or in the private imperialist fantasy of the businessman who comes to enjoy the sheer power manipulation of buying and selling companies long after he has met the financial needs of his family. Many scientists recognize that the very acts of setting up hypotheses about the structure of the universe and testing these through astronomical measurements often have an element of game playing and pretending, the creation of a smaller world from the vast one that looms off into infinity.

Rules games often become interwoven with pretend. Watching eight-year-old boys playing whiffle baseball on our street we observe that they each assume special identities, Sam Rice, Reggie Jackson, Fred Lynn. They describe the plays, imitating radio announcers and even simulate the roar of the crowd! Here our observations suggest that Piaget underestimated the persistence of symbolic play well into middle childhood and even early adolescence. It may become more social but make-believe continues to emerge even in solitary play.

Adaptive Features of Play

While all children in our society engage in some forms of play as part of their natural development, recent studies suggest that there are wide individual differences. Analysis of the consequences of imaginative play, for example, suggest that children who engage in more of such play show advantages in general positive emotionality (happiness, liveliness and interest), fluency of speech, persistence at tasks, ability to distinguish reality from fantasy, empathy and cooperation with other children, leadership and the ability to resist temptation or tolerate delays (D. Singer & J. Singer, 1980; J. Singer and D. Singer, 1976, 1981; Shmukler, Note 2; Smilansky, 1968). When children play at make-believe they practice new combinations of imagery and of verbal expression; they learn to take turns (Garvey, 1977). They are forced by the necessity of keeping the make-believe story going to try out different roles, to persist at the task because of the inherent logic (beginning, middle, and end) of the plot, and to anticipate consequences (Singer, 1973).

Children who had not developed the tendency to engage in much imaginative play often seem restless. They can't amuse themselves in waiting rooms or during periods of necessary delay before receiving food or some other reward. Singer (1955, 1961) has shown that imaginativeness can be a useful method for children to learn to tolerate delays. Mischel and Moore (1977) have demonstrated that children can resist temptation most effectively when encouraged to engage in playful distracting imagery, e.g., thinking of desired marshmallows as "fluffy white clouds" rather than focussing their thoughts directly on the food.

ENHANCING IMAGINATIVE PLAY

There have been extensive studies demonstrating that children can be "trained" to increase the amount or type of their spontaneous imaginative play. Generally preschoolers or early elementary school age children respond well to teachers who initiate fantasy games and then back out of the game leaving the children to elaborate on these further. A few weeks of such training leads to a general increase in the level of such play (Freyberg, 1973; Saltz, Note 1; D. Singer & J. Singer, 1976; Shmukler, Note 2; Smilansky, 1968). Even daily exposure for two weeks to a television program which emphasizes make-believe like Mister Rogers' Neighborhood has been shown to lead to increase in make-believe play and to more positive, "good" feelings among nursery school children (D. Singer & J. Singer, 1976; Tower, Singer, Singer, & Biggs, 1979).

FAMILY INFLUENCES

If make-believe play tendencies can be increased experimentally it is likely that particular family or cultural influences may also enhance such behavior in young children. Available evidence suggests that children who show more spontaneous imaginative play have a history of "secure attachment" (Matas, Arend, & Sroufe, 1978). They are more likely to have at least one parent who spent time with them telling them stories or playing make-believe games with them (Singer, 1961; Singer & Singer, 1976; Shmukler, Note 2). Studies of white middle class children in South Africa carried out by Shmukler, for example, indicate that preschoolers who engage in imaginative play or who show more inner fantasy, e.g., in having make-believe playmates, usually have mothers who interact warmly with their children, initiate play but then allow the child to forge ahead on its own while the mothers become preoccupied with their own thoughts. It seems likely that children need some encouragement from parents to develop their interest in fantasy games and they also need ideas for the content of such play. A hovering or over-concerned parent impedes the child from moving along in its game spontaneously.

Parental values and interest patterns seem to be transmitted at very early ages to children and are reflected in their play. A group of children who played in preschool were rated for degree of imagination and playfulness. Those who showed more make-believe proved to have mothers who scored higher on a measure of creative and independent thinking values. The children who showed little imaginativeness but who were more likely to be aggressive had mothers who emphasized social relationship values rather than inner thought (D. Singer & J. Singer, 1976). A very careful study by Tower (Note 3) examined parental values along three dimensions validated by a multitrait, multimethod analysis, Resourcefulness (Creativity, Independence, Imagination), Relatedness (Sociability), and Responsibility (Stability and Conformity). The more imaginative boys generally reflected either a family background of parental agreement on values or a parent pattern where the mother expecially valued Resourcefulness and the father emphasized Relatedness.

TELEVISION, IMAGINATION AND PLAY

Piaget does not seem to have taken notice of television. Now we can no longer ignore it. Television-viewing is a major source of input in the consciousness of children growing up today. It is probably a major contributor to plot material for play. Often the habit of dependence on TV for providing immediate, packaged fantasy may impede the child in practicing its own play skills. Children who are extremely heavy TV-viewers are often less likely to develop imaginary playmates or elaborate imagery tendencies. They may charge into the preschool play group shouting "I'm Batman" or "I'm Godzilla" and proceed to knock over others' blocks or to attack the children physically thereby evoking counterattacks or the wrath of the teachers. Children who play more extensively are less likely to be aggressive, use many themes besides television, and are more likely to be cooperative and pleasant. They are also less likely to be heavy viewers of TV, or, if they do watch, they may emphasize the more "benign" public television programming (D. Singer & J. Singer, 1980; J. Singer & D. Singer, 1981).

PLAYFULNESS AS A PERSONALITY TRAIT

By three and four years of age children are already showing fairly consistent differences in play patterns. Boys show more involvement in games of adventure and exploration, girls in games of nurturance and domesticity even in this period of "women's lib" (J. Singer & D. Singer, 1981). Although girls are now adopting more elements of boys' games in their play, e.g., playing garage or superheroes, boys (perhaps because of our society's fears of demasculinizing boys) show little trend towards playing with dolls or identifying even with female TV superheroes such as Wonder Woman.

Three factor analytic studies of spontaneous play patterns over a year's time have identified distinct styles of naturally-occurring behavior. Some children consistently show a tendency to play at games of pretending and they are, as suggested above, also more likely to be lively and smiling, cooperative and interactive with the other children and to be leaders in play groups. They talk more and use more complex language even when IQ differences are controlled (J. Singer, D. Singer, & Sherrod, 1980; D. Singer & J. Singer, 1980; Shmukler, Note 2).

Lieberman (1977) carried out an extensive study of kindergarten children and examined differences in physical spontaneity, social spontaneity, cognitive spontaneity, manifest joy, and sense of humor. She found factor analytic evidence supporting a consistently playful behavioral style, children who were regularly more joyful, made up jokes and stories and showed more make-believe play. These children also showed more capacity for divergent or creative responses to special tests. A study of high school adolescents who were rated for their behavior by their teachers revealed a similar playfulness dimension, identifying students who were consistently more humorous, cheerful and laughing, enthusiastic and imaginative. Lieberman suggested that "bubbling effervescence" in adolescents might reflect the continuation of the kindergartener's playfulness. Actual longitudinal studies focusing on this dimension to see if it does persist from the preschool years have not yet been carried out.

Studies of adult personality make it clear that playfulness can be identified as a style of relatedness. Meehl, Lykken, Schofield, and Tellegen (1971), in a factor analysis of personality descriptions emerging from the case records of psychotherapists, found a strong factor called Surgency/Pleasure/Play. Items and descriptions such as jocular, cheerful, enthusiastic, smiles often, colorful personality, and stimulating were linked together. They felt that their results fit in well with the extensive factor work of Raymond B. Cattell to identify a major dimension of personality, playfulness. The recent studies of children suggest therefore that this enthusiastic and colorful personality pattern is already evident by the third or fourth year of life and it may be related to particular parental styles and values.

EARLY THEMES OF PLAY

In a recent study Dorothy Singer and I have examined recurrent themes of play from the protocols gathered between six and eight times over a year's period of systematic observation of 80 four year olds. There were equal numbers of boys and girls and the socioeconomic status of the children ranged from lower class through middle class socioeconomic status (SES). Detailed protocols of ten minutes of spontaneous play were recorded by two independent observers. These protocols were then scored by other raters trained to high levels of agreement on a series of dimensions such as location of play, types of play from games of mastery, rules to make-believe, specific themes such as family games, occupations etc. A factor analysis of our data yielded evidence that generally supported Piaget's distinctions of games of mastery from make-believe and from games with rules. With some differences for the social class groups (the Lower SES being more traditionally distinct in sex role play), the patterns that emerged suggest that children show adventurous fantasy play and domestic fantasy play as two facets of a more general make-believe play style, involvement in art versus physical mastery play, ritual games such as dancing and singing, and, finally, games with rules, which are just beginning to emerge.

While all children may play all of these ways, the separation into factors suggests clearly that there are consistent individual styles in emphasis on the various patterns already in evidence by age four. It is important to note that children rated by direct observers as more consistently imaginative over a year's time are also those rated from the protocols as playing either the adventure games, the games of "house" or "doctor" or "school," or both types of make-believe.

Of interest is the evidence that the highly and consistently imaginative children (based on consistency of make-believe play over a year's time) are not restricted in play to solitary games or to a purely fantastic side of play. The High Imaginatives also show more social play and participate, if anything, even more than Low Imaginatives in the ritual games and singing or dancing that occur in the spontaneous play of the preschoolers. Indeed, according to the protocols, children from the High Imagination group are rated as significantly less likely to play alone. The Imaginative children are also significantly higher on the variable of "initiates play." This is also a suggestive result. In the subsequent study with 200 preschoolers, we introduced a variable defined as Leadership. This score correlated significantly and positively over the year with Imaginativeness of Play. Thus, the child who is consistently high in make-believe play in the nursery school is by no means a solitary, withdrawn, or defensive child. Rather, he or she is more likely to be social and to show leadership in stimulating play in others.

TELEVISION AND PLAY THEMES

Our data make it clear that television has a major influence on the content of the imaginative play of our children. The most frequent references to characters and adventures that occur are drawn from TV shows, cartoons, and so-called fantasy-action shows such as Six Million Dollar Man, Wonder Woman, etc. Since children are not yet reading and it is clear from parent interviews that the stories they are read or told by parents are not drawn from comic books, the emphasis on specific superheroes reflects directly the TV influence.

Despite the widespread viewing and commonality we see some differences emerge as a function of the extent of TV-viewing. High TV-viewers, irrespective of imaginative level, are rated from play protocols as significantly higher on the variables "initiates attack," "reacts to attack with aggression," and "withdraws, weeps or cowers in response to aggression." Clearly the heavier viewers seem to be more uncomfortable, aggressive or impulsive in their play. These data point perhaps to an ominous influence of television. We cannot refute with confidence the alternative possibility that the more aggressive or fearful children are simply attracted more to heavy TV-viewing, at least from this particular set of data drawn from the larger study. Results from the full sample of middle class and lower SES children appear to rule out the likelihood that aggressive children simply prefer violent TV (D. Singer & J. Singer, 1980; J. Singer & D. Singer, 1981).

CHANGES IN PLAY OVER THE YEAR

Finally, our data allow us to look more closely at changes in play over the year. The protocols make it clear that there is a decrease over the year in gross physical activity or larger motor activity and a significant increase in the direction of more art play and more ritual play or singing and dancing. Play also becomes more social although this trend levels off by mid-year and seems then at a new plateau. Finally, with respect to play themes we see an increase in reference to sexuality that closely parallels the increase in and then leveling off of social play. By contrast, the themes of "danger, disaster, physical mutilation, etc." show a steady increase over the year. This last finding may reflect: a) an increasing awareness of children of the real dangers that confront them in life; b) an increased ability to express such fears verbally; c) an increased response of fearfulness occasioned by the comparable increase in TV-watching over the year, since Gerbner and Gross (1976) have shown that heavy TV-viewing is associated with overestimation of the world dangers by children and adults, or d) the fact that increased capacities for plot formation in play increase also the likely references to dangers that make for interesting story-lines. Considerably more research is needed to help us understand which of these or other possibilities can explain such an increased representation of fear in the preschool years.

TOWARDS THE PLAY OF LATER CHILDHOOD AND ADULT FANTASY

In this chapter I have so far emphasized what appear to me to be the beginnings of the fantasy life of the older child and of the adult. The fact is that systematic research and careful observation of large samples (as distinct from the suggestive speculations of clinicians treating individual clients) tell us little about the fantasy lives of middle childhood and only somewhat more about adolescence or early adult life. Make-believe play and pretending seems to be at its peak during the fifth year in American children and then, with the restrictions on talking out loud imposed by teachers and parents, the make-believe seems to go underground to be interiorized as interior monologue and fantasy (Piaget, 1962; Singer, 1973). Are the children who already were more imaginative in kindergarten those who become the readers and fantasizers of the preadolescent period? There are some suggestions that this may be the case (Singer and Singer, 1976b), especially from the reports of creative adults. What role does peer culture or "lollipop" music play in the further development of fantasy as a resource, escape, or even sexual stimulant for the nine or ten-year-old? Here certainly lies a very fertile area of future research.

The evidence cited in this chapter point to some issues that the clinician who seeks to use fantasy or imaginative procedures must confront. If by four years of age children already show consistent differences in extent of recourse to pretending and in style or content of fantasy, isn't it likely that such variations may be relatively crystallized in the adult? The clinician who asks clients to produce fantasies or to launch themselves on imagery trips must be prepared to confront wide differences in predisposition and capacity or skill to enter this pretend realm. We may have to give increasing attention to the problems of identifying in adults specific patterns of recurrent fantasy or the limitations of such behavior. In additon, we may have to pay more heed to the question if training adults in their imaginative tendencies can be enhanced. The data from early childhood suggest definite benefits to be accrued from entering temporarily into the world of make-believe. Adults often unwittingly seek such experiences even if by means of the prepackaged form of television soap operas. A recent newspaper article indicated that hundreds of irate phone calls were received by Phoenix TV stations when the afternoon fiction of soap operas was interrupted by the "reality" of news items about the fate of the American hostages in Iran (Arizona Daily Star News report, January 22, 1981). Are those people who are so strongly drawn to externally-generated fantasy-persons whose private fantasy capacities have not been sufficiently developed? Certainly it seems likely that the capacity for regulating one's own fantasies rather than depending on the external sources would have some intrinsic benefits. Clearly much remains to be learned!

REFERENCE NOTES

1. Saltz, E. Training for thematic-fantasy play in culturally disadvantaged children. Annual report to the Spencer Foundation, Wayne State University, 1976.

2. Shmukler, D. The origins and concomitants of imaginative play in young childhood. Unpublished doctoral dissertation, University of Witwatersrand, Johannesburg, South Africa, 1978.

3. Tower, R. B. The influence of parents' values on preschool children's behavior. Unpublished doctoral dissertation, Yale University, 1980.

REFERENCES

Fein, G. A transformational analysis of pretending. Development Psychology, 1975, 11, 291-296.

Freyberg, J. Increasing the imaginative play of urban disadvantaged kindergarten children through systematic training. In J. L. Singer (Ed.), The child's world of make-believe. New York: Academic Press, 1973.

Garvey, C. Play. Cambridge, MA: Harvard University Press, 1977.

Gerbner, G., and Gross, L. Living with television: The violence profile. Journal of Communication, 1976, 26, 173-199.

Lieberman, N. J. Playfulness. New York: Academic Press, 1977.

Maretski, T., and Maretski, J. Taira: An Okinawan Village. In B. Whitney (Ed.), Six cultures. New York: Wiley, 1963.

Matas, L., Arend, R. A., and Sroufe, L. A. Continuity of adaptation in the second year: The relationship between quality of attachment and later competence. Child Development, 1978, 49, 547-556.

Meehl, P. E., Lykken, D. T., Schofield, W., and Tellegen, A. Recaptured item technique (RIT): A method for reducing somewhat the subjective element in factor naming. Journal of Experimental Research in Personality, 1971, 5, 171-190.

Mischel, W., and Moore, B. Effects of attention to symbolically presented rewards on self control. Journal of Personality and Social Psychology, 1973, 28, 172-179.

Piaget, J. Play, dreams and imitation in childhood. New York: Norton, 1962.

Schwartzman, H. B. Transformations. The anthropology of children's play. New York: Plenum, 1978.

Singer, D. G., and Singer, J. L. Family television viewing habits and the spontaneous play of preschool children. American Journal of Orthopsychiatry, 1976, 46, 495-502.

Singer, D. G., and Singer, J. L. Partners in play. New York: Harper & Row, 1977.

Singer, D. G., and Revenson, T. A. A Piaget primer: How a child thinks. New York: New American Library, 1978.

Singer, D. G., and Singer, J. L. Television viewing and aggressive behavior in preschool children: A field study. In F. Wright, C. Bahn, & R. Rieber (Eds.), Annals of the New York Academy of Sciences: Forensic Psychology and Psychiatry (Vol. 347). New York: New York Academy of Sciences, 1980.

Singer, J. L. Imagination and waiting behavior in young children. Journal of Personality, 1961, 29, 396-413.

Singer, J. L. The child's world of make-believe. New York: Academic Press, 1973.

Singer, J. L., and Singer, D. G. Can TV stimulate imaginative play? Journal of Communication, 1976, 26, 74-80. (a)

Singer, J. L., and Singer, D. G. Imaginative play in early childhood: Some experimental approaches. In A. Davids (Ed.), Child personality and psychopathology. New York: Wiley, 1976. (b)

Singer, J. L., and Singer, D. G. Television, imagination and aggression: A study of preschoolers. Hillsdale, N. J.: Erlbaum, 1981.

Singer, J. L., Singer, D. G., and Sherrod, L. R. A factor analytic study of preschooler's play behavior, Academic Psychology Bulletin, 1980, 2, 143-156.

Smilansky, S. The effects of sociodramatic play on disadvantaged preschool children. New York: Wiley, 1968.

Sutton-Smith, B. Play, creativity, and moving. In E. Han and W. Preising (Eds.), Human movement. Schorndoff, Germany: Verlag Karl Hoffman, 1976.

Tower, R. B., Singer, D. G., Singer, J. L., and Biggs, A. Differential effects of television programming on preschoolers' cognition, imagination, and social play. American Journal of Orthopsychiatry, 1979, 49, 265-281.

DEVELOPMENTAL ASPECTS OF MENTAL IMAGERY:

A THEORY OF THEMATIC DISSONANCE

Dan Tomasulo

Yeshiva University

New York City, New York

How Does Imagery Develop?

Usually cited as the principal exponents of cognitive theories on the ontogenetic evolution of imagery are Piaget and Inhelder (1971) and Bruner (1964). Both theories follow the line of reasoning that cognitive maturity develops from "concrete" conceptual organization to more "abstract" abilities in the processing of information.

Piaget (1962) and Piaget and Inhelder (1971) argued that the symbolic process of imagery parallels the development of sensory and motor exploration of an object, with imagery being the internalized imitation resulting from perceptual-motor coordination of information about an object. In general, the development of the process of mental imagery is viewed by Piaget and Inhelder as subordinate to the function of intelligence, with imagery being classified as either reproductive or anticipatory. Reproductive images are subdivided into three categories: (1) static (motionless), (2) moving, and (3) transformational. Anticipatory images have two subdivisions relating only to movements or transformations.

The series of studies undertaken by Piaget and Inhelder and their colleagues indicated that reproductive images (particularly the static images) are present at the earlier stages of the preoperational period of cognitive development, and mark the beginning of symbolic functioning. The establishment of anticipatory images emerges at the operative stage (concrete operations) during the seventh or eighth year, and allows for the use of a dynamic symbolic process, indicative of more abstract symbolic functioning.

Bruner (1964) describes three modes of representation in a developmental sequence. The first is the enactive mode, in which past events are represented through motor responses (roughly related to Piaget's sensorimotor period of cognitive development). The second is the ikonic stage, in which the child can represent the world to itself via an imaginal reconstruction independent of the motor responses needed in the enactive stage. (Again this ikonic stage parallels Piaget's notion of representational imagery emerging at the onset of the preoperational period.)

The third mode of representation for Bruner is the symbolic (or linguistic) system, which corresponds in age-related fashion to the emergence of anticipatory images and the operative stage of cognitive development noted by Piaget. The striking parallel is that those theorists have determined that at about the age of six, a decisive developmental stage is reached with respect to the ability to use imagery. It is this parallel that serves as the point of departure for the theoretical underpinnings to support the present research.

Berlyne (1965) distinguished between "situational" and "transformational" thoughts. Situational thinking refers to intermediate or conclusional stages of thought, while transformational thinking refers to the dynamic process involved in moving from one situational representation to the next. The distinction is similar to the notion Piaget and Inhelder have elaborated on in their defining of the qualitative difference between reproductive (especially static) imagery and anticipatory images. Bruner (1964) is also concerned with the anticipation of transformations in conceptualizing his symbolic (linguistic) stage of representation. He regards the images of the ikonic stage as being relatively concrete and static, and views language as the system of symbolic activity most involved with the anticipation of transformations. If we can then use Berlyne's distinction as a way of bridging our understanding of these two theorists, one may integrate their findings and geralize the results. In doing this, we find a static-dynamic conceptual distinction that is made relative to the use of symbolic processes after the age of six. This leaves us with the problem of trying to identify those features of the symbolic process that rest at the core of the static-dynamic conceptual distinction. The work of several theorists will aid our understanding of this problem. Their research is interpreted as it relates to the following questions: (1) What elements are responsible for the construction of a static imaginal representation and (2) what role do these elements play in the development of more dynamic processes?

The Mediational Image

Roger Shepard in a recent article (1978) offers experimental evidence as well as a theoretical rationale for a cognitive link between perception and imagery. There are several interesting features of his remarks, the first of which involves the paradigm of what is referred to as a second-order isomorphism. This paradigm proposes that "the functional relations among objects as imagined must to some degree mirror the functional relations among those objects as actively perceived" (P. 131). In experiments employing visual imagery (Shepard and Chipman, 1970; Shepard, Kilpatric, and Cunningham, 1975) subjects proved to do equally well describing objects whether they were physically present or only imagined. Further, Shepard suggests that if the same neural circuitry is used for both perception and imagination, then imagining a particular object should produce "a unique state of readiness for the actual perception of the particular object" (P. 132). In other experiments (Shepard and Metzler, 1971; Cooper, 1975) reaction time was used to test the effectiveness of having subjects form a preparatory visual image of the relevant stimulus. These researchers have consistently found that the reaction time was faster and responses more accurate when an appropriate visual image had been formed. Shepard and his colleagues also found that there was a direct linear relationship between the length of time required to mentally transform an imagined object and the degree to which there was spatial transformation (i.e., rotation).

Shepard has hit on the very core of our questions. His contribution has been to show that in both static and dynamic images, there is a perceptual link to the imaginal process. His research indicates that the neural circuitry used in visually perceiving information about an object or event is the same circuitry used in cognitive imagery. While the cognitive-developmental nature of this perceptual-developmental link is not a direct concern of Shepard's work, this research is of great value when combined with the work of Katherine Nelson.

In a recent paper, Tomasulo (1980) reviewed the work of Katherine Nelson (1974) with reference to a perceptual-developmental link to imagery. Nelson proposes a conceptual model which accounts for a child's initial translation of meanings into words. The structure of the model raises a now familiar distinction relating to static and dynamic information. The important difference with this use of terms by Nelson is that her theory of conceptual development notes that children attain their natural concepts from a world of "complex, dynamic events" (P. 269). As such, it is assumed that children abstract relevant cues from "the complex dynamic perceptual array" (P. 270) and then recombines them to form a concept. In other words, the static concept (which I will later argue is the base for "static" imagery) is actually formed via a perceptually dynamic process. Nelson suggests the nine- to twenty-four-month-old infant is developing the concept of an object by directly experiencing an object and noting all of its dynamic functional attributes (i.e., the rolling, bouncing, and throwing qualities of a ball, for instance). Over a period of time, this process allows for a synthesis of the various functional relationships that will create the core of the child's concept. If we incorporate Shepard's perceptual-imaginal link with Nelson's perceptual-conceptual model, then it seems we are prepared to offer an explanation to our first question on the development of static imagery based on the child's cognitive abstraction of the object's functional attributes.

Before a conclusion can be drawn, a review of the conceptual models of imagery (Pylyshyn, 1973; Bower, 1972; Anderson and Bower, 1973) is necessary. Our hypothesized extension of Nelson's conceptual development model seems sanctioned by these theorists as they suggest that the concept of a particular object or idea is represented through an image. In this regard, Brainard (1971) asserts that an image is a conscious form that functions as the dependent variable indicative of the activation of the conceptual representation. This view holds that the image is mediational in that it represents a conscious form of internalized concept. In this mediational contest, the image serves as a mnemonic representation reflective of a known concept. In combining the thinking of the above theorists, for the purpose of forming a developmental hypothesis we would suspect that at the origin of its ontogenetic evolution, an image reflects a perceptually learned associative connection to a concept. In addition, we can further hypothesize that this associative connection between an image and a concept is rooted in a cognitive appreciation of functionally relevant features. This hypothesis then seems to provide us with the tools to answer the second question. If the image develops from what is an associative connection to a dynamic perceptual process, then the mnemonic potential of the image should be sensitive to the dynamic or transitional changes that occur in those features responsible in the formation of the image (i.e., functional elements of the objects).

On the surface of this premise, we find evidence to support a relational organization of an image as a facilitative component in associative imagery. Bower (1972) has shown that when objects are imagined interacting they are recalled more readily by adult subjects than when a comparison group imagined objects that did not interact. This finding is comparable to the findings of an earlier experiment (Epstein, Rock, and Zuckerman, 1960) where two objects depicted in spatial interaction were more readily recalled by subjects than when paired in noninteracting positions. Extending the trend, Rohwer (1966) found that nouns in a paired-associate learning task, when connected by prepositions and verbs, are recalled better than if conectives were used. These findings prompted Bower to note "that this recall pattern with pictures, images, and words is probably being produced by the same relational generating system." (Pg. 81). It is not a mere coincidence that Nelson uses a "relational concept" theory as the term to describe the process of concept development prior to acquisition of language.

The use of the term relational for Bower and Nelson may be best understood if we note that the elements that compose meaningful entities (i.e., concepts and images) are cognitively organized according to specific rules. In other words, the rules or organization concerning information relevant to the development of a concept and subsequent images is responsible for determining the thematic nature of those elements. If an image is a mnemonic representation reflecting an unknown concept as stated above, then the mnemonic potential of this mediational image in evoking a concept should be best when the elements of the concept are cognitively appreciated and match the thematic structure of the image.

To date, one of the foremost theories that incorporates the mnemonic power of an image is put forth by Paivio in his "Conceptual Peg Hypothesis" (1971). He proposes that the more concrete the stimulus term in a paired association, the better (stronger) the associated response will be. In this type of associative connection, the stimulus term functions as a "peg" on to which an associated response term is hung. The stimulus member is rated as having an imagery value that relates to the degree to which mental imagery acts as a mediator in the association. The higher the imagery-arousing value of the stimulus term, the higher its mnemonic potential. Stimuli that are rated as being more concrete are therefore rated higher in their imagery-arousing value. The more abstract the stimulus term, the lower its mnemonic potential. In Paivio's hypothesis, imagery-arousing stimuli then are rated on a continuum, based on their level of concreteness. Objects themselves are the most concrete stimulus terms having the highest imagery-arousing value, with pictures of the object being the next most concrete. Concrete nouns are listed next on the continuum with abstract nouns having the lowest imagery-arousing value and least mnemonic potential.

After reviewing the literature with respect to the mnemonic potential of verbal material, Bower (1972) concludes "...that imagery concreteness of the stimulus word is the most potent attribute in paired associate learning yet identified." (Pg.77) While other research (Anisfeld, 1970; Goldfarb, Wirtz, and Anisfeld, 1973) has shown other variables to be responsible for this phenomenon, we will limit our explanation to Paivio's hypothesis, since it appears most relevant for a discussion of imagery. In particular, Paivio's view that an image is an irreducible psychological construct has prompted his investigation of the most minimal perceptual (i.e., color, size, orientation) as well as the minimal cognitive abilities (i.e., attention, memory, etc.) that will evoke the image.

But what of our hypothesis of the image as being mediational in reflecting a thematically organized concept? In this view, if the thematic or relational quality of the elementary components of a concept are changed, then the image that mediates the concept must eventually become altered as well. Thus, we would assume that a change in the organization of a concept's elements allows for a qualitatively different mediational image to emerge. The altered concept is not a new one, but rather the alternate view of the concept's elements is associated into the existing thematic organization. Again the image reflecting the new conceptual organization is not, in essence, a new image; we would expect, however, (and the present research will demonstrate) that the psychological significance of the image, specifically, its mnemonic potential, would change dramatically. Such effects would seem to indicate that an image is sensitive to changes that tamper with those elements present at the origin of its ontogenetic evolution. This argument, then, is for a view of imagery as a psychological construct whose qualities vary as a function of manipulation of initial conceptualization. Ultimately, the identification of those initial features allows us to understand imagery as a psychological construct with diverse psychological significance.

The Relationship of Imagery to Intelligence

The ability to use more dynamic forms of imagery via transformations is generally considered subordinate to the process of cognitive maturity. This explains why Piaget and Inhelder (1971) and Bruner (1964) agree so closely on the age of transformational ability. However, if our hypothesis is correct and imagery development is directly related to concept development, as proposed above, then we may expect imagery to serve as a facilitative component superordinate to cognitive maturity. This expectation is a reasonable assumption if we consider the first issue of resolution in cognitive development to be the deciphering of thematically related functional elements. This would be in keeping with the concrete-abstract continuum of cognitive development in that "concrete" imagery representations are those relating most directly to the initial concept. Moving toward the "transformational" or "abstract" dimension of this continuum, we would expect thematically dissonant stimuli to evoke a less mnemonically powerful image to mediate the cognitive appreciation of a concept. This chicken-egg dilemma between cognition and imagery is viewed in a clearer perspective if we understand cognitive growth to be in a state of process rather than in the midst of a qualitative change. This implies that the cognitive developmental process is constantly seeking avenues through which this process may continue. Imagery, in this context, provides what appears to be a most direct route.

Measuring Imagery

We have hypothesized that the elements that compose a mental image are derived from the process of conceptual development. This hypothesis is further expanded upon by noting that the neurological network employed in perceiving an object or event will be the same network used in generating an image. If the process of conceptual development allows for a relational organization of functionally dynamic elements as explained by Nelson, then the composition of the image generated by the same system must correspond to the rules initially employed in concept development.

Thus we should find that the image that mediates the link between a concept and conscious recognition of a concept should have its greatest mnemonic (associative) potential when the relational organization of the concept and the thematic appreciation of the image are synchronized. A dissonant representation of the thematic nature of an image's functional elements should result in an initial reduction in the image's mnemonic potential. We should then suspect that a distorted or dissonant reproduction of an object's function (as in functionally bizarre relationships) should result in poorer memory for such relationships. In this way, the measure of an image's mnemonic power is tested with the dependent variable of memory for variously related associated pairs of objects.

The Relationship of Imagery to Age

The concept of mental age and its relationship to chronological age has been so firmly rooted in our thinking about an individual's cognitive abilities that separate discussions for these topics may be perceived as being potentially naive. However, such a question is necessary due to our previous argument of imagery as a facilitative component superseding cognitive growth. It may prove to be more fruitful for an investigation of imagery development if we study age-related as well as cognitively-related differences in the ability to use images. If our hypothesis is correct, we should find such differences at ages where no qualitative changes in cognitive growth have been noted as occurring.

The Age of Transformational Ability with Imagery

A study by Tomasulo (1980) tested twenty-eight male and female children from a New Jersey day care program on a paired-associate memory task. Black and white line-drawn pictures of objects were depicted in various interacting positions that had been previously rated by adult subjects on a forced-choice scale and assigned to one of three conditions. The normal condition depicted two items interacting in a normal manner where the functional attributes of both objects were being displayed in their usual manner (a match lighting a pipe, for instance). A low bizarre condition was indicated when the two objects were depicted in a relationship where the functional attributes of the items were slightly absurd (e.g., a pipe in a frying pan). The high bizarre condition was represented by uniquely absurd interactions where the relationship of the two items was considered highly dissonant (e.g., a fish smoking a pipe).

Fourteen of the children had an average age of approximately three years, six months, with a standard deviation of nearly six and one half months. The other fourteen children had an average age of four years, seven months, with a standard deviation of nearly four months. Each child was exposed to all three conditions in alternating presentation schedules.

The findings indicated that there were no significant differences across any of the three conditions with the four-year, seven-month-old children when tested for recall of an associated item. In contrast, the younger children scored significantly lower on the low bizarre and high bizarre conditions than on the normal conditions. These results indicate that both groups of children do equally well on memory tasks when objects are depicted in their normal functioning positions but that the younger children have great difficulty using a mediational image as an associative peg when the functional elements of two objects create a thematically dissonant arrangement.

There are two important issues that are brought to light by this experiment. First, the degree to which objects' functional attributes deviated from a normally interacting relationship was found to have a significant impact on the mnemonic potential of the mediational image in the associative pairing with the younger children. This supports our argument that isolating and manipulating the functional elements of an object is an appropriate method for testing the developmental nature of transitional or dynamic forms of imagery. Secondly, the finding of this developmental difference between the ages of 42 months and 55 months with respect to the ability to use imagery is unique in that the qualitative difference in imagery occurs during a time when no major cognitive development distinction has been recognized. This lends support to our hypothesis that imaginal processing facilitates and precedes cognitive develpomental stages.

Practical Implications for the Retarded

The above experiment was also conducted with twenty-eight community-based retarded adults (Tomasulo, 1980). Half of this group had an average I.Q. of 30.57 with a standard deviation of 7.72. The other half had a mean I.Q. of 68.79 with a standard deviation of 7.32. The results paralleled the findings with the children. The higher I.Q./higher-functioning retarded adults were similar to the four-year, seven-month-old children in that there were no differences across the three conditions. In contrast, the lower I.Q./lower-functioning group performed comparably to the three-and-one-half-year-old normal children. The more dissonant the thematic relationship of the functional attributes of the objects, the poorer the mnemonic potential of the mediational images. This suggests several strategies for employing imagery techniques to enhance training programs for the retarded. Suggestions relevant for the lower-functioning include the labeling of closets, refrigerators, drawers, cabinets, etc., with line-drawn pictures that depict the desired object in a functionally dynamic way. Milk should be pouring, knives cutting, salt and pepper shakers shaking, etc. In this way, the normal functional association will be portrayed, which allows for a stronger association to be made to the conceptual labelling of the objects.

Word accentuation, such as flames on top of the word "hot" and snow caps on the word "cold" for the appropriate water faucet, employ a dynamic functional element of the concept in a visual form. As an example, the "o" in the word "on" is made to look like a lighted bulb to show that when the switch is turned in this direction it will bring about this function.

Daily living skills such as brushing teeth or washing hair may be taught by using a series of pictures (Tomasulo, Sullivan, and Biango, 1978) that depict the stages of completing the task by showing objects using their natural functions; e.g., toothpaste being squeezed out of a tube and onto a brush, and a brush brushing teeth, as opposed to more static representations.

Vocational skills may also be taught with such a method (Tomasulo, 1976). Those retarded individuals who are not ready to enter a vocational setting have been able to profit from a sequentially arranged picture-cuing system where the tasks needed to be performed were depicted in their normal, functional setting.

With higher-functioning retarded adults we have found that imagery training for using mnemonic pegs has been extremely helpful in improving memory skills. As an example, after training people to use highly functionally bizarre imagery associations, we were able to help them recall a variety of tasks which, until such training, had eluded their sphere of competence. In one such instance, we trained one individual to imagine an exceptionally large pill in his bed just before he retired in the evening. This thematically dissonant imagery association provided a powerful mnemonic trigger which allowed the individual to autonomously regulate his intake of a needed medication.

<u>Summary: A Theory of Thematic Dissonance</u>

A theory of thematic dissonance is proposed with respect to ontogenetic evolution of imagery. The theory advances our understanding of the imaginal process in three main issues.

1. An image is hypothesized to conform to the same rules of development that formulates a concept. In using the same neural circuitry that was responsible for taking in the information for concept development, the image is generated via the same thematic relationship as the concept. This identifies the dynamic functional attributes of the item in question as the central units in the developmental continuum from concrete to abstract thought.

2. At the early stages of cognitive growth, the more dissonant the representation of the thematic nature of these elements, the poorer the mnemonic potential of the mediational image. This is in keeping with the concrete-abstract continuum in that the more concretely the image relates to the concept it portrays, the stronger its associative value in the earlier stages of cognitive development.

3. The age and level of cognitive maturity necessary to display the ability to synthesize thematically dissonant concepts is shown to occur sooner than the usually considered time at which the concrete-abstract dimension is achieved. This ability has been demonstrated within the imaginal process at a time when the cognitive-developmental process is not undergoing any major qualitative change. As such, once the imaginal process has begun, it is theorized to precede and facilitate cognitive maturity.

ACKNOWLEDGEMENTS

The author would like to thank Ms. Nancy Razza for her typing and review of the manuscript. Gratitude is also extended to the staff of the instructional development lab at Brookdale Community College, under the direction of Mr. Charles Burton; to the staff and residents of the Westchester County Group Homes operated by Young Adult Institute, under the direction of Mr. Philip Levy; and to the staff and students of the Children's Educational Learning Lab, Brookdale Community College.

REFERENCE NOTES

1. Tomasulo, D., Imagery and cognitive development. Unpublished manuscript, 1980.

2. Tomasulo, D., Sullivan, A., and Razza, N. Pictures as cues for functional skills training. Unpublished manuscript, 1978.

REFERENCES

Anisfeld, M. False recognition of adjective-noun phrases. Journal of Experimental Psychology, 1970, 86, 120-122.

Anderson and Bower, Human associative memory. Washington, D. C.; Winston, 1973.

Berlyne, D. E., Structure and direction in thinking, New York; Wiley, 1965.

Bower, G., Mental imagery and associative learning. In . . Gregg (Ed.), Cognition in Learning and Memory. New York: Wiley, 1972.

Brainard, C., Imagery as a dependent variable. American Psychologist, 1971, 26, 599-600.

Bruner, J., The course of cognitive growth, American Psychologist, 1964, 19, 1-15.

Cooper, C., Mental transformation of random two-dimensional shapes. Cognitive Psychology, 1975, 7, 20-43.

Epstein, W., Rock, I., and Zuckerman, C., Meaning and familiarity in associative learning. Psychological Monographs, 1960, 74 (4, Whole No. 491).

Goldfarb, C., Wirth, J., and Anisfeld, M., Abstract and concrete phrases in false recognition. Journal of Experimental Psychology, 1973, 98, 25-30.

Metzler, J., and Shepard, R. Transformational studies of the internal representation of three dimensional objects. In R. Solso (Ed.), Theories in Cognitive Psychology: The Loyola Symposium. Potomac, MD: Erlbaum 1974.

Nelson, K. Concept, word, and sentence: Inter-relations in acquisition and development. Psychological Review, 81, 4, 1974.

Paivio, A., Imagery and verbal processes. New York: Holt, Rinehart and Winston, 1971.

Piaget, J., Play, dreams and imitation in childhood. New York: Norton, 1962.

Piaget, J., and Inhelder, B. Verbal imagery in the child. London: Routledge and Kegan, 1971.

Pylyshyn, Z. What the mind's eye tells the mind's brain: A critique of mental imagery. Psychological Bulletin, 1973, 80, 1.

Shepard, R., The mental image. American Psychologist, 1978, 33, 125-137.

Shepard, R., and Chipman, S., Second order isomorphism of internal representations: Shapes of states. Cognitive Psychology, 1975, 7, 82-138.

Shepard, R., and Metzler, J. Mental rotation of three dimensional objects. Science, 1971, 171, 701-703.

Tomasulo, D., An economical approach to the development of a training program for porters. Mental Retardation, 1976, 14, 3.

Tomasulo, D. Functional attributes of mediational imagery: A developmental view toward habilitation of retarded adults. In J. E. Shorr, J. Connella, G. Sobel, and P. Robin, (Eds.) Imagery: Its many dimensions and applications. New York: Plenum, 1980.

LIFE-SUSTAINING SYSTEMS AND CONSCIOUSNESS

Albert R. Gilgen

University of Northern Iowa

Cedar Falls, IA

INTRODUCTION

American psychology is fragmented, in part because mind, consciousness, and, to some degree, affect were driven underground from about the 1920's to the 1960's by behavioral and operational orientations. While research on such mentalistic states or processes as sensation, perception, and cognition continued vigorously, each was usually considered in isolation rather than as a particular aspect of mind or consciousness. With the re-legitimation of mind by the late sixties and consciousness by the seventies, there is now some hope that psychology can become a more integrated discipline; there is even a slim chance that a paradigm, i.e., some sort of comprehensive unifying model, may eventually emerge.

In order for the full integrative potential of the concepts mind and consciousness to become manifest, however, it is necessary to reconsider and perhaps reconceptualize the structural and functional aspects of both; for only then will it be possible to understand the roles played by individual mentalistic or psychological processes and states. As a step in that direction it is the purpose of this paper to examine some of the more obvious functions served by consciousness in helping organisms survive. The assumption is made that the capability of being conscious evolved in certain life forms because it is adaptive. George Miller puts it succinctly when he states "the function of consciousness is to guide action" (Miller, 1963, P. 141). While the focus of the paper is on consciousness rather than mind, mind is considered the guidance system of any organism capable of generating a three-dimensional representation of its surround, and consciousness the three-dimensional representation actually generated. It is assumed that many of the processes of mind operate unconsciously. No attempt is made here to review previous functional analyses of consciousness (e.g., James, 1890; Angell, 1906), or analyses of particular conscious modalities or states in particular perceptual phenomena (Brunswik, 1949; Ittelson & Cantril, 1954; Gibson, 1950, 1966, 1979).

Consciousness can be investigated by introspective and retrospective analyses of one's own experiences; by examining such residues of conscious activity as language, art, technology, and the products of everyday living; by physiological and biochemical research; by looking for reasonable models of mentalistic processes; and by asking such functional questions as "how does consciousness aid survival?" As Hilgard points out in a recent Annual Review article (Hilgard, 1980), a new introspectionism has emerged since the 1970's characterized by the following five procedures for obtaining information about inner experiences: "questionnaires, thinking out loud, thought sampling (descriptive), thought sampling (using ratings), and event recording" (P. 17).

The present analysis, while primarily functional, also of necessity makes assumptions concerning the structure of consciousness based mostly on the examination of personal experience and some consideration of the concepts used to classify what are apparently the major conscious states, namely sensation, percept, image, feeling, dream, and perhaps thought. There is some question about thought because the term may refer to an underlying process rather than a type of conscious experience.

THE STRUCTURE OF HUMAN CONSCIOUSNESS

As stated before, consciousness is here considered a three-dimentional representation of its surround generated by an organism. The primary characteristic of consciousness, therefore, is its three dimensionality; there is a three-dimensional space occupied by three-dimentional objects including the organism itself. Another important characteristic of consciousness is focus and background: not all aspects of the three-dimensional matrix are sharp and clear, only those in attention at the moment; and the attentional focus shifts rapidly and continually. It is the continual shifting of attention that generates what William James referred to as the "stream of thought" (James, 1890). Consciousness is also, as we have said before, composed of a variety of discriminable states including sensation, percept, image, dream, and feeling, with each having a somewhat different referent and function. Finally, the content of awareness changes and is added to by experience. While a more detailed discussion of the structure of consciousness is, of course, possible, the foregoing provides enough of a framework for the functional analysis that follows.

A TAXONOMY OF LIFE-SUSTAINING SITUATIONS

The basic structural unit of life is the cell; the basic functional unit is the essential exchange carried on between a cell and its surround. Life is sustained if a cell can ingest the nutrients it needs and expel the waste products produced. For convenience, life-sustaining systems are subdivided into three types: (1) single or small groups of nonencased cells immersed in liquids containing all of their nutrients; (2) nonmobile encased cell aggregates (e.g., plants); and (3) mobile encased cell aggregates (most complex animals). With this taxonomy in mind, we shall now examine each life-sustaining situation and try to determine whether or not consciousness (a three-dimensional representation of surround) is necessary for survival.

Cells Immersed in Liquid Containing All Nutrients

In a quiescent nutrient broth, cells have a reasonable chance of surviving long enough to reproduce if they can move even randomly. Some movement is of course necessary or the cells would become separated from nutrients by their own waste products. In a changing liquid surround, cells would not even have to move in order to survive. See Figure 1. In both of these situations there is clearly no need for a guidance system of any kind; such creatures are therefore without mind or consciousness.

Nonmobile Encased Cell Aggregates

Figure 2 depicts the second type of life-sustaining situation, which in reality is represented by most land-dwelling plants. Such

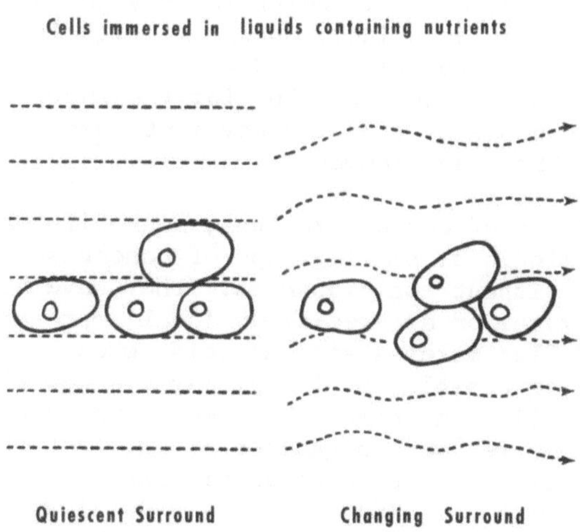

Figure 1

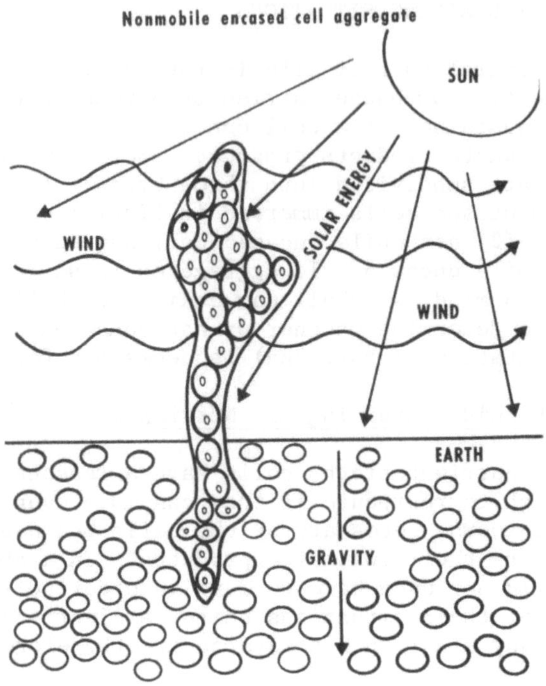

Figure 2

essentially nonmobile cell aggregates survive because they are capable of alignment with the major external energy sources, namely the sun, the earth, and the moving air. In doing so they get all of the resources needed to provide each individual cell with its nutrients. Developmental sensitivity to the sun and earth represents a crude guidance capability in the long run, but for the short run cell groups of this type are incapable of directed movement toward or away from specific aspects of their environments.

Within the context of our assumptions, nonmobile encased cell aggregates are, like single or small groups of nonencased cells immersed in nutrient broths, without consciousness. They have no need for either a guidance system or a three-dimensional representation of their surrounds. Miller makes a similar point when he states: "Imagine that by some impossible, Druidical magic a new kind of tree is created. This tree, like an animal, has sense organs connected by sensory nerves to a large, well organized brain. But the tree does not have any motor nerves or any muscles or glands. It must stand immobile, moving only with the wind, as trees have always stood. Now, here is the question: Does this remarkable tree have any advantage over an ordinary tree?" (Miller, 1963, P. 142). Miller concludes that "a sentient but immobile intelligence would not, could not, develop anything resembling the state of consciousness that you and I recognize as our own" (ibid., P. 142). Such cell aggregates also, incidentally, have little freedom because their existence is directly determined by the major external energy sources. They must grow toward the sun and into the earth or die.

Mobile Encased Cell Aggregates

Figure 3 represents a mobile encased cell aggregate of the type that might exist on the surface of the earth. Unable to extract nutrients from the soil or use the sun directly for energy, such organisms need to move with directional control toward nutrient sources and mates and away from dangers. They clearly require guidance systems sensitive to information in the external energy fields which encompass them. They need to be able to do more than align themselves with the earth and sun.

Are then all mobile encased cell aggregates characterized by guided movement capable of consciousness? Probably not; at least we shall argue that it depends on the nature of their guidance systems.

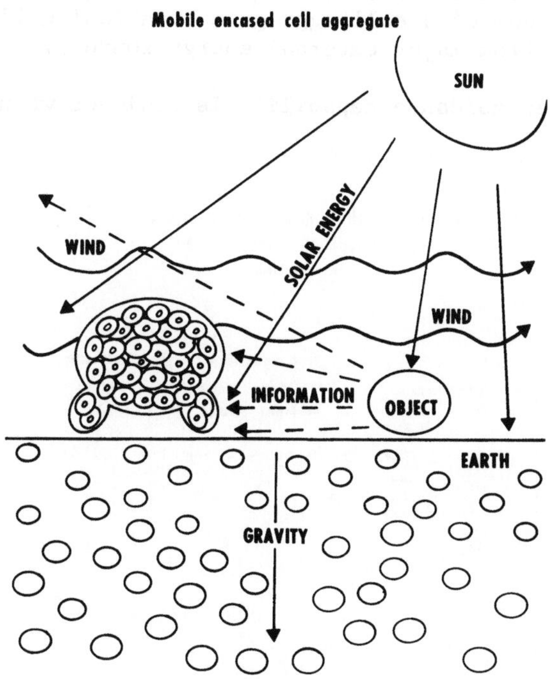

Figure 3

Let us examine some of the ways that guided or controlled movement (behavior) can be achieved and in each case try to determine whether or not consciousness is necessary.

HYPOTHETICAL GUIDANCE SYSTEMS

In general, guidance is achieved whenever an organism is able to use energy patterns (information) to direct its movements. Some of the information has to be of the organism's surround though some of it may also be of the organism itself, e.g., the internal environment. Sensitivity to information in itself does not, however, constitute a guidance system; the information must have an influence over the organism's movement-producing systems. This is possible, as Miller, Galanter, and Pribram (1960) point out, because both cognitive as well as behavioral processes involve sequences of change in the nervous system, thus allowing for the interaction of the two sets of events.

The most rudimentary guidance system orients an organism toward those things in the environment it needs for survival on the basis of a single type of energy change (information). See Figure 4. A simple detection-alignment device such as this would not seem to require a complex central nervous system capable of generating consciousness, that is, a three-dimensional representation of a creature's surround. It is interesting to note that even the simplest guidance mechanism increases the freedom of a cell aggregate by allowing living things some independence from major external energy sources.

A more complex guidance capability is achieved when an organism

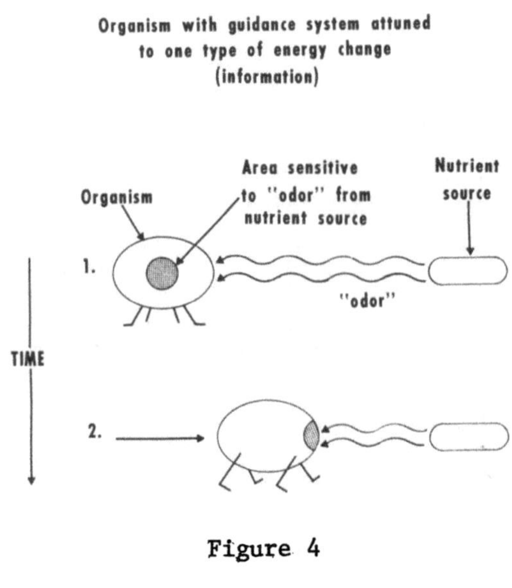

Figure 4

is able to use two or more sources of information to control its activities. If, for example, the movements of a cell aggregate can be directed by chemical changes in the air and light patterns, then guidance is probably enhanced and chances of survival increased. Would an organism with such a detection-alignment device necessarily be capable of consciousness, i.e., would this control mechanism require a central nervous system able to generate a three-dimensional representation of the organism's surround? Probably not, particularly if only one source of information at a time controls movement. For instance, if the sensitivity to chemical changes in the air controls movement until a certain light pattern impinges on the creature, at which time control shifts automatically to the light-sensitive system, then there would be no need for a three-dimensional representation of the organism's surround (see Figure 5).

Simple detection-alignment systems are adaptive if nutrient sources are plentiful and easily detected. If an organism, however, has to make many discriminations in order to get its food, find sexual partners, and avoid dangers, then it needs to evolve a guidance system based on additional information. Since patterned light contains more detailed information of the environment than any other energy source, successful adaptation to a situation requiring refined discrimination probably results in the evolution of highly developed visual systems that include the ability to generate, within an increas-

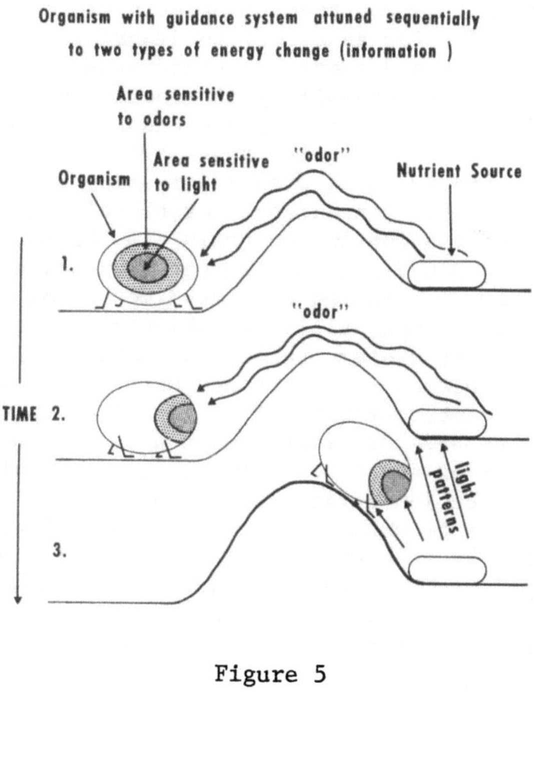

Figure 5

ingly complex brain, three-dimensional representations of the surrouding environment. When this happens, a creature has, according to our criteria, developed the capability to be conscious. That is not to say that the waking state of such an organism would be the same phenomenologically as that of a human being; it would share with us some sort of awareness of structured three-dimensional space, but the details of the structure would vary among species.

We must remember, however, that a three-dimensional representation of an organism's surround, or any other informational display, does not in itself comprise a guidance system; there must be a mechanism whereby the information can influence the organism's movement-control systems. In simple detection-alignment devices, such a mechanism is probably a relatively uncomplicated homeostat; but if the information is in the form of a three-dimensional representation, a more involved linkage between information and organismic control is required. The linkage is apparently accomplished by a focusing mechanism that places movement under the control of information in the total configuration most relevant to survival at a particular moment. Phenomenologically, this is what gives human consciousness its focus-background character; the information in focus determines whatever it is we are attending to.

The evolution of consciousness, however, most likely depends on more than the development of a highly refined visual system, because vision alone does not provide enough information for survival. Sensitivity to the chemical composition of objects via taste and smell is also required in order for an animal to discriminate among those things it needs to ingest and those it should avoid. It is assumed that any life form with the capability of generating a three-dimensional representation of its surround, and thus being conscious, has evolved a central nervous system within which highly structured visual information is intercorrelated with information provided by its other sensory systems. For convenience let us call the configuration of intercorrelated information in the brain the "Primary Information Configuration" (PIC). See Figure 6. We can then say that it is the PIC that generates for an organism a three-dimensional representation of the surrounding environment filled by objects with qualities determined by whatever sensory systems the organism has evolved. If a creature is aware of objects at a distance with shapes and odors, then the PIC represents an intercorrelation of visual and olfactory information; if the objects have distinct sounds as well, then auditory information is also part of the PIC. A guidance system with a PIC is superior to simple detection-alignment mechanisms because it is based on more information and because there is a redundancy of information. The "objects" created by the intercorrelation of information can be recognized via shape, smell, sound, and so forth. This reduces dependency on any single information source. Such an arrangement also provides a prototype for a symbolization process in that one type of information can <u>stand for</u> another; an odor, for example, can stand

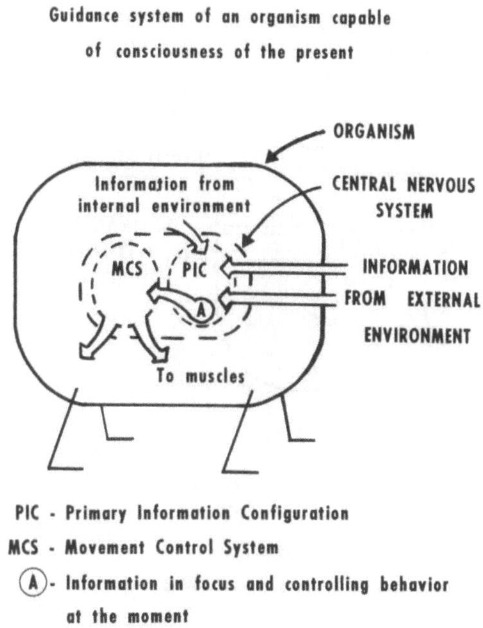

Figure 6

for a shape and so forth.

With regard to freedom, an organism with such a guidance capability, i.e., one capable of consciousness, is freer than one dependent on a simple detection-alignment mechanism because it has many more options. It is, however, still locked into the present; the PIC is made up of information concerning the internal and external environments of the organism as they are at the moment. Transcendence of the present depends on modification of the guidance system by past experience. The degree to which species can free themselves of information _of the present_ undoubtedly varies, and it would seem that _homo sapiens_ has moved farthest in that direction.

A model of _human_ consciousness would therefore have to include a highly developed information-storage system, one in which residues of the intercorrelated information in the Primary Information Configuration (PIC) are stored. There would, in other words, need to be a Secondary Information Configuration (SIC), structured by aspects of informational patterns briefly displayed in the PIC. See Figure 7. In order for such a dual information-configuration arrangement to provide movement control, the focusing device described earlier would have to be capable of shifting back and forth between the PIC and the SIC. Phenomenologically, when the focus is on information in the SIC,

Guidance system of an organism capable of consciousness of the past as well as the present

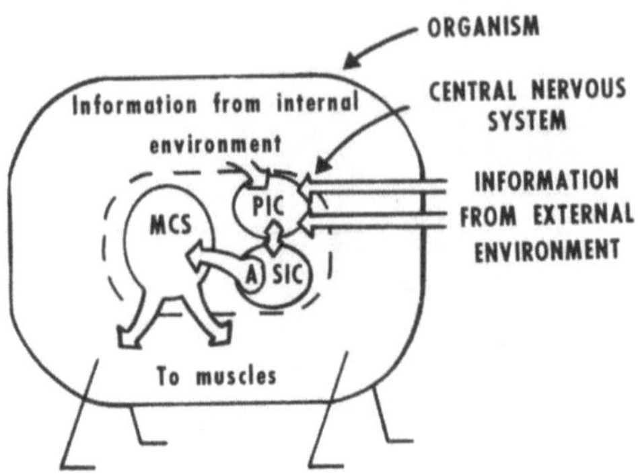

PIC - Primary Information Configuration

SIC - Secondary Information Configuration

MCS - Movement Control System

(A) - Information in focus and controlling behavior at the moment

Figure 7

then a person would be daydreaming, imagining, or thinking; if the focus is on information in the PIC which is of the surround, then the focus of attention would be perceptual; and, if the focus is on information in the PIC concerning the present state of the body, the person might feel or sense a stomach discomfort, a pain in the foot, or a state of relaxation.

While attention can shift between information of the past as reflected by the SIC and events in the present as represented in the PIC, it seems, on the basis of personal introspection, that the information in the PIC almost always provides a context within which all changes in attention take place. There is in awareness what some existentialists have called a sense of "being-in-the-world." The adaptive importance of such an arrangement is obvious, for it is within the context of the information in PIC, i.e., the information of the present (phenomenologically, sensations, percepts, and feelings associated with these states) that movements take place. The world outside and the internal environment must still be monitored even when we are deep in thought or imagination. The only time that information in the PIC does not provide a sense of being-in-the-world is when we are asleep and dreaming. When we are sleeping, of course, we do not plan to go anywhere (we do not need guided movement); and if we have chosen to sleep at the right time and place, we still survive.

To recapitulate, a guidance system capable of accounting for human consciousness must include a highly developed Secondary Information Configuration (SIC) constructed gradually from residues of informational patterns in the PIC, which in turn represent intercorrelations of information of the present from two or more information sources, including a highly developed visual system. Such an arrangement allows the focus of attention to shift from information of the present (in the PIC) to information of the past (in the SIC).

The adaptive value of such a guidance system rests in the fact that for an organism that must exist a long time in order to perpetuate the species, the present states of the internal and/or external environments are not always the best guides for behavior. It is often more adaptive for a person, for instance, to plan his or her next move at least partially on the basis of a frame of reference free from "the now." The very act of planning requires an attentional referent free of present conditions. The ability to plan, imagine, or think is also adaptive because it saves energy: it allows us to consider a variety of behavioural options without having to do very much.

Can the full richness of human consciousness be accounted for by the type of guidance capability just described and depicted in Figure 7? Perhaps, but only if we realize that the complexity of human experience is a function of both the residues, in the brain, of previous information configurations and relatively permanent transformations of the external environment such as words, books, art works, buildings, roads, clothing, appliances, tools, and so forth, which represent residues of collective behavior. The primary environmental pressure for the evolution of a brain capable of complex thought may, in fact, have been provided by these cumulative external residues of our ancestors' activities. Perhaps humanity's superior intelligence evolved not because people made tools but because they shaped and scratched stones, which, being very durable, accumulated over generations and created an increasingly complex heritage and environment.

In conclusion, mobile encased cell aggregates depend on a variety of guidance systems for survival, from simple present-oriented detection-alignment mechanisms to complex information-processing capabilities structured partly by past organism-environment encounters. Consciousness, it is argued, emerges when an organism evolves a central nervous system capable of intercorrelating information from a highly developed visual system with information from at least one other sensory source; such a development is adaptive because it creates a guidance system based on a great deal of redundant information. The systems discussed are not, however, meant to account entirely for the directional-control capability of any particular species, for it is probably the case that rudimentary guidance mechanisms are often retained even when an organism develops more sophisticated control over its activities. While we can be conscious and highly versatile mentally, for example, some of our behavior is still under the control of simple detection-alignment mechanisms (reflexes).

EPILOG

This analysis of consciousness casts a rather interesting light on the free-will-versus-determinism issue. It proposes that as cell aggregates become less dependent on the direct influence of the sun, earth, and air, they attain more freedom. A plant, for example, has little freedom because its existence depends on its direct alignment with the sources of solar and gravitional energies. A simple mobile creature sensitive to information concerning the structure of its present state and surround, on the other hand, gains some freedom because it can move and still survive. And, finally, an organism capable of transcending information of its present state and surround is even freer. Humans by this reasoning are the freest of living things, except perhaps single or nonencased groups of cells lazing about in nutrient broths.

REFERENCES

Angell, J. R. The province of functional psychology. Presidential address before the American Psychologica Association, 1906. In Hillgard, E. R. (Ed.), American psychology in historical perspective. Washington, D.C.: American Psychological Association, 1978.

Brunswik, E. Systematic and representative design of psychological experiments. Berkeley: University of California Press, 1949.

Gibson, J. The perception of the visual world. Boston: Houghton-Mifflin, 1950.

Gibson, J. The senses considered as perceptual systems. Boston: Houghton-Mifflin, 1966.

Gibson, J. The ecological approach to visual perception. Boston: Houghton-Mifflin, 1979.

Hilgard, E. R. Consciousness in comtemporary psychology. Annual Review of Psychology, 1980, 31, 1-26.

Ittelson, W. H., and Cantril, H. Perception: A transactional approach. Garden City, NJ: Doubleday, 1954.

James, W. The principles of psychology (Vol. I). New York: Holt, 1890.

Miller, G. A. Thinking, cognition, and learning. In B. Berelson (Ed.), The behavioral sciences today. New York: Basic Books, 1963.

Miller, G. A., Galanter, E., and Pribram, K. H. Plans and the structure of behavior. New York: Holt, Rinehart and Winston, 1960.

A PHILOSOPHICAL CRITIQUE OF PIAGET'S VIEW OF IMAGES AS INTERIORIZED ACTIONS

Dennis M. Senchuk

Indiana University

Bloomington, IN

Mental imagery, according to Piaget, is a matter of 'interiorized imitation.' Since imitation is an activity, his view amounts to the suggestion the images are interiorized actions. But what does that mean? This paper is a philosophical exploration of Piaget's account of mental images, an attempt to clarify and critically examine his account rather than to offer any alternative theoretical conception of images. I shall try to determine whether Piaget's views on the subject make any sense, whether they fit together well, and whether they accord with plausible philosophical observations about the nature of mental images.

It should be noted at the outset that after-images and physical representations, such as photographs, are not the locus of Piaget's concern. Instead, he is interested in what might be referred to (albeit obscurely) as mental representations; and Piaget (1962) alerts us to a possible further ambiguity that could infect the discussion of this topic. "Representation," he tells us, can be understood in two different senses: either broadly as "identical with...all intelligence which is based on a system of concepts or mental schemas..." or narrowly, as "restricted to the mental or memory image, *i.e.*, the symbolic evocation of absent realities" (P. 67). But Piaget insists that the two kinds of representation are related: first, because images as concrete symbols are the signifiers of concepts and, so, are implicated in all thinking in terms of concepts; and, second, because both kinds of representation develop concurrently. In any case, this

---

This work was supported, in part, by a grant from the Spencer Foundation.

paper will restrict itself to a consideration of his account of representations in the narrow sense, i.e., internal models or memories (hereafter, mental images).

Piaget's account of mental images is a genetic, developmental one. According to that account, the infant at birth is equipped with a repertoire of reflexes. Wherever possible, the infant tries to assimilate its environment to the reflexes--sucking and grasping everything in reach. Whenever necessary, the infant accommodates the reflexes to its environment, gradually modifying them to cope with features of that emvironment. Mental development is understood as progress toward a stable equilibrium between these complementary processes of assimilation and accommodation. But before this equilibrium is reached, there is a supremacy either of assimilation or of accommodation. It is this latter sort of dominance that interests us here, since it is said to result in representative imitation, which in turn is said to evolve into mental imagery. As Piaget (1962) puts the matter, "if the subject's schemas of action are modified by the external world without his utilizing this external world, i.e., if there is primacy of accommodation over assimilation, the activity tends to become imitation" (P. 5). So let's trace his account of the development of imitation from reflex action to genuine mental imagery.

Piaget argues that, at the level of pure reflexes, there is no imitation. His first argument for this conclusion seems weak: he defines imitation as the reproduction of a model, points out that such an activity presupposes something acquired by experience, and concludes that pure reflexes, which presumably haven't acquired anything from experience, can't support imitation.

However, if there were an imitative reflex (or instinct), it might well be set off by exposure to appropriate models previously unexperienced by the subject; so we can hardly concur with Piaget that imitation at the level of pure reflexes is ruled out even by his own definitions.

Piaget's interpretations of certain observations he makes of his own infant children make it plain, however, that his main reason for denying imitation at this level lies elsewhere. He says that when an infant cries in response to someone else's crying, the other's crying may well be just a noxious stimulus that causes it to cry rather than a model the infant reproduces. But this sounds as though Piaget is denying the one possibility only because there is another possibility not controverted by any evidence. So it is still possible--however unsubstantiated by any positive evidence--that infants are born with imitative reflexes. And, we must remember, it is equally unsubstantiated by evidence that, as Piaget insists, infants are born with nonimitative reflexes.

But let us not dwell on what, in the present context, is a relatively minor issue. Whatever the truth is about whether or not imitation is innate, the fact remains that Piaget does sketch an interesting and informative story of the development of imitation. He considers the appearance of imitation to be dependent upon the appearance not just of reflexes but of what he calls "circular reactions." These are said to arise when reflex responses become differentiated--when, e.g., crying becomes wailing or whimpering (or whatever). These differentiated reactions are said to be circular when they are reproduced for their own sake, when the very activity, say, of wailing seems to stimulate itself--as if the wailing reaction were self-reinforcing. Now the inception of true imitation is said to be an outgrowth of these circular reactions--the only difference being that, with imitation, someone else's sounds serve as the model for the reproduction for its own sake. In other words, sort of vocal contagion takes place: sounds produced by others are assimilated to ones produced by the infant and are then reproduced by the infant.

At first this contagion only occurs when the infant has itself produced the same sound right before the other person does. Later on, the infant will reproduce sounds it has not been making recently, provided only that it does have those sounds in its repertoire. Still later, in the case of gestures, the infant can reproduce wholly new gestures, provided they can be produced by parts of its own body that are visible to it. This is followed by (often crude) attempts to imitate movements not visible to the infant itself, such as sticking out its tongue. Next, the infant imitates behavior not previously in its repertoire. And finally, the infant's imitation is said to be deferred, in that it reproduces behavior in the absence of the original model for that behavior.

It is this final development in the evolution of the infant's ability to imitate that most needs to be examined if we are to understand and assess the merits of Piaget's account of the genesis of mental imagery; for, as Gruber and Vonéche (1977) explain it in their sketch of Piaget's account of deferred imitations, such "imitations take place in the absence of the model because of internalization by the child of his own movements. This last form of imitation is a symbolic evocation, because it does not lean upon the presence of the model" (P. 486). In other words, the infant's ability to engage in deferred imitation is explained by its reliance upon a mental representation of the behavior to be imitated. And this mental representation or image is itself understood as an internalized imitation. Accordingly, deferred imitation is really supposed to be a sort of double imitation: first an internalized one, then an externalized reproduction of that internalized model. Let us think this through philosophically.

The very idea of a double imitation may seem a bit peculiar, but it should not be faulted on that basis alone. Indeed, once we remember that imitation depends on circular reactions, with their characteristic tendency to keep themselves going--to reinforce themselves--the idea of the double imitation might seem less odd. Indeed, for Piaget, double imitation amounts to little more that one circular reaction giving rise to another, very similar circular reaction. The only problem might then seem to be that of understanding why two circular reactions are said to be involved instead of one, but the answer would doubtless be that the first is an interiorized imitation of an external model, while the second is an "exteriorized" version of the interiorized model.

Before we explore what Piaget means by interiorization here, let us consider whether the notion of an interiorized imitation, a mental representation, is really needed in order to account for the possibility of deferred imitation. Piaget's reasoning about this matter, although largely unstated, seems patent. He assumes that since the original model to be imitated is not present in the case of deferred imitation, there must be some other, less public model around for the infant to copy. Since imitative behavior is always a copy of some original behavior, it seems reasonable to conclude that, in deferred imitation, this less public model is itself some sort of interiorized imitative behavior.

But this reasoning is subject to some rather serious objections. For one thing, it ought to apply with equal vigor even to the earliest stages in the development of imitation. After all, even some of the earliest cases of vocal imitation do not quite overlap the sounds being imitated; and if there is any temporal gap whatever between model and imitation, the cases qualify as ones of deferred imitation. But we do not seem to feel the need to explain these cases in terms of intermediary, interiorized imitation. These earlier bits of mimicry seem aptly characterized merely as delayed reactions, the explanation of which might well be given in exclusively physiological terms. Indeed, it would hardly be a very plausible explanation of delayed reactions in general to say that they are really <u>immediate</u> reactions--especially when those immediate reactions are said to be virtually identical to the delayed reactions. Thus, it would hardly make much sense to say that the dynamite that explodes moments after impact has really exploded, inwardly, immediately upon impact. Still, it must be admitted that just such an explanation is far more plausible in the case of delayed imitation, given Piaget's view that circular reactions are involved in imitation: since such reactions are supposed to be self-perpetuating, it is not beyond the realm of possibility that they could fill the gap between action and apparently delayed reaction.

But consider the consequences of using inner circular reactions to account for deferred, outer circular reactions. If these inner versions are to fill the gap, they must fill it completely. But is it really very plausible to suppose that, when one of Piaget's children screams, shakes her play-pen, and stamps her foot in deferred imitation of another child, she has been doing all this in an interiorized fashion ever since seeing the other child do it? If that does not strain credulity, let me point out further that a whole day has passed between the original behavior and its deferred imitation. But surely Piaget does not mean to say that an interiorized circular reaction has been taking place from the moment the other child stopped his tantrum, continuing on through lunch, dinner, and even sleep, until the time when the deferred imitation of that tantrum goes public. Circular reactions may tend to be self-perpetuating; but there are some temporal limits to the monotonous repetition of any particular pattern of overt behavior, so there is some reason to expect comparable limits in the case of covert behavior as well. Besides, during the period of delay, the other activities that occupy the child would seem in some cases (e.g., eating) to interfere with ongoing covert activity and in other cases (e.g., dreamless sleeping) to be incompatible with such activity.

Given the apparent absurdity of suggesting that the interiorized imitation occurs continuously during the interim between an action and its overt imitation, one might be inclined to conclude that Piaget surely does not mean to suggest any such thing. Perhaps, instead, he merely introduces these interiorized imitations as immediate precursors of their exterior reproductions. In other words, perhaps these inner models do not have to be on the scene until the deferred imitation itself is about to begin. This would, of course, make it easier for Piaget's daughter to eat and sleep in the meantime.

But this suggestion is no less absurd than the one it replaces. The comforting illusion that such mental representations might serve as contemporaneous models for deferred imitation is quickly dispelled once we realize that these inner models are themselves supposed to be imitations. After all, if we need an inner imitation to serve as a ready model for the deferred outer imitation, what will serve in the capacity of such a model for the deferred inner imitation itself? And if it does not stand in need of a model, then neither does the outer imitation. If it does stand in need of one, then we are faced once again with the prospect of continuous inner imitation; for if each imitation stands in need of a presently available model, then--although an infinite regress of models is not a problem--there cannot be <u>any</u> time between the original model and any of its successive reproductions. And if now, in retrospect, the idea of such continuous imitation seems more attractive than the alternative of having the appeal to interior imitation do no explanatory work at all, then perhaps we should consider one more absurd consequence of that earlier idea. It implies that whenever we set out, successfully, to give a deferred imitation of anything, we are in fact already giving such an imitation. And if we consider the number of things we might be prepared to imitate, however badly, at any given moment, we quickly realize that our inner lives would have to be far more densely active than they seem to be. Pity the poor professional impressionist, who, on this view at least, must not only imitate Chevalier, Cagney, and

Gable serially, but simultaneously.

But are we so badly impaled on the horns of this dilemma? Certainly not if we abandon the idea of interiorized imitation altogether. To see whether this is a viable alternative, let us begin by taking the heroic course--seeing, while remaining in the Piagetian framework, whether deferred imitation requires any inner representation whatever, be it an interior imitation or not. Given the other elements of Piaget's account of imitation, what is really needed is something to set off the circular reaction that is supposed to be the underlying mechanism of imitative behavior. But why should we assume that only another model, either the original or a mental reproduction of it, can serve as an appropriate detonating device? The causative factor might well be a physiological one of which we are totally unaware. Or, if we insist on a conscious, mental determination in the case of imitation, then we might consider the possibility of some sort of cue, a phenomenon that is associated for us with the behavior to be imitated and that elicits the circular reaction that in some sense constitutes our (deferred) imitation. Either alternative seems quite in keeping with the spirit of Piaget's theory, since it is basic to his conception of intellectual development that action schemata can come to be set off by different stimuli than the ones that first serve that purpose. Reflexes evolve into circular reactions because of this assimilative tendency on the part of those reflexes, so why not postulate an analogous occurrence in the case of those circular reactions that constitute imitations?

Of course it might be objected that unless some actual model provokes the circular reaction, that reaction cannot very well qualify as an imitation. But if there is some causal chain of events connecting the original model with the physiological factor or the conscious cue, then perhaps this would be grounds enough to affirm the existence of a genuine imitation.

Still, we might be a bit reluctant to speak of imitation save in cases where there is intentional reproduction of a model. Imitation proper seems all too willful. Piaget seems to be getting at some such point when he emphasizes that even the first, most rudimentary attempts at imitation are not involuntary circular reactions: the child who engages in vocal imitation, Piaget (1962) stresses, "must be interested in the sounds he hears, in which case the contagion is in no way automatic, but is a kind of spontaneous circular reaction" (P. 10). The child who imitates a sound is thus consciously setting out to produce a sound similar to one already heard. And while we may sometimes speak of unconscious mimicry or imitation, these are nevertheless cases where we do not readily suppose a total lack of responsibility and intent. The author who unwittingly imitates another's writings is thought to have done something rather suspect, and the child who imitates another child's speech, gestures and other behavior is quickly accused by his peers of being a "copy-cat." Accordingly, the automatic, causally determined reproduction of a given piece of behavior may not even count as genuine imitation, except in special, theoretically tendentious, psychological usage. And if it does not, then the proffered alternatives to Piaget's dilemma are themselves highly questionable, since they fail to account for cases of genuine imitation.

But, once again, this tends to make the notion of an interior model, by comparison, a more compelling alternative; for if someone deliberately sets out to reproduce a given model, the absence of any version of that model would seem to pose a serious challenge--one that could not be met by any factor that merely triggered a reaction similar to the original model. Such a chain of events would not qualify as a bona fide imitation unless the reaction were itself a consciously controlled reproducing of the original. Thus, if someone inhales helium in order to bring about a vocal response similar to the sound of Donald Duck's voice, that does not qualify as an imitation of Donald Duck. Therefore, it might be thought that the only way to bring off a true imitation is to have some model of the thing to be imitated right before the senses or the mind; for if some model is on the scene, then the reproduction can be a consciously controlled undertaking. The would-be imitator consults the model in order to have some appropriate feedback--the model serves as a standard against which the efforts at imitation are gauged.

One way of avoiding some of the earlier objections against understanding such a model as an interiorized imitation is to suggest that the interior version is not a full-fledged imitation. Perhaps it could be suggested instead that the inner model is just an automatic circular reaction causally tied to the original model. (Since the inner model is supposed to provide the genetic basis for the "semiotic function," to serve as a symbolic representation developmentally prerequisite to the development of linguistic representation, there is some obvious affinity between the suggested view of that model and what has come to be called the "causal theory of reference." According to that theory, words refer to things provided our use of these words is causally tied to the dubbing of those things with these words (Kripke, 1972).

But while this suggestion preserves any benefits that may accrue to Piaget's view of images as circular reactions, it still runs afoul of what is known, in philosophical circles, as Meno's paradox of inquiry. In Plato's Meno (1961) the observation is make that it makes no sense to inquire about the nature of (say) virtue, since if one already knows, the inquiry is pointless, and if one does not know, one will not recognize the nature of virtue even if one stumbles upon it. The above view of the inner model is up against the first horn of this paradoxical dilemma, since there seems to be little point in our intentionally reproducing a model that we are or were already automatically reproducing. On the other horn, if we hope to dispense with any inner model, we are apparently stuck without any way of controlling our deferred imitation--even if we do get it right, we will not have any way of knowing that we do.

Before we try to decide between these unpalatable alternatives, let us consider briefly some ancillary benefits and deficits of Piaget's view of images. One strong point in favor of this view is that it explains the development of mental imagery as a gradual evolution out of pre-existing capabilities rather than as a sudden emergence out of nothing. Another benefit is its construal of imagery in active, dynamic terms, rather than in the more customary static terms employed by views of images as perceptual copies. Such an active view might well help to make more sense out of the notion that the activity of thinking consists in a succession of images; and, according to Piaget, this active view of images holds some promise of explaining the acquisition of language, the anticipation in thought of action, and the ability to solve certain problems. Thus, to give an illustration of this last sort of application, we might mention one of Piaget's (1977) own favorite examples:

> ...in trying to open a box of matches that is nearly shut, the subject gropes for a while, then pauses, looks attentively at the aperture which has to be made bigger, opening and shutting his mouth as he does so, until finally he puts his finger in the slit and thus solves the problem (Pp. 60-61).

Each of these proposed applications deserves careful consideration. Some of them seem subject to the paradox of inquiry in much the same way as the account of deferred imitation does. Thus, the account of problem-solving might seem to explain little by suggesting as it does that the problem has already been solved by way of an imitative representation of that solution. But all of these applications are quite fascinating and are suggestive of further empirical as well as philosophical investigation.

A major drawback of Piaget's view of images would seem to be the notion of interiorization, which appears to suggest some mysterious process of evolution from external, physical and publicly observable action to internal, mental and only privately accessible action. This mysterious transition seems even more incomprehensible as it is claimed that the interior activity is, nonetheless, very similar to its exterior prototypes. But these sticking points may rest on a misunderstanding of Piaget's notion, since he describes "internalized imitation" of body movements as something "by which they are reproduced in outline, complete reproduction being held back by inhibition" (Piaget, 1977, P. 657). In other words, such things as the initial muscular contractions that, if carried to completion, would result in gross movement of limbs, are what Piaget seems to mean by interiorized activity. This activity is not something mental as opposed to physical, and it could even be publicly detected, given suitable aids to observation. Of course there remain some questions about the character of one's subjective experience of such a "motor adumbration of...movement"

(Piaget, 1977, P. 657), but Piaget does not really have much to say about this subject--his interest in images seems more functional than metaphysical. Here, too, is a topic worthy of further philosophical inquiry, but this is not the time to pursue it.

Enough has been said, I think, to show that Piaget's view of images should not be readily dismissed. Still, we should not be led by our favorable disposition toward the view to ignore its faults as an account of deferred imitation. As such, it seems firmly stuck on the first horn of Meno's paradoxical dilemma. The alternative suggestion, that deferred imitation requires no mental imagery, is threatened, of course, by the other horn of that dilemma; but I am inclined to think that this danger is more easily avoided.

Suppose we set out to imitate a particular person's characteristic ways of talking, smiling, and so on. If that person is a famous movie star or other public figure, there may be filmed or videotaped records of his or her behavior. But if these are presently unavailable to us we are forced, I suppose, to rely on our memories. And if we construe all memories as images, it begins to seem that mental representations are unavoidable elements of deferred imitations. But this is not, or at any rate need not, be what happens.

Sometimes we just strike a pose or intone a few syllables in direct imitation of the absent model, without the obvious intervention of any images. We may or may not get it right on the first trial--sometimes it seems to capture a feature of the person, sometimes it seems a little off. In the former case, we make an effort to go further in the same direction; in the latter, we try to improve upon our past performance. We do not always compare our performance with some inner representation of the original; we do not have to. Memory serves us well in calling forth our initial efforts and in guiding those efforts in the future. When we do try to improve upon our first stumbling attempts, we may do so because we recognize that those attempts are faulty: they do not really remind us of the person; or, perhaps, they seem only partly right. We are engaged in a process of reconstruction from memory. Our imitative efforts are themselves integral to that process; and we imitate successfully not so much as a result of first correctly remembering--correctly imagining--the model, but rather by remembering as we go along that what we are doing is like--is reminiscent of--the original. By the same token, when our performance reminds others of the person we hope to imitate, they need not compare our performance with their own images in order to be thus reminded.

I hope I have said enough to make plausible the suggestion that it is possible to engage in deferred imitation without recourse to imagery. This is not to say, however, that such imitation never involves internal models. Thus, if we set out to imitate Burt Lancaster's persona, who among us can resist a preliminary appeal to an image of his broad, beaming grin? Of course if we still wish to retain Piaget's view of images, even this preliminary peek is really a sort of "motor adumbration" of that grin, our own internalized imitation of it. And this suggests a possible release from the first horn of the dilemma, too. For if the internal model is a mere shadow of the later external performance, we might construe that model as an early phase of the process of reconstruction, as an anticipation of the fuller version to follow. If that first reproduction seems to make the later version pale by comparison, perhaps it is for much the same reason as our humming a familiar tune seems to outshine our subsequent efforts to vocalize it, or the same reason our rough sketches can sometimes hold out a greater promise than our meager talents at precise draftsmanship can fulfill.

REFERENCES

Gruber, H. E., and Voneche, J. J. The essential Piaget. New York: Basic Books, 1977.

Kripke, S. A. Naming and necessity. In D. Davidson, and G. Harmon (Eds.), Semantics of natural language. Boston: D. Reidel, 1972.

Piaget, J. Play, dreams and imitation. New York: Norton, 1962.

Piaget, J. Mental images. In H. E. Gruber, and J. J. Voneche (Eds.), The essential Piaget. New York: Basic Books, 1977.

Plato. Meno. In E. Hamilton, and H. Cairns (Eds.), Plato: The collected dialogues. New York: Pantheon Books, 1961.

IMAGES, PROPOSITIONS, AND NATURAL SIGNS

Charles J. List

University of Iowa

Iowa City, Iowa

Russell in his 1919 paper, "On Propositions: What They Are and How They Mean," argues that there are two kinds of propositions--word-propositions and image-propositions and that word-propositions "mean" image-propositions (Russell, 1971). As Russell says: "The problem of the meaning of words is reduced to the problem of the meaning of images" (P. 303). Furthermore, Russell continues, the "'meaning' of images is the simplest kind of meaning, because images resemble what they mean, whereas words, as a rule, do not" (P. 303). Taken together, these claims determine a familiar position on the relation between words and images: words mean images and images resemble what they mean. What makes my statement about <u>him</u> a statement about him is its relation to an images I have of him; and what makes my image of him an image of him is its resembling him.

The problem this view faces can be put initially like this: either an image is a natural sign in that its meaning is in need of no further analysis in terms of other relations or objects, or an image is a conventional sign, one that does depend on prior knowledge of rules and conventions in determining its meaning. An image, I shall argue, is not a natural sign. If an image is a conventional sign, Russell's analysis of meaning is incomplete without an analysis of image-meaning, i.e., resemblance. What this analysis shows I shall argue is that images cannot be assigned an explanatory role in analyses of meaning, belief, and truth, as Russell asserts. This point is worth making because at least one recent defender of mental images, Alastair Hannay, fails to appreciate its force. Hannay briefly discusses Wittgenstein's criticism along these lines but fails to appreciate the way in which it calls into question the necessity of a defense of mental images (Hannay, 1971). In outline, what I shall do in this paper is this: first,

I shall fill in some of the detail of Russell's view. Second, I shall raise a traditional objection to any image theory of meaning. Third I shall argue that resemblance is not a kind of natural signification and that thus images are not natural signs.

IMAGE-PROPOSITIONS

Russell's express reason for embracing image-propositions is his dissatisfaction with the behaviorism of Watson. Russell argues against Watson that meaning is primarily a relations which passes through a mental intermediary and that therefore behaviorists miss the essential point about meaning when they attempt to analyze it solely in a causal-physical way (Kaplan and Copilowish, 1939; Russell, 1940). Russell discusses two criticisms of behaviorism. First, it is empirically undeniable that there are images. Yet, behaviorism at least appears to deny their existence. Second, behaviorism seems incapable of accounting for the use of words in the absence of their objects. The first is an objection of fact, the second an objection of theory. Russell finds only the first criticism acceptable: "If, therefore, images were not empirically undeniable, I should not consider them theoretically necessary in order to account for the occurrence of words in the absence of their objects" (P. 299). Russell thinks the advantage of his view is that image-propositions are elements of experience, and that it "rejects everything mythological or merely schematic" (P. 307).

"Logicians," Russell says elsewhere, "have done very little toward explaining the nature of the relation called 'meaning', nor are they to blame in this, since the problem is essentially one for psychology" (P. 290). What Russell means to imply by this is that the entities and relations which constitute meaning must be "empirically observable."

If the problem of meaning is a psychological one, the first question to ask is which brand of psychology best solves the problem. For Russell, this is a choice between the behaviorism of Watson and the neutral monism of William James. Russell chooses James and says that he has made "great endeavors to believe" James' theory (P. 299). Although Russell ultimately rejects behaviorism, he says that there is much that is true and important in it. In particular, the behaviorist's account of meaning is right _as far as it goes_. Behaviorism is adequate to explain our understanding the meaning of words in four common situations. We understand a word, according to the behaviorist, if, (1) we use the word properly on suitable occasions, (2) when we hear it we act appropriately, (3) we associate the word with another word which has the appropriate effect on behavior, or finally, (4) we associate the word with some object that has the same causal effects as the word itself. Insofar as these are meanings of "meaning" or "understanding," the behaviorist is certainly correct in emphasizing them.

However, as Russell points out, there is another sense of "meaning" which "cannot be fully dealt with on behaviorist lines" (P. 303). The follwoing is a case in point. Suppose, for example, that a child relates an incident that happened on his birthday: "I remember that I blew out the candles." Russell says about this situation:

> It is clear that, insofar as the child is genuinely remembering, he has a picture of the past occurence, and his words are chosen so as to describe the picture, and insofar as the hearer is genuinely apprehending what is said, the hearer is acquiring a picture more or less like that of the child. (P. 302)

This "narrative" use of language is intended to describe or to cause images. Russell reinforces the importance of this use of language as follows:

> And this is really the most essential function of words: that, primarily through their connection with images, they bring us into touch with what is remote in time or space. When they operate without the medium or images, this seems to be a telescoped process. Thus the problem of the meaning of words is reduced to the problem of the meaning of images. (P. 303)

But what is the difference between the meaning of words and the meaning of images? "The meaning of words differs, as a rule, from that of images by depending upon association, not upon similarity" (P. 300). Words are associated by causal relationships with other words, with actions, and with images. Images, on the other hand, resemble their "prototypes." This resemblance, though hard to define, is characterized by Russell in the following way:

> If an object _0_ is the prototype (or a prototype, in the case of vagueness) of an image, then, in the presence of _0_, we can recognize it as what we had an image 'of.' We may then say that _0_ is the 'meaning' (or a meaning, in the case of vagueness) of the image. (P. 304)

Let us now move to propositions. Word-propositions are complexes of words (of course, not just any complex) and image-propositions are complexes of images:

> As a general rule, a word-proposition "means" an image-proposition; this is the case with false propositions as well as with true ones, since image-propositions are as capable of truth and falsehoods as word-propositions. I shall not speak of the fact which makes a proposition true or false as its "meaning," because this usage would be confusing in the

> case of falsehood. (Pp. 308-309)

Meaning has a dual aspect: the meaning of word-propositions is accounted for in terms of association; the meaning of image-propositions is accounted for in terms of resemblance.

In order to better understand the nature of Russell's images, let us raise the following probelm. The possibility of communication requires that multiple speakers be able to find the same meaning in a given word or sentence. This meaning cannot be a particular mental entity: that is not publicly accessible in the required way. Russell's image-propositions do not seem to meet the requirement of publicity.

Russell, although he does not explicitly deal with this objection, says some things which may be taken as tonics to ease its force. He discusses this problem with publicity in the context of a general mistrust of introspective evidence. But he argues that this mistrust is too selective and it should not be if the anti-introspectionist is to be consistent:

> If privacy is the main objection to introspective data, we shall have to include among such data all bodily sensations. A toothache, for example, is essentially private. (P. 294)

Yet, Russell continues, cavities have been correlated with toothaches in a perfectly acceptable manner useful for both dentists and patients. Similarly, other bodily aches or pains provide essential data for physicians. So why can we not trust introspective data? We do trust them all the time.

Community or belief and communication require "public" data. Images are not "public." Therefore, they will not do. Another reply to this argument questions the first premise: what does this dichotomy public-private amount to? Russell says that underlying the public-private distinction is the concept of localization. Introspective data "are not localized at all, or they are localized in a place already physically occupied. . ." (P. 295). If we can <u>place</u> something, it is public; if not, it is private. The problem with this, Russell thinks, is that there is a gradually diminishing degree of publicity in various data of introspection. The data of sight and hearing are the most public, smell is less so than these, touch even less so, and visceral data are hardly public at all. These gradually diminishing degrees of publicity are familiar upon reflection.

Let us be clear that these data are <u>sensations</u>, not yet <u>images</u>. Images, Russell asserts with Hume, are copies of sensations. Thus "when we consider the localization of images, we find a difference according to the nature of the image" (P. 295). Some images, of pains of feelings, can be localized, e.g., a stomachache or the resembrance of one, in the stomach. But visual and auditory images are not thus localizable. These images are not public, yet they undoubtedly occur. Thus,

> it seems that the physical world does not include all that we are aware of, and that introspection must be admitted as a source of knowledge distinct from sensation. (P. 296)

To summarize Russell's probable reply to the publicity problem: he says, first, that we often do trust our private sensations and images, so there is nothing on this score which would persuade us to begin mistrusting images. But, second, the fact that images, especially visual and auditory ones, are not localizable does not show that they are untrustworthy; rather it shows that we must countenance a new source of knowledge.

AN INFINITE REGRESS

Russell, as we have seen, distinguishes word-propositions from image-propositions. He further says that as a general rule, a word-proposition means an image-proposition. The difficulty with this view is well stated in these words from Ayer (1947):

> . . .The assumption that understanding consists in having images leads to a vicious infinity regress. For these images must themselves be symbols if they are to do the work required of them; and in that case further images will have to be supplied for their interpretation and so on *ad infinitum*. (P. 21)

If, to understand a work-proposition, I must understand an image-proposition, and if an image-proposition is a "symbol" in the same way a word-proposition is a symbol, then I must understand another image-proposition before I can understand the first. If a word-proposition *means* an image-proposition, and if we may in the same sense be in doubt about the meaning of an image-proposition, it seems that we never escape the realm of images, and thus we never can find out what anything, word or image, means.

Are images symbols in the same sense that words are symbols? There are certain important features they share. Russell notes that the causes of the word or image, the effects of the word or image, and the relation that constitutes meaning must be kept distince. He says, "It is fairly clear that 'meaning' is a relation involving causal laws, but it involves also something else which is less easy to define" (P. 300). Russell attempts to capture this something else in terms of the difference between association and resemblance. In effect, Russell is arguing that the sense in which *words* have meaning (dependent upon mere association) is different from the sense in which images have meaning. Images mean by way of resemblance, while words mean by way of conventional association. This, then, is Russell's reply to the infinite regress argument: images are not symbols in the same sense that words are symbols. To understand an image, one need not have any other images; the image is understood "straightoff." No interpretation is necessary.

But are images thus natural signs? Let us consider a contrary opinion. The idea for this objection is explicit in Wittgenstein's later work. Wittgenstein says for example in the Blue Book:

> One is tempted to imagine that which gives the sentence life as something in an occult sphere, accompanying the sentence. But whatever accompanied it would for us just be another sign.[1] (1958, P. 5)

In Wittgenstein's terms such an object as a natural sign "shows its sense." One of the things Wittgenstein argues is that no image and hence no image-proposition is capable of showing its sense, since images like pictures can be interpreted in various ways. Thus, Russell is mistaken in that image-propositions are not natural signs, but just other conventional signs.

How shall we decide this issue? One party is saying, "Image-propositions are intrinsically meaningful--subject to only one interpretation." The other party replies, "No, your image-propositions are signs, just like word-propositions and are therefore subject to a variety of interpretations."

Russell wants to hold that words and sentences mean images and image-propositions. The objection used the generic term "sign" for words and images. These are signs because they "stand for" something else. The signs are conventional. So, the objection restates the original position as all signs mean images or image-propositions. But images themselves are signs, i.e., they "stand for" something else, namely, prototypes. But Wittgenstein points out that all signs may mean images, but signs are always subject to a variety of interpretations. Thus words may be "interpreted" in one way by one image or set of images. But as images themselves are signs, they too may be interpreted in a variety of ways. Thus, this second objection concludes, images cannot do the task set for them: to be natural signs.

Now there is an obvious reply to these related criticisms. I have already said that Russell in effect avails himself of it. What Russell does is to distinguish the sense in which words "mean" images from the sense in which images "mean" something. That is, he first agrees that both images and words are "signs" in the broad sense of standing for something else. Here the similarity ends. Words are signs in that they are conventionally attached to images.

Images are signs in that they resemble, or copy their "meanings." They look or sound like the things and facts they represent. So, the straight reply to the objection above is that it equivocates on "sign," where it should make a distinction. We might use the term "symbol" for a word-sign and "picture" for an image-sign. Then what Ayer and Wittgenstein have failed to take account of is the possibility of analyzing the meaning of symbols in terms of pictures, and the meaning of pictures in terms of resemblance.

RESEMBLANCE AS NATURAL SIGNIFICATION

Our discussion of Russell has reached the following point. If Russell is to stop the infinite regress argument raised by Ayer and Wittgenstein, then he must maintain that resemblance--the kind of meaning unique to images--is a kind of natural signification. There can be no question of meaning or interpretation left over once we have image _qua_ natural sign before us; a natural sign _means_ straight off. So the question now before us is whether or not resemblance is sufficient to stop the infinite regress.

It may be helpful to have a tolerably clear statement of the criterion for an object's being a natural sign. Ockham recommends the following:

> We can decide to alter the signification of a spoken or written term, but no decision or agreement on the part of anyone can have the effect of altering the signification of a conceptual term. (P. 50)

A conceptual term is a natural sign. Other characterizations of natural signs have picked out such features as that natural signs "mean straight off" or "show their sense" or "stand in an internal relation to an interpretation." All of these characterizations emphasize the fixed nature of the meanings of natural signs: there is no way to alter their meaning. I shall argue that we can and do alter the signification of images, and thus that images are not natural signs.

There are three basic reasons images cannot be natural signs. First, resemblance is subject to degrees. We might call the first problem a problem of _vagueness_. Vagueness does not make images less useful in thinking. On the contrary, it accounts for the versatility of images as well as of words. It is a virtue of images that they may be used for different purposes. Unfortunately, this virtue is what denies to images the possibility of being natural signs.

Consider first the vagueness of images. How much resemblance is necessary for an image to mean something? Suppose that at one time I have a stick figure image of a dog and at another I have a full color photographic image of the same dog. Which better resembles the dog? If you are tempted to pick the photographic image, what would you say about a black and white photograph? At what point does the image optimally resemble a dog? This question, I submit, is unanswerable. But the very fact that we can wonder about the degree of resemblance of an image at all shows that resemblance is not a kind of natural signification. Something more is required than mere resemblance to make an image mean something.

But even if we could determine the optimum point of resemblance there is other problematic feature of images, problematic, that is, for Russell's point of view. Images are ambiguous in that they resemble too much. An image of a dog resembles a mammal, an animal, and an organism. The image of a dachshund resembles a sausage; a bar of soap resembles a hunk of cheese. Such examples are clear exceptions to the thesis that images are natural signs. As Prince points out, "a symbol which symbolizes by resemblance must be ambiguous, just because it does symbolize in that way."[2] (P. 270) If an image resembles a dog, it is bound to resemble a mammal. It is precisely this feature that makes images so useful. They are capable of resembling different things.

Oddly enough Russell seems to agree with the foregoing characterization of images as vague and ambiguous:

> The question what a given image 'means' is partly within the control of our will. The image of a printed word may mean, not the word, but what the word means. The image of a triangle may mean one particular triangle, or triangles in general. In thinking of dogs in general, we may use a vague image of a dog, which means the species, not any individual. (1971, P. 303)

However, if images are not natural signs, it is difficult to see how Russell can avoid the force of the infinite regress argument. If something else is required to make the meanings of images determinate, clearly images alone are not sufficient to make the meanings of words determinate.

My third criticism is that resemblance is neither a necessary nor a sufficient condition for one thing being a sign for another, ignoring for the moment the further limitations on natural signs. Resemblance is not necessary because there are many things that are taken to be signs that do not resemble what they are signs of: a barrel hoop is a sign of wine, a fever a sign of infection, etc. Neither is resemblance a sufficient condition for one thing's being a sign of another. A painting may resemble another painting closely, yet not be a sign of it. Identical twins resemble one another, yet few things are signs of themselves. So, even if we can say that images are signs in some sense, we cannot say this is so solely in virtue of any resemblance they bear to their prototypes.

Even though I must not reject Russell's theory, there is one point worth holding firm on. We do have images and use images in thinking. Image-propositions as complexes of images do exist, and their use in thinking remains to be determines. My suspicion is that images must be considered to be signs on a par with verbal signs. But that is another story. Images may not be natural signs but they are signs whose meaning demands explanation.

Let me now summarize the main points of this paper. Bertrand Russell, in keeping with scientific psychology, has presented a central feature of which is the image-proposition. If image-propositions are to be meanings, they must themselves mean "straight off." If not, an infinite regress threatens. I have argued that images are not natural signs and that therefore Russell's view fails in its primary purpose.

FOOTNOTES

1. For a related criticism see Goldberg, 1968.

2. H. H. Price, Thinking and Experience (Cambridge, Massachusetts: Harvard University Press, 1953), P. 270. Price himself discusses the infinite regress which seems to be involved in what he calls "The imagist theory of thinking," P. 257. Cf. Roger Brown, Words and Things (The Free Press of Glencoe, 1958), Pp. 83-89.

REFERENCES

Ayer, A. J. Thinking and meaning. London: Lewis, 1974.

Brown, R. W. Words and things. New York: Free Press, 1958.

Goldberg, B. The correspondence hypothesis. Philosophical Review, 1968, 77, 438-454.

Hannay, A. Mental images--A defense. New York: Humanities Press, 1971.

Kaplan, A., and Copilowish, I. M. Must there be propositions? Mind, 1939, 48, 478-484.

Ockham, W. Ockham's theory of terms: Part I of the Summa Logicae (M. J. Loux, trans.). Notre Dame: University of Notre Dame Press, 1974.

Price, H. H. Thinking and experience. Cambridge, MA: Harvard University Press, 1974.

Russell, B. An inquiry into meaning and truth. Baltimore: Penguin, 1940.

Russell, B. On propositions: What they are and how they mean. In R. C. Marsh (Ed.), Logic and Knowledge. New York: Capricorn, 1971.

Wittgenstein, L. The blue and brown books. New York: Harper Colophon, 1958.

II. MEASUREMENT OF IMAGERY

IMAGERY MEASUREMENT IN CLINICAL SETTINGS:

MATCHING THE METHOD TO THE QUESTION

Roni Beth Tower

Yale University

New Haven, CT

The increased use of imagery in as varied a range of clinical interventions as traditional behavioral techniques (e.g., Cautela's covert conditioning, 1971, 1977; Wolpe's systematic desensitization, 1969); psychodynamically oriented imagery therapies (Shorr's psycho-imagination therapy, 1972; Reyher's emergent uncovering therapy, 1978; Leuner's Guided Affective Imagery, 1977, 1978) and more physiologically-oriented interventions (e.g., biofeedback, bioenergetics, hypnosis, some Gestalt techniques, occasionally psychodrama--see Singer, 1974; Singer & Pope, 1978) has precipitated a resurgence of interest in imagery measurement. Qualitative and quantitative indices have been sought. This interest in assessment for clinical purposes can focus on diagnostic questions, can reflect needs of the intervention itself, or can grow from a desire to evaluate progress. Thus the function of the question being asked of the measure can vary.

In addition, the dimension of imagery at issue is important. It is meaningless to measure vividness of visual imagery when what one wants to know is the sequence of images surrounding a maladaptive behavior pattern or unpleasant affective experience. This paper will (1) suggest a schema for identifying dimensions of imagery that may be of interest, (2) consider some clinical questions that an imagery measure might be useful in answering, (3) briefly survey the types of measures that have been developed, and (4) offer a summary for helping to match the questions to the methods.

IMAGERY DIMENSIONS

Horowitz (1970) has suggested four profitable approaches to the study of imagery, delineating: properties of images, contexts in which they occur, the relation of imagery to perception, and the content of an image. Further aspects of imagery of imporance when asking clinical questions are whether the image being sought is passive or active in genesis and whether it is consciously or unconsciously experienced. Finally, questions concerning individual differences in imagery and the process of imagining may be of interest. These issues have been considered extensively elsewhere (Tower and Singer, 1980) and will only be briefly discussed here.

Properties of Images

By far the most researched properties of images are vividness, controllability, and modality (see Tower and Singer, 1980, for a summary). In addition, Tondo and Cautela, (1974) have noted the importance of ease of evocation of an image, regardless of clarity, and also of an image's affective tone. These aspects of imagery are critical to the success of behavioral interventions. Assessment of them can help in diagnosing the availability of imaginal skills, measuring the effectiveness of any imagery-skill building that might be instituted, and in identifying cognitive-affective factors critical to outcome both during sessions and across treatment. For example, the value of calling as many imaginal and affective responses into play as possible in attaining a therapeutic goal has become clear. From this standpoint, the variety of modalities available to a person is important. The work of Merrill Anderson (note 1) suggests that increased attention to detail in an image creates increased vividness. To the extent that such vividness bears a linear relationship to conscious awareness (e.g., Reyher, 1977, Reyher & Morishige, 1969; Morishige & Reyher, 1975), its assessment could also be useful in determining progress in therapies designed to broaden conscious awareness of unconscious experience.

Contexts of Images

The contexts of images can be important clinically in two major ways: First, the type of context within which imagery takes place may be critical in both improving imaging skills and in therapies designed for "growth," or the expansion of human consciousness. It is likely that imagery development is easier in low-stimulation contexts: thus meditation, sensory deprivation, immediate presleep or postsleep (hypnagogic and hypnopompic imagery), actual sleep states, or drug-induced alterations in consciousness may facilitate the emergence of imagery, its parctice, and the ease of evocation, vividness, controllability, frequency, and range. Second, the situational contexts of ongoing thought with its richness of images and ideas can be of central interest if the clinical questions center around meaning--for example, identifying themes that preoccupy a person; one's associations to a particular person, event or thing; the sequences by which one organizes experience and behavior; the rules of organization that govern such sequences; and the ability to intensify or modify implicit rules. Indeed, the phenomenon of changing maladaptive beliefs and behaviors through imaginal explorations of alternatives is a cornerstone to multiple therapeutic interventions, varying from improvisational psychodrama to structured decision-making.

Relation to Perception

The two areas in which the relation of imaging to perception can be of clinical interest focus on perceptual distortions, when the perceptual reality is substantially modified in its representation, and in perceptual deficits, in which the information available to the senses is simply not being adequately grasped. The first amounts to biased scanning for information and distortions (through lack of adequate attention to contextual features) of that which is filtered in; the second is more easily conceptualized as a learning diasability, in which a specific deficit in perceptual or cognitive capacity rather than overvalent ideational concerns, avoidance of anxiety, or a maladaptive information processing organization is the central problem. Assessment can be useful as a diagnostic tool for measuring objective visual or spatial imaginal skills, for providing feedback in intervention, and for evaluating the outcome of remedial programs.

Content

The content of images has long been of clinical interest. It can be used to reconstruct a person's perception of him- or herself and his or her past, to identify conflictual areas and current concerns, to regulate arousal by using more or less affect-laden images, and to identify both symbolic transformations that distort reality and associative sequences in which thoughts, feelings and behaviors become embroiled. Assessment of all these dimensions can be derived from a careful content analysis of free or semistructured imagery reports.

Type of Involvement

A fifth dimension of imagery to be considered when selecting an assessment approach concerns the extent to which a person is passively or actively involved in the iamgery creation and, if necessary, manipulation. There is evidence (e.g., Worthington, 1978) that client-generated images are far more powerful in predicting positive outcome in behavioral interventions than are experimenter- or clinician-dictated images. Thus, if clients are to be expected to generate their <u>own</u> images during treatment, evaluation of the extent to which they can do so and of their success during intervention is more appropriate than evaluation of images conceived by others. On the other hand, perhaps identification of strengths and weaknesses in other-generated imaging could be used to facilitate training through shaping procedures when spontaneous imaging skills are weak. In addition, in many behavioral interventions and in those dynamically-oriented therapies that rely on providing a superior resolution in imagination, the ability to generate and manipulate appropriately therapist-determined imagery is important. Measures should be selected accordingly.

Level of Consciousness

The extent to which one's imagery is or becomes conscious may be of clinical interest. Behavioral interventions tend to stress imagery that can be grasped consciously; other techniques aim at bringing that which is arousing but unconscious into awareness. The level of arousal, reactivity, and ability of a client to regulate such arousal and reactivity can be of great interest--both in state situations, and as general strategies for dealing with internal experience.

Individual Differences

Finally, many imagery measures must take into account the range of individual differences. State information can be helpful in identifying imagery content interactions with specific contexts--but trait information can tell how characteristically a person responds in such a way--and the extent of flexibility he or she has over responding.

Persuasibility may be of great interest, since there is mounting evidence that those people who show more hypnotic susceptibility also have a freer imaginal flow and are more easily absorbed into whatever they do (e.g., Crawford, 1978; Tellegen & Atkinson, 1974; Wilson & Barber, Note 3 and this volume). This skill bodes well for the success of an intervention; indeed, recent data of Peter Lang (Note 4) suggests that those who merely verbally report greater vividness in imagery without a concommitantly greater physiological arousal are also more responsive to intervention.

Last, cognitive style, particularly along a verbalizer-visualizer continuum, may be useful clinical infomation. It can be helpful diagnositically in identifying a person's characteristic modes of dealing with information in his or her life, in decidng on what type of intervention is indicated and how it should be carried out, and in setting reasonable limits to therapeutic goals. These ideas are substantially expanded elsewhere (Tower and Singer, 1980).

CLINICAL QUESTIONS CONCERNING IMAGERY

Organizing one's questions concerning imagery can profitably proceed along two lines: the type of question and the purpose of the question ought be considered.

Type of Question

Imagery questions, like all other kinds, can address functional, structural or genetic issues. Is the function of the image of relevance, the role it plays in creating, sustaining or changing an affect, cognition or behavior? If so, then assessments should take into account sequence and contextual features as well as parameters (such as vividness) that may mediate function. Interests, values, and style may also be relevant (cf. Chowdhury and Vernon, 1964). If the structure of the image is of primary interest, either in terms of the form of imaging or content, then elements of form such as modality, vividness, or context may be relevant as well as direct affective and cognitive content and the source of the content (internally generated or externally requested). Finally, if the process of imaging is central to a clinician's questions, then dimensions such as sequence, associations, persuasibility, reactivity, arousal, regulation, and style are being asked. Attributes of images as mediated by process could be important.

Purpose of the Question

Imagery questions might be asked for diagnostic, intervention, or evaluation purposes.

Diagnostic. Diagnostic questions most clearly appropriate for imagery assessment include using imagery to help identify (a) the nature of problems, (b) their meaning to the client, (c) symbol-systems evolved in dealing with or engendering problems, (d) associative chains that trigger difficulties or preclude change and thus the role of imagery in maintaining maladaptation, (e) the extent to which reality is distorted in representation, (f) the imaginal resources one has for dealing with problems, and (g) an information-processing style, along with other organized tendencies to response.

Intervention. In therapeutic work, imagery assessments can be useful in (a) understanding contextual triggers of images and the effects of their evocation; (b) expanding one's varieties of experience or range of consciousness; and (c) providing feedback to aid in the regulation of arousal (or other physiological processes) or the production of imagery, or to change its very nature to being more or less arousing, depending upon the therapeutic task.

Evaluation. Finally, assessment can be useful in determining the effectiveness of an intervention and the attainment of broader therapeutic goals. Changes in the structure of a client's imagery, the functions it serves, and the processes by which it takes place may all be of interest in judging the extent to which goals have been met.

A BRIEF SURVEY OF POPULAR MEASURES

A summary table of many imagery measures or assessment methods appears in Table 1. These are discussed in detail elsewhere (Tower

Table 1. Summary of Imagery Measures

Type of Measure	Name of Measure	Author(s)	State or Trait[1]	Type of Imagery	Dimension(s)	Source[2]
Questionnaire	Betts QMI	Betts, 1909 Sheehan, 1967	T	multi-modality	vividness	E
Questionnaire/ Interview	Gordon's Test of Visual Imagery Control	Gordon, 1949	T	visual	control	E
Questionnaire	Vividness of Visual Imagery Questionnaire (VVIQ)	Marks, 1973	T	visual	vividness control	E
Interview	Brower Self-Report Test	Brower, 1947	T	multi-modality	vividness	E
Questionnaire	Imagery Survey Schedule (ISS)	Tondo & Cautela, 1974	T	multi-modality	presence ease vividness pleasantness	E
Questionnaire	Imagery Research Question.	Lane, 1977	T	multi-modality	control ease	E
Questionnaire	Personal Imagery Question.	McSweeny & Baer, Note 5	T	multi-modality	ease vividness pleasantness	S
Questionnaire	Survey of Mental Imagery	Switras, Notes 6,7	T	multi-modality	presence vividness control	E
Questionnaire	Individual Differences Q'aire	Paivio, 1971	T	verbal, visual	style	E
Questionnaire	Verbalizer-Visualizer Q'aire	Richardson, 1977	T	verbal, visual	style	E
Questionnaire	Imaginal Processes Inventory	Singer & Antrobus, 1972	T	visual auditory	daydreaming dimensions	E
Questionnaire	Creative Imagination Scale	Wilson & Barber, 1978	S/T	multi-modality	persuasibility vividness	E
Naturalistic	Logs, Reports	Singer, 1978 Klinger, 1978 Csikszentmihalyi, 1975	S	multi-modality	conditions sequence associations	S

Type of Measure	Name of Measure	Author(s)	State or Trait[1]	Type of Imagery	Dimension(s)	Source[2]
Naturalistic	Experiential Analysis Technique	Sheehan, McConkey and Cross, 1978	S/T	multi-modality	associations affect themes stop-rate	S
Behavioral-Spatial	Cube Problem	Short, 1953	T	spatial	problem-solving	E
	Flags Test	Thurstone & Jeffrey, 1959				
	Minnesota Paper Form Board	Likert & Quasha, 1970				
	Space Relations Test	Bennett, Seashore & Wesman, 1963				
	Visual Matrix Task	Barratt, 1956				
	Chinese Characters	Durndell & Wetherick, 1976				
	Estimation Tasks	Kosslyn, 1980				
Behavioral-Visual	Pictures	Marks, 1973	T	visual	memory	E
	Photographs	Rehm, 1973				
	Replicate Block Designs	Danaher & Thoreson, 1972				
	Benton Test of Visual Memory	Benton, 1963				
Behavioral-Verbal	Verbal Learning Tasks	Paivio, 1970	T	visual	associative learning	E
	Onomotopoeia & Images	Khatena, 1975	T	multi-modality		
Behavioral-Thought	Analogical Thinking	Cooper & Shepard, 1975	T	sensory images	reaction time	E
Interests, Values	Strong-Campbell Interest Inventory	Campbell, 1977	T	inferred	interests	E
	Study of Values	Allport, Vernon, & Lindzey, 1960	T	inferred	values	E
Projective	Shorr Imagery Test	Shorr, 1974	S/T	visual	themes affect associations symbols	S
Projective	Thematic Apperception Test	Murray, 1943	S/T	visual	themes affect association symbols	S

(continued)

Table 1 (continued)

Type of Measure	Name of Measure	Author(s)	State or Trait[1]	Type of Imagery	Dimension(s)	Source[2]
Projective	Rorschach "M" Response	Rorschach, 1942/51	T	kinesthetic	uses of imagery	S
Physiological	Breathing, Heart Rate		S/T	multi-modality	arousal regulation	S/E
Physiological	Muscle Tension		S	multi-modality	affect reactivity effectiveness	S/E
Physiological	Eye Movement Laterality		S	multi-modality	attention focus reactivity sequences	S/E
Physiological	Brain Waves (alpha on/off)		S	multi-modality	arousal	S/E

[1]S = State; T = Trait

[2]S = Subject-generated; E = Experimenter-generated

& Singer, 1980), with reports on reliability, validity, applications, and research done using them to be found in that place. Here I should only like to point out that there are essentially four types of measure and the type selected limits the kinds of information that can be obtained from its use. Self-report measures include questionnaires, structured interviews, and naturalistic reports of ongoing thought. They all assume that one's subjective experience of the images is of primary importance (rather than the match to any objective criterion) and that this experience is at a conscious level. Behavioral measures can be useful in tapping actual perceptual abilities and certain cognitive skills such as memory, problem-solving, and associative learning. Projective tests furnish a rich source of information concerning unconscious organization of thought and images, with concomitant themes, associations, symbols, affects, and, potentially, processes by which images emerge and are dealt with along with parameters determining and regulating those processes. Physiological measures provide perhaps the best pipeline to both conscious and unconscious state reactions to imaginal productions. While precise measurement is unfeasible in most clinical situations, observation of lateral eye shifts, muscle tensions, and heart and breathing rates is not difficult and can furnish data on multiple aspects of the imaging process and perhaps also on function.

MATCHING THE MEASURE TO THE QUESTION

Table 1 offers a summary of imagery measures by type, whether the measures assess state or trait imagery, the modalities available through the measures, dimensions tapped by each of them, and whether a measure implies self- or clinician-generated imagery. By clarifying the purpose of the question (What use shall I make of the information?), the type of question (Am I asking about imagery as it exists, as it operates, as it affects other functions?), and the dimension of imagery at issue, the clinician can hope to match the question being asked to a measure that will provide optimally useful information in answering it.

SUMMARY

Understanding the content and/or processes of a client's imaginal life may be essential to answering diagnostic questions, designing and conducting an intervention, or evaluating its effectiveness. The current paper surveys the questions that might be of relevance when carrying out these tasks and suggests a matching of imagery measure or method to the specific questions being asked. Self-report (questionnaire, interview, phenomenological), projective, behavioral and physiological measures and techniques are reviewed and examined from the perspective of their relevance to particular diagnostic, intervention, or outcome issues.

REFERENCE NOTES

1. Anderson, M. P. Oualities of imagery: A content-analytic approach to vividness and detail. Paper presented at the annual meeting of the American Association for the Study of Mental Imagery. Minneapolis, June, 1980.

2. McSweeny, A. J. An initial evaluation of an imagery questionnaire designed to assess imagery vividness in behavior therapy situations. Paper presented to the Association for the Advancement of Behavior Therapy, New York, 1976.

3. Wilson, S. C., and Barber, T. X. Vivid fantasy and hallucinatory imagery of very good hypnotic subjects. Paper presented at the annual meeting of the American Association for the Study of Mental Imagery. Minneapolis, June, 1980.

4. Lang, P. J. Image and emotion: Perceptual and conceptual structure in affective cognition. Paper presented at the annual meeting of the American Association for the Study of Mental Imagery. Minneapolis, June, 1980.

5. McSweeny, A. J. and Baer, P. The Personal Imagery Questionnaire. Unpublished manuscript, 1976. (Available from A. J. McSweeny, Department of Psychology, West Virginia University, Morgantown, WV 26506.)

6. Switras, J. E. Survey of Mental Imagery. Unpublished manuscript, 1975. (Available from J. E. Switras, 143 Linden Dr., Fairmont, MN 56031.)

7. Switras, J. E. Survey of Mental Imagery test manual. Unpublished manuscript, 1979.

REFERENCES

Allport, G. W., Vernon, P. E., and Lindzey, G. Study of Values. Boston: Houghton-Mifflin, 1960.

Barratt, P. E. Use of the EEG in the study of imagery. British Journal of Psychology, 1956, 47, 101-114.

Bennett, G. K., Seashore, H. G. and Vesman, A. G. Differential Aptitude Tests. New York: Psychological Corporation, 1963.

Benton, A. L. Revised Visual Retention Test: Manual. New York: Psychological Corporation, 1963.

Betts, G. H. The distribution and functions of mental imagery. Teachers College Columbia University Contributions to Education, 1909, No. 26, 1-99.

Brower, D. The experimental study of imagery: I. The relation of imagery to intelligence. Journal of Genetic Psychology, 1947, 72, 229-231.

Campbell, D. P. Manual for the Strong Vocational Interest Blank/ Strong-Campbell Interest Inventory (2nd ed.). Stanford, California: Stanford University Press, 1977.

Cautela, J. R. Covert conditioning. In A. Jacobs and L. B. Sacks (Eds.), The psychology of private events. New York: Academic Press, 1971.

Cautela, J. Covert conditioning: Assumption and procedures. Journal of Mental Imagery, 1977, 1, 53-64.

Chowdhury, K., and Vernon, P. An experimental study of imagery and its relation to abilities and interests. British Journal of Psychology, 1964, 55, 355-364.

Cooper, L. A., and Shepard, R. N. Mental transformations in the identification of left and right hands. Journal of Experimental Psychology: Human Perception and Performance, 1975, 1, 48-56.

Crawford, H. J. Relationship of hypnotic susceptibility to imagery vividness, absorption, and daydreaming styles. Hypnosis Research Memorandum #152, June 20, 1978, Stanford University.

Csikszentmihalyi, M. Beyond boredom and anxiety. San Francisco: Jossey-Bass, 1975.

Danaher, B. G., and Thoresen, C. E. Imagery assessment by self-report and behavioral measures. Behavior Research and Therapy, 1972, 10, 131-138.

Durndell, A. J., and Wetherick, N. E. Reported imagery and two spatial tasks. Perceptual and Motor Skills, 1976, 43, 1050.

Gordon, R. An investigation into some of the factors that favor the formation of stereotyped images. British Journal of Psychology, 1949, 39, 156-167.

Horowitz, M. J. Image formation and cognition. New York: Appleton-Century-Crofts, 1970.

Khatena, J. Relationship of autonomous imagery and creative self-perceptions. Perceptual and Motor Skills, 1975, 40, 357-358.

Klinger, E. Modes of normal conscious flow. In K. S. Pope and J. L. Singer (Eds.), The stream of consciousness: Scientific investigations into the flow of human experience. New York: Plenum, 1978.

Kosslyn, S. Imagery and mind. Cambridge, Massachusetts: Harvard University Press, 1980.

Lane, J. B. Problems of assessment of vividness and control of imagery. Perceptual and Motor Skills, 1977, 45, 363-368.

Likert, R., and Quasha, W. H. Revised Minnesota Paper Form Board Test. New York: Psychological Corp., 1970.

Leuner, H. Guided affective imagery: An account of its development. Journal of Mental Imagery, 1977, 1, 73-92.

Leuner, H. Basic principles and therapeutic efficacy of Guided Affective Imagery. In J. L. Singer and K. S. Pope (Eds.), The power of human imagination. New York: Plenum, 1978.

Marks, D. F. Visual imagery differences in the recall of pictures. British Journal of Psychology, 1973, 64, 17-24.

McSweeny, A. J. Imagery as a variable in the efficacy of systematic desensitization. Unpublished doctoral dissertation, Northern Illinois University, 1975.

Morishige, H., and Reyher, J. The alpha rhythm during three conditions of visual imagery and emergent uncovering psychotherapy: The critical role of anxiety. Journal of Abnormal Psychology, 1975, 84, 531-538.

Murray, H. A. Thematic Apperception Test Manual. Cambridge, Mass.: Harvard University Press, 1943.

Paivio, A. On the functional significance of imagery. Psychological Bulletin, 1970, 73, 415-421.

Paivio, A. Imagery and verbal processes. New York: Holt, Rinchart, and Winston, 1971.

Rehm, L. P. Relationships among measures of visual imagery. Behavior Research and Therapy, 1973, 11, 265-270.

Reyher, J. Emergent uncovering psychotherapy: The use of imagoic and linguistic vehicles in objectifying psychodynamic processes. In J. L. Singer and K. S. Pope (Eds.), The power of human imagination. New York: Plenum, 1978.

Reyher, J. Spontaneous visual imagery: Implications for psychoanalysis, psychopathology, and psychotherapy. Journal of Mental Imagery, 1977, 2, 253-274.

Reyher, J., and Morishige, H. Electroencephalogram and rapid eye movements during free imagery and dream recall. Journal of Abnormal Psychology, 1969, 74, 576-582.

Richardson, A. Verbalizer-visualizer: A cognitive style dimension, Journal of Mental Imagery, 1977, 1, 109-126.

Rorschach, H. Psychodiagnostics. New York: Grune and Stratton, 1951. (First published in 1942.)

Sheehan, P. W. A shortened form of Betts' questionnaire upon mental imagery. Journal of Clinical Psychology, 1967, 23, 386-389.

Sheehan, P. W., McConkey, K. M., and Cross, D. Experimental analysis of hypnosis: Some new observations on hypnotic phenomena. Journal of Abnormal Psychology, 1978, 87, 570-573.

Shorr, J. E. Shorr Imagery Test. Los Angeles: Institute for Psycho-Imagination Therapy, 1974.

Short, P. L. The objective study of mental imagery. British Journal of Psychology, 1953, 44, 38-51.

Singer, J. L. Imagery and daydreaming methods in psychotherapy and behavior modification. New York: Academic Press, 1974.

Singer, J. L. Experimental studies of daydreaming and the stream of thought. In K. S. Pope and J. L. Singer (Eds.), The stream of consciousness: Scientific investigation into the flow of human experience. New York: Plenum Press, 1978.

Singer, J. L., and Antrobus, J. S. Daydreaming, imaginal processes, and personality: A normative study. In P. W. Sheehan (Ed.), The function and nature of imagery. New York: Academic Press, 1972.

Singer, J. L., and Pope, K. S. (Eds.). The power of human imagination. New York: Plenum, 1978.

Tellegen, A., and Atkinson, G. Openness to absorbing and self-alterning experiences ("absorption"), a trait related to hypnotic susceptibility. Journal of Abnormal Psychology, 1974, 83, 268-277.

Thurstone, L. L., and Jeffrey, T. G. Space thinking (flags). Chicago: Education-Industry Service, 1959.

Tondo, T. R., and Cautela, J. R. Assessment of imagery in covert reinforcement. Psychological Reports, 1974, 34, 1271-1280.

Tower, R. B., and Singer, J. L. The measurement of imagery: How can it be clinically useful? In P. C. Kendall and S. D. Hollon (Eds.), Assessment strategies for cognitive-behavioral interventions. New York: Academic Press, 1980.

Wilson, S. C., and Barber, T. X. The Creative Imagination Scale as a measure of hypnosis. American Journal of Clinical Hypnosis, 1978, 20, 235-249.

Wolpe, J. The practice of behavior therapy. New York: Pergamon, 1969.

Worthington, E. L. Jr. The effects of imagery content, choice of imagery content, and self-verbalization on the self-control of pain. Cognitive therapy and research, 1978, 2, 225-240.

IMAGERY ASSESSMENT THROUGH CONTENT ANALYSIS

Merrill P. Anderson

Houston Cardiovascular Rehabilitation Center

Houston, Texas

One of the most frustrating areas in imagery research is assessment. A wide variety of assessment approaches have been used, ranging from rating scales of one's own imagery, to questionnaires about thinking habits, to spatial reasoning tests, to verbal memory tests, to psychophysiological measures. In general, the relationship of scores on these measures to outcome measures of imagery-based therapeutic procedures has been minimal or inconsistent.

With some trepidation I ventured into this area and developed yet another approach to imagery assessment. This approach is based on the content analysis of verbal reports of imaginal contents. This report begins with a review of the theoretical background of the approach, followed by a description of the assessment system itself. The report concludes with a brief summary of a study in which this system was used.

THEORETICAL BACKGROUND

The content analysis system that I developed was designed to assess the amount of <u>detail</u> contained in verbal reports of imaginal experiences. This approach was grounded in two recent theoretical thrusts in cognitive psychology: the propositional interpretation of imagery (Kieras, 1978; Pylyshyn, 1973), and Neisser's (1976) recent theorizing about perceptual processes.

The fundamental issue with which the propositional interpretation of imagery is concerned is the nature of the format in which information is stored or represented. The issue is whether information is stored in quasisensory imaginal and/or verbal codes, or in a more abstract, common format. The propositional position argues that information is stored in a common format that has a propositional structure. Propositions are thought of as informational units containing knowledge about relations, meanings, concepts, and properties. A simple proposition might consist of two concepts or properties linked by a relation. Simple propositions can be linked in network fashion to represent the information contained in a given stimulus field. Propositional representations are not thought of as exclusively semantic in nature, in spite of the fact that words must be used to communicate the idea. It is knowledge of the meanings and relations communicated by words and pictures that is stored in propositional structures. Thus, the informational structures underlying images are more like descriptions of the original stimulus situations than photographs of them, in that a description contains information about the structure of a picture.

An implication of this view is that images of different quality would be associated with propositional networks that differ in the amount of descriptive detail or information they contain. Following this line of reasoning further, one way of assessing the quality of images would be to use the relative amount of detail that people can report from their imaginal experience as an index of the quality of the underlying representation. (Peter Lang (1977) made the same suggestion on the basis of this literature.)

The second source of ideas for the present approach to imagery assessment is the view of imagery contained in Neisser's recent theorizing about perceptual processes (Neisser, 1976). Neisser thinks of perception as an interaction of cognitive, behavioral, and environmental feedback factors. The cognitive factors are thought of as schemata that function to "anticipate" the general form of the stimulus to be perceived. Neisser thinks of imaginal activity as the activation of one of these schemas in the absence of an environmental stimulus appropriate to it. Neisser states that "the experience of having an image is just the inner aspect of a readiness to perceive the imagined object, and differences in the nature and quality of people's images reflect differences in the kind of information they are prepared to pick up" (Neisser, 1976, p. 131). He adds that "a description of a visual image is a description of what one is ready to see" (p. 168).

The implications of this view of imagining for imagery assessment are similar to those derived from the propositional approach: images may be qualitatively differentiated by the information people can report from them. The difference between the two views of imagery is that Neisser's conceptualization seems to underline the importance of the kind of information included in the imagery, and the propositional approach emphasizes the amount of information. Both are probably important. Imagery that includes relevant, detailed information may have more impact on behavior and emotion in a given situation than imagery containing either sketchy relevant information, or detailed irrelevant information. Thus, these two theoretical perspectives on imagery suggest that the amount and kind of information that is processed may be important functional dimensions of mental images. These dimensions could be assessed by quantifying the amount and kind of descriptive detail contained in narrative reports of imaginal activity.

While formal assessment techniques based on this idea have not been developed, there is evidence in the literature that researchers and clinicians have used narrative detail as an index of the quality of people's imagery for informal assessment and training purposes. For example, Joseph Wolpe, the originator of systematic desensitization, reports that clients often are unable to construct sufficiently realistic scenes for the therapy to be effective (Wolpe, 1973). He advises the therapist to describe the scenes in progressively more detail until the client reports he has achieved a satisfactory degree of realism. Cautela and McCullough (1978) outlined an imagery training program used prior to treatment with a covert conditioning therapy. Several aspects of their training program are based on the idea of a close relationship between vividness and detail. First, clients are urged to construct images in multisensory, rather than merely visual, detail. Second, the client may be asked to glance around the office, and then to describe the office in as much detail as possible with their eyes closed. Third, clients are encouraged to practice by attending to events and situations during the day, and then later to reconstruct them imaginally with as much multisensory detail as they can remember. Fourth, clients are asked to write about some of their experiences in as much detail and with as much realism as they can muster. Cautela and McCullough do not provide data to evaluate the effectiveness of this training program, but the components of their program indicate that at the level of clinical practice it has been useful to assume a relationship between vividness and descriptive detail. To summarize, clinicians interested in improving the quality of clients' imagery have found the amount of descriptive detail reported from the imagery to be a useful index. The particular kind of detail that is of interest varies according to the specific clinical or research purposes, but the amount of detail reported seems to be widely used index of quality.

THE CONTENT ANALYSIS SYSTEM

For the purposes of developing a formal assessment procedure, content analysis of verbal reports of imaginal contents is the most appropriate methodology for determining the amount of detail included. It should be acknowledged that there are undeniable problems with using verbal reports of conscious states as data in scientific investigations. However, because of the kinds of information about imaginal content that are available through them, there is almost no substitute for relying on them to some extent. Thus, it is necessary for cognitively oriented investigators to develop methodologies for obtaining and quantifying verbal reports that take into account the problems inherent in them.

This content analysis system is designed to assess the amount of detail or information contained in a person's retrospective report of his or her imagery. There is evidence that subjective ratings of vividness and detail are correlated (Klinger, 1978), implying that the amount of information imagined may be a component of vividness. However, the two dimensions should be kept conceptually distinct. The extent to which the amount and kind of detail reported are related to impressions of vividness and/or have functional importance in their own right must be determined by empirical research.

The coding categories in this system (Table 1) are grouped into two broad classes based on Lang's distinction between stimulus and response propositions (Lang, 1977). Stimulus propositions include all references to objects, events, or features of the person's imagined environment. In other words, they include things the person would have perceived with his external senses were he present in the imagined situation. Response propositions include all references to the person's own imagined motor behavior, cognition, affect, and somatic processes.

This system is an example of a classical content analysis system in that coding involves a minimum of inference and is based on the

Table 1. Coding categories

Stimulus Detail	Response Detail
Setting	Motor Behavior
Objects	Properties of Own Behavior
Properties of Objects	Posture
Object Movement	Sense Organ Adjustment
People	Processing Characteristics
Properties of People	Body Parts
Verbal Behavior of People	Verbal Behavior
Motor Behavior of People	Thoughts
Properties of Behavior	Emotions
Behavioral Outcomes	Visceral Parts
Spatial	Bodily States
Temporal	

sematic meanings in the report. The coder's primary task is to determine the size of the units into which the content of the report is to be divided, assigning them to categories, and calculating the category frequencies. To enhance reliability, coding categories are as precise as possible, consistent with avoiding generating a mass of sematic trivia. That is to say, an attempt was made to have the categories reflect meaningful informational units. The categories of the present system vary in the size of units they cover, with some of them covering single words, and some entire sentences. Only information that clearly describes the content of the person's imagery is coded. The system excludes segments that either evaluate or explain the content, as well as a variety of phrases that are more a function of the way in which the subject communicates the information verbally than of the content of the imaginal activity.

Most coding situations can be resolved by the basic category definitions. An additional set of guidelines and conventions was developed for handling frequently encountered problem situations. Some representative guidelines include the following: (1) With the categories Verbalizations and Thoughts, each complete thought segment is coded as one unit. In other words, simple sentences are coded as one unit, compound or run-on sentences are subdivided into simple sentences, and complex sentences are divided into major and subordinate clauses. The point of this guideline is that the coding system captures the fact that the person imagined the occurrence of a unit of verbalization or thought. The specific content of the verbalization or thought is not coded. (2) The Processing Characteristics category is used to code references to properties of the person's _imagined_ cognitive processing. Statements that evaluate the quality of the imagery experience as a whole are not coded because they are not part of the content that was imagined. Examples of this latter type of statement would include the following: "The scene was crystal clear," or, "The scene was very detailed." Since the purpose of the coding system is to make inferences about properties such as these, they should not be included in the coding. (3) If the status of an object or person remains the same in the imagery, its presence is coded only once even though it may be mentioned repeatedly. New properties of a previously coded object or person may be coded separately. (4) The most difficult coding decisions had to do with the Spatial category. Prepositions generally communicate spatial information. It can be hard to determine when a preposition communicates meaningful spatial detail for the purposes of this system and when it is more a function of the structure of the language the person used to communicate the content of imagery. With prepositions such as _over_, _under_, and _beside_, the decision is easy. However, it is more difficult with prepositions such as _in_, _at_, and _on_. In order to be systematic, the decision was made to always code the preposition and its object separately (providing the object had not been coded previously), even though this could result in some overcoding.

Usually it is advisable to forewarn the imagers that a request for a report will be made and to instruct them about what it should contain. The exception would be when the clinician/researcher either has explicit interest in the content of an unexpected report, or has good reason to expect that forewarning would contaminate in some way the variables of interest. Assuming, however, that the imager is forewarned, the initial narration instructions should be the most detailed ones the person receives. When reports of specific images are requested, the time lag between the end of the imaging and the beginning of the report will be critical. Giving the detailed instructions initially and not repeating them when the report is requested minimizes this lag.

The request for report should be limited to a simple instruction such as "Describe your scene." The request should be nonspecific about content areas to be included in the report in order to minimize the delay between experience and report, and to minimize the demand on the subject to include things that are of interest to the clinician/researcher, but were not actually part of the subject's imagery. There must be a balance between the pre- and postimagery instructions such that subjects are forewarned about the content areas of interest (the initial instructions) but do not feel compelled to include all of them in their report regardless of their actual occurrence. When postimagery requests are nonspecific about content areas the content reported is more likely to be the content actually imagined and less likely to be biased by the content suggested in the request for the report.

AN EXPLORATORY STUDY

This content analysis system was used by Anderson and Borkovec (1980) in an investigation on the effects of having speech-anxious college students repeatedly imagine two types of anxiety-arousing scenes. This represented an exploratory application of the content analysis procedure, designed to test its feasibility for research and to obtain initial data on its utility and validity for assessing therapeutic imagery. Our study was inspired by Lang's thesis that imagery scripts that included response information would be more effective in eliciting arousal and fear reduction than scripts limited to stimulus information. We addressed two major questions: (1) What is the relative fear-reducing ability of stimulus and stimulus -plus- response scripts when subjects repeatedly imagine scenes relevant to a fear they had, and (2) what changes occur in imagery over repeated visualizations?

In a 2 x 4 x 5 repeated-measures design one group of subjects imagined four scenes presented only in terms of stimulus propositions, and another group imagined four scenes described in terms of both stimulus and response propositions. Each scene was imagined a total of five times. Heart rate was recorded throughout the procedure, with samples taken from the 10 seconds immediately preceding presentations of each scene and from the first 10 seconds of each 20-second scene visualization. Subjects rated each scene visualization on vividness, detail, and fear. They described their imaginal contents on the first and last presentation of each scene. Descriptions were tape recorded, transcribed, and coded according to the procedures outlines above.

We found no support for the proposition that imagining stimulus -plus- response scripts reduces either physiological or subjective measures of fear more than does imagining just stimulus scripts. Consistent with these findings, there were no differences between the two script groups in the amount of response detail they reported. While we certainly expected the stimulus-plus-response group to report more response detail, the fact that they did not offers an explanation for the lack of group differences on the two fear measures: subjects simply may not have imagined scenes that were as different on the relevant dimension as we had hoped.

Because of the exploratory nature of the content analysis system, we decided to take a closer look at the narrative data in order to determine whether in fact there were group differences that had not been reflected in the measures we derived from the coding. We identified a reduced set of coding categories under each heading that we felt might lead to more sensitive measures of the relevant kinds of detail. Accordingly, we retained only those categories that unambiguously reflected either clearly perceptible stimulus detail or references to emotional, somatic, or cognitive arousal. The categories that were retained for Stimulus Detail were Objects, Properties of Objects, People, Properties of People, and Movement. The reduced set of Response Detail categories included Processing Characteristics, Body Parts, Emotion, Visceral Parts, and Bodily Arousal. Repeating the analysis of variance with these new measures, we again did not find group differences.

A final post hoc exploration of the data did yield a group difference. We calculated the proportion of reports in each condition that contained <u>any</u> reference to one of the reduced set of <u>response detail</u> categories. A test for the significance of the difference between two proportions was significant, $p < .001$. A higher proportion of subjects in the stimulus-plus-response script group, .94, made at least one reference to response detail than those in the stimulus script group .77. While this difference did reach statistical significance, the practical conclusion is that our imagery inductions did not result in imaginal contents that differed as greatly as we had intended. Alternatively, perhaps the initial narration instructions placed too much emphasis on reporting response components of the imagery, thus creating a demand on the subjects to report them regardless of their actual occurrence. Future research could address these questions.

The second question addressed by this study concerned changes that occurred imagery over repeated visualizations of scenes. The most interesting results were obtained with the subjective ratings of vividness, detail, and fear. Over repetitions of scenes, vividness and detail increased significantly while fear declined significantly. On the other hand, collapsing across repetitions of scenes and looking at the effect for scenes only, vividness and detail declined significantly, while fear increased. The inverse relationship between quality of imagery and fear that is reflected in these results suggests that to some extent fearful arousal is antagonistic to high quality imagery. Perhaps this is because fearful arousal competes for attention with the task of constructing an imaginary scene. No significant changes over repetitions were found in the narrative measures (reduced set of categories). Stimulus Detail decreased significantly over scenes, and Response Detail increased significantly over scenes. The latter result is consistent with the hierarchical order in which the scenes were presented.

A final set of analyses explored the relationships among the different measures. A unique aspect of this study was its assessment of imaginal processing from three perspectives: physiology, subjective experience, and content. We were interested in how our measures of these different response systems covaried. Because we were most interested in changes that occurred over repetitions of scenes, we derived mean change scores over repetitions of scenes for each kind of dependent variable. Our most intriguing results were with the mean change score for Response Detail. These scores correlated significantly with the scores for heart rate responsiveness and fear ratings, $r = .32$ and $r = .30$, respectively, both $p < .05$. The change score for Stimulus Detail was not signigicantly related to the score for heart rate responsiveness, indicating some specificity in the relationship between the response detail and heart rate measures. The correlations are low, but given the different response systems and measurement techniques, they are not unreasonably low. They indicate that as the amount of response detail imagined increases or decreases, so do the physiological and subjective measures or fear. This is what one would expect if Lang is correct in his idea that the amount of response information that is processed is causally related to physiological reactivity.

To summarize, this study modeled an approach to investigating imagery processing that attempted to go beyond simple ratings of vividness. We found some support for a relationship between imagining response information and fearful arousal. We refined a content analysis system for coding imagery content. Further work is obviously needed on this approach. We also learned that if one wishes to do careful empirical work in the area of imagery treatments it is mandatory to devise means of maximizing the probability that subjects imagine contents consistent with the manipulations. Premanipulation imagery training programs are one way of accomplishing this. More detailed imagery induction scripts are another. Finally, to ensure interpretability of results, imagery investigators would be well advised to include in their procedure some check on the content actually imagined. The content analysis system described in this chapter offers one means of obtaining such information.

REFERENCES

Anderson, M., and Borkovec, T. Imagery processing and fear reduction during repeated exposure to two types of phobic imagery. Behavior Research and Therapy, 1980, 18, 537-540.

Cautela, J., and McCullough, L. Covert conditioning. A learning theory perspective on imagery. In J. L. Singer & K. S. Pope (Eds.), The power of human imagination. New York: Plenum, 1978.

Kieras, D. Beyond pictures and words: Alternative information processing models for imagery effects in verbal memory. Psychological Bulletin, 1978, 85, 532-554.

Klinger, E. Modes of normal conscious flow. In K. S. Pope and J. L. Singer (Eds.), The stream of consciousness: Scientific Investigations into the flow of human experience. Plenum: New York, 1978.

Lang, P. J. Imagery in therapy: An information processing analysis of fear. Behavior Therapy, 1977, 8, 862-886.

Neisser, U. Cognition and reality: Principles and implications of cognitive psychology. San Francisco: Freeman, 1976.

Pylyshyn, Z. What the mind's eye tells the mind's brain: A critique of mental imagery. Psychological Bulletin, 1973, 80, 1-22.

Wolpe, J. The practice of behavior therapy (2nd ed.). New York: Pergamon, 1973.

III. HYPNOSIS AND IMAGERY

HYPNOTIC RESPONDING: AUTOMATIC DISSOCIATION OR SITUATION-RELEVANT COGNIZING?

Nicholas P. Spanos

Carleton University

Ottawa, Canada

Social behavior is strategic. People continually moderate their interpersonal behavior in conformance with the changing cues and expectations generated by the situations in which they find themselves. Such behavior involves planning, attention to social contingencies, and coordinated decision-making. In short, social behavior involves the kinds of processes that, in everyday life, we think of as being voluntary (cf. Goffman, 1959).

Hypnotic behavior usually occurs in an interpersonal context and involves communication between hypnotist and subject. Nevertheless, responsive hypnotic subjects typically do _not_ define their behavior as voluntary. Instead, they define it as occurring effortlessly and automatically (Spanos, Rivers, & Rose, 1977; Weitzenhoffer, 1978). For example, "good" hypnotic subjects who respond to a suggestion that their arm is rising do not report that they voluntarily raised it. Instead, they typically report that the arm rose by itself. Their arm rising is experienced _not_ as something they did, but rather, as something that happened to _them_ (Spanos, 1971; Spanos & Barber, 1972).

Traditionally, investigators in this area have taken subjects at their word. Because hypnotic subjects report that their responses _feel_ automatic, investigators have assumed that these responses _are_ automatic. In this respect hypnotic behavior has been conceptualized as being fundamentally different from other kinds of social behavior.

I thank D. Addey, L. Della Malva, D. Dubreuil, P. Golding, C. McNeil, H. L. Radtke, and H. J. Stam for critically reading earlier versions of this paper.

Special psychological processes like "trance" and "dissociation" have been postulated to explain this supposed automaticity of hypnotic responding (Gill & Brenman, 1959; Janet, 1907; Hilgard, 1977, 1979; Kihlstrom, 1978). These traditional approaches do not deny that situation-specific motivational and attitudinal factors influence hypnotic responding. However, the influence of these variables is usually seen as being indirect. Positive attitudes and motivations set the stage; they produce a readiness that allows for the development of "trance" or for the occurrence of a "dissociation between cognitive subsystems." It is these latter factors however, that supposedly produce automatic responding to suggestion (Hilgard, 1977).

In this paper I shall argue that conceptualizations of hypnosis that view responses to suggestion as automatic occurrences and posit special cognitive processes like dissociation to explain such automaticity are fudamentally misleading. I shall also endeavor to show that hypnotic behavior can be better understood if it is regarded, first and foremost, as social behavior. According to this perspective, responsive hypnotic subjects are not automatons. They are persons actively involved in adopting and maintaining the definition of the situation contained in the suggestions and other communications they are administered (Barber, 1969; Barber, 1972; Barber, Spanos & Chaves, 1974: Coe & Sarbin, 1977; Sarbin, 1950; Sarbin & Coe, 1972; Spanos, 1971; Spanos et al., 1977). I shall illustrate my thesis by discussing some recent research carried out by my colleagues and me on two phenomena traditionally considered to be hallkards of hypnotic responding: suggested analgesia and suggested anmesia.

SUGGESTED ANALGESIA

Most experimental studies dealing with suggestion-induced pain reduction have used ice water as the pain stimulus. Typically, subjects immerse an arm in ice water for a brief period (e.g., 60 sec) and at various points during the immersion make numerical estimates of pain intensity. Frequently, subjects immerse the arm more than once. The first immersion serves as a baseline and provides an estimate of subjects' pain responses before the intervention of any treatment procedures. Later immersions (posttests) usually follow some treatment such as a hypnotic induction procedure or suggestion for analgesia (Barber & Hahn, 1962; Evans & Paul, 1970; Hilgard & Hilgard, 1975; Spanos, Barber, & Lang, 1974; Spanos, Radtke-Bodorik, Ferguson, & Jones, 1979). Although a good many studies have assessed the effects of hypnosis and suggestion on reducing pain, very few have examined the cognitive activities presumed to mediate such reductions. Moreover, even these few studies (Chaves & Barber, 1974; Spanos et al., 1979; Stam & Spanos, in press) have focused on subjects' cognitive activities during posttesting.

Some recent work in our own laboratory has focused on the cognitive activities carried out by subjects during their baseline immersion as well as during posttesting (Spanos, Stam, & Brazil, Note 1; Spanos, Brown, Jones, & Horner, Note 2). Using questionnaires and interviews we assessed the extent to which subjects spontaneously engaged in coping and catastrophizing cognitions during baseline testing, and the manner in which these cognitive activities were modified by suggestion. Coping cognitions refer to such activities as imagining events inconsistent with the noxious stimulation (e.g., imagining lying on the beach basking in the sun) and engaging in self-distraction. Positive self-statements like "this isn't so bad" and "as long as I take it easy this will be ok" are also classified as coping activity (Spanos et al., 1979; Meichenbaum, 1977). Catastrophizing refers to worrying about and exaggerating the noxious aspects of the situation and imagining negative consequences. For instance, catastrophizing would be indexed by reports like "oh God, I have to get out of here," "I think the blood has stopped circulating to my hand," "what if I get frostbite" (Lazarus, 1974; Spanos et al., 1979).

In one recent study (Spanos et al., Note 1), subjects estimated their degree of pain following 60 sec of immersion on a baseline test and afterwards rated the extent of their coping and catastrophizing cognitive activity during the immersion. A multiple regression analysis indicated that 34% of the variance in subjects' baseline pain ratings could be accounted for by knowing their scores on coping and catastrophizing scales. Clearly, subjects do not experience a baseline immersion either passively or in a uniform manner. Some try to cope actively with the situation while others catastrophize, and subjects' degree of involvement in these cognitive activities affects the degree of pain they report.

What happens when subjects are administered a suggestion for pain reduction following baseline testing? Usually, analgesia suggestions invite subjects to engage in imaginings that are inconsistent with pain. For instance, subjects may be asked to imagine that their arm is numb and insensitive, like a piece of rubber (e.g., Spanos et al., 1974). A large number of studies have consistently indicated that suggestions of this type produce decrements in reported pain (Barber & Hahn, 1962; Evans & Paul, 1970; Spanos et al., 1974, 1979). Recently, we compared the effectiveness of an analgesia suggestion with a distraction task (Spanos et al., Note 1). Subjects in the distraction condition tracked a moving light with one hand while their other arm was immersed in ice water. The tracking task required continuous attention, but not imaginative involvement. Subjects given the suggestion showed a significant decrement from baseline to posttest in the rate at which pain grew during 60 sec of immersion. Distraction subjects showed the same rate of pain growth on baseline and posttest. Moreover, suggestion subjects showed significant increments on all measures of coping and significant decrements on all measures of catastrophizing from baseline to posttest. On the other hand, distraction subjects did not show consistent changes on these measures.

The results of this study (Spanos et al., Note 1) were also assessed in a different manner. Subjects were collapsed across treatments and divided into those who had (a) engaged predominantly in coping activity during both the baseline and the posttest, (b) engaged predominantly in catastrophizing on the baseline but coped on the posttest, and (c) catastrophized on both the baseline and posttest. Subjects who coped on both immersions and those who catastrophized on the first immersion but coped on the second reported significant decrements in pain from baseline to posttest. However, those who catastropized on both immersions reported the same high level of pain on both baseline and posttest immersions. In a related study Spanos et al. (Note 2) found that analgesia suggestions were associated with reductions on reported pain when they transformed subjects from baseline catastrophizers into posttest copers. The suggestions had no effect when subjects remained catastrophizers on both immersions.

Combined, these data indicate that suggestions that invite subjects to become involved in coping imagery may be more effective than a distraction task in reducing reported pain. Moreover, suggestions appear to produce their effects by enhancing cognitive coping and reducing catastrophizing. Subjects' reports do not indicate that suggestions induce unique or unusual processes. On the contrary, they seem to reinforce the coping activities that many subjects spontaneously engage in during baseline testing.

Hypnotic Analgesia

The studies discussed thus far did not involve hypnotic procedures. What happens if suggestions for analgesia are preceded by the administration of a hypnotic induction procedure? Basically, nothing different happens under these circumstances. Most studies indicate that a hypnotic induction procedure coupled with a suggestion (hypnotic analgesia) is no more effective than a suggestion alone (waking analgesia) in reducing reported pain (Barber & Hahn, 1962; Evans & Paul, 1970; Spanos et al., 1974, 1979). Nevertheless, several studies (Evans & Paul, 1970; Spanos et al., 1979, Note 1) indicate that general responsiveness to hypnotic procedures (i.e., hypnotic susceptibility) is correlated with degree of pain reduction following analgesia suggestions both in hypnotic subjects (i.e., those given a hypnotic induction plus a suggestion) and in nonhypnotic subjects (i.e., those given a suggestion alone).[1]

Recently, we investigated the relationships among subjects' cognitive activity, their hypnotic susceptibility, and the administration of an hypnotic induction procedure in affecting pain reductions (Spanos et al., 1979). All subjects were tested in a baseline and posttest immersion as described above. Immediately after the baseline immersion (but before posttesting), subjects were assigned to one of four treatments; (a) hypnotic induction plus analgesia suggestion, (b) hypnotic induction alone, (c) analgesia suggestion alone, (d) no induction and no-suggestion (control). Within each of these treatments one third of the subjects were high, one third medium, and one third low on hypnotic susceptibility. Following their treatment manipulation, subjects were posttested and then interviewed about their experiences during the second immersion.

As in previous studies, subjects given hypnotic analgesia and those given waking analgesia showed equivalent reduction in reported pain. Furthermore, these reductions were greatest for the high susceptible subjects and smallest for the low susceptibles. Examination of interview testimony indicated that hypnotic and nonhypnotic subjects given an analgesia suggestion reported equivalent use of coping strategies. Furthermore, subjects given an analgesia suggestion used more coping strategies than those not given a suggestion, and those high in susceptibility used more coping strategies than low susceptibles. When collapsed across treatments, subjects classified as catastrophizers reported more pain on the posttest than those who did not catastrophize. Among the noncatastrophizers, those who used numerous coping strategies reported greater baseline-to-posttest pain reductions than those who did not engage in coping cognitions. In short, hypnotic and nonhypnotic subjects given an analgesia suggestion appeared to reduce reported pain for the same reasons; they did not catastrophize, and they became involved in coping cognitions. Rather than automatically inducing "dissociation among cognitive subsystems," analgesia suggestions (in both hypnotic and nonhypnotic subjects) appear to be effective when they lead subjects to stop catastrophizing and successfully encourage them to become involved in coping ideation.

Treatment Expectancies and Hypnotic Analgesia

The analgesia studies described thus far assigned different subjects to hypnotic and nonhypnotic treatments. In a different group of experiments (Hilgard, Macdonald, Morgan, & Johnson, 1978; Stacher, Schuster, Bauer, Lahoda, & Schulze, 1975), the same subjects were given both waking analgesia and hypnotic analgesia at different times. For instance, Hilgard et al. (1978) required high susceptible subjects to immerse an arm in ice water three times. The first immersion was a baseline test, the second followed suggestion alone, and the third followed a hypnotic induction procedure plus suggestion. Under these circumstances, subjects showed significantly more pain reduction during hypnotic analgesia than they did during waking analgesia. Hilgard (1977, 1979) interpreted these results to mean that hypnotic analgesia is intrinsically more effective than waking analgesia in reducing pain. He argued that hypnotic analgesia involves the dissociation of pain from conscious awareness while waking analgesia does not. Purportedly, hypnotized subjects continue to experience pain at an unconscious level. However, the pain is somehow separated from conscious awareness by an amnesic barrier. In short, hypnotically analgesic subjects are thought to experience events at two levels of consciousness simultaneously. At one level, they are aware of greatly reduced pain while, at a different level, hidden from conscious awareness, they experience the pain at more or less its full intensity.

Hilgard (1977) contends that nonhypnotic subjects given an analgesia suggestion do not dissociate. These subjects may be able to reduce their felt pain somewhat by employing conscious procedures like distraction, but they do not experience the more profound pain reduction that occurs when pain is dissociated from conscious awareness.

Hilgard's (1977, 1979) dissociation hypothesis cannot parsimoniously account for the equivalent reduction in reported pain found for hypnotic and waking analgesia treatments in studies that assigned different subjects to these two treatments (Barber & Hahn, 1962; Evans & Paul, 1970; Spanos et al., 1974, 1979). On the other hand, Hilgard et al.'s (1968) findings can be accounted for parsimoniously and without recourse to the notion of dissociation if the social context in which experiments on hypnotic analgesia are carried out is taken to consideration. When the same high-susceptible subjects are given both waking analgesia and hypnotic analgesia, they are aware that these two treatments are being compared. High susceptible subjects have a strong investment in validating their role performance as <u>good hypnotic</u> subjects (Dolby & Sheehan, 1977; Sarbin & Coe, 1972; Spanos, Stam & D'Eon, Pawlak, & Radtke-Bodorik, in press). Therefore, they may perform less than optimally when given a suggestion alone so that they can improve significantly with hypnosis (Spanos, McPeake, & Carter, 1973; Zamansky, Scharf, & Brightbill, 1964).

Figure 1 shows the results of a recent study (Stam & Spanos, in press) that examined these ideas. We tested four groups of high susceptible subjects, all of whom immersed their arms in ice water for 60 sec on three different trials. For each immersion subjects rated their degree of pain at 60 sec. Subjects in one group received the order of treatments used by Hilgard et al. (1978): baseline, suggestion alone, hypnosis and suggestion (B/S/H&S). As indicated in Figure 1, the results of the Hilgard et al. (1978) study were replicated. We found significantly more pain reduction with hypnotic analgesia than with waking analgesia. Subjects in our second group were not given a hypnotic procedure. Instead, they received a baseline test and then two immersions following suggestion alone (B/S/S). As Figure 1 indicates, these subjects showed as much pain reduction with waking analgesia as those in Group 1 showed with hypnotic analgesia. Moreover, during Immersion 2 more pain reduction with waking analgesia was shown by subjects in the B/S/S treatment than by those in the B/S/H&S treatment. In short, subjects who received waking analgesia while knowing that hypnotic analgesia was to follow seem to have performed less than optimally during the suggestion alone so that they could later show an improvement with hypnosis.

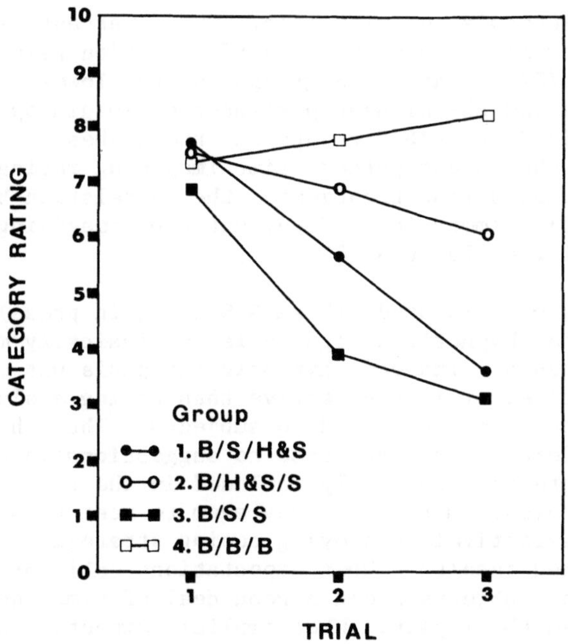

Figure 1. Mean category scale pain ratings for the four groups of high susceptible subjects in the Stam and Spanos (in press) experiment. (B = baseline, S = suggestion, H = hypnosis).

Our third group was designed to counter the usual expectation of heightened pain reduction during hypnotic analgesia. After baseline testing, these subjects were given hypnotic analgesia followed by waking analgesia (B/H&S/S). Immediately before receiving the hypnotic analgesia treatment, they were told that they would later receive waking analgesia. They were also told that they would probably experience less pain reduction with hypnosis than with suggestion alone. In order to buttress this counter-expectational idea, they were told that hypnosis produced drowsiness which tended to interfere with the concentration necessary for pain reduction. Figure 1 shows that our expectancy manipulation reduced responding to both hypnotic and waking analgesia. It seems that subjects were not certain how to respond and, therefore, chose the conservative option of responding minimally to both treatments. It is worth noting that the second immersion hypnotic analgesia treatment given to the B/H&S/S subjects was less effective than the corresponding waking analgesia suggestion given to the B/S/S subjects. Subjects in our fourth group simply underwent the baseline procedure on all three immersions (B/B/B). The data from this group indicate that practice at ice water immersion did not, in and of itself, lead to reductions in reported pain.

Following the pain testing sequence, we obtained subjects' estimates of the percentage of time during their third immersion that they imagined events inconsistent with pain. These percent-time imagining scores closely paralleled subjects' third immersion pain ratings. Subjects in the B/S/H&S and B/S/S groups had the lowest third immersion pain ratings and the highest percent-time imagining ratings. Those in the B/H&S/S and B/B/B groups had the highest third immersion pain ratings and the lowest percent time imagining ratings. When subjects were collapsed across treatments, the correlation between pain ratings on the third immersion and percent time imagining estimates was a substantial $r = .70$, $p < .01$.

The findings of this study (Stam & Spanos, in press) contradict the hypothesis that hypnotic analgesia is intrinsically more effective than waking analgesia. Instead, hypnotic analgesia was equally effective, more effective, or less effective than waking analgesia depending upon the expectations conveyed to subjects. Thus, high-susceptible subjects moderate their response to suggestions in terms of expectations that are not explicitly included in the test suggestions they are administered. Moreover, they seem to meet these implicit expectations by selectively employing coping strategies that will lead to the desired results. When expectations call for high levels of pain reduction, subjects spend a good deal of time engaged in imaginings that lessen their pain. When implicit expectations do not call for pain reduction (despite the explicit requests of an analgesia suggestion), subjects engage only minimally in coping imagery and thereby experience relatively high degrees of pain. These data paint a picture of the highly susceptible hypnotic subjects as an actively cognizing individual who is attuned to subtle social expectations and who modifies his or her imaginative activities to meet these expectations. All of this is quite different from the automatic responding envisioned by a dissociation hypothesis of hypnosis.

Hypnotic Analgesia and the Hidden Observer

The evidence most frequently cited in support of the hypnosis-as-dissociation hypothesis comes from a series of "hidden observer" studies conducted by Hilgard and his colleagues (Knox, Morgan, & Hilgard, 1974; Hilgard, Morgan, & Macdonald, 1975; Hilgard, Hilgard, Macdonald, Morgan, & Johnson, 1978). According to Hilgard (1977, 1979), pain during hypnotic analgesia continues to be felt at an unconscious level at more or less its full intensity. However, this unconscious or dissociated pain experience is hidden from conscious awareness by an amnesic barrier. Hilgard (1977, 1979) contends that the experimenter can contact the hidden part of the hypnotically analgesic subject and obtain pain intensity estimates from this hidden part (i.e., hidden pain estimates). At the same time, the conscious part of the hypnotically analgesic subject can estimate the degree of pain that "it" feels (i.e., overt pain estimates).

In a typical hidden observer experiment (e.g., Hilgard et al., 1975) high-susceptible subjects are given a baseline limb immersion during which they verbally estimate their pain intensity every five seconds. Later, subjects are administered a hypnotic induction procedure and instructed that there is a hidden part of them that is aware of experiences that their hypnotized part is unaware of. These hidden observer instructions are quite explicit. For instance:

> When I place my hand on your shoulder, I shall be able to talk to a hidden part of you that knows things that are going on in your body, things that are unknown to the part of you to which I am now talking. The part of you to which I am now talking will not know what you are telling me... (Knox et al., 1974, P. 842).

Subjects are also given a good deal of practice at performing two tasks simultaneously while supposedly maintaining one of the tasks outside of awareness. For example, on one task subjects name colors verbally while they "unconsciously" tap out a pattern on a key-pressing device. In later limb immersion sessions, subjects are given a hypnotic induction procedure and an analgesia suggestion. They are also instructed to give two types of pain reports every five seconds: overt (verbal) reports that index the pain felt by their hypnotized part and hidden reports (numbers tapped out in a key-pressing code) that reflect the pain experienced by their hidden part.

Hilgard and his associates (Hilgard et al., 1975, 1978; Knox et al., 1974) have consistently found that (a) overt reports from subjects' hypnotized part indicate reduced pain relative to reports from baseline immersions and (b) hidden reports indicate more pain than overt reports and about the same degree of pain as baseline reports. According to Hilgard (1977, 1979), hidden reports do not result from suggestion. The experimental instructions employed in his studies are not seen by him as communications that teach subjects to behave as though they have hidden parts. Instead, hidden reports are thought to reflect the intrinsic characteristics of a dissociated state, and the experimental instructions used in these studies are thought to create a structured setting in which these intrinsic characteristics can come to light (Hilgard, 1979).

Recently, we (Spanos & Hewitt, in press) proposed an explanation for the hidden observer effect that does not revolve around the notion of dissociation. We argued that hidden reports were engendered and shaped by the interpersonal communications contained in hidden observer experiments. From our perspective, hidden reports more closely approximate experimental creations than the discovery of a novel psychological phenomenon. If this social expectancy hypothesis is accurate, then we reasoned that we could obtain hidden reports indicating either more or less pain than overt hypnotic analgesic reports by manipulating the expectations that subjects were given. These ideas were tested by assigning high susceptible subjects to two treatment conditions (Spanos & Hewitt, in press). Those in one group received Hilgard et al.'s (1975) procedures for eliciting hypnotic analgesia and overt and hidden pain reports. Subjects in the second group received similar instructions, but with one important difference. They were informed that their hidden part was so deeply hidden that it would be even less aware of what was being experienced than was their hypnotized part. In short, our two groups were provided with opposite expectations concerning the experiences that would be felt by their hidden parts. Those in our "more aware" hidden observer group were implicitly informed that their hidden part would experience more pain than their hypnotized part while those in our "less aware" hidden observer group were informed that their hidden part would experience less pain than their hypnotized part. Figure 2 plots our findings. The graph on the left displays the data from our "more aware" subjects and clearly indicates that we replicated the pattern of results observed by Hilgard et al. (1975): higher hidden pain than overt pain. Comparing the graphs for our two groups indicates that our social expectancy hypothesis was clearly confirmed. "More aware" and "less aware" subjects showed hidden observers with opposite characteristics: high sensitivity to pain in one case and greatly reduced sensitivity to pain in the other.

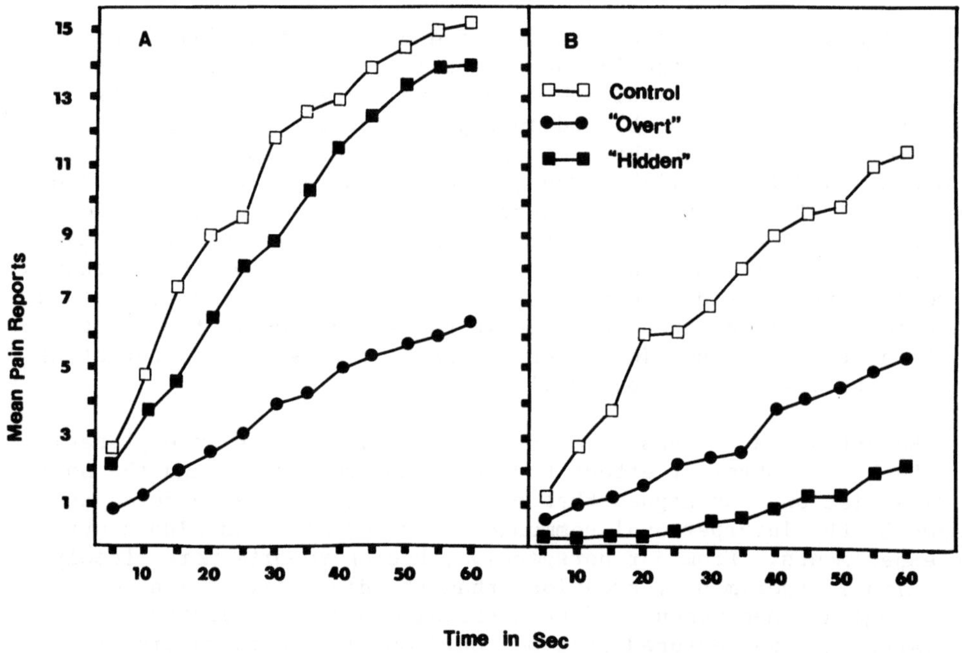

Figure 2. Mean category scale pain ratings for the more aware and less aware treatment groups in the Spanos and Hewitt (in press) experiment (A = More aware treatment, B = Less aware treatment).

Spanos and Hewitt's (in press) data seem to indicate that the experimental procedures used in hidden observer studies do not simply provide a context that allows the intrinsic characteristics of a dissociated subsystem to become manifest. Instead, these procedures provide willing subjects with information and expectancies that encourage them to construe and describe their experiences in terms of dissociated parts that have particular characteristics.

Taken together, the findings discussed above are inconsistent with the notion of hypnotic analgesia as an automatic result of a dissociative process. On the contrary, they indicate that hypnotic analgesia, like waking analgesia, is something that subjects actively achieve by gearing their cognitive activity to the expectations and coping strategies contained in the suggestions they are administered.

Recall that for Hilgard (1977, 1979) pain reduction following a waking suggestion involves distraction and other attention-deployment procedures, while hypnotic analgesia involves the automatic construction of an amnesic barrier that separates the pain experience from conscious awareness. One implication of these ideas is that hypnotic amnesia involves automatic dissociative processes that differ fundamentally from such attention-deployment procedures as self-distraction. It is to a fuller consideration of hypnotic amnesia that we now turn.

SUGGESTED AMNESIA

Suggested amnesia is usually defined as a temporary, suggestion-induced inaccessibility of available information (Nace, Orne, & Hammer, 1974; Spanos & Radtke-Bodorik, 1980). The temporary nature of this recall deficit is demonstrated by its reversibility. Amnesic subjects are able to recall the forgotten material without practice or relearning when they are provided with a prearranged cue that cancels their amnesia (Spanos & Bodorik, 1977). When suggestions for amnesia are preceded by a hypnotic induction procedure, the resulting recall deficit is labeled hypnotic amnesia. This phenomenon has held a central place in theories of hypnosis for over a century (Ellenberger, 1970; Spanos & Gottlieb, 1979). Traditionally, investigators have explained it by positing processes like repression and dissociation that are conceptualized as somehow automatically blocking recall (Clemes, 1964; Hilgard, 1977; Kihlstrom, 1978). For example, Kihlstrom and Shor (1978) have argued that hypnotically amnesic subjects are unable to generate the retrieval cues that will reinstate recall and have described such amnesia as "...a dissociation of memories from conscious control." (Pp. 346-347).

Our own research suggests a very different conception of this phenomenon. From our perspective, amnesia can be conceptualized in terms of attention deployment, its occurrence being determined by what subjects attend to and ignore during designated aspects of a standardized testing sequence (Spanos & Radtke-Bodorik, 1980; Spanos, Radtke-Bodorik, & Stam, 1980; Spanos et al., in press). Typically, however, the amnesia testing situation is ambiguous. Therefore, the events that subjects attend to are largely determined by the way in which they construe the conflicting demands inherent in this situation.

THE STRUCTURE OF THE AMNESIA TESTING SITUATION

The amnesia testing sequence typically employed in our own laboratory illustrates the ambiguous nature of this situation. Following a hypnotic induction procedure or task-motivation instructions (brief control instructions that ask subjects to try their best), subjects in our amnesia studies (Radtke-Bodorik, Planas, & Spanos, 1980; Radtke-Bodorik, Spanos, & Haddad, 1979; Spanos & Bodorik, 1977; Spanos et al., in press; Spanos, Radtke-Bodorik, & Shabinsky, 1980; Spanos, Radtke-Bodorik, & Stam, 1980) usually learn a short list of words to a stringent criterion. They are then exposed to amnesia testing sequence that can be divided into three parts. First, they are given a suggestion informing them that they will be unable to recall the words they just learned until they are given an explicit signal that cancels their amnesia. Second, before receiving the cancellation signal subjects are challenged to try to recall the words and are given an opportunity to do so. Third, the cancellation signal is presented and subjects are again asked to recall all of the words. Subjects are defined as amnesic if they recall fewer words after the challenge than after presentation of the cancellation signal and if they report postexperimentally that they actually forgot (as opposed to remembered but withheld) the words that they failed to recall following the challenge.

One source of ambiguity in this situation involves the challenge to remember that is given before the cancellation signal. Subjects frequently interpret the amnesia suggestion as a cue to shift attention away from the target material during the amnesia testing period (Spanos et al., 1980). Therefore, these subjects can interpret the challenge to remember in one of two ways: either as a serious request to refocus attention on the task of recalling the words (active-recall interpretation) or as a request to recall any words that happen to "come to mind" while simultaneously maintaining attention elsewhere (passive-recall interpretation). We recently tested the hypothesis that subjects would show amnesia to the extent that they interpreted the challenge as a request for passive recall and thereby maintained attention away from the target material until given the cancellation signal (Spanos et al., in press, Experiment 1). Hypnotic and task-motivated subjects were assigned to three preexperimental instructional conditions. Those in one condition were told about the list-learning-amnesia-suggestion sequence they were about to undergo and were explicitly instructed to interpret the remember challenge as a serious request to actively try to recall the words. Those in a second condition were asked to interpret the challenge as an invitation to passively recall words that came to mind, but not to actively try to retrieve words or interfere with the forgetting process. A third group was given no special instructions. Under the no-instruction condition hypnotic subjects showed more amnesia than task-motivated subjects. This finding was predicted, because our previous amnesia studies (Radtke-Bodorik et al., 1979, 1980; Spanos & Bodorik, 1977; Spanos, Radtke-Bodorik, & Shabinsky, 1980; Spanos, Radtke-Bodorik, & Stam, 1980) had also shown more amnesia for hypnotic subjects than for task-motivated subjects. For both hypnotic and task-motivated subjects given the preliminary instruction to try actively to remember when challenged, amnesia was practically eliminated. On the other hand, the instructions to recall passively when challenged affected hypnotic and task-motivated subjects differently. Task-motivated subjects in this condition showed more amnesia than corresponding task-motivated subjects in the no instructions condition. However, hypnotic subjects in the passive-recall and no-instructions conditions showed equivalent levels of amnesia.

These results indicate that amnesia can be greatly reduced by instructing subjects to consider the remember challenge as a serious request for active recall. They also indicate that hypnotic and task-motivated subjects who have been given no special instructions frequently interpret the remember challenge differently. Moreover, these differing interpretations may account for the higher level of amnesia usually shown by hypnotic as compared to task-motivated subjects. Under no-instructions conditions task-motivation subjects seem to interpret the remember challenge as an instruction to focus attention actively on recall of the words and, therefore, show relatively little amnesia. Hypnotic subjects seem to interpret the challenge as a request to recall passively and, therefore, special instructions to this effect are redundant.

The remember challenge constitutes only one source of ambiguity in the amnesia testing situation. Another occurs in the wording of amnesia suggestions. These suggestions frequently imply that subjects are to participate actively in forgetting the target material (e.g., "I want you to forget..."). However, they also imply that forgetting will occur effortlessly and automatically (e.g., "The words will be gone, gone completely from your mind."). Thus, some subjects may interpret these suggestions as requests to direct attention away from recall of the target material, whereas others may interpret them as requests to continue attending to this material and to wait for amnesia to happen. In a second experiment (Spanos et al., in press, Experiment 2), we eliminated this ambiguity by explicitly instructing hypnotic and task-motivated subjects to interpret the amnesia suggestion as a request to direct and maintain attention away from the target material until they received the cancellation signal. Both the hypnotic and task-motivation subjects given these instructions to attend away showed substantially more amnesia than corresponding hypnotic and task-motivation subjects assigned to a no-instructions condition. When collapsed across hypnotic and task-motivation treatments, 75% of the attend-away subjects showed some amnesia as compared to only 36% of the no-instructions subjects. In short, the results of these studies are consistent with our hypothesis of amnesia as inattention. Both hypnotic and task-motivated subjects showed large increments in amnesia when they were induced to maintain attention away from target recall. Furthermore, amnesia was virtually eliminated when these subjects interpreted the remember challenge as a serious request to attend to the target material. These findings also suggest that wide individual differences in amnesia occur not because some subjects become dissociated while others do not, but because the testing situation is ambiguous and therfore subjects interpret it in different ways.

"Breaching" Amnesia

As mentioned earlier Spanos et al. (Experiment 1, in press) virtually eliminated amnesia when subjects were instructed to interpret the remember challenge as a request to refocus attention actively on the recall task. This finding was obtained using subjects who were unselected with respect to hypnotic susceptibility. In other words, relatively few of the subjects in that experiment obtained high scores on hypnotic susceptibility. On the other hand, two studies (Howard & Coe, in press; Kihlstrom, 1975) have found that high susceptible amnesics continued to show forgetting despite various instructions aimed at "breaching" their amnesia. For instance, Kihlstrom (1975) challenged high susceptibles to recall target material twice before presenting the cancellation signal. Before the second challenge, subjects were told either to try their best to remember, to employ an organizational retrieval strategy to aid recall, or given no special (control) instructions. Subjects given the various breaching instructions were no more likely than the controls to show increments in recall following the second challenge. Subjects in all groups showed further increments in recall after presentation of the cancellation cue. In other words, high-susceptible subjects given instructions aimed at overcoming their amnesia continued to show as much amnesia as uninstructed control subjects. Kihlstrom (1975) did not present data concerning his subjects' experiences during amnesia. Nevertheless, he interpreted his findings to mean that "the hypnotized amnesic subject appears to be trying about as hard as he can [to recall the 'forgotten material']...there is some impediment in retrieval that prevents him from easily and efficiently recollecting any more of the available memories" (P. 75).

Our social psychological perspective suggests a very different interpretation of such findings. As we pointed out earlier, high susceptible subjects are particularly intent on successfully fulfilling the requirements of the role of the good hypnotic subject. Moreover, these subjects respond in terms of what they believe these requirements to be even when the requirements are explicitly contradicted by other aspects of the experimental situation (Orne, 1971; Dolby & Sheehan, 1977). We have already seen, for example, that high-susceptible subjects will respond less than optimally to the requests of an analgesia suggestion in order to report large pain reductions when later tested under a hypnotic procedure. In an amnesia testing situation responding to the remember challenge by actively refocusing attention on the task of recalling the target material (even when explicitly instructed to do so) conflicts with maintaining the role of a good hypnotic subject. If high susceptible subjects actively attend to and try to recall the target material, they will remember it. However, if they remember it, they violate the role requirements for being good hypnotic subjects.

These considerations led us to conduct a study that compared high-susceptible hypnotic subjects given preliminary instructions to attend actively when challenged to target recall with corresponding high-susceptibles given preliminary control instructions (Spanos et al., Experiment 3, in press). As we anticipated, subjects in the two treatments showed equivalent degrees of amnesia. More important, however, rating scale data and interview testimony indicated that, despite their preliminary instructions, the "active recall" subjects continued to show as much evidence of inattention following the challenge as did controls. Thus, instead of refocusing their attention on the recall task as instructed, the "active recall" subjects reported experiences like the following during their amnesia: "I concentrated on driving very fast down an open highway repeating 'I cannot remember' and just concentrating on moving ahead quickly..." or "I went over and over in my mind saying 'forget' over and over..." (Spanos et al., Experiment 3, in press). In short, when high-susceptibles were faced with the choice of following preliminary instructions that would lead to role violation or ignoring those instructions in order to meet role requirements, they tended to choose the latter course of action. They ignored their preliminary instructions and, thereby, did not invalidate their status as good hypnotic subjects.

These findings are not consistent with dissociation formulations that view amnesia as an automatic process that somehow prevents recall (Hilgard, 1977; Kihlstrom, 1975, 1978). Notions like "dissociated" imply an inability to recall despite sustained attention and effort directed toward the recall task. Our findings suggest, instead that subjects remain amnesic to the extent that they maintain attention away from rather than toward the recall task. Moreover, these findings emphasize that the responding of hypnotic subjects is determined by their interpretations of the experimental situation. For the high susceptible individual, performing as a good hypnotic subject is an important consideration. Therefore, for such a person instructions that conflict with good hypnotic performance tend to be ignored, reinterpreted, or relegated to a status of secondary importance.[2]

Recall Organization During Suggested Amnesia

Modern information processing approaches to memory frequently emphasize the notion of recall organization (Puff, 1979; Sternberg & Tulving, 1977). Suppose, for example, that subjects are given a series of trials to learn a list of words that fall into several taxonomic categories (e.g., birds, flowers). The words are presented in a different random order on each trial, and subjects are told that they can recall the words in any order they like. Under these circumstances, subjects do not typically recall the words in their order of presentation. Instead, they tend to cluster their recall; to recall together words from the same category (Bousfield, 1953; Murphy, 1979; Shuell, 1969). Many investigators interpret the occurrence of clustering as a strategy that aids recall (e.g., Murphy, 1979; Slamenka, 1972). Thus, organizing a word list into clusters may be one way in which subjects enhance the accessibility of the list words. If this is true, the converse may also be the case; subjects who temporarily fail to organize their recall might be expected to experience a temporary difficulty in accessing the list words.

A series of studies carried out in our laboratory indicate that suggested amnesia for a categorized word list is associated with a temporary "breakdown" in subjects' tendency to cluster their recall (Radtke-Bodorik et al., 1979, 1980; Spanos & Bodorik, 1977; Spanos, Radtke-Bodorik, & Stam, 1980). The responses of subjects to an amnesia suggestion can be classified into three major groupings. Complete amnesics do not recall anything following the remember challenge. Partial amnesics recall some of the words at this time but fewer than they recall after the cancellation signal. Full recallers show as much recall after the remember challenge as after the cancellation signal, despite being given the suggestion. The clustering of recall cannot be measured in complete amnesics because there is no recall to measure. It can, however, be measured in partial amnesics and in full recallers. We have measured clustering at three different points for each subject; (a) immediately before the amnesia suggestion (on the last learning trial), (b) following the remember challenge, and (c) after the cancellation signal. Partial amnesics cluster significantly less following the remember challenge than they do either before the suggestion or after the cancellation signal. On the other hand, full recallers continue to cluster to the same high degree before the suggestion, following the challenge, and after the cancellation signal (Spanos & Bodorik, 1977; Spanos, Radtke-Bodorik, & Stam, 1980). The tendency for partial amnesics to cluster less during amnesia than before it or after it is labeled "disorganized recall." Hypnotic and task-motivated partial amnesics show equivalent degrees of disorganized recall and high susceptible partial amnesics are more likely than low susceptible partial amnesics to show such disorganization (Spanos et al., 1980). Among hypnotic partial amnesics a clustering breakdown occurs even when the word list is long and incompletely learned (Radtke-Bodorik, 1980) and when recall is written rather than spoken (Radtke-Bodorik et al., 1979). Spanos, Radtke-Bodorik, and Stam (1980) demonstrated that the disorganized recall associated with partial amnesia was not a statistical artifact produced by reduced recall and that such disorganization did not occur when nonamnesic subjects were simply instructed to withhold (rather than forget) part of their recall. In short, disorganized recall is a robust phenomenon reliably associated with suggested amnesia. How is it to be explained?

Evans and Kihlstrom (1973) have described disorganized recall as a defining characteristic of hypnotic amnesia.[3] More recently, Kihlstrom (1975, 1978; Kihlstrom & Shor, 1978) argued that amnesic subjects are unable to recall the target material (despite serious efforts to do so) because thay are unable to organize their recall. He also argued that amnesia involves a dissociative process and implied that disorganized recall reflects such dissociation. As we saw above, however, there is no convincing evidence to support the notion that amnesic subjects are unable to recall. They fail to recall when they interpret the suggestion as a request to consistently maintain attention away from the recall task. When subjects choose to attend to the recall task, they recall the target material. These findings suggest that the organization of subjects' recall following the remember challenge will also be a function of attention deployment.

From our perspective, disorganized recall is not a defining characteristic of hypnotic amnesia. Neither a hypnotic procedure, amnesia suggestions, nor high susceptibility are necessary conditions for producing disorganized recall. In fact, any procedure that temporarily diverts subjects' attention from the recall task should lead to both reduced recall and disorganization (Spanos & Radtke-Bodorik, 1980). We recently tested these ideas in an experiment that involved three groups of subjects (Spanos & D'Eon, in press). Those in the first group were high-susceptibles who were administered a hypnotic induction procedure and tested in our standard list learning-amnesia suggestion paradigm. A second group of high-susceptibles did not receive a hypnotic induction procedure and carried out an attention diversion task in place of the amnesia suggestion. These subjects learned the same word list as those in our first group. However, in place of the amnesia suggestion they counted backwards by threes in writing and tried to recall the words orally at the same time. They were instructed preexperimentally to focus on counting efficiently, but to say any words that "came to mind" as they counted. A third group consisted of low-susceptibles given the same attention diversion treatment as those in Group two. Within each group, we divided subjects into those who recalled all of the words despite the suggestion or attention-diversion task and those who showed partial recall at this time. As in earlier studies, clustering was measured before the suggestion/attention diversion, following the remember challenge, and after cancelling the suggestion/attention diversion. The partial recallers in all three groups showed an equivalent breakdown in clustering following the remember challenge. The full recallers in all three groups failed to show a clustering breakdown. In short, diverting attention from the task of recall not only led to reduced recall, it also produced the same degree of disorganization as an amnesia suggestion given to high-susceptible hypnotic subjects. These findings are consistent with our hypothesis that suggested amnesia results from inattention to the task of recall. Furthermore, they indicate that disorganized recall cannot be used as an unambiguous index of the type of automatic, nonconscious blocking of retrieval functions implied by concepts like dissociation.[4]

Taken together, our findings concerning suggested analgesia and suggested amnesia argue strongly against the notion that hypnotic responding occurs automatically. Subjects' interpretations and expectations do not simply provide a readiness that allows for the automatic emergence of dissociative processes. Instead, these variables determine the attentional shifts, imaginings, and other cognitive processes that subjects selectively carry out in order to meet the implicit and explicit demands in the test situation. In short, hypnotic analgesia and hypnotic amnesia are not events that happen to subjects. They are experiences that subjects must strategically bring about (Barber et al., 1974; Coe & Sarbin, 1977; Spanos et al., in press; Stam & Spanos, in press).

Having stated (and hopefully demonstrated) that the responses of hypnotic subjects are not automatic, I will return briefly to the issue that began this essay. Namely, that regardless of how strategic the responses of good hypnotic subjects may in fact be they often <u>feel</u> automatic to these subjects.

THE PHENOMENOLOGY OF SUGGESTED RESPONSES

Spanos et al. (1979) asked subjects postexperimentally whether they did anything to reduce pain during their second ice water limb immersion. Fifty-six percent of the subjects who had been rated as using one or more coping strategies during this immersion stated that they did nothing to help reduce their pain. For example, one subject was classified as engaging in distraction on the basis of the following report, "I was counting in my head, sort of counting off seconds. It was just a way of sort of changing the subject, taking your mind off it..." (Spanos et al., 1979, P. 286). When explicitly asked, this subject stated that he did nothing to help himself feel less pain.

All of our amnesia studies have included postexperimental interviews designed to assess subjects' experiences. Some of the amnesic subjects in these studies reported that their forgetting felt effortless, while others stated that it required effort. The effortful forgetters reported that they tried to forget the words by purposefully shifting attention to other things. However, the effortless forgetters insisted that they did not do anything to forget; "the words just seemed to go away by themselves." Effortful and effortless forgetters did not differ either in extent of amnesia or in the extent to which their recall was disorganized (Radtke-Bodorik et al., 1979; Spanos & Bodorik, 1977; Spanos, Radtke-Bodorik, & Stam, 1980).

Despite their insistence that they did nothing to produce forgetting, the testimony of effortless forgetters often revealed that they attended to events other than the recall task during amnesia, but failed to define their inattention as self-generated distraction. For instance, the following subject, after stating explicitly that he did nothing to make himself forget, reported that "I just let myself think of things other than the words...my mind wandered to other things." Clearly, this subject shifted his attention away from the task of recalling the list words. Nevertheless, he defined this attentional shift as occurring effortlessly.

We believe that it is important to make a clear distinction between the variables that account for subjects' responses to suggestion and those that account for how subjects define their responses to suggestion. For example, the forgetting that occurs during hypnotic amnesia appears to be due to temporary, suggestion-generated inattention. However, subjects' reports of their forgetting occurring effortlessly or effortfully result from a different set of variables. These reports can be conceptualized as reflecting attributions that subjects make about the causes of their own behavior. Thus, effortful forgetters attribute their recall deficit to their own voluntary self-generated activity (i.e., "I did it.") while effortless forgetters attribute it to events external to their own self (i.e., "It happened to me."). These attributions appear to be a function of such variables as preconceptions concerning hypnosis, expectations for effortless responding implicit in the wording of hypnotic procedures and test suggestions, and in some cases patterns of imaginative activity that accompany response to many types of suggestion (Spanos et al., 1977; Spanos et al., in press).

The role of preconceptions and expectations in affecting reports of effortless amnesia was assessed by Spanos et al. (in press). Subjects who had been instructed preexperimentally to regard an amnesia suggestion as a request to distract themselves were less likely than uninstructed subjects to define their forgetting as effortless. Hypnotic procedures implicitly and explicitly inform subjects that their responding is supposed to occur automatically. On the other hand, task-motivating instructions ask them to try their best to experience suggested effects and, thereby, carry fewer implications of effortless responding. Several studies (Radtke-Bodorik et al., 1979; Spanos & Bodorik, 1977) found that hypnotic amnesics were more likely than task-motivated amnesics to define their forgetting as occurring effortlessly. These findings are consistent with the notion that experimentally generated expectations affect subjects' tendency to apply attributions of effortlessness to their behavior.

The role of imaginings in affecting subjects' attributions of effortlessness or involuntariness have been investigated with "motoric" suggestions. Suggestions that call for a specific motor act (e.g., arm levitation, arm lowering, arm rigidity) typically imply that the act should occur involuntarily (e.g., "your arm is rising" as opposed to "raise your arm"). Motoric suggestions frequently elicit imaginative activity as well as the overt act requested. Moreover, some subjects imagine specific situations that are congruent with the idea of their overt behavior occurring involuntarily. For example, a subject given a suggestion that his or her arm is rising might imagine that the arm is being pumped up with air or that it is attracted to an overhanging magnet. Imaginings of this type, which are congruent with the implicit expectations for involuntary responding contained in the suggestion, are called "goal-directed fantasies" (Spanos, 1971). When given identical suggestions, subjects who reported such fantasies were more likely than those who did not to define their overt responses as involuntary occurrences (Spanos & McPeake, 1977; Spanos, Spillane, & McPeake, 1976; Spanos et al., 1977). Moreover, the degree to which subjects became absorbed or involved in imaginings of this type correlated significantly with the degree of involuntariness that they attributed to their behavior (Spanos & McPeake, 1974). Spanos and Barber (1972) found that subjects' attributions of involuntariness were related to the wording of the suggestion they were administered. Hypnotic subjects were given a suggestion that instructed them either to imagine a balloon pulling up their arm or simply to raise their arm. Arm-raising occurred with equal frequency for the two groups, but subjects asked to imagine were more likely than those asked simply to raise their arm to engage in goal-directed fantasy and also to rate their arm-rising as feeling involuntary. Taken together, these findings do not indicate that subjects' imaginings cause their overt response to suggestion. They do suggest, however, that the attributions of involuntariness applied by subjects to their behavior are, at least in part, determined by their concurrently occurring imaginative activity.

The systematic assessment of variables that affect subjects' reports of effortlessness and automaticity has only just begun. Nevertheless, this preliminary work supports the utility of conceptualizing such reports as the outcome of an attribution process rather than the reflection of dissociated mental subsystems that produce automatic behavior.

CONCLUSIONS

The view that hypnotic behavior occurs automatically extends back to 18th century conceptions of the "magnetized" individual as an automation acted upon by forces emanating from the superior powers of the "magnetizer" (Deluze, 1825/1879; Spanos & Gottlieb, 1979). The notion of automaticity was accepted by almost all 19th Century investigators and survived the theoretical transition from magnetism to hypnosis. Even late 19th Century antagonists like Charcot and Bernheim, despite their many disagreements, took for granted that hypnotic behavior occurred automatically (Weitzenhoffer, 1978). Specific explanations for automaticity did, of course, change with the scientific Zeitgeist. Fluids, vital energies, and animal electricity that emanated from the magnetizer (e.g., Deluze, 1825/1879; Dods, 1865; Grimes, 1845) were gradually replaced with notions like dual consciousness and dissociation: forces or entities operating within the person, but more or less independently of his or her dominant will, self, or consciousness (Bramwell, 1903/1956; Janet, 1907; Prince, 1908/1957). The modern notion of dissociation propagated by Hilgard (1977, 1979) and others appears to be little more than a restatement of such 19th century ideas expressed in the modern jargon of information processing and cognitive psychology. If anything, the modern notion is somewhat less amenable to empirical test than was the 19th century idea.[5]

Investigators who make use of notions like dissociation (or trance, or hypnotic state) attempt to account for hypnotic behavior by positing a host of ill-defined mental entities (e.g., cognitive subsystems) that operate semi-independently of subjects' "normal consciousness" (e.g., their plans, intentions, stated expectancies). From this perspective, the role of contextual factors in influencing behavior is downplayed (e.g., these simply create a "readiness" for dissociation), and subjects are implicitly construed as passive responders, as individuals in whom amnesic barriers are automatically constructed, and cognitive subsystems divided (Coe, 1980; Coe & Sarbin, 1977). This perspective is misleading to the extent that hypnotic subjects can be described accurately as actively cognizing individuals who are attuned to variations in context (some quite subtle) and who modify their interpretations and enactments in terms of these variations. The evidence from our laboratory concerning the role of expectations and other cognitive factors in analgesia and amnesia, as well as related work by others (e.g., Barber, 1969; Orne, 1977; Sarbin & Coe, 1972; Sheehan, 1980) indicates that such a description of hypnotic subjects is accurate. Historically, one aspect of a good hypnotic role enactment has involved subjects coming to define their own behaviors and experiences as occurring automatically. These attributions of involuntariness do not indicate that good hypnotic subjects somehow begin functioning as automatons. On the contrary, they indicate that these individuals are attuned to the implicit communications they receive, are able and willing to deploy attention and generate imaginings that are consistent with these communications, and as a result convince both themselves and their audience (e.g., hypnotic investigators) that their responses "just seemed to happen automatically."

FOOTNOTES

[1]Hypnotic susceptibility is usually measured on one of several standardized scales that consist of a hypnotic induction procedure followed by a number of test suggestions. The suggestions vary in difficulty and call for responses such as arm levitation, limb rigidity, hallucination, and amnesia. Subjects typically obtain a single hypnotic susceptibility score that reflects the number of suggestions they responded to successfully. The psychometric properties and theoretical adequacy of these scales have been reviewed by Tellegen (1979). One of the few person variables found to correlate consistently with susceptibility is labeled "absorption" (Tellegen, 1979) and reflects the tendency of individuals to become immersed or involved in such everyday imaginative activities as daydreaming, novel reading, and so on (Davis, Dawson, & Seay, 1978; Spanos & Barber, 1974; Spanos & McPeake, 1975; Spanos, Rivers, & Gottlieb, 1978; Tellegen & Atkinson, 1974). High-susceptible subjects may be particularly adept at reducing pain with analgesia suggestions because their imaginative skills enable them to easily become absorbed in the coping imagery called for by these suggestions (Spanos et al., 1979).

[2]Kihlstrom (1978) has stated explicitly that his dissociation formulation is unable to account adequately for two of the most important aspects of suggested amnesia: why amnesia suggestions lead to forgetting and why the cancellation cue restores recall. "What is it about hypnosis, and the administration of the amnesia suggestion, that allows posthypnotic amnesia to occur? And how does the reversibility cue function to restore access to the critical memories? It is premature to offer any detailed speculations in this regard: we simply do not know enough yet about memory, amnesia and hypnosis" (Kihlstrom, 1978, P. 259). In our opinion, this dead-end in Kihlstrom's theorizing stems not from a lack of information about hypnosis or memory, but from the misleading questions he is forced to deal with when adopting a dissociation perspective. For example, how can a brief verbal instruction lead suddenly and automatically to a dissociation of target material from conscious control, and how can a cancellation signal just as suddenly reverse such an automatic process? From our perspective, questions of this type are simply irrelevant to an understanding of suggested amnesia. Both suggestion-induced forgetting and its subsequent reversibility can be accounted for parsimoniously in terms of situationally cued attention deployment. Suggested amnesia can begin and terminate as a function of verbal cues precisely because it is <u>not</u> automatic.

[3]Evans and Kihlstrom (1973) did not investigate categorical organization during amnesia. They focused instead on temporal organization in the recall of unrelated material during amnesia testing. Their findings suggested a correlation between hypnotic susceptibility level and degree of temporal disorganization during amnesia. Unfortunately, two recent studies by independent investigators have been

unsuccessful at replicating their major results (Radtke & Spanos, Note 3; St. Jean & Coe, Note 4).

[4]Elsewhere we (Spanos & Radtke-Bodorik, 1980; Spanos et al., (1980) have pointed out that our inattention hypothesis is consistent with what Tulving (1974) has labeled the principle of encoding specificity. According to this notion, recall will be successful to the extent that retrieval cues present at the time of recall match those that were associated with the target material at the time of its encoding (Tulving, 1974; Tulving & Thomson, 1973). In other words, the recall of list words is likely to be successful only to the extent that the "cognitive environment" present during recall matches the "cognitive environment" that was present during initial learning (Tulving, 1974). By shifting their attention away from the recall task following the suggestion, subjects are, in effect, altering their "cognitive environment." To the extent that they maintain their inattention, the retrieval cues that were present during encoding will not be present during recall. For this reason, recall will occur less efficiently than usual (i.e., subjects will display amnesia). Among the important cues used to initially learn a categorized list are the category labels infered from the list. However, because partial amnesics are paying relatively little attention to these or other retrieval cues, category labels are less likely than usual to provide a structure for the organization of their recall. Thus, the inefficient recall of partial amnesics will tend to be disorganized.

[5]As originally formulated, the notion of dissociation held that subjects could perform two complex tasks simultaneously: one consciously, the other unconsciously. Supposedly, the unconscious task did not interfere with performance of the conscious one. However, Hull and his students demonstrated experimentally that socalled unconscious tasks did, in fact, interfere with conscious performance (reviewed by Hull, 1933). Hilgard dealt with these findings by positing that dissociations are usually partial and, therefore, "unconscious" tasks may interfere with conscious ones. Hilgard's theoretical modification was, of course, post hoc and has served to make the concept of dissociation less amenible to direct empirical test.

REFERENCE NOTES

1. Spanos, N. P., Stam, H. J., and Brazil, K. The effects of suggestion and distraction on coping ideation and reported pain. Unpublished manuscript, Department of Psychology, Carleton University, 1980.
2. Spanos, N. P., Brown, J. M., Jones, B., and Horner, D. Cognitive mediation of suggested analgesia. Unpublished manuscript, Department of Psychology, Carleton University, 1980.
3. Radtke, H. L., and Spanos, N. P. Temporal sequencing during posthypnotic amnesia: A methodological critique and failure to

replicate. Unpublished manuscript, Department of Psychology, Carleton University, 1980.

4. St. Jean, R., and Coe, W. C. Disrupted retrieval in recognition recall. Paper presented at the 86th annual meeting of the American Psychological Association, Toronto, August, 1978.

REFERENCES

Barber, T. X. Hypnosis: A scientific approach. New York: Van Nostrand, 1969.

Barber, T. X. Suggested ("hypnotic") behavior: The trance paradigm versus an alternative paradigm. In E. Fromm and R. E. Shor (Eds.), Hypnosis: Research developments and perspectives. Chicago: Aldine-Atherton, 1972.

Barber, T. X., and Hahn, K. W. Jr. Experimental studies in "hypnotic" behavior: Physiological and subjective effects of imagined pain. Journal of Nervous and Mental Disease, 1964, 139, 416-425.

Barber, T. X., Spanos, N. P., and Chaves, J. F. Hypnosis, imagination and human potentialities. New York: Pergamon, 1974.

Bousfield, W. A. The occurrence of clustering in the recall of randomly arranged associates. Journal of General Psychology, 1953, 49, 229-240.

Bramwell, M. Hypnotism, its history, practice and theory. New York: Julian Press, 1956. (Originally published, 1903.)

Chaves, J. F., and Barber, T. X. Cognitive strategies, experimenter modelling, and expectation in the attenuation of pain. Journal of Abnormal Psychology, 1974, 83, 356-363.

Clemes, S. Repression and hypnotic amnesia. Journal of Abnormal Psychology, 1964, 69, 62-69.

Coe, W. C. On defining altered states of consciousness. The Bulletin of the British Society of Experimental and Clinical Hypnosis, 1980, 3, 8-10.

Coe, W. C., and Sarbin, T. R. Hypnosis from the standpoint of a contextualist. Annals of the New York Academy of Sciences, 1977, 296, 2-13.

Davis, S., Dawson, J. G., and Seay, B. Prediction of hypnotic susceptibility from imaginative involvement. American Journal of Clinical Hypnosis, 1978, 20, 194-198.

Deleuze, J. P. F. Animal magnetism. Translated with an appendix of notes and letters added by T. Hartshorn. New York: Wells, 1879. (Originally published, 1825.)

Dods, J. B. Philosophy of Mesmerism. New York: Fowler and Wells, 1865.

Dolby, R. M., and Sheehan, P. W. Cognitive processing and expectancy behavior in hypnosis. Journal of Abnormal Psychology, 1977, 86, 334-345.

Ellenberger, H. The discovery of the unconscious. New York: Basic Books, 1970.

Evans, F. J., and Kihlstrom, J. F. Posthypnotic amnesia as disrupted retrieval. Journal of Abnormal Psychology, 1973, 82, 317-323.

Evans, M. B., and Paul, G. L. Effects of hypnotically suggested analgesia on physiological and subjective response to cold stress. Journal of Consulting and Clinical Psychology, 1970, 35, 362-371.

Gill, M. M., and Brenman, M. Hypnosis and related states. New York: International Universities Press, 1959.

Goffman, E. Presentation of self in everyday life. New York: Doubleday, 1959.

Grimes, S. J. Etherology; or the philosophy of Mesmerism and phrenology. New York: Saxton and Miles, 1845.

Hilgard, E. R. Divided consciousness. New York: John Wiley and Sons, 1977.

Hilgard, E. R. Divided consciousness in hypnosis: The implications of the hidden observer. In E. Fromm and R. E. Shor (Eds.), Hypnosis: Developments in research and new perspectives (2nd ed.). New York: Aldine, 1979.

Hilgard, E. R., and Hilgard, J. R. Hypnosis in the relief of pain. Los Altos, CA: William Kaufman, 1975.

Hilgard, E. R., Hilgard, J. R., Macdonald, H., Morgan, A. H., and Johnson, L. S. Covert pain in hypnotic analgesia: Its reality as tested by the real-simulator design. Journal of Abnormal Psychology, 1978, 87, 655-663.

Hilgard, E. R., Morgan, A. H., and Macdonald, H. Pain and dissociation in the cold pressor test: A study of hypnotic analgesia with "hidden reports" through automatic key-pressing and automatic talking. Journal of Abnormal Psychology, 1975, 84, 280-298.

Howard, M. L., and Coe, W. C. Contextual factors in breaching posthypnotic amnesia. Journal of Personality, in press.

Hull, C. L. Hypnosis and suggestibility: an experimental approach. New York: Appleton-Century-Crofts, 1933.

Janet, P. The major symptoms of hysteria. New York: Macmillan, 1924.

Kihlstrom, J. F. The effects of organization and motivation on recall during posthypnotic amnesia (Unpublished doctoral dissertation, University of Pennsylvania, 1975). Dissertation Abstracts International, 1975, 36, 2473B-247b. (University Microfilms No. 75-24082).

Kihlstrom, J. F. Context and cognition in posthypnotic amnesia. International Journal of Clinical and Experimental Hypnosis, 1978, 26, 246-267.

Kihlstrom, J. F., and Evans, F. J. Memory retrieval processes during posthypnotic amnesia. In J. F. Kihlstrom and F. J. Evans (Eds.), Functional disorders of memory. Hillsdale, NJ: Lawrence Erlbaum Associates, 1979.

Kihlstrom, J. F., and Shor, R. E. Recall and recognition during posthypnotic amnesia. International Journal of Clinical and Experimental Hypnosis, 1978, 26, 330-349.

Knox, V. J., Morgan, A. H., and Hilgard, E. R. Pain and suffering in ischemia: The paradox of hypnotically suggested anesthesia as contradicted by reports from the "hidden observer." Archives of General Psychiatry, 1974, 30, 840-847.

Lazarus, R. S. Psychological stress and coping in adaptation and illness. International Journal of Psychiatry in Medicine, 1974, 5, 321-333.

Meichenbaum, D. Cognitive-behavior modification. New York: Plenum Press, 1977.

Murphy, M. D. Measurement of category clustering in free recall. In C. R. Puff (Ed.), Memory organization and structure. New York: Academic Press, 1979.

Nace, E. P., Orne, M. T., and Hammer, A. G. Posthypnotic amnesia as an active psychic process: The reversibility of amnesia. Archives of General Psychiatry, 1974, 31, 257-260.

Orne, M. T. The simulation of hypnosis: Why, how, and what it means. International Journal of Clinical and Experimental Hypnosis, 1971, 19, 183-210.

Orne, M. T. The construct of hypnosis: Implications of the definition for research and practice. Annals of the New York Academy of Sciences, 1977, 296, 14-33.

Prince, M. The dissociation of personality. New York: Meridian, 1957. (Originally published, 1905.)

Puff, C. R. (Ed.) Memory organization and structure. New York: Academic Press, 1979.

Radtke-Bodorik, H. L., Planas, M., and Spanos, N. P. Suggested amnesia, verbal inhibition, and disorganized recall for a long word list. Canadian Journal of Behavioral Science, 1980, 12, 87-97.

Radtke-Bodorik, H. L., Spanos, N. P., and Haddad, M. G. The effects of spoken versus written recall on suggested amnesia in hypnotic and task-motivated subjects. American Journal of Clinical Hypnosis, 1979, 22, 8-16.

Shuell, T. J. Clustering and organization in free recall. Psychological Bulletin, 1969, 72, 353-374.

Sarbin, T. R. Contributions to role theory: Hypnotic behavior. Psychological Review, 1950, 57, 255-270.

Sarbin, T. R., and Coe, W. C. Hypnosis: A social psychological analysis of influence communication. New York: Holt, Rinehart and Winston, 1977.

Sheehan, P. W. Factors influencing rapport in hypnosis. Journal of Abnormal Psychology, 1980, 89, 263-281.

Slamecka, N. J. The question of associative growth in the learning of categorized material. Journal of Verbal Learning and Verbal Behavior, 1972, 11, 324-332.

Spanos, N. P. Goal-directed fantasy and the performance of hypnotic test suggestions. Psychiatry, 1971, 34, 86-96.

Spanos, N. P., and Barber, T. X. Cognitive activity during "hypnotic" suggestibility: Goal-directed fantasy and the experience of non-volition. Journal of Personality, 1972, 40, 510-524.

Spanos, N. P., and Barber, T. X. Toward a convergence in hypnosis research. American Psychologist, 1974, 29, 500-510.

Spanos, N. P., Barber, T. X., and Lang, G. Cognition and self-control: Cognitive control of painful sensory input. In H. London and R. E. Nisbett (Eds.), Thought and Feeling: Cognitive alteration of feeling states. Chicago: Aldine, 1974.

Spanos, N. P., and Bodorik, H. L. Suggested amnesia and disorganized recall in hypnotic and task-motivated subjects. Journal of Abnormal Psychology, 1977, 86, 295-305.

Spanos, N. P., and D'Eon, J. L. Hypnotic amnesia, disorganized recall and inattention. Journal of Abnormal Psychology, in press.

Spanos, N. P., and Gottlieb, J. Demonic possession, mesmerism and hypnosis: A social-psychological perspective on their historical interrelations. Journal of Abnormal Psychology, 1979, 88, 527-546.

Spanos, N. P., and Hewitt, E. C. The hidden observer in hypnotic analgesia: Discovery or experimental creation? Journal of Personality and Social Psychology, in press.

Spanos, N. P., and McPeake, J. D. Involvement in suggestion-related imaginings, experienced involuntariness, and credibility assigned to imagining. Journal of Abnormal Psychology, 1974, 83, 687-690.

Spanos, N. P., and McPeake, J. D. Involvement in everyday imaginative activities, attitudes toward hypnosis, and hypnotic suggestibility, Journal of Personality and Social Psychology, 1975, 31, 594-598.

Spanos, N. P., and McPeake, J. D. Cognitive strategies, reported goal-directed fantasy, and response to suggestion in hypnotic subjects. American Journal of Clinical Hypnosis, 1977, 20, 114-123.

Spanos, N. P., McPeake, J. D., and Carter, W. The effects of pretesting on response to a visual hallucination suggestion in hypnotic subjects. Journal of Personality and Social Psychology, 1973, 28, 293-297.

Spanos, N. P., and Radtke-Bodorik, H. L. Integrating hypnotic phenomena with cognitive psychology: An illustration using suggested amnesia. Bulletin of the British Society of Experimental and Clinical Hypnosis, 1980, 3, 4-7.

Spanos, N. P., Radtke-Bodorik, H. L., Ferguson, J. D., and Jones, B. The effects of hypnotic susceptibility, suggestions for analgesia and the utilization of cognitive strategies on the reduction of pain. Journal of Abnormal Psychology, 1979, 88, 282-292.

Spanos, N. P., Radtke-Bodorik, H. L., and Shabinsky, M. A. Amnesia, subjective organization, and learning of a list of unrelated words in hypnotic and task-motivated subjects. International Journal of Clinical and Experimental Hypnosis, 1980, 28, 126-139.

Spanos, N. P., Radtke-Bodorik, H. L., and Stam, H. J. Disorganized recall during suggested amnesia: Fact not artifact. Journal of Abnormal Psychology, 1980, 89, 1-19.

Spanos, N. P., Rivers, S. M., and Gottlieb, J. Hypnotic responsivity, meditation and laterality of eye movements. Journal of Abnormal Psychology, 1978, 87, 566-569.

Spanos, N. P., Rivers, S. M., and Ross, S. Experimental involuntariness and response to hypnotic suggestions. Annals of the New York Academy of Sciences, 1977, 296, 208-221.

Spanos, N. P., Spillane, J., and McPeake, J. D. Cognitive strategies and response to suggestion in hypnotic and task-motivated subjects. American Journal of Clinical Hypnosis, 1976, 18, 252-262.

Spanos, N. P., Stam, H. J., D'Eon, J. L., Pawlak, A. E., and Radtke-Bodorik, H. L. The effects of social psychological variables on hypnotic amnesia. Journal of Personality and Social Psychology, in press.

Stacher, G., Schuster, P., Bauer, P., Lahoda, R., and Schulze, D. Effects of relaxation or analgesia on pain threshold and pain tolerance in the waking and in the hypnotic state. Journal of Psychosomatic Research, 1975, 19, 259-265.

Stam, H. J., and Spanos, N. P. Experimental designs, expectancy effects are hypnotic analgesia. Journal of Abnormal Psychology, in press.

Sternberg, R. J., and Tulving, E. The measurement of subjective organization in free recall. Psychological Bulletin, 1977, 84, 539-556.

Tellegen, A. On measures and conceptions of hypnosis. American Journal of Clinical Hypnosis, 1979, 21, 247-236.

Tellegen, A., and Atkinson, G. Openness to absorbing and self-altering experiences ("absorption"), a trait related to hypnotic susceptibility. Journal of Abnormal Psychology, 1974, 83, 268-277.

Tulving, E. Cue-dependent forgetting. American Scientist, 1974, 62, 74-82.

Tulving, E., and Thomson, D. M. Encoding specificity and retrieval processes in episodic memory. Psychological Review, 1973, 80, 352-375.

Weitzenhoffer, A. M. What did he (Bernheim) say? In F. H. Frankel and H. S. Zamansky (Eds.), Hypnosis at its bicentennial. New York: Plenum, 1978.

Zamansky, H. S., Scharf, B., and Brightbill, R. The effect of expectancy for hypnosis on prehypnotic performance. Journal of Personality, 1964, 32, 236-248.

VIVID FANTASY AND HALLUCINATORY ABILITIES IN THE LIFE HISTORIES OF EXCELLENT HYPNOTIC SUBJECTS ("SOMNAMBULES"): PRELIMINARY REPORT WITH FEMALE SUBJECTS

Sheryl C. Wilson and Theodore X. Barber

Cushing Hospital

Framingham, MA

Throughout the history of hypnosis, excellent hypnotic subjects (sometimes referred to as somnambules or somnambulists) have been studied in terms of how they respond and what they experience when given suggestions to hallucinate, to age regress, to experience anesthesia, to go into a trance, etc. Although their behavior in a hypnotic or suggestive setting has been looked at extensively, there has been very little research in which they were intensively interviewed to discover how their extremely high responsiveness to suggestions is related to their life histories.

One of the few relevant studies in this area is the important investigation carried out by Josephine Hilgard (1970, 1979). In this project, she conducted individual two-hour interviews with 187 college students to delineate events in their lives that might be related to their hypnotic responsiveness. Each student was also assessed on the Stanford Hypnotic Susceptibility Scale, Form C. Hypnotic susceptibility was found to be related to ability to become involved in an imaginative way in one or more of the following seven areas: reading, dramatic arts, religion, sensory experiences, imagery, imaginary companions (during childhood), and physical and mental adventures. These results were congruent with other lines of investigation that suggested that there is something about the imaginative-fantasy abilities of individuals that is related to their responsiveness to suggestions in hypnotic and non-hypnotic situations (Andersen, 1963; As, 1962; As, O'Hara, & Munger, 1962; Atkinson, 1971; Barber & Glass, 1962;

This research was supported in part by a grant from Proseminar Institute.

Coe, 1964; Coe & Sarbin, 1966; Davis, Dawson & Seay, 1978; Diamond & Taft, 1975; Lee-Teng, 1965; Sarbin & Lim, 1963; Sheehan, 1972; Shor, Orne & O'Connell, 1962; Spanos & McPeake, 1975; Sutcliffe, Perry & Sheehan, 1970; Tellegen & Atkinson, 1974).

In this paper, we present a preliminary report of a long-term research project in which we are conducting extensive in-depth interviews with excellent hypnotic subjects. During the past two and a half years we have been able to find 19 "somnambulistic" hypnotic subjects who respond quickly and profoundly, with or without a hypnotic induction, to the kinds of suggestions that have been traditionally associated with hypnosis--e.g., anesthesia, age regression, visual and auditory hallucinations, blindness, deafness, and other negative hallucinations, amnesia, post-hypnotic behaviors, etc.

The preliminary results of our project confirm Josephine Hilgard's findings. Our superb hypnotic subjects do become involved imaginatively in the seven areas Hilgard delineated and, with some exceptions, they have strong imaginative involvements not just in one or two of the areas but in six or all seven.

However, our most significant and surprising findings are as follows. Not only do our excellent hypnotic subjects become involved imaginatively in reading, drama, etc., but they also have an overriding extreme involvement in <u>fantasizing per se</u>. In fact, they are so involved in fantasy that they could be labeled without exaggeration as "fantasy addicts". Related to their addiction to fantasy is the surprising finding that they are able to "hallucinate" at will. Their fantasy is "hallucinatory" in all sensory modalities; they "see," "hear," "smell," "touch," and fully experience what they fantasize. Their fantasy appears to be as vivid as reality; and they appear to experience what they fantasize in the same way that they experience reality. Their ability to "hallucinate" seems to be related to their extensive practice in fantasizing and also to their surprisingly thorough memory of almost everything they have experienced in their lives.

METHOD

<u>Subjects</u>

As of now, we have completed interviews with 19 excellent hypnotic subjects, all females who have attended or are attending college. One has an M.D. (psychiatrist), one a Ph.D. (psychologist), 11 have B.A.'s or M.A.'s in psychology or counseling, 3 have B.A.'s in other areas, and 3 are college students. Their age range is 21 to 47 with a mean of 33. With one exception, they are either married or have a close relationship with a boyfriend.

As a comparison group, we have also interviewed in the same way 25 unselected female college students and graduates among whom are poor, fair, and good hypnotic subjects but no excellent (somnambulistic) hypnotic subjects. The nonexcellent hypnotic subjects manifested a pattern in their answers to our interview questions different from that of our excellent subjects. Data from the interviews with the 25 "nonsomnambulistic" subjects will be presented in future publications. In this preliminary report, the nonexcellent subjects will serve as background while we focus on our most surprising and significant findings with our "somnambulistic" hypnotic subjects.

Procedure

We tested the subjects for hypnotic responsiveness by administering in varying order the Creative Imagination Scale (Wilson and Barber, 1978), traditional and nontraditional hypnotic induction procedures (Barber, 1978b, 1979a, 1979b; Barber & Wilson, 1978), the Barber Suggestibility Scale (Barber and Wilson, 1978/79), representative suggestions from the Stanford Hypnotic Susceptibility Scales (Weitzenhoffer & Hilgard, 1959, 1962), plus suggestions that are not included on any of the above scales (such as past life regression, suggestions to experience a super-conscious or mystical state, suggestions to experience extreme happiness, etc.).

Our criterion for designating a subject as excellent was simply that she convincingly experienced the classical hypnotic phenomena. For instance, the 19 subjects easily and quickly responded to suggestions for negative hallucinations, amnesia, and posthypnotic behavior and to suggestions to go into a deep trance (which were usually given towards the middle of the session); and they also reported unambiguously experiencing (a) a hand as cold, then hot, then immovable, then numb, (b) themselves in elementary school, in the future, and in a past lifetime, and (c) the sights, sounds, smells, and other sensory qualities of whatever had been suggested.

About one third of our excellent subjects were tested as described above in individual sessions, one third in group sessions (in workshops given by the second author), and one third in both group and in individual sessions. These 19 subjects were selected as the best female hypnotic subjects from an original population that we tested of approximately 900 male and female subjects.[1]

Interview

After being tested for hypnotic responsiveness, each subject was interviewed individually on the Memory, Imagining, and Creativity Interview Schedule. This interview schedule, which we constructed for this study, was derived in the following way.

First, we became very well acquainted with two women who were excellent hypnotic subjects and who were in psychotherapy with us for overweight and phobias, respectively. During the course of the therapy sessions, we obtained in-depth data pertaining to their early memories, their past and present fantasies, and many other aspects of their lives. As we became well acquainted with both individuals, we realized that although they differed markedly in many respects, they had some highly unusual characteristics in common and that these characteristics were related to their hypnotic susceptibility.

Next, we conjectured that perhaps other excellent female hypnotic subjects also have the same characteristics that are shared by the two whom we were seeing in therapy. To test this conjecture, we first constructed an interview schedule with 88 questions, of which 73 pertained to those characteristics shared by our two therapy clients who were "somnambulistic" subjects. These 73 questions covered areas such as the following: early memories, childhood and adult beliefs and fantasies, empathy and role playing as a child and as an adult, feelings about self, sleep behaviors, hypnagogic hallucinations, psychosomatice and hysterical illnesses, extrasensory experiences, out-of-the-body experiences, and eidetic imagery. In addition, we included 15 items derived from Josephine Hilgard's (1970) interview schedule. These questions, which came from those she had found to be correlated with hypnotic susceptibility, pertained to imaginative involvements in seven areas and to identification with parents of the opposite sex, severity of punishments experienced as a child, and positive motivation for hypnosis. As we continued interviewing additional subjects, we occasionally added new questions and, as a result, the Memory, Imagining, and Creativity Interview Schedule now contains 100 items.

The length of time required to interview the subjects varied drastically, depending upon the extensiveness of their memories and their fantasy life. Interviews of excellent hypnotic subjects required a minimum of four hours and, with the two most verbal, as much as 32 hours. The not-so-good-hypnotic subjects could be interviewed in much less time, about two hours, since they answered simply "No" to many of the questions and thus their responses could not be probed for details.

RESULTS

The findings supported our conjecture that other excellent female hypnotic subjects might also share the characteristics we found in the two female "somnambules" we were seeing in therapy. Although our 19 excellent subjects differed markedly on various personality characteristics--e.g., some were extroverted whereas others were extremely introverted--all had certain unusual characteristics in common. These shared characteristics fall together into a syndrome which we have labeled as "addiction to fantasy."

Shared Characteristics During Childhood

As children, they all lived in a make-believe world much or most of the time. Sixteen of the 19 believed that their dolls and stuffed animals were alive, and that they had their own feelings and personalities. Consequently, they would take turns sleeping next to each doll and stuffed animal so that none would have hurt feelings. Also, they felt sorry for their dolls and stuffed animals when they left them home alone because they believed they would feel lonely.

When they were children, 17 of the 19 believed in fairies, leprechauns, elves, and other such "magical" beings. The strength of these beliefs is illustrated by one subject's statement that, when she was finally convinced that Santa Claus was a fabrication, she could not understand why adults had tried to "make up" one when there were so many real magical beings around such as tree spirits, etc. Their beliefs in elves, leprechauns, fairies, tree spirits, and other magical beings did not terminate during childhood; as adults they either still believe in them or they are not absolutely convinced that they really do not exist.

Eleven of our 19 "somnambulists" spent a large part of their time during childhood playing and interacting with imaginary companions (fantasized people or animals), which they report they clearly saw, heard, and felt in the same way they perceived living people and animals. Those who as children were most isolated from other children and most lonely tended to have not just one, but rather a whole world of imaginary companions. For instance, one subject had a score of imaginary animals and another had two dozen imaginary children whom they played with continuously.

As children, they became so absorbed in their pretending and their fantasies that what they were fantasizing became reality for them and the real world faded. Eighteen of the 19 would pretend they were someone else such as an orphan, a princess, an animal or bird, a fairy tale character such as Cinderella or Snow White, etc. They became so absorbed in these roles that they would feel as if they were the character they were pretending to be. One of our subjects believed not that she was pretending to be a princess but that she was a princess pretending to be an ordinary child doing things ordinary children do, such as going to school, etc. In the same way, another subject believed not that she was pretending to be a bird but rather that she was a bird pretending to be a child.

Their extremely realistic childhood pretending and fantasizing caused problems for our excellent hypnotic subjects. For instance, the "princess" was accused of lying by her school friends when she brought them to see her fantasized castle (actually her middle-class home). She was shocked that they could not see it; it was absolutely real to her.

The potential dangers involved in the fading of external reality are illustrated in the following example. One of our subjects described for us a time when she was 11 years old and was "lost" in a fantasy in which she was walking with her imaginary pet lamb through an imaginary meadow. As she was concentrating on stepping with deliberately high steps through the tall grass, she was startled out of her fantasy by the sounds of horns honking. She was startled to find herself standing surrounded by traffic in the middle of a busy city street. She decided at that moment to always maintain some awareness of the actual world whenever she was in a potentially dangerous situation.

Shared Characteristics as Adults

Now that they are adults, the extensiveness of their fantasizing has not clearly decreased. From very early in life and continuing into the present, they spend a large part of their time fantasizing. In fact, they say they practically live their lives in fantasy. Seventeen subjects were asked to estimate what percent of their waking day they spent in fantasizing. Eleven said they fantasize at least 90% of the time, two estimated at least 75% of the time, three estimated more than half the time, and only one estimated less than half the time. They typically found it easier to estimate the amount of time they do not fantasize. For instance, one subject said she does not allow herself to fantasize while driving but otherwise she fantasizes all the time. She is able to work and to interact with others while her fantasies continue without interruption; for instance, while interacting with a male co-worker whom she likes very much, she has a continuously ongoing fantasy of love-making and sexual intercourse with him.

These subjects view imagining-fantasizing as a necessary and integral part of their lives. It is as necessary for them as sleeping and eating. We asked what it would be like for them if they were never able to imagine and fantasize again (even though they still would be able to think and to plan for the future). All 19 found this question very distressing; they just could not imagine life without fantasizing. All indicated that without imagining-fantasizing, they would not be the same person; they would be basically different. A typical reply was: "Forget it! Take away my food or my clothes. Fantasizing is more important to me than any of these. Without fantasy, I'd be someone I don't like." Many added that either they would rather be dead or it would be like being dead.

Fantasy is immensely important to them and they see it as the most wonderful thing in life. When asked during the interview what fantasy means to them, our most verbal subject spontaneously blurted out the following: "Fantasy is being anything you can be, could be, or are. It's possibilities made possible. It's soaring, thrilling, living. Who's to say what's happening right now is reality? Fantasy is your own private reality, your own private world. You set the stage. You make it. It's being God-like. Anything you believe, if you believe it, it's true."

The contents of their fantasies as adults are varied and creative. The following are examples of some of the kinds of fantasies they experience:

1. During a conversation, while they are speaking or while they listen to the other person speak, they "see," "hear," "smell," and "feel" what is being described.
2. When they are taking a shower, the shower might become a waterfall in the Caribbean.
3. When they hear the word Egypt, they might imagine in detail their life as the wife of a Pharaoh.
4. When they are bored at a social gathering, they might escape from the boring situation by imagining that the people are clowns or by fantasizing themselves alone with a lover on an exotic tropical island.
5. When they have free time, they may sit down or lie down and fantasize for fifteen minutes, or half an hour, or one or two hours. Even though they fantasize throughout the day, they may also set aside a special time and place solely for fantasizing.
6. When they are alone for a weekend, they might spend the entire weekend in fantasy.
7. When they are watching a bird or looking at a tree, they may suddenly lose the sense of their body and feel they are the bird or tree.

An impressive characteristic shared by all 19 of our subjects is that they have very vivid sexual fantasies. They experience these fantasies so realistically that they usually obtain greater satisfaction and enjoyment from these fantasied sexual relations than from actual sexual relations. Of the 17 subjects asked, 14 reported that they have orgasms produced <u>solely</u> by sexual fantasies.

A characteristic shared by at least 12 of our subjects (two were not asked) is that as adults they still occasionally pretend to be someone else. While they are pretending, they lose their own identity and feel they really are the character just as they did when they were children. Six of our subjects enjoy telling strangers about their (pretend) selves. For instance, while riding on a bus just the day before the interview, one of our subjects from New York introduced herself as an Eskimo to the person sitting next to her and then proceeded to tell the intrigued stranger all about her (imagined) life in Alaska.

Another impressive shared characteristic is that their fantasies have an automatic, involuntary quality. It is almost as though they have imagined and fantasized so much in their lives that their imagination has become like a well-developed muscle. Their ability to fantasize easily and automatically is analogous to the apparent effortlessness in lifting a very heavy weight shown by a highly trained weight lifter. Their fantasies seem to be produced automatically in response to their conscious and unconscious thoughts and feelings. As they describe it, they "set the stage", that is, they begin with certain characters, settings, or themes, and then they sit back and watch the drama unfold. The automatic quality of their fantasies has its drawbacks, however. Twelve of our subjects report having difficulty driving since anything they think or feel, consciously or unconsciously, might be "seen" in front of them on the road as if it is actually there. For example, if any one of these 12 subjects happens to think to herself while driving, "I better be careful because a child or animal might dart into the street", then she is very apt to "see" an imaginary child or animal "run" into the street.

An additional shared characteristic is the life-like quality of their fantasies; they feel the fantasy is reality and what they are fantasizing is actually there. In fact, their fantasies are so realistic that, with the exception of only two subjects, they tend to confuse their memories of their fantasies with their memories of actual events. For instance, when one of our subjects fantasizes interactions with her boyfriend while he is away, her fantasized interactions are so realistic that later she will have difficulty determining which of her remembered interactions with him actually occurred and which were fantasy.

A striking characteristic shared by 16 of our subjects is that their fantasies are associated with physical effects. Eleven spontaneously reported that they become ill whenever they see violence on TV or in the movies. They cannot let themselves fantasize anything with violence because they are certain they will become sick. Although we did not directly ask this in the interview, fourteen told us that imagined heat and cold affect them in the same way as actual heat and cold. For instance, one subject described how she was freezing as she sat bundled up in a blanket in a warm living room while she was watching Dr. Zhivago in Siberia on TV.

Our subjects also seem to be "naturals" at biofeedback. Biofeedback involves transmitting continuous information ("feedback") to individuals pertaining to changes in their heart rate, blood pressure, skin temperature, and other bodily processes of which they are normally unaware and not able to control voluntarily (Barber, 1976). When individuals are exposed to biofeedback in a series of practice and training sessions, they commonly learn to voluntarily control (to increase and to decrease at will) their heart rate, blood pressure, skin temperature, etc. However, some of our subjects are able to exert voluntary control over these physiological processes without biofeedback training. Four of our excellent hypnotic subjects, independently of our study, were involved in clinical or experimental biofeedback. Those who were to administer the biofeedback were all impressed by their abilities, manifested prior to the biofeedback training, to either speed up and slow down their heart rate, raise and lower their blood pressure, or increase and decrease their skin temperature.

A surprising number--11 of the 14 who were asked--have had pseudocyesis (false pregnancy) at least once. They believed they were pregnant and they had many of the symptoms. In addition to amenorrhea (stoppage of menstruation), they also typically experienced at least four of the following: breast changes, abdominal enlargement, morning sickness, cravings, and fetal movements. With two exceptions, the false pregnancies terminated quickly when negative results were received from pregnancy tests. The remaining two went for abortions following which they were told no fetus had been found.

Fifteen of the 19 have had illnesses that seem to be directly related to their thoughts, feelings, and fantasies. For example, most of them had become physically ill when they thought (incorrectly) that they had eaten spoiled food, and several developed an uncomfortable and continuous itch when they (incorrectly) believed they had been contaminated with lice.

A characteristic shared by all of our excellent hypnotic subjects is their unusually vivid memory extending back to a very early age. Their memories appear to be reinstatements of original experiences so that when they are asked to recall some past event they do not just remember it, they seem to relive it. Their memory appears to be "hallucinatory" in all senses; they seem to "see," "hear," "tastes," "smell," and "feel" the events they are recalling.

A surprising aspect of their extrememly vivid memories is that they seem to have little childhood amnesia. They all report vivid early memories dating back to age two or earlier. Seven of our subjects report clear memories of some (and possibly many) events that occurred when they were one-year-olds, and an additional seven subjects report clear memories of some events that occurred when they were less than one year of age.

When they try to remember their very early life, they appear to re-experience the sensations and feelings, including the feeling of being in their baby body. For example, as one of our subjects was describing her memory of her first birthday, she vividly re-experienced her father singing "Happy Birthday," her mother standing behind her encouraging her to try to blow out the candle, and her sister sitting next to her. She could feel herself sitting in her highchair and could feel herself in her body as it was at that time ("with my big, fat tummy"). Immediately following this experience, she cried out to us, "Life was wonderful back then!"[2]

As far back as they can remember, our 19 excellent subjects were "into" fantasy. This raises the question: How did they become so involved in fantasy at an apparently very early age? Looking carefully at their early lives, three patterns seemed to emerge: 1) most were encouraged to fantasize by significant adults; 2) some fantasized because they were isolated and lonely; and 3) some fantasized in order to escape from a bad environment. Most of our subjects had two of these three patterns in their lives. Let us look a little more closely at each pattern in turn.

1. Sixteen of our 19 subjects were encouraged to fantasize by a significant adult. This adult was either a parent, an aunt, an uncle, a grandmother, a grandfather, a friend's mother, or a neighbor. The adult directly encouraged the child to fantasize by means of one or both of the following: (a) The adult read to the child or told the child fairy tales and fantasy stories. (b) The adult treated the child's dolls and stuffed animals as if they were alive, thus encouraging the child to believe they were alive; for example, the adult might pick up the child's doll Mary and begin conversing with the doll in the following manner, "How are you feeling today Mary? [Pause] That's too bad. Maybe Janie [the child] can help you feel happier."

2. Nine had been very lonely and isolated as children and they became involved in fantasy for both companionship and entertainment. Three of these "overcame" their isolation by having many imaginary companions.

3. Seven had a hard early life (e.g., some were physically abused) and they used fantasy to escape from their environment. We were surprised to learn that four of these seven had a secret hiding place (e.g., in a nearby meadow or behind the sofa) where they would habitually "hide" in order to be undisturbed while they lived an entirely different life in fantasy.

All 19 of our excellent hypnotic subjects report numerous psychic experiences. All report what they firmly believe are precognitive experiences and telepathic experiences and, with one exception, they all see themselves as "psychic". In addition, 12 report impressive experiences of encountering apparitions. In general, these subjects have seen only one, two, or a few ghosts, but one subject saw the same apparition ("an elderly white-haired man with sad blue eyes") often during her childhood. Of the 19 subjects, 15 have had vivid out-of-the-body experiences. (One subject has realistic out-of-the-body experiences every day--usually during the time she sets aside for "meditation" or fantasy--and she has had such experiences almost daily as far back as she can remember.) Finally, eight of the subjects have experienced automatic writing or "spirit" writing. All eight have written poems, and 5 of the 8 have also written songs or philosophical material, which they felt at the time were being written not by them but by someone else writing through them.

These people all state that they are eager for new experiences. They have all tried to experience the world in new ways via altered states of consciousness. Seventeen had thought of hypnosis as one means for attaining an altered state and, thus, hypnosis was appealing to them. In order to achieve a new state of consciousness, 15 of the 19 have at some time in their life experimented with drugs, and 16 (of the 17 asked) have tried some form of meditation.

DISCUSSION

As we accumulated our data, we realized that the reason some individuals are excellent hypnotic subjects is that their addiction to fantasy leads them naturally to experience hypnotic phenomena in their own lives. Perhaps this is the "secret" of hypnosis. The experiences and behaviors traditionally categorized as "hypnotic phenomena" are in the behavioral repertoire of "somnambules" prior to their having any formal experience with hypnosis. Hence, when we give them "hypnotic suggestions", e.g., suggestions for age regression, anesthesia, hallucinations, and amnesia, we are asking them to do for us what they can do independently of us in their daily lives. "Hypnosis" provides them with a social situation in which they are encouraged to do what they usually do only privately. For instance, when we suggest age regression during hypnosis, how difficult is this suggestion for someone like our subject who vividly reexperienced her first birthday when recalling it during our interview session? In fact, age regression (reliving previous experiences) is something our 19 excellent subjects do naturally in their daily lives since (a) they relive the past, to a surprisingly vivid extent, when they recall it, and (b) they have vivid memories of their experiences extending back to their very early life.

Another "classical hypnotic suggestion" is the suggestion to hallucinate visually, acoustically, or in all sensory modalities. This is not difficult for our subjects. These individuals experience "hallucinations" numerous times each day since their fantasies are "hallucinatory" in all sensory modalities and they fantasize at least half their waking day.

The hypnotist also commonly suggests various sensory phenomena, for instance, that a limb feels either heavy, light, cold, or numb and that the subject is lying on a beach and feels the warm sand. Once again, these suggestions are not difficult for our subjects who have very vivid ("hallucinatory") memories in all sensory modalities and are able, whenever they wish, to remember vividly and reexperience a time when they were lying on a beach or when they felt their hand either heavy, light, cold, or numb.

Other kinds of suggestions that involve bodily changes, e.g., increasing the blood flow and thus increasing the temperature of a limb, raising or lowering the heart rate, removing warts or producing blisters (Barber, 1970; Barber, 1978a) are not especially difficult for individuals whose everyday sexual fantasies can produce orgasms, whose fantasies of pregnancy can produce pseudocyesis, or whose fantasies of eating spoiled food can produce illness. When people's daily fantasies are capable of producing orgasms, temperature changes, heart rate changes, nausea, vomiting, etc., it is not too difficult to conclude that what they are asked to fantasize during hypnosis might also result in bodily changes.

Similarly, if we suggest automatic writing during hypnosis, we might expect that they might comply since about half of them have naturally experienced automatic writing or "spirit" writing in the course of their lives.

In brief, individuals who can be labeled as "fantasy addicts" have many experiences, as part of their ongoing lives, that are very similar to those that have been associated with "hypnosis". We would conjecture that these are the people who are the subjects when we hear dramatic accounts of hypnotic phenomena. We would also conjecture that throughout the history of hypnotism, when these individuals were the subjects, most hypnotists and observers believed (incorrectly) that they hallucinated, age regressed, experienced past lives, performed automatic writing, etc., because they were in "hypnosis". Apparently most hypnotists did not realize that these "somnambules" were able to have vivid hypnotic experiences primarily because they had had extensive practice in having such experiences during their daily lives. Our data indicate that the hypnosis setting provides a situation in which those with a secret "fantasy addiction" can publicly demonstrate their special abilities or talents. In the hypnosis situation, their ability to fantasize with hallucinatory intensity is not only socially permissible, it is also rewarded.

We cannot overemphasize that our 19 excellent hypnotic subjects are socially aware and they work, love, and function much like other highly educated American women. They range in "emotional stability" or in "mental health" all over the normal curve; three are very well functioning, "self-actualized" individuals, and two have "emotional problems," but the great majority appear to others to be more-or-less typical college-educated American women.

Because they are socially aware, our excellent subjects have told no one about the extent to which they fantasize or the hallucinatory quality of their fantasies. Their fantasy life has been their well-guarded secret. Nevertheless, during the course of our interviews with them, they told us secrets that they had never told anyone. They revealed their secrets to us because (a) we clearly communicated to them our belief that fantasy is creative and valuable and (b) they all felt fantasy is extremely important, useful and "wonderful" in their own lives.

LIMITATIONS OF THE DATA

Since the conclusions presented in this paper are based on only 19 "somnambules" (and a comparison group of 25 "nonsomnambules"), they may need to be revised as we expand the research with larger groups of subjects. We may find excellent hypnotic subjects who do not possess the characteristics shared by our first 19 "somnambules." We may also find "nonsomnambules" who have the "fantasy addiction" and "hallucinatory abilities" that we now believe are unique to "somnambules." Also, since the subjects we have interviewed up to now are all females, our preliminary findings may not be applicable to male "somnambules." In brief, we have just begun to probe into how the life of "somnambules" is related to their dramatic hypnotic performance, our early findings with a small sample must be considered as tentative, and much more work needs to be done.

SUMMARY

We are conducting intensive, in-depth interviews with excellent hypnotic subjects ("somnambules") to discover how their extremely high level of responsiveness to suggestions is related to their life histories. At this time, we have completed interviews with 19 female "somnambules" (and 25 female "nonsomnambule" controls).

Our preliminary results are consistent with earlier findings by Josephine Hilgard; our excellent hypnotic subjects become involved imaginatively in most of the following: reading, dramatic arts, religion, sensory experiences, imagery, imaginary companions, and physical and mental adventures.

Our most important finding is that our 19 superb hypnotic subjects have a series of characteristics in common that go far in explaining their very high hypnotic responsiveness. In general, all or nearly all of these 19 subjects share the following characteristics that are not shared by our control subjects: their involvement in fantasy is so extreme that they can be labeled as "fantasy addicts". During childhood, they lived in a make-believe world most of the time; and, at present, they typically spend 50% or more of their time fantasizing.

They experience their fantasies in the same way that they experience reality. From very early life, and continuing into the present, their fantasies are so vivid in all senses that they can be labeled as "hallucinatory". Their fantasies, which tend to have an automatic, involuntary quality, can give rise to physical effects, e.g., a sexual fantasy can give rise to an orgasm.

As children, they believed their stuffed animals and dolls were alive and had feelings. Also, as children, they believed in elves, fairies, leprechauns, tree spirits, and other "magical" beings and as adults, they are not certain that these beings do not exist. During childhood, they typically had imaginary companions whom they "saw", "heard", and "felt" in the same way they perceived real people. Both as children and now as adults, they feel they "become" the characters they are pretending to be, and at times they have difficulty differentiating fantasied from nonfantasied events and persons.

When they remember past events, they relive them with all the sights, sounds, smells, feelings, etc. Their vivid ("hallucinatory") memory extends back to a surprisingly early age.

They have had many psychic experiences and they see themselves as psychic. They also seek new experiences and they wish to experience altered states of consciousness. They see hypnosis, and also drugs and meditation, as means for experiencing new states of consciousness.

Their life-long involvement in "make-believe" and fantasy, their ability to "hallucinate at will," their ability to recall past experiences vividly, and their other special talents go far in explaining why they are able so easily to experience the classical hypnotic phenomena.

FOOTNOTES

1. We limited this preliminary study to females because (as will be described below) the first two "somnambules" whom we interviewed thoroughly were women, and we decided first to determine if other female excellent hypnotic subjects had the same characteristics that were shared by the first two. For the same reason, in this preliminary study, we included only female subjects in our control group of "nonsomnambules". Now that we have ascertained that at least 19 female "somnambules" have a set of characteristics in common, such as "addiction to fantasy," we are now proceeding to test the conjecture that male "somnambules" also have the same characteristics.

2. We are aware that these early memories may be fantasies instead of realities. We will keep this question open as we continue the research.

REFERENCES

Andersen, M. L. Correlates of hypnotic performance: An historical and role-theoretical analysis. Unpublished doctoral dissertation, University of California, Berkeley, 1963.

As, A. Nonhypnotic experiences related to hypnotizability in male and female college students. Scandinavian Journal of Psychology, 1962, 3, 112-121.

As, A., O'Hara, J. W., and Munger, M. P. The measurement of subjective experiences presumably related to hypnotic susceptibility. Scandinavian Journal of Psychology, 1962, 3, 47-64.

Atkinson, G. A. Personality and hypnotic cognition. Unpublished doctoral dissertation, University of Minnesota, 1971.

Barber, T. X. LSD, Marijuana, Yoga, and Hypnosis. Hawthorne, NY: Aldine, 1970.

Barber, T. X. Introduction. Self-control: Temperature biofeedback, hypnosis, yoga, and relaxation. In T. X. Barber, L. V. DiCara, J. Kamiya, N. E. Miller, D. Shapiro, and J. Stoyva (Eds.), Biofeedback and Self-Control 1975/76. Hawthorne, NY: Aldine, 1976.

Barber, T. X. Hypnosis, suggestions, and psychosomatic phenomena: A new look from the standpoint of recent experimental studies. American Journal of Clinical Hypnosis, 1978, 21, 13-27. (a)

Barber, T. X. Positive suggestions for effective living and philosophical hypnosis (Cassette tape). Medfield, MA: Medfield Foundation, 1979. (b)

Barber, T. X. Hypnotic suggestions for weight control and smoking cessation (Cassette tape). Medfield, MA: Medfield Foundation, 1979. (a)

Barber, T. X. Hypnotic and self-hypnotic suggestions for study-concentration, relaxation, pain control, and mystical experiences (Cassette tape). Medfield, MA: Medfield Foundation, 1979. (b)

Barber, T. X., and Glass, L. B. Significant factors in hypnotic behavior. Journal of Abnormal and Social Psychology, 1962, 64, 222-228.

Barber, T. X., and Wilson, S. C. Hypnotic inductions, mental relaxation, and permissive suggestion (Cassette tape). Medfield, MA: Medfield Foundation, 1978.

Barber, T. X., and Wilson, S. C. The Barber Suggestibility Scale and the Creative Imagination Scale: Experimental and clinical applications. American Journal of Clinical Hypnosis, 1978/1979, 21, 84-108.

Coe, W. C. The heuristic value of role theory and hypnosis. Unpublished doctoral dissertation, University of California, Berkeley, 1964.

Coe, W. C., and Sarbin, T. R. An experimental demonstration of hypnosis as role enactment. Journal of Abnormal Psychology, 1966, 71, 400-405.

Davis, S., Dawson, J. G., and Seay, B. Prediction of hypnotic susceptibility from imaginative involvement. American Journal of Clinical Hypnosis, 1978, 20, 194-198.

Diamond, M. J., and Taft, R. The role played by ego permissiveness and imagery in hypnotic responsivity. International Journal of Clinical and Experimental Hypnosis, 1975, 23, 130-138.

Hilgard, J. R. Personality and hypnosis. Chicago: University of Chicago Press, 1970.

Hilgard, J. R. Imaginative and sensory-affective involvements: In everyday life and in hypnosis. In E. Fromm and R. E. Shor (Eds.), Hypnosis: developments in research and new perspectives. Hawthorne, NY: Aldine, 1979.

Lee-Teng, E. Trance-susceptibility, induction-susceptibility, and acquiescence as factors in hypnotic performance. Journal of Abnormal Psychology, 1965, 70, 383-389.

Sarbin, T. R., and Lim, D. T. Some evidence in support of the role-taking hypothesis in hypnosis. International Journal of Clinical and Experimental Hypnosis, 1963, 11, 98-103.

Sheehan, P. W. Hypnosis and the manifestations of "imagination." In E. Fromm and R. E. Shor (Eds.), Hypnosis: Research developments and perspectives. Chicago: Aldine-Atherton, 1972.

Shor, R. E., Orne, M. T., and O'Connell, D. N. Validation and cross-validation of a scale of self-reported personal experiences which predicts hypnotizability. Journal of Psychology, 1962, 53, 55-75.

Spanos, N. P., and McPeake, J. D. The effects of involvement in everyday imaginative activities and attitudes towars hypnosis on hypnotic suggestibility. Journal of Personality and Social Psychology, 1975, 31, 594-598.

Sutcliffe, J. P., Perry, C. W., and Sheehan, P. W. Relation of some aspects of imagery and fantasy to hypnotic susceptibility. Journal of Abnormal Psychology, 1970, 76, 279-287.

Tellegen, A., and Atkinson, G. Openness to absorbing and self-altering experiences ("absorption") a trait related to hypnotic susceptibility. Journal of Abnormal Psychology, 1974, 83, 368-277.

Weitzenhoffer, A. M., and Hilgard, E. R. Stanford Hypnotic Susceptibility Scale, Forms A and B. Palo Alto, CA: Consulting Psychologists Press, 1959.

Weitzenhoffer, A. M., and Hilgard, E. R. Stanford Hypnotic Susceptibility Scale, Form C. Palo Alto, CA: Consulting Psychologists Press, 1962.

Wilson, S. C., and Barber, T. X. The Creative Imagination Scale as a measure of hypnotic responsiveness: Applications to experimental and clinical hypnosis. American Journal of Clinical Hypnosis, 1978, 20, 235-249.

IV. SYNAESTHESIA

A COMPARISON OF SYNESTHETES AND NONSYNESTHETES

Charles M. Rader * and Auke Tellegen **

*Arnold Vinson & Associates; **University of Minnesota

*St. Paul, Minnesota; **Minneapolis, Minnesota**

Synesthetes, those endowed with synesthesia (the phenomenon in which sense experiences in one modality are associated with imagery in another), have been described as everything from bright and imaginative to deeply disturbed. For example, Galton (1883) characterized synesthetes as creative and intelligent. However, E. R. Jaensch (1938) regarded synesthesia as a type of perceptual slovenliness and, consistent with his Nazi ideology, considered it a likely result of a "racially mixed heredity." He viewed synesthetes as degenerates who could not keep their senses straight!

To be sure, in spite of the early research, a good deal of it before the 20th Century, really not much is known about the personality characteristics and intelligence of synesthetes. Almost all of the published research consists of either case studies on individual synesthetes or psychophysical studies (for example, Marks' more recent studies designed to identify universal synesthetic "translation" principles). We have learned two main things from the previous research about visual-auditory synesthesia (color hearing), the associating of visual images with sound stimuli. These two findings were extremely helpful in the design of our own investigaion comparing synesthetes and nonsynesthetes. First, individual differences exist in the vividness of imagery associated with sound stimuli. Some people represent sound or music in visual images that are extremely vivid. Such individuals are traditionally referred to as synesthetes. It may be noted that in general "having synesthesia" typically refers to a certain mode of experiencing and responding to stimuli, namely, with vivid images in a different sense modality.

A second important finding is that the particular colors used to represent or describe sound stimuli are related to particular stimulus qualities. For example, bright colors tend to be associated with higher-pitched sounds whereas dark colors tend to be associated with lower-pitched sounds. Loud sounds are perceived as large whereas soft sounds are felt to be small. Joyful music is often associated with bright colors such as yellow, and sad music with black or gray. Thus, the translation of sounds into colors appears to follow universal laws as delineated by Marks (1975, 1978).

It is important to distinguish between what we will call the "experiential" component of synesthesia, a term we will use to refer to the imagery or feelings engendered by the stimuli, and the "translation" component, the term we will use to refer to the representation or depiction of sounds with colors. At the present time we do not know whether synesthetes (vivid imagers) would use different colors to describe sound stimuli than nonsynesthetes (poor imagers).

RESEARCH QUESTIONS AND HYPOTHESES

Our investigation was designed to answer the following questions: (1) do synesthetes and nonsynesthetes translate in a similar fashion; (2) how do the personality characteristics of synesthetes and nonsynesthetes differ, and (3) are synesthetes more intelligent than nonsynesthetes? We hypothesized that since synethetes were probably quite experienced at using colors to describe sound stimuli, they could be more skillful translators than nonsynesthetes. We also predicted that since they would be more sensitive to subtleties in the sound stimuli, they probably would tend to use more colors when describing sounds. Karwoski and Odbert (1938), for example, reported that subjects in their complex synesthete group showed a capacity for translating more aspects of auditory stimuli into visual sensory content than any subjects from their other groups. With regard to personality characteristics, we believed that synesthetes would show a greater inclination toward imaginative involvement and a better capacity for absorbed attention than nonsynesthetes. We did not expect a higher incidence of maladjustment than among nonsynesthetes. Lastly, we did not expect synesthetes and nonsynesthetes to differ in intelligence.

METHOD AND PROCEDURE

We decided to assess both synesthetic translation ability and vividness of imagery by incorporating into one comprehensive battery a variety of tasks traditionally used in synesthesia studies, as well as a set of paper-and-pencil tasks which we anticipated would tap synesthetic translation ability. Such a comprehensive battery had never been used before.

We also decided that visual-auditory synesthetic functioning could best be assessed by asking subjects to listen to vowels, tones, classical and popular music, to describing each stimulus by selecting appropriate colors and to rate the vividness of their color experiences. Five vowels and twelve pure tones were included as they appeared to be simpler, less "culturally-loaded" stimuli than musical selections. In addition, we selected ten classical and ten popular musical selections which we judged to be representative of different moods. We considered the musical selections to be more complex, meaningful and culturally-loaded than the vowels and tones. These four tasks, the vowel, tone, classical and popular tasks, were termed the "auditory" tasks.

The auditory stimuli were presented to the subjects using a tape recorder. For each stimulus, a subject was allotted five "points" that he or she was asked to assign to one or more of 11 colors (identified verbally only): red, orange, yellow, green, blue, purple, brown, white, pink, grey and black. Each test had its own rating grid. The subject was asked to distribute the five points over the colors in the manner he or she thought best described the stimulus. For example, if a subject felt that a musical selection was mostly red with a little black, he or she could allot four points to red and one to black. Subjects were asked to use all five points and not to use fractions of points. The assignment of points is a novel procedure which we believed would reflect individual differences more sensitively than asking subjects to select just one color, the procedure followed in most previous studies.

The subjects rated the degree or intensity of their color experience using a rating scale devised by Lehman (1972). For each stimulus, they were instructed to indicate a "yes" or "no" in response to questions whether they "saw colors," "thought of colors," "felt like colors make them feel," "had other types of experiences," or "had no experience at all." Unlike the inquiry adopted in other investigations, the present study allowed for subjects to use several rather than just one category. Thus, a subject could endorse both the "see" and "feel" categories. In this way, it was possible to assess more adequately the complexity of a subject's experience. The scores for each of the four categories were summed across each of the four subtests to derive total experience scores after factor analyses indicated that such a procedure was justified. Interestingly, an examination of the "see" score distribution seemed to indicate that the ability to translate sound stimuli into vivid images is indicative of a continuously rather than typologically distributed skill. It appears that most subjects possess some, albeit limited, ability to associate sounds with images: thus, henceforth when using the term "synesthetes" or "seers" we are referring to individuals high in this ability. We do not mean to imply a discrete typology or special class of individuals.

We believed that the three paper-and-pencil tasks included in the study, the mood-color, line-mood, and line-color tasks, would provide further measures of synesthetic translation skill. Two of the tasks, the mood-color task and the line-mood task, were similar to tests used in previous investigations. We expected these tasks to be relatively easier for the subjects than the line-color test.

For the mood-color test, subjects were asked to describe 11 moods selected to comprise major dimensions of affectivity (angry, tired, proud, peaceful, surprised, sad, excited, tender, ashamed, joyful and scared), in terms of the 11 colors used during the auditory portion of the test. The same five-point distribution system was utilized. Except for this feature, our task was comparable to that used by Odbert, Karwoski and Eckerson (1942) in their large scale synesthesia study. Wexner (1954) had also used a similar task and replicated their results.

For the line-mood test, subjects were asked to characterize 18 lines used in a study by Poffenberger and Barrows (1924) in terms of the 11 moods used in the mood-color test. Again the five point allocation system was utilized. The Poffenberger and Barrows lines were used since they included the major types of lines investigated in the past (fast and slow curves, fast and slow jagged lines) and allowed one to determine what effect tilting the lines up or down might have on the emotions they convey. In the past, such tasks as the line-mood one have been described by such investigators as Scheerer and Lyons (1957) as measures of physiognomic perception, a term used by Werner (1948) to describe the dynamic apprehension of the world prior to the differentiation of the senses When one perceives physiognomically, objects such as landscapes may appear animate and express some inner for of life. Werner also noted that synesthesia preceded sensory differentiation.

The line-color test was, as far as we know, never formally used in previously published research. Using the five-point allocation system, subjects were asked to describe the 18 Poffenberger and Barrows lines in terms of one or more of the 11 colors.

In addition to these synesthesia tasks, subjects were also asked to fill out a short synesthesia questionnaire designed to assess the possible frequency and intensity of a subject's synesthetic experiences outside of the experimental situation. Since the correlation of this measure with the "see" score derived from the experiment was .37 for females and .50 for males, we decided to use a composite experimental-nonexperimental synesthesia score to select our high and low seers. Thus, we would be able to select those most likely to have synesthetic experiences both within and outside an experimental setting.

Finally we asked the subjects to complete the Differential Personality Questionnaire (DPQ), a 300-term personality inventory

(Tellegen, Note 1), and a modified version of the Mill-Hill Vocabulary test, a brief intelligence test. The DPQ is designed to reflect major self-descriptive dimensions of both "healthy" and clinical populations. It consists of 11 primary scales measuring traits labeled Well Being, Social Potency, Achievement, Social Closeness, Stress Reaction, Alienation, Aggression, Control, Harm Avoidance, Authoritarianism and Absorption. The DPQ also provides measures of three higher-order dimensions, namely Positive Affectivity, Negative Affectivity and Constraint Acceptance.

We administered our battery to 385 subjects, 206 females and 179 males, most of whom participated in the study to gain supplementary course points. Using the composite synesthesia score, we decided to choose approximately the top and bottom 15% of the females and males (separately). After the composite scores were examined, 28 female highs and lows and 26 male highs (some scores were tied or extremely close) and 25 male lows were selected.

RESULTS

The first step in our analysis involved computing, for both females and males, means and standard deviations for each of the 11 colors and moods for all of the auditory and paper-and-pencil tests. The data were analyzed separately for males and females. An examination of the results indicated that the data were quite orderly, and the male and female responses to the different stimuli very similar.

For both sexes, the color means varied systematically from stimulus to stimulus in accordance with differing stimulus properties, and our findings were consistent with those of previous investigators reviewed by Marks (1975, 1978). On the basis of the arrangement of the colors in "factor space" we arrived at the following color sequence which appears to reflect the dominance of brightness differences among the colors: white, pink, yellow, red, orange, green, blue, purple, brown, grey, and black. When we examined the color responses to the tones, the darker colors were mostly associated with the lowest tones, the middle ones with middle tones, and the lightest ones with the highest tones. The vowel responses were also quite orderly. (For a more detailed discussion of these findings the reader can refer to Rader, Note 2.)

Not only did we replicate previous findings for the simple stimuli, but using our musical selections, we found the same mood-color relationships as Odbert, Karwoski and Eckerson (1942). For example, red was used to describe exciting, vigorous music; yellow, joyful music; blue, tender music; and black and grey, sad music. The paper-and-pencil mood-color test results were consistent with this pattern. Furthermore, the line-mood findings were similar to those of Lundholm (1921) and Poffenberger and Barrows (1924). Lastly, subjects tended to select specific colors to describe particular lines in the line-color test. For example, a curve characterized as "peaceful" in the line-mood test was rated "blue," which in turn is the color used to describe "peaceful" on the mood-color test.

Comparisons of Seers' (Synesthetes') and Nonseers' (Nonsynesthetes') Translation Skill

Since our stimulus-color findings were consistent with those of previous investigators and with the generalizations arrived at by Marks (1975, 1978), we decided to adopt the group means as standards against which the "precision" of individual responses could be evaluated. Thus, we decided to compute a "translation" score (or "performance" score) for each subject for each stimulus based upon how closely her or his auditory and visual test responses matched those of the group as a whole. Precision was measured inversely, namely, as the sum of the absolute (color or mood response) deviations from the group mean. This score enabled us to measure how closely the individual's translation performance conformed to the collective norm. A factor analysis of the "performance" variables ("translation" scores) for females and males indicated that each of the seven tests behaved as a functional unit, justifying the representation of each of these tests by a single score. (A factor analysis using these seven variables in turn indicated a "higher-order" general translation factor.)

The seers' and nonseers' performance scores for the seven tests were compared, and no systematic differences were found. The data did suggest a slight interaction between sex. "seeing," and performance, as the female seers tended to be slightly more unconventional in their translating than the female nonseers, while the male seers tended to be more conventional than the nonseers.

As a means of testing for more subtle differences between seers and nonseers, a Q-correlational analysis was also performed in order to assess the possibility of distinctive translator "types" within the seer or nonseer group, but the results were not confirmatory. We also computed color bias scores to determine whether seers or nonseers would tend to favor certain colors in carrying out their translations. No systematic color translation bias differences between the two groups were observed. Overall, then, the results did not support our hypothesis that seers would tend to be more skillful translators than nonseers: both groups appear to translate in a similar fashion.

Differentiation Score Comparisons

In order to test our hypothesis that seers would tend to use more colors when describing stimuli, we computed response complexity scores (which we called differentiation scores) designed to reflect how a subject "spreads out" her or his five points over the 11 colors. Since assigning five points to one color is the least complex response, and assigning one point each to five different colors is the most complex, we devised a scoring rule which expressed quantitatively the relative complexity of response: for every pair of points she or he had assigned to two different colors, the subject received a point on her or his differentiation score, the maximum score therefore being 10 points, the minimum zero (which we later changed to 4 because of the skewed distribution). A factor analysis of the differentiation variables suggested that we could compute five "total" differentiation scores, one each for the simple auditory stimuli, the musical selections and the three paper-and-pencil tests.

When the seers' and nonseers' differentiation scores were compared, the only significant difference to emerge was for females for the musical differentiation score, the female seers producing more differentiated translations ($t = 3.16$, $p < .05$). The male group's difference in mean scores on this variable was in the same direction and approached significance ($t = 1.84$, $p = .079$). These findings confirm to some extent the expectation of greater complexity of response to musical stimuli on the part of synesthetes, as suggested by Korwoski and Odbert (1938). This suggests that seers are more sensitive to subtle nuances of musical stimuli than nonseers.

Comparison of Seers' and Nonseers' Personality and Intelligence Scores

The Differential Personality Questionnaire scale scores for the seers and nonseers were computed and standardized in accordance with the female and male group norms for this study ($M = 100$, $SD = 10$) in order to facilitate interpretation.

Our major hypothesis regarding the personality functioning of seers was borne out by the data: On the Absorption scale, female ($M = 107.74$) and male ($M = 107.23$) seers scored significantly higher than female ($M = 91.94$) and male ($M = 92.87$) nonseers ($t = 7.36$ and $\underline{t} = 6.22$, respectively, $\underline{p} < .001$). (These results are consistent with the correlations between the "see" scores derived from the experiment and the Absorption scores, .42 for females and .39 for males and the Synesthesia Questionnaire "see" score-Absorption correlations, .40 for females and .46 for males.) The results suggest that the most outstanding personality features of the seer groups are their imaginative ability, their enjoyment and quest for imaginative experiences, their artistic interests and their appreciation of interesting sights, sounds, stories, etc., as well as their capacity for absorbed attention. The nonseers, on the other hand, are probably somewhat lacking in these qualities.

An examination of the other seer-nonseer personality score differences suggested that seers, on the whole, obtained higher scores than nonseers on measures related to a positive self-view, although none of the differences were as striking as the Absorption differences. From these findings, one may conclude that, overall, the personality profile of the seers tends to refute the longstanding myth that synesthesia is correlated with maladjustment.

Lastly, male and female seers and nonseers did not differ with respect to intelligence. Thus, the longstanding belief of greater intelligence in synesthesia was also not supported.

DISCUSSION

Despite the novelty of our tasks, the subjects' responses yielded results that were quite orderly, demonstrating meaningful and systematic associations between reactions to color and those to sound, to color and emotion, and to lines and emotion. Furthermore, a subject's skill in using colors to describe stimuli is not related in any systematic way to the subjective intensity of the perceptual-imaginative experience. Thus, both seers and nonseers tended to use the same colors to describe stimuli, although the translation process may, of course, have differed for the two groups. Nothing in the results refutes Marks' contention that "synesthetes align dimensions on different modalities in ways that are qualitatively similar to the ways that nonsynesthetes align them" (Marks, 1975, p. 303). His information-processing theory of synesthesia, based upon the work of investigators such as Werner (1948), Osgood, Suci and Tannenbaum (1967), Bruner (1964), Richardson (1969) and Paivio (1971), helps in part to explain why the end products of the translation processes, the color responses, are similar for seers and nonseers.

Drawing on Marks' generalizations and on our own finding that seers as a group score significantly higher on Absorption, we may speculate on how seers might translate sounds into colors. To begin with, we assume that even though synesthetes and nonsynesthetes may use the same colors to describe stimuli, their process of translation may differ from that of nonsynesthetes. Following Marks, we may assume that synesthetes can avail themselves of both language and vivid visual imagery for encoding sensory inputs, while nonsynesthetes are apt to rely more exclusively upon language. Thus, seers probably have more varied means of processing information at their disposal than nonseers. Transforming sounds info vivid visual representations probably involves a more extensive process of construction and transformation than when preexisting linguistic categories are used to describe them. We may liken the seers to Piaget's "assimilators" in that they act upon the stimuli they perceive and transform it, perhaps in novel ways, in carrying out their translations. Thus "seeing" colors probably represents a much more "active" perceptual process than not "seeing" them. It is interesting to note in this connection that Arieti (1976), in his book Creativity, The Magic Synthesis, observed that imagery can be a springboard to creativity in that it is the first function that permits the human being not to adapt passively to reality and in a sense to transcend the limitations it imposes. One may surmise that synesthetes tend to be more creative than nonsynesthetes.

Following Tellegen and Atkinson's (1974) discussion of Absorption, we may postulate that synesthetes transform, enrich, store and encode stimuli in a variety of sensory modalities. Furthermore, for "good" synesthetes, the "enactive" nature of their representations may be highly involving and "real" in that sense.

Synesthetes probably encode more information about stimuli than nonsynesthetes. Marks (1975, P. 326) noted: "Synesthetic cross-modal, sensory cognition is both less abstract and more dense in informational content." It is likely that the method of allocating five points was too confining for fully describing the complexity of their representations and limited their assessment. At any rate, as noted, the female synesthetes responded to the classical and popular music in a more complex (differentiated) way than the nonsynesthetes. The trend was in the same direction for males. It is probable that the seers became especially absorbed by complex auditory stimuli. However, their differentiation scores for the vowels and tones did not suggest that they enrich their translations for these tasks any more than the nonseers.

With regard to how seers might develop their images, one should distinguish between spontaneous, unbidden images and those which have been elicited as in our study. It seems likely that the individuals constituting the seer groups (combined scores) are disposed not only to develop images in response to explicit demands but also to have more spontaneous and effortless imaginal experiences.

In view of the observed relationship between Absorption and synesthetic experience, we propose the following hypotheses to be verified by future studies: (1) seers will tend to be good hypnotic subjects. This hypothesis is based on the frequently observed positive correlation between hypnotic responsiveness and Absorption (Sheehan, 1979). (2) Seers are likely to be more creative than nonseers. Judging from their high Absorption scores, seers may have the ability to suspend ego control, an ability hypothesized to be an integral part of the creative process (Bowers, 1979). (3) Seers will probably show a history of learning to become involved in a variety of activities which have kept alive the imaginative involvements of childhood. Josephine Hilgard's developmental-interactive theory of hypnotic susceptibility (Hilgard, 1979) may shed light on how early synesthetic ability may be maintained. Thus, a developmental study of synesthetes would certainly prove useful.

REFERENCE NOTES

1. Tellegen, A. The Differential Personality Questionnaire. Unpublished personality inventory, 1976.

2. Rader, C. Explorations in synesthesia. Unpublished doctoral dissertation, University of Minnesota, 1979.

REFERENCES

Arieti, S. Creativity: The magic synthesis. New York: Basic Books, 1976.

Bowers, K., and Bowers, P. Hypnosis and creativity: A theoretical and empirical rapprochement. In E. Fromm and R. Shor (Eds.) Hypnosis: Developments in research and new perspectives (2nd ed.). New York: Aldine, 1979.

Bruner, J. S. The course of cognitive growth. American Psychologist, 1964, 19, 1-15.

Galton, E. Inquiries into human faculty and its development. London: Macmillan, 1883.

Hilgard, J. Personality and hypnosis: A study of imaginative involvement (2nd ed.). Chicago: University of Chicago Press, 1979.

Jaensch, E. R. Der Gegentypus. Leipzig: Barth, 1938.

Karwoski, T. F., and Odbert, H. S. Color-music. Psychological Monographs, 1938, 50 (2, Whole No. 222).

Lehman, R. A multivariate model of synesthesia. Multivariate Behavioral Research, 1972, 7, 403-439.

Lundholm. H. The affective tone of lines: Experimental research. Psychological Review, 1921, 28, 43-60.

Marks, L. On colored-hearing synesthesia: Cross modal translations of sensory dimensions. Psychological Bulletin, 1975, 82, 303-331.

Marks, L. The unity of the senses: Interrelations among the modalities. New York: Academic Press, 1978.

Odbert, H. S., Karwoski, T. F., and Eckerson, A. B. Studies in synesthetic thinking: I. Musical and verbal association of color and mood. Journal of General Psychology, 1942, 26, 153-173.

Osgood, C., Suci, G., and Tannenbaum, P. The measurement of meaning.

Urbana: University of Illinois Press, 1957.

Paivio, A. Imagery and verbal processes. New York: Holt, Rinehart and Winston, 1971.

Poffenberger, A. T., and Barrows, B. E. The feeling value of lines. Journal of Applied Psychology, 1924, 8, 187-205.

Richardson, A. Mental imagery. London: Routledge & Kegan Paul, 1969.

Scheerer, M., and Lyons, J. Line drawings and matching responses to words. Journal of Personality, 1957, 25, 251-273.

Sheehan, P. W. Hypnosis and the process of imagination. In E. Fromm and R. Shor (Eds.) Hypnosis: Developments in research and new perspectives (2nd ed.). New York: Aldine, 1979.

Tellegen, A., and Atkinson, G. Openness to absorbing and self-altering experiences ("absorption"), a trait related to hypnotic susceptibility. Journal of Abnormal Psychology, 1974, 83, 268-277.

Werner, H. Comparative psychology of mental development. New York: International Universities Press, 1948.

Wexner, L. The degree to which colors (hues) are associated with mood tones. Journal of Applied Psychology, 1954, 38, 432-435.

[illegible] Ohio State University, [illegible]

[illegible]

[illegible]

CHROMESTHETIC RESPONSES TO THE MUSIC OF G. F. HANDEL

Donald J. Polzella and Audrey M. Kuna

University of Dayton

Dayton, OH

> Presented with a tone pitched at 50 cycles per second and an amplitude of 100 decibels, S. saw a brown strip against a dark background that had red tongue-like edges. The sense of taste he experienced was like that of sweet and sour borscht, a sensation that gripped his entire tongue...Presented with a tone pitched at 500 cycles per second and having an amplitude of 100 decibels, he saw a streak of lightning splitting the heavens in two. When the intensity of the sound was lowered to 74 decibels, he saw a dense orange color which made him feel as though a needle had been thrust into his spine. (Luria, 1968, P. 23)

This vivid account describes one of the most unusual forms of mental imagery, synesthesia. It is defined as "production, from a sense-impression of one kind, of an associated mental image of a sense-impression of another kind" (Synaesthesia, 1970, P. 373). Synesthesia can theoretically occur among any sense modalities. However, it does occur more frequently between some modalities than others. In this paper, we are concerned with chromesthesia or colored hearing, a particular form of synesthesia in which color images (photisms) are evoked by auditory stimuli.

Marks (1975) has reviewed the extensive scientific literature on chromesthesia, which dates back over 2000 years. The association between auditory stimuli and color photisms is complex, but there are several general relationships that are common to normal people as well as to synesthetes. The most frequent reports of chromesthesia are color photisms produced by speech sounds. In these cases the brightness of the photism is a direct function of the pitch of the vowel. For example, acute (high-pitched) vowels like /i/ and /e/ tend to evoke bright colors, while grave (low-pitched) vowels like /o/ and /u/ tend to evoke darken colors. More subtle linkings occur between the ratio of the frequencies of the second to first formants of the vowel and the redness and greenness of the photism. For example, compact vowels like /a/ and /o/ tend to evoke red, while diffuse vowels like /y/ and /i/ tend to evoke green.

Color photisms can also be evoked by musical stimuli, which is the specific concern of this paper. The relationships here are similar to those for colored vowels. The brightness and size of the photisms are a function of the pitch and loudness of the stimuli; however, the relationships are clearest for colors and single tones (Wicker, 1968). When the stimuli are actual pieces of music the photisms are a function of the interaction of many stimulus attributes and are less reliable (Karwoski & Odbert, 1938), but they appear to be mediated by a "cognitive space" that is common to both music and color (Lehman, 1972; Odbert, Karwoski, & Eckerson, 1942).

The purpose of the present study is to determine if color photism can be reliably evoked by the complex stimulus attributes that characterize musical compositions. One such attribue is tonality or musical key:

> In its broadest sense tonality refers to the fact that most musical compositions, whether Western or non-Western, primitive or avant garde, melodic or harmonic, have a primary pitch about which they are structured. This pitch is the <u>tonal center</u> and serves as the tone to which other tones ultimately return. It comes to serve as the ultimate musical expectation within the piece, both melodically and harmonically. (Radocy & Boyle, 1979, P. 122)

In most Western music written since the 18th century, two complementary tonal systems predominate, major and minor. Both systems are based on a scale of seven notes, which are chosen from the twelve semitones that divide the Western octave. The scales differ in the pitch intervals between the successive notes. (The familiar <u>do</u>-<u>re</u>-<u>mi</u>-<u>fa</u>-<u>sol</u>-<u>la</u>-<u>ti</u>-<u>do</u> is merely a major scale. A minor scale is formed by lowering <u>mi</u> and <u>la</u> one semitone.) Both systems comprise twelve keys. Each key has a different tonal center since it is based on a scale that begins on a different one of the twelve semitones dividing the octave (Machlis, 1963, Pp. 257-268).

There are clear affective differences between the two systems (modes). Stimuli in the major mode are judged happy, merry, graceful, and playful, while stimuli in the minor mode are judged sad, dreamy, and sentimental (Lundin, 1967, P. 172). Notwithstanding the beliefs of several well known composers, Jeans (1937/1968) argues that the affective differences are not inherent in the music, but are merely subjective. Meyer (1956) agrees:

> Eventually all these theories are faced with the single overwhelming fact that the minor triad has no peculiarly affective significance, carries no sad connotations in non-Western music, in folk music, or in the music of primitives. This would seem to indicate...that like most musical responses the one to the minor mode is not natural or universal but learned. (P. 223)

Regardless of their origins, psychological differences do exist between the major and minor modes. Moreover, there is anecdotal evidence that colors are associated with various tonalities. For example, Beethoven called the key of B-minor black, and Scriabin and Rimsky-Korsakov, both synesthetes, agreed that D-major is yellow (Marks, 1975). Noncomposers Carroll and Greenberg (1961) show considerable agreement in associations between all twelve major keys and colors. The purpose of the present study is to determine whether color photisms can be experimentally evoked as a function of the major/minor distinction.

METHOD

Subjects

The subjects were 216 Introductory Psychology students. They participated as part of a course requirement.

Stimuli

The stimuli were taped excerpts (1-2 min.) from each of the twelve Concerti Grossi (Opus VI) by G. F. Handel (Haendel, 1739/1968). Downes (1976) calls the concertos "the crowning orchestral achievement of one of the greatest composers who ever lived. Together with the 'Brandenburg' Concertos of J. S. Bach, they represent the peak of late Baroque orchestral writing" (P. 367).

The twelve excerpts were equivalent in scoring (string orchestra) and tempo (allegro), but they differed in musical key. Four of the excerpts were in major keys, four in minor keys, and four in mixed keys. (It is common for Western composers to "mix" keys by shifting from one to another within a section of music. This is known as modulation, and composer Arnold Schoenberg likens it to "a change of scenery" [Machlis, 1963, P. 265].) The major excerpts were from Concerti 1 (Pp. 3-5), 7 (Pp. 95-96), 9 (Pp. 119-120), and 11 (Pp. 152-153). The minor excerpts were from Concerti 4 (Pp. 54-55), 6 (Pp. 88-91), 8 (P. 117), and 12 (Pp. 169-171). The mixed excerpts, with major/minor or minor/major modulations, were from Concerti 2 (Pp. 20-21), 3 (Pp. 34-35), 5 (Pp. 72-73), and 10 (Pp. 139-142).[1] The performances were conducted by Jean-Francois Paillard (Musical Heritage Society, MHS 806-809).

Procedure

The subjects read the following instructions:

In this experiment, you will hear brief excerpts from twelve pieces of classical music. As you listen to each excerpt, think about the predominant color and the strength of your color images. Attached to these instructions is an answer sheet. After you hear each excerpt, please make three responses. First, choose one color, red, yellow, green or blue as the one that was most apparent while you were listening. Please choose a color even when you are not sure. Second, rate the strength of the evoked color on a 1 to 5 scale. Third, rate the degree to which you enjoyed listening to the excerpt on a 1 to 5 scale. Indicate your responses by circling the appropriate choices on the answer sheet.

The subjects chose the color of their photisms by circling R, Y, G, or B. They indicated their ratings by circling 1 (very weak), 2 (moderately weak), 3 (moderate), 4 (moderately strong), or 5 (very strong) for image strength, and 1 (disliked), 2 (disliked somewhat), 3 (neutral), 4 (liked somewhat), or 5 (liked) for enjoyment. The subjects were tested in groups of 20-30. Each group heard the excerpts in either of two random orders.

RESULTS

Color Photisms

Table 1 lists the proportion of subjects who chose a particular color for each excerpt. Chi square analyses indicated that the observed distributions of color responses were significantly different than chance in every case ($p < .01$). The pooled data are plotted in Figure 1. In general, major excerpts evoked yellow and green photisms, while minor excerpts evoked blue. The photisms were least consistent for the mixed excerpts.

The results were also interpreted using analysis of variance for a 3 X 4 (Mode X Excerpt) nested design with repeated measures on both factors. Separate analyses were computed for each color; the data were dichotomous, 1 if the color was evoked, 0 if it was not. (See Lunney, 1970 and Winer, 1962 for support for this approach.) The tests of significance were conservatively biased as a precaution against heterogeneity of covariance (Myers, 1972, Pp. 176-178).

The modality of the excerpt significantly affected the incidence of red photisms. They were most frequent for mixed excerpts, least for major excerpts, $F(1,215) = 13.81$, $p < .001$, $w^2 = .06$. The incidence of yellow photisms was also affected. They were most frequent for major excerpts, least for minor excerpts, $F(1,215) = 22.21$, $p < .001$,

Table 1

Proportion of Responses to Excerpts from G. F. Handel's Concerti Grossi (Op. VI)

Concerto Number	Color of Photisms			
	Red	Yellow	Green	Blue
Major Excerpts				
1	.13	.38	.31	.18
7	.18	.35	.29	.19
9	.17	.32	.31	.20
11	.17	.33	.27	.22
Mean	.16	.34	.30	.20
Minor Excerpts				
4	.14	.22	.29	.36
6	.21	.17	.26	.36
8	.40	.08	.26	.25
12	.14	.34	.16	.36
Mean	.22	.20	.24	.33
Mixed Excerpts				
2	.18	.36	.30	.16
3	.30	.13	.28	.29
5	.31	.37	.18	.14
10	.27	.15	.33	.25
Mean	.27	.25	.27	.21

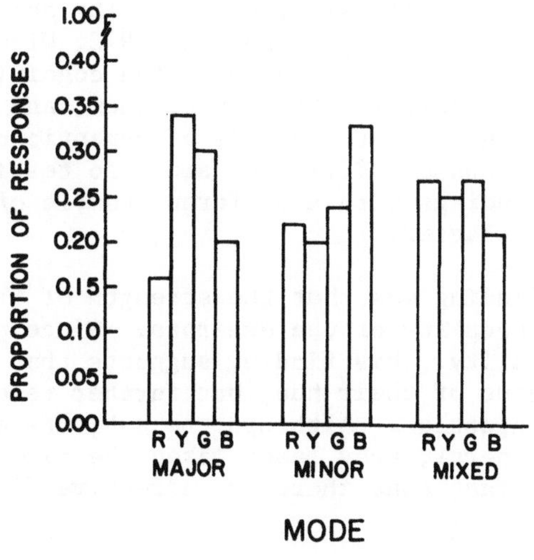

Figure 1. The proportion of red, yellow, green, and blue photisms evoked by major, minor, and mixed musical excerpts.

$w^2 = .09$. Modality did not significantly affect green photisms, $F(1,215) = 3.00$, $p > .05$, $w^2 = .01$, but it did affect blue photisms. They were most frequently evoked by minor excerpts, $F(1,215) = 23.08$, $p < .001$, $w^2 = .10$.

Strength of Photisms

These results were interpreted using the analysis of variance. The raw data were responses on a 5-point scale ranging from "very weak" to "very strong." The mean strength of photisms to major, minor, and mixed excerpts was 3.16, 3.20, and 3.27, respectively. These means were not significantly different, $F(1,216) = 3.26$, $p > .05$, $w^2 = .01$.

Enjoyment of Excerpts

These results were also interpreted using the analysis of variance. The raw data were responses on a 5-point scale ranging from "disliked" to "liked." The mean enjoyment of major, minor, and mixed excerpts was 3.74, 3.53, and 3.73, respectively. These means were significantly different, $F(1,215) = 21.49$, $p < .001$, $w^2 = .09$. In general, subjects liked listening to the music, but the minor excerpts were liked the least.

DISCUSSION

The results indicate that specific color photisms are linked to the different tonalities of Handel's Concerti. The most reliable associations were between major excerpts and yellow, and minor excerpts and blue. Mixed excerpts evoked the least consistent pattern of photisms. This is not surprising since the tonality shifted in these excerpts. Based on previous studies (Lehman, 1972; Wicker, 1968), we expect that there are similarities between the cognitive structures of the colors and the modalities that evoke them, and we are exploring this possibility through factor analysis of semantic differential data (Osgood, Suci, & Tannenbaum, 1957). We are also testing the generality of the present findings with a different sample of music (J. S. Bach's Well-Tempered Clavier).

An important finding was that the strength of the photisms was not affected by the modality of the excerpts. Since photisms changed as a function of modality, this finding suggests that the strength of photisms is independent of their hue, but further research is necessary to test this suggestion. Although the subjects enjoyed listening to the excerpts in general, they least liked the minor excerpts. This finding supports the fact that there are affective differences between the two modes.

A final consideration lies in the applicability of these findings to aesthetics. We share Omwake's (1940) belief that the principles of visual-auditory synesthesia "should be investigated on a larger scale to discover the extent to which auditory and visual factors should be combined to produce a heightened and unified emotional effect" (P. 481).

SUMMARY

This experiment explored chromesthetic imagery, i.e., colored-hearing synesthesia, evoked by 12 excerpts from G. F. Handel's Concerti Grossi, Opus 6. The excerpts were equivalent in scoring and tempo but they systematically varied in tonality (key). After listening to each excerpt, the subjects (216 Introductory Psychology students) chose the predominant color (red, yellow, green, or blue) of the evoked photism. They also rated the strength of the photism and their enjoyment of the excerpt. In general, excerpts in major keys evoked yellow, and excerpts in minor keys evoked blue. Mixed excerpts, in which tonality was modulated, evoked the least consistent pattern of photisms. The strength of the photisms was unrelated to tonality suggesting that the strength and hue of color photisms are independent. Minor excerpts were enjoyed the least, which supports earlier findings that there are affective differences between major and minor modes. The findings have practical relevance to the extent that auditory and visual factors can be combined to produce heightened aesthetic experience.

FOOTNOTE

1. The authors wish to thank Dr. Richard P. Benedum, Music Division, University of Dayton, for analyzing the tonality of the excerpts.

REFERENCES

Bekesy, G. V. Similarities between hearing and skin sensations. Psychological Review, 1959, 66, 1-22.

Carroll, J. B., and Greenberg, J. H. Two cases of synesthesia for color and musical tonality associated with absolute pitch ability. Perceptual and Motor Skills, 1961, 13, 48.

Downes, E. The New York Philharmonic guide to the symphony. New York: Walker, 1976.

Haendel, G. F. Twelve concerti grossi, opus 6 (2 vols.). New York: Edwin F. Kalmus, 1968. (Originally composed, 1739.)

Howells, T. H. The experimental development of color-tone synesthesia. Journal of Experimental Psychology, 1944, 34, 87-103.

Jeans, J. Science & music. New York: Dover, 1968. (Originally published, 1937.)

Karwoski, T. F., and Odbert, H. S. Color-music. Psychological Monographs, 1938, 50 (2, whole No. 222).

Lehman, R. S. A multivariate model of synesthesia. Multivariate Behavioral Research, 1972, 7, 403-439.

London, I. D. Research on sensory interaction in the Soviet Union. Psychological Bulletin, 1954, 51, 531-568.

Lundin, R. W. An objective psychology of music (2nd ed.). New York: Ronald, 1967.

Lunney, G. H. Using analysis of variance with a dichotomous dependent variable: an empirical study. Journal of Educational Measurement, 1970, 7, 263-269.

Luria, A. R. The mind of a mnemonist. New York: Basic Books, 1968.

Machlis, J. The enjoyment of music (rev. ed.). New York: Norton, 1963.

Marks, L. E. On colored-hearing synesthesia: cross-modal translations of sensory dimensions. Psychological Bulletin, 1975, 82, 303-331.

Meyer, L. B. Emotion and meaning in music. Chicago: University of Chicago Press, 1956.

Myers, J. L. Fundamentals of experimental design (2nd ed.). Boston: Allyn and Bacon, 1972.

Odbert, H. S., Karwoski, T. F., and Eckerson, A. B. Studies in synesthetic thinking: I. musical and verbal associations of color and mood. Journal of General Psychology, 1942, 26, 153-173.

Omwake, L. Visual responses to auditory stimuli. Journal of Applied Psychology, 1940, 24, 468-481.

Osgood, C. E., Suci, G. J., and Tannenbaum, P. H. The measurement of meaning. Urbana, IL: University of Illinois Press, 1957.

Radocy, R. E., and Boyle, J. D. Psychological foundations of musical behavior. Springfield, IL: Charles C. Thomas, 1979.

Synaesthesia. The Oxford english dictionary (Vol. X). Oxford: Clarendon, 1970.

Wicker, F. W. Mapping the intersensory regions of perceptual space.

American Journal of Psychology, 1968, 81, 178-188.

Winer, B. J. Statistical principles in experimental design. New York: McGraw-Hill, 1962.

V. IMAGERY AND COGNITIVE PROCESSES

BRAIN HEMISPHERICITY AND RESPONSE TO THE IMAGINAL PROCESSES INVENTORY

Paul Bakan and William G. Glackman

Simon Fraser University

Burnaby, B.C., Canada

The concept of hemisphericity was introduced by Bogen (1969) to relate the findings of functional hemispheric asymmetry of the brain to individual differences in cognitive functioning. It is now well established that the right and left hemispheres of the human brain, despite a superficial similarity in appearance, are quite different in mode of functioning. Functional asymmetry, first noted in the greater specialization of the left hemisphere for language, has now been extended to a number of other cognitive and affective variables including perception of music, faces, emotional tone, visuo-spatial skills, dreaming, depression and other personality variables. The concept of hemisphericity denotes the characteristic tendency of an individual to rely on one or the other (right or left) hemispheric modes of processing regardless of task requirements.

The application of hemisphericity in a typological sense requires some indicator of hemisphericity, i.e., some way to establish the characteristic tendency of an individual to rely on the right or left hemisphere in psychological functioning. Bakan (1969) has suggested an indicator of hemisphericity based on the direction of lateral eye movements made by an individual as he or she begins to reflect on the answer to a question. Day (1964) had earlier observed that if you face an individual and ask a question, his or her eyes move laterally, either to the right or left, as he or she begins to think of the answer to the question. The direction of the eye movement is generally consistent for an individual. Day also noted certain differences in behavior between those whose eyes move to the left and those whose eyes move to the right. Bakan (1969, 1971, 1978) has suggested that differences in eye movement direction, as well as associated differences in behavior, are due to hemisphericity. According to the Bakan model, eye directionality is an indicator of a relative dominance of one hemisphere over the other in the overall psychological fucntioning of an individual. Since stimulation of the right frontal lobe leads to left eye movements, and stimulation of the left frontal lobe leads to right eye movements, Bakan argued that the direction of conjugate lateral eye movements (CLEMS) is "symptomatic of easier triggering of activity in the hemisphere contralateral to the direction of eye movement". Subsequent research has shown a number of correlates of CLEM direction, and hence possibly of hemisphericity, if left movers are considered to favor the right hemisphere and right movers are considered to favor the left hemisphere. Differences between left and right movers have been reported in hypnotic susceptibility, dream recall, personality variables, defense mechanisms, values, aptitudes, physiological variables, and cognitive variables (Bakan, 1978; Ehrlichmann & Weinberger, 1978; Gur & Gur, 1977).

There has been considerable interest in the relationship between imagery and the hemispheres. In a recent review of imagery-hemisphere relationships (Bakan, 1980), I considered the evidence for an intimate relationship between imagery and the right hemisphere; but I also noted some results from our laboratory that appear paradoxical, namely, that in certain aspects of imagery, such as vividness of directed imagery, the use of imagery mediators in learning, and spatial visualization ability there was a superiority of right eye movers over left eye movers. Thus according to the CLEM hemisphericity model, those subjects showing a preference for use of the left hemisphere were performing at a higher level in these aspects of an imagery task.

These results suggested that both hemispheres have a role in the performance of imagery tasks, and that the hemispheres are differentially involved in different aspects of imagery. My conceptualization of the relationship between imagery and the hemispheres was summarized as follows:

> The right hemisphere does indeed have a primary role in imagery, in that it is crucial for the production of raw images. This basic ability to produce images is what gets lost after certain right hemisphere brain injuries. It appears spontaneously under certain conditions such as sleep, muscular relaxation, free association, mind wandering, and under the influence of certain drugs, it has primary process qualities and may be described as regressive, affective and illogical.
>
> When the hemispheres are in good communication, there may be processing or cooking of the raw right hemisphere imagery by the left hemisphere; the left hemisphere may take hold of raw imagery and bring to bear on it some form of logical, analytic or reality-oriented processing.

With the possibility that both hemispheres may be differentially involved in various aspects of imagery, it was decided to compare the performance of right and left eye movers on the Singer-Antrobus Imaginal Processes Inventory (IPI), an inventory whose 400 items arranged into 28 subscales taps a wide range of behaviors having to do with the content or structure of daydreaming and imaginal processes, as well as some measures of curiosity and patterns of attention (Singer & Antrobus, 1963, 1972).

There has been one previous study of this type by Meskin and Singer (1974). That study differed from the present one in that it was done with a male sample only, and it made use of a score based on only one factor from the scales (positive-vivid daydreaming) combined with a measure of repression-sensitization of Byrne to define a concept called "inner-attentive". Using these measures it was found that high inner attentive males were more likely to be left movers.

METHOD

400 item version of the IPI was administered to a group of right-handed students in an introductory psychology course. There were 110 subjects, 68 male and 42 female. Each subject was seen by an experimenter individually, so that he could evaluate the direction of lateral eye movements (CLEMS). The experimenter had no knowledge of subjects' test scores when he did this.

During the recording of CLEM direction the subject was seated across a desk from the experimenter. Directly behind and above the experimenter's head was a video camera supported by a tripod. The subject was told that the study was intended to relate cognitive processes during problem solving with performance in another experimental task. The subject was told that there might not be a single correct answer to the questions that he or she would be asked. The experimenter read each of 20 questions that had been previously shown to have no tendency to elicit eye movements predominately in one direction. The questions used to elicit CLEMS are listed in Table 1.

Just before the end of each question the experimenter activated a video recording system with a foot switch. He noted the direction of the subject's first eye movement after the end of each question as a number from 1 to 12, indicating the direction of the movement on an imaginary clock face superimposed around the subject's eyes. One to five o'clock are scored as left eye movements, and seven to eleven o'clock as right eye movements. As a check on interviewer reliability the video tapes were viewed by a second trained rater who also recorded the clock direction as the first interviewer did. The correlation between the two ratings was .77, indicating good reliability of the CLEM direction ratings.

RESULTS

The number of questions eliciting a right lateral eye movement

Table 1

Questions used to Elicit Conjugate Lateral Eye Movements (CLEMS)

1. What is the meaning of the proverb: A watched pot never boils?
2. What is the meaning of the proverb: It is an ill wind that blows no one good fortune?
3. Make up a sentence using two forms of the same verb.
4. Tell me two verbs beginning with "N".
5. What is the meaning of the proverb: A poor worker blames his tools?
6. Spell "therapeutic".
7. What is the meaning of the proverb: Call no man happy till he's dead?
8. List two adverbs.
9. What is the meaning of the proverb: Lend your money and lose your friends?
10. What is the meaning of the proverb: More than enough is too much?
11. List two prepositions.
12. What is the meaning of the proverb: Words should be weighed, not counted?
13. What is the meaning of the proverb: He is rich who has few wants?
14. Define the word "inflation".
15. What is the meaning of the proverb: A rolling stone gathers no moss?
16. Make up a sentence using two adverbs.
17. Tell me two verbs beginning with "R".
18. What is the meaning of the proverb: The hardest work is to go idle?
19. What is the meaning of the proverb: What saddens a wise man gladdens a fool?
20. Define the word "economics".

was divided by the total number of the 20 questions eliciting a lateral eye movement to provide a measure of proportion of right eye movements (PRE). This measure was correlated with scores for each of the 28 scales of the IPI, for males and females separately, and for all subjects combined. Results of this analysis are presented in Table 2.

Males

Three of the scales show relationships with CLEM direction significant at the 5% level (two-tail test) or better. These scales and their correlations with proportion of right eye movements (PRE) are: Need for external stimulation (-.251), Curiosity-interpersonal (-.239),

Table 2

Correlation Coefficients Between Proportion of Right Eye Movements and Imaginal Process Inventory Scale Scores

Scale	Male	Female	All Subjects
1. Daydream frequency	-.068	.011	-.038
2. Night dream frequency	.037	.008	.028
3. Absorption in DD[a]	.087	.071	.082
4. Acceptance of DD	.099	.161	.129
5. Positive reactions in DD	-.011	.064	.020
6. Frightened reactions to DD	.107	-.157	.020
7. Visual imagery in DD	.189	.236	.209**
8. Auditory imagery in DD	.120	.132	.126
9. Problem solving through DD	.048	.228	.118
10. Present orientation in DD	-.239**	-.069	-.164*
11. Future orientation in DD	-.113	.231	.025
12. Past orientation in DD	-.220*	-.283*	-.236***
13. Bizarre improbable DD	.140	.121	.128
14. Mind wandering in DD	.057	.126	.085
15. Achievement oriented DD	-.112	.364**	.080
16. Hallucinatory vividness of DD	.051	-.159	-.022
17. Fear of failure in DD	-.018	-.323**	-.152
18. Hostile aggressive DD	-.038	-.202	-.102
19. Sexual DD	.174	-.048	.080
20. Heroic DD	.048	.189	.099
21. Guilt DD	.093	-.358**	-.113
22. Curiosity--interpersonal	-.239**	.184	-.075
23. Curiosity--impersonal/mechanical	.139	.305**	.193**
24. Boredom	-.009	-.185	-.077
25. Mentation rate	-.031	.297*	.121
26. Distractibility	-.030	.115	.015
27. Need for external stimulation	-.251**	.045	-.116
28. Self-reporting tendencies	.044	-.143	-.033

a DD = Daydreams
* P < .10
** P < .05
*** P < .01

and Present orientation in daydreams (-.239). A fourth scale, Past orientation in daydreams (-.220) is significantly related to PRE at the 8% level. Taking into account the negative sign of these correlations, the results mean that right movers tend to score lower than left movers on Need for external stimulation, Curiosity-interpersonal, Present orientation in daydreams, and Past orientation in daydreams.

The left mover tends to score higher on Need for external stimulation. Items correlating with this scale include: "I like to spend my holidays where there are all kinds of things to do and places to go." and "I do not like to do dangerous or daring things" (scored negatively). The left mover male tends to score higher on Curiosity--interpersonal. This scale measures curiosity about people and their relationships. Positive responses to items such as the following are related to higher scores on this scale: "I often notice a person at a restaurant or bar and wonder what he does for a living or what kind of person he is", and "I often wonder about the life of a person I happen to see standing at the window of an apartment building".

The left mover tends to score higher on Present orientation in daydreams and Past orientation in daydreams. The Present orientation scale deals with a primary focus in daydreaming on the current events in one's life. Items correlating with this scale include: "I am very much concerned with the present in my daydreams", and "My thoughts are never far removed from my everyday problems". The Past orientation scale taps the degree to which reminiscence plays a role in daydreaming. Items showing good correlation with this scale include: "I sometimes daydream about people and places I was familiar with when I was younger", and (keyed negatively) "I do not think about scenes from my earlier years".

Females

Four of the scales show relationships with PRE, that is, the tendency to make right CLEMS. Of the four scales showing relationships significant at the 5% level (two-tail), two yield positive correlations and two yield negative correlations. These scales and their correlations with PRE are: Achievement oriented daydreams (.364), Curiosity--impersonal/mechanical (.305), Guilt daydreams (-.358), and Fear of failure in daydreams (-.323). Two other scales approach significance (p equal to .056 and .070 respectively). A scale with a positive relationship to right CLEMS is the Mentation rate scale (.297), and another correlating negatively with PRE or right CLEMS is the Past orientation in daydreams scale (-.283). This means that females tending to make right CLEMS score higher on scales measuring Achievement oriented daydreams, Curiosity--impersonal/mechanical, and Mentation rate. Females tending toward left CLEMS score higher on Guilt daydreams, Fear of failure daydreams, and Past orientation in daydreams.

Right moving females tend to score higher on Achievement oriented daydreams, Curiosity--impersonal/mechanical, and Mentation rate. The Achievement oriented daydream scale taps an important area of daydream content, the achievement of difficult tasks or outstanding accomplishment. Items correlating with this scale include: "In my idle thoughts I picture myself receiving an award for outstanding achievement in my field", and "I imagine receiving the highest honor in my field of work".

The Curiosity--impersonal/mechanical scale was designed as a contrast to the Curiosity--interpersonal scale (discussed above as a scale that male left movers score higher on). It taps interest in the world of natural or mechanical structures in contrast to interest in human relationships. Items correlating with scores on this scale include: "I often wonder about how a particular mechanical or electrical device works", and "I have always liked to take things apart to see what makes them work."

The Mentation rate scale was designed to tap the degree to which active thoughtfulness or awareness of considerable ongoing mental activity is associated with daydreaming. It is a measure of mental activity as represented by items such as the following: "My mind is always on the go," and "My mind is always active."

The next three scales to be considered correlate negatively with proportion of right eye movements, and therefore are scales on which left movers tend to do better. The Guilt daydream scale may be described as representing a facet of daydreaming tied to obsessional rumination, self doubt and guilt. Items correlating with the Guilt daydream scale include: "In my daydreams I am always afraid of being caught doing something wrong," and "I imagine myself running away from someone who is going to punish me."

The Fear of failure in daydreams scale taps a profound self-doubting "tortured self-concern" in daydreams. Items correlating with this scale include: "I imagine myself failing those I love," and "In my daydreams I lose my job and am financially in debt and feel worthless."

The Past orientation in daydreams scale has already been discussed in the results section for males where it was also found that male left movers tended to score higher on this scale.

Combined Sample of Males and Females

In order to study the relationship between CLEM direction and the IPI scales the male and female samples were combined. Correlations between proportion of right eye movements and scale scores were significant at the 5% level (two-tail) for three scales and at the 9% level for one scale. The four scales and their correlations with proportion of right eye movements are Past orientation in daydreams (-.236), Visual imagery in daydreams (.209), Curiosity--impersonal/mechanical (.193), and Present orientation in daydreams (-.164).

Considering Past and Present orientation in daydreams, it has already been shown that Past orientation was characteristic of both male and female left movers. Male and female left movers both tend to score higher on the Present orientation in daydreams scale but this is significant only for the males and for the sexes combined.

With respect to the Visual imagery in daydreams scale, the right mover males and females both show higher scores on this scale and though the correlations for each sex (.189 for males and .236 for females) do not attain significance at the 5% level, the correlation for the combined sample (.209) does reach that level of significance. This scale was designed as a measure of the degree to which a visual imagery component is important in daydreaming. Items correlating with this scale include: "Visual scenes are an important part of my daydreams," and "The pictures in my mind seem as clear as photographs."

The Curiosity--impersonal/mechanical scale yielded higher scores for right moving males and females, with the correlation being statistically significant (5% level) only for females and for the combined sample.

DISCUSSION

The results of this study indicate that there is a relationship between direction of CLEMS and response to the scales of the Imaginal Processes Inventory (IPI). Of the 28 scales ten are significantly (10% level, two-tail) related to CLEM direction either for males, females, or the total sample.

Most of the scales of the IPI refer to daydreaming; one refers to night dreaming, and seven are related to general aspects of curiosity, attention, and self-reporting tendency. Considering the results on daydreaming first, it appears that the male left mover shows a greater inclination toward a past or present orientation than does the male right mover. There are some statistically insignificant trends suggesting more visual imagery in daydreams, more bizarre improbable daydreams, and more sexual daydreams for male right movers than for male left movers (Table 2).

Results for the non-daydreaming scales show a greater need for external stimulation and greater interpersonal curiosity for male left movers than for male right movers. There is an insignificant trend toward greater impersonal/mechanical curiosity for male right movers. This combination of results suggests a bias toward extraversion in male left movers.

There are more marked differences between female right and left movers in the daydreaming scales. The daydreams of female left movers appear to be loaded with negative affect in light of their higher scores on scales concerned with fear of failure in daydreams and guilt in daydreams. Like the left mover male, the female left mover shows a greater orientation to the past in daydreams. In contrast to the negative affect of the female left mover is a more positive tone in the daydreams of female right movers as seen in the higher scores on the scale of Achievement oriented daydream.

There are some statistically insignificant relationships suggesting more frightened reactions to daydreams, more hostile aggressive daydreams, and greater hallucinatory vividness in daydreams for female left movers. These trends confirm the negative affect that seems characteristic of daydreams of female left movers. Insignificant trends for female right movers include greater acceptance of daydreams, more visual and auditory imagery in daydreams, more use of daydreams in problem solving, more future orientation in daydreams, more bizarre improbable daydreams, more mind wandering, and more heroic daydreams. There is an absence of negative affect in the daydreams of female right movers.

The difference between female right and left movers in the degree of negative affect associated with daydreaming is supportive of the hemispheric model of CLEM direction where right moving is associated with left hemisphericity and left moving with right hemisphericity. There is a body of research (Flor-Henry, 1976; Hommes and Panhuysen, 1971; Rossi and Rosadini, 1967) suggestive of an association between negative emotion and the right hemisphere, and between positive emotion and the left hemisphere.

On the nondaydreaming scales the female right mover tends to higher scores on the Curiosity--impersonal/mechanical scale and the Mentation rate scale. This curiosity scale has been described (Singer and Antrobus, 1972) as reflecting "male" interests or curiosity. This raises the intriguing possibility that CLEM direction, and possibly hemisphericity, may be related to a masculinity-femininity dimension independent of the biological dichotomy. Following this line, the tendency for male left movers to score higher on interpersonal curiosity could mean a higher degree of "feminine" interests for male left movers.

The higher mentation rate scores for female right movers can be interpreted as a greater tendency for these females to be "manic" in their thinking. The combination of manic type thinking with absence of negative affect in female right movers, combined with a left hemisphericity, and the presence of negative affect in those with right hemisphericity, may have a bearing on theoretical approaches to manic-depressive conditions in terms of hemispheric dynamics (Flor-Henry, 1976).

With male and female subjects combined the right movers tend to score higher on visual imagery in daydreaming, and the left movers tend to have daydreams more characterized by past and present orientation. There are non-significant trends toward higher scores on the Fear of failure in daydreams scale for left movers, and toward higher scores on scales measuring Acceptance of daydreaming, Auditory imagery in daydreaming, and Bizarre improbable daydreaming for right movers. On the nondaydream scale of Curiosity--impersonal/mechanical the right movers tend to score higher.

The scales on the original IPI were given their names largely on the basis of face validity. It might be argued that the factor structure based on the interrelationships between the IPI items might throw more light on the information presented by responses to the items. Giambra (1980) has recently reported on an extensive factor analytic study of these scales and items. He describes the results in terms of these scales and items. He describes the results in terms of 33 factors. When these factors are named they come surprisingly close to the names of the 28 scales originally named by Singer and Antrobus.

For seven of the ten scales found related in some way to CLEM direction (10% level) there is practically complete overlap between the scale name and Giambra's factor name based largely on the items constituting the IPI scales. These scale names and the associated factor names are Present orientation in DD (the Present in daydreams), Past orientation in DD (Past in daydreams), Achievement oriented DD (Achievement oriented daydreams), Curiosity--interpersonal (interpersonal curiosity: intimate-private), Curiosity--impersonal/mechanical (Curiosity: impersonal/mechanical), Mentation rate (Mentation rate), and Need for external stimulation (Need for external stimulation: activity).

Two of the scales on which female left movers tend to score higher, the Fear of failure DD and the Guilt DD scales collapse in Giambra's factor analysis to one scale that he calls "Negative or guilt attached daydreaming". This factor seems to capture the negative affect associated with the daydreams of female left movers.

The Visual imagery in DD scale becomes part of a factor called "Daydream imagery-Visual-Auditory." Though the Auditory imagery in DD scale was not significantly related to CLEM direction, it was correlated positively with proportion of right eye movements for both males and females just as was the Visual imagery in DD scale.

CLEM direction is clearly related to various aspects of daydreaming and other dimensions tapped by the IPI scales. The relationships seem to interact with the sex of subject. To the extent that CLEM direction is an indicator of hemisphericity, the present results offer a number of leads to our understanding of the relationships between hemispheric functioning, individual differences in hemispheic dynamics, and a number of cognitive dimensions.

REFERENCES

Bakan, P. Hypnotizability, laterality of eye-movements and functional brain asymmetry. Perceptual and Motor Skills, 1969, 28, 927-932.

Bakan, P. The eyes have it. Psychology Today, April 1971, 64-67 and 96.

Bakan, P. Two streams of consciousness: a typological approach. In K. S. Pope and J. L. Singer (Eds.), The stream of consciousness: Scientific investigations into the flow of human experience. New York: Plenum, 1978.

Bakan, P. Imagery, raw and cooked: A hemispheric recipe. In J. E. Shorr, J. Connella, G. Sobel, and P. Robin (Eds.), Imagery: Its many dimensions and applications. New York: Plenum, 1980.

Bogen, J. E. The other side of the brain. II: An appositional mind. Bulletin of the Los Angeles Neurological Societies, 1969, 34, 135-162.

Day, M. E. An eye-movement phenomenon related to attention, thought and anxiety, Perceptual and Motor Skills, 1964, 19, 443-446.

Ehrlichmann, H., and Weinberger, A. Lateral eye movements and hemispheric asymmetry: a critical review. Psychological Bulletin, 1978, 85, 1080-1101.

Flor-Henry, P. Lateralized temporal-limbic dysfunction and psychopathology, Annals of the New York Academy of Sciences, 1976, 280, 777-795.

Giambra, L. M. A factor analysis of the items of the Imaginal Processes Inventory. Journal of Clinical Psychology, 1980, 36, 383-409.

Gur, R., and Gur R. Correlates of conjugate lateral eye movements in man. In S. Harnad, Lateralization in the nervous system. New York: Academic Press, 1977.

Hommes, O. R., and Panhuysen, L. Depression and cerebral dominance. Psychiatria, Neurologia, Neurochirurgia, 1971, 74, 259-270.

Meskin, B. B., and Singer, J. L. Daydreaming, reflective thought, and laterality of eye movements. Journal of Personality and Social Psychology, 1974, 30, 64-71.

Rossi, G. F., and Rosadini, G. Experimental analysis of cerebral dominance in man. In F. L. Darley (Ed.), Brain mechanisms underlying speech and language, New York: Grune and Stratton, 1967.

Singer, J. L., and Antrobus, J. S. A factor analytic study of daydreaming and conceptually related cognitive and personality variables. Perceptual and Motor Skills Monograph Supplement, 1963, 17, 187-209.

Singer, J. L. and Antrobus, J. S. Daydreaming, imaginal processes, and personality: A normative study. In P. W. Sheehan (Ed.) The function and nature of imagery. New York: Academic Press, 1972.

IMAGERY, INCUBATION, AND RIGHT HEMISPHERIC LEARNING STYLE AS RELATED TO DIVERGENT THINKING

David Sarnoff

University of Kentucky

Lexington, Kentucky 40502

Psychotherapists such as May (1975), and Rogers (1961) have recognized a relationship between the therapeutic process and the creative process. The goals of therapy are often to facilitate within the client the ability to think to things in new ways, to come up with new ideas that can lead to changes in thoughts, feelings, and behavior. This ability has been called divergent thinking (Guilford, 1967). Examining the creative process may reveal ways to increase divergent thinking in clients. Various writers, such as Haefele (1962), have identified four stages of the creative process, namely, preparation, incubation, illumination, and verification. In preparation the person thinks about a problem, looks at it from many angles, and attemts logical solutions. In incubation, the person puts the problem aside, no longer consciously working on it, allowing some sort of unconscious processing to take place. This leads to the illumination in which a new idea in the mind of the person leads to a satisfying solution to the problem. Verification means making sure that the new idea does indeed lead to a solution that is satisfying. In this process incubation is a key step because one often meets an impass after long periods of preparation with no illumination forthcoming, and once illumination does come, it usually is accompanied by sufficient emotional energy to sustain the person through the stage of verification (Vargiu, 1974). One way of facilitating the incubation stage could be through the use of imagery (Gowan, 1979) that has been considered a link to the unconscious (Watkins, 1977).

There has indeed been evidence that imagery production is related to creativity (Khatena, 1976a; Khatena, 1975; Kubzanski, 1961). The exact nature of that relationship is still unknown. However, Torrance and others (1978) have done studies showing that right hemispheric styles of thinking are associated with greater creativity and also with the ability to produce imagery. Fulgosi and Guilford (1976) conducted a study in which a 20 minute incubation period significantly increased subjects' divergent thinking scores. Leonard and Lindauer (1973) found a positive correlation between participation in creative activities and vividness of imagery. Khatena (1976b) found divergent thinking to be greater in subjects with more autonomous imagery. Hershey & Kearns (1979) found that divergent thinking was enhanced in a group of gifted elementary students by eight weekly half hour guided imagery sessions. Dwindell & Wetherick (1976) found divergent thinking to be positively associated with subjects reports of ability to control imagery and with use of imagery during the divergent thinking task. They did not find a significant relationship between vividness of imagery and divergent thinking.

More research is needed to establish firmly the effectiveness of incubation in increasing quantity and quality of divergent thinking. More research needs to be done in the area of imagery and creativity; conclusions to date are largely speculative, based upon a few studies.

Incubation is seen by the researcher as a time when a process within the mind that helps solve a problem previously worked on at a time when the person is unaware of this process taking place. Further, it is assumed that imagery is a product of the same part of the mind that is capable of unconscious processing. By changing the way in which a person images, one could possibly change the ways in which the incubation process is occurring within that person. More specifically, it is possible that through imagery training incubation will better enhance the quantity and quality of the ideas produced afterwards.

A series of three studies of the relationship between imagery and divergent thinking was conducted to see how imagery could be used to facilitate creativity.

STUDY 1

The specific hypotheses of this study were: (1). Divergent thinking is positively correlated with right hemispheric learning style. (2). The mean scores on the second five minutes of a divergent thinking task (adjusted for scores on the first five minutes), are greater for each of 2 incubation groups than for a control. (3). This mean is higher for a group using imagery during incubation than for a group receiving a lecture on creativity during incubation. (4). There is an interaction between the imagery treatment and right hemispheric learning style; the treatment is more effective for subjects with high right-hemispheric learning style.

Method

Subjects. Subjects were 70 student volunteers, mostly freshmen and about half male and half female, in introductory psychology labs at the University of Kentucky.

Materials. Right hemispheric learning style was measured using Torrance's (1978) Your Style of Learning and Thinking scale.

Divergent thinking was measured using a uses task from Torrance's (1966) Tests of Creative Thinking. In this study the task was thinking of uses for tin cans.

Procedure. Three groups of subjects were given a ten minute divergent thinking task; one randomly assigned group had a half-hour imagery-training session right in the middle of the ten minutes; another had a lecture on creativity during this incubation period; the control had no incubation during the ten minute task. All subjects had been previously scored on the hemispheric learning style scale. The imagery group were told during incubation to close their eyes, relax by taking deep breaths, and look into their imaginations. There were three separate imagery "trips"; one to a beautiful outdoor place of their choice, one flying into space and landing anywhere in the world they chose, and one in a movie theatre with a movie they had never seen before.

Results

The first hypothesis was confirmed. A significant correlation of +.40 was found between right hemispheric learning style and divergent thinking. The analysis of variance for the regression line predicting the total divergent thinking scores from the scores for Right Learning Style yielded an $F\ (1,\ 68)$ of 13.2 ($P < .01$).

The data failed to support Hypotheses 2 and 3. However the adjusted mean divergent thinking scores of Groups 2 and 3 were significantly different ($P < .05$).

The data also failed to support hypothesis 4.

Discussion

The confirmation of Hypothesis 1 adds to the growing body of knowledge about the hemispheric learning styles. There is a positive relationship between preference for right hemispheric learning and thinking, and ability to produce ideas.

The significant difference between the lecture group and the control group could be evidence of the effectiveness of incubation in divergent thinking. The lack of a significant difference between the control and imagery groups could be explained by a tiring hypothesis: The use of the right hemisphere in producing images tired that hemisphere, making the incubation less effective.

The lack of a significant interaction between right hemispheric learning style and the treatments leaves us uncertain as to how these variables are related, if at all. It is possible that with more refined measuring instruments, and a larger subject sample, an interaction could be detected.

STUDY 2

The purpose of this study was to explore the relationships among five variables; amount of imagery, vividness of imagery, autonomy of imagery, right hemispheric learning style, and divergent thinking. The aim of this study was not to manipulate imagery in any way, but rather to investigate the types of imagery already present, in order to gain greater understanding of the cognitive processes involved.

The hypothesis of this study was that the variables would be related according to the path diagram model presented in Figure 1.

Figure 1

Hypothesized Path Model: Study 2

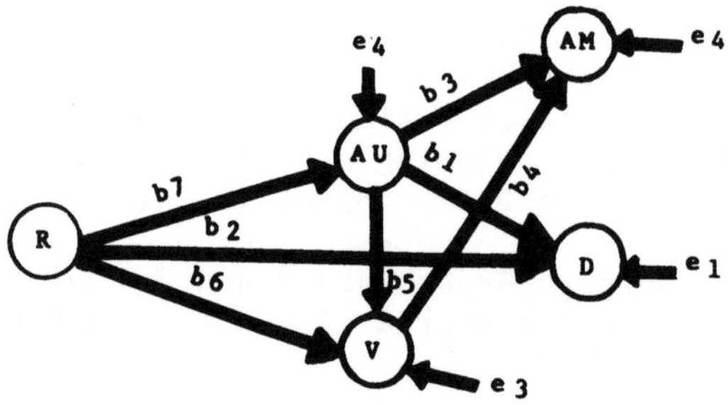

Structural equations:

R = Right Hemispheric Learning Style

AU = Autonomy of Imagery

V = Vividness of Imagery

AM = Amount of Imagery

D = Divergent Thinking

$$D = b_1 AU + b_2 R + e_1$$

$$AM = b_3 AU + b_4 V + e_2$$

$$V = b_5 AU + b_6 R + e_3$$

$$AU = b_7 R + e_4$$

The bi are parth coefficients and the ei are error terms. Arrows represent the direction of causality.

This model hypothesized that the right hemispheric style affects divergent thinking directly and also indirectly through its effect on the autonomy of imagery. Autonomy of imagery is hypothesized to be a central feature of imagery affecting the vividness and the amount of imagery experienced. It further hypothesizes that right hemispheric learning style has no direct effect on the amount of imagery and that neither the amount nor the vividness of the imagery affect divergent thinking.

Method

Subjects. Subjects were 35 students in introductory psychology labs at the University of Kentucky. They were mostly freshmen and equally divided between the sexes. Subjects volunteered for the study as an educational experience and received no other incentive to participate.

Materials. Same as in Study 1.

Procedure. Subjects were administered the divergent thinking task as in Study 1. Then they were led through two of the guided imagery trips as in Study 1: first the trip to a beautiful place, then were asked to record the amount of imagery they saw during the session on a scale of one to four (1= 0 - 25%, 2= 26 - 50%, etc.), the vividness of the imagery on a scale of one to ten (1= very dim, almost imperceptable, 10= extremely vivid, almost like real life), and the autonomy of the imagery on a scale from one to ten (1 = stuck, no motion, need to force the images to change, 10 = images flow freely as if they have a life of their own).

Results

The correlations among the five variables are presented in Table 1. The finding of Study 1 that divergent thinking is positively correlated with right hemispheric learning style was replicated. The correlation between autonomy of imagery and divergent thinking approached significance. Five additional significant correlations were found.

The hypothesized path model was tested for "goodness of fit" by the LISREL program (Joreskog, 1978). A chi square of 3.32 was obtained with an associated probability level of .35 which means that the model can not be rejected on the basis of this data.

The hypothesis that the paths from R to AM, from V to D, and from AM to D are nonexistent was tested using a t test, results of which are presented in Table 2. Since none of the t values obtained were in the critical region, the hypothesis that these paths are 0 can not be rejected on the basis of this data.

Table 1. Correlations: Study 2

	D	AM	V	AU
AM	-.07			
V	.02	.53**		
AU	.27+	.51**	.47**	
R	.36*	.18	.35*	.35*

Note. D = Divergent thinking; AM = Amount of Imagery; V = Vividness of Imagery; AU = Autonomy of Imagery; R = Right Hemispheric Learning Style.

+P = .058

*P < .05

**P < .005

Table 2. T-Test: Study 2

Path	Path coefficient	Standard Error	t
R → AM	.08	.15	.52
AM → D	.24	.19	1.25
V → D	.13	.19	.69

Note. Critical value of t = 1.96 (P = .05); R = right hemispheric learning style; AM = amount of imagery; D = divergent thinking; V = vividness of imagery.

Discussion

As Duncan (1975) points out, path analysis can not confirm a theory, it only tells us if the model fits the data. Other models could fit as well, and some paths may actually be nonzero but small enough so that their difference from zero is undetected by a small sample. Therefore, these results only indicate that the model proposed is still a possibility given the data obtained. Much more research in this area is needed in order to build a stronger theory, which is what is really required by path analysis. Also, ideally, larger samples should be used.

The notion of causality explicit in path analysis may eventually be found to be too primitive when dealing with elements of consciousness. Is someone's divergent thinking score caused by the autonomy of that person's imagery? Perhaps a notion such as synchronicity (Jung 1973) would be more appropriate. However, it is possible that construction and experimentation with causal models in this area can lead to greater understanding of cognitive processes, just as Newtonian physics advanced our understanding of physical reality even though it was later replaced with Einstein's theory of relativity (Kuhn, 1970).

The fact that autonomy of imagery was positively correlated with divergent thinking while amount of imagery and vividness of imagery were almost uncorrelated with divergent thinking seems worthy of note and further study. Also of interest is the finding that right hemispheric learning style is positively correlated with every measure except the amount of imagery. This suggests that there are some forms of imagery associated with a left hemispheric learning style. Bakan's (1980) notions of "raw" and "cooked" imagery could be a partial explanation for this.

STUDY 3

The purpose of this study was to investigate the subjective experience of imagery trips of high and low scorers on the divergent thinking task in order to detect any differences for future imagery training in attempts to increase divergent thinking. This was an exploratory study with no specific hypotheses.

Method

Subjects. Subjects were 18 students in a section of the human development course required of undergraduate education majors at the University of Kentucky. They volunteered for the study during regular class time with no incentive for participation other than its educational value. The majority of students in this section were seniors, 13 female and 5 male.

Procedure. Subjects were given the divergent thinking task and the two imagery trips as in Study 2. Then they were asked to write down what they experienced during the second trip, in as much detail as possible, including both what they saw and how they felt.

Results

The four high scores on the divergent thinking task had 15, 15, 14, and 13 ideas. The four low scores had 3, 4, 5, and 6 ideas.

The mean number of ideas was 8.5.

The reports of the imagery experiences of these 8 subjects are as follows:

Subject 1: "A World Travel Fantasy: I dreamed of being transported to a place that was different, exotic, a warm latitude where all was mystery. I fantasized a mid or lost Asian jungle - and a coastal city of forty-50 thousand. There was frequent heavy vegetation - it was a bright sunny day. Most of all I would sense a feeling of being unknown and different from the environment. In this privacy I felt a real comfort - like I could travel on and on not have to know or be known by others. All moves would be of my imagination - totally in my own control."

Subject 2: "I saw the entire U. S., then flew to Italy, to Rome. I saw the ancient ruins, the theatres that once existed. I saw the small tiny cars traveling on narrow roads. Then, I flew to Greece and saw beautiful gardens, full of bright colorful flowers, and sweet smelling trees. I saw how grapes exist and how wine is made. Then, I flew to Egypt and saw the old pyramids. They were large in statue and built of thick rock. I also went and saw the black sea and thrones and palaces where the Kings once lived. I then went to England, where everything appeared hazy and muggy. The people there dressed in an extreme casual manner - rugged old blue jeans that seemed as if they hadn't been washed for a while. The kids were sloppy. The city was dirty. Then I flew home.

Subject 3: "When I first started getting higher it was real. I saw all the land under me Lexington and surrounding areas. The green, the houses, the water, etc. When rising to see the United States and the world I found the difficulty of resisting and see it as it was with everything connected. United States, Africa, Incia, Europe, all these diverse lands, people, and cultures sitting right next to each other. They think they are divided by imaginary lines but ha ha! I can see them all together!!! The jungles, deserts, oceans, cities, all different colors and textures flowing into each other, all at an arms length. I can go and talk with any of these people, savages and presidents."

Subject 4: "At first I got the image of being on a plane very close to the ground but everything still looked like toys. Then I felt like I was flying through cities right down the streets all kinds of cities U. S. and Europe mostly. For some reason I kept drifting off to Iran and having a scared feeling it seemed, very real and clear through it all."

Subject 5: "As I took off, I saw the campus and Kentucky perfectly, then the Country and the broad rims of the world. Then I found myself in a high grass land area with brush and a few trees off in the distance, rolling meadows with animal noises all around. I climbed a tree and a tiger was on top of a branch. I wasn't afraid for it was like I was at peace with nature. Then, I took off from there into a still world forgetting everything even myself and I was still, motionless in a new creation but still traveling onward."

Subject 6: "On to Jerusalem - The wailing was immense - many people praying - Throught the small gate called "The eye of a Needle". Up the way of surroundings, crowded with hungry ragged children - to Golgotha - sad not many visitors there on to Gethsemene pretty garden - it was night when we visited - water dangerous to drink. Out to East gates of the city - when suddenly Mt. of Olives split and great light was all around and Jesus returned to Jerusalem just as prophisized long ago - So happy. All family there."

Subject 7: "I went to visit many people. I went to Venezueala, it was a lot like U. S. I met people I've been wanting to meet. Then I went to Hawaii it was colorful and fun but I go bored. Then I went to see my boyfriend in Indiana. Then to see friends in Tenn., Ariz., Iowa, Ill., Va., and Louisville. When I got to Lexington all the neighbors & my mom were looking at our class in the air. My mom was telling me to get down from there and go to school so. . . Here I am. Everywhere I went was colorful and very realistic. I could feel the hugs from my friends. Before I came home I went to heaven to visit some people. Then I came back. The weather was beautiful - hot - everywhere. When I was up high I saw a clear view of everything."

Subject 8: "I floated rather quickly and effortlessly to Africa and landed in the jungle.., standing up and on my feet... it didn't hurt to land. I sort of floated around while still walking through the tiny trail. I could hear the jungle sounds of monkeys and wild birds. The sun was blocked by the overhanding trees and sticky, large plants had to be waded through. I saw huts and heard people talking. I climbed a tree and tried to swing from a vine (like Tarzan); it was scary and I burned my hands while holding on. I hit the other tree with my left side and made a great bruise on my thigh, I then scraped my leg and arm trying to get a foothold. Then I fell and landed in a bunch of dried grass and had the wind knocked out of me. I was gasping for breath when I was called back to school. . . I came back very quickly and was very tired. It took even less effort to come back than to go."

The report of a subject who scored around the average on the divergent thinking task (8 ideas) follows:

Subject 9: "Exploration of the world was very interesting. I traveled to Scotland where I explored the landscape which was lush and green. From there I went to London, Germany, Greece and Russia. I saw several different landscapes and different people. These people brought me to my homeland where I met with old friends that I hadn't seen for a while. Then the journey brought me back to an evaluation of myself and where I stand in relation to my world."

Discussion

A common theme appears to emerge upon reading these reports. The first four from the low scorers on divergent thinking appear to be uninvolved in any interaction with the images; they are "unknown and different", sightseeing, "at an arms length," and "drifting off to Iran and having a scared feeling". In contrast the second four reports from the high scorers on the divergent thinking task appear to indicate greater involvement with the images in that the subjects image themselves as being actively interacting with the other images. They are climbing a tree, swinging on a vine, or hugging friends. Subject 6 seems to be an exception in as far as physical interaction with the images is concerned. However she appears to be intensely emotionally and spiritually involved in the scene.

It is possible that training people to become more actively involved in interacting with their image worlds could increase their divergent thinking ability. It is possible that theraputic techniques such as Gestalt (Perls, 1969) and Psychosynthesis (Assagioli, 1971) which get people actively involved in interaction with their images owe their success in part to a cognitive process where by these interactions lead to a greater divergency of thoughts and feelings which in turn leads to better creative solutions to life problems.

It is interesting to note that subject 9, an average scorer on the divergent thinking task reported that the journey brought her to "an eveluation of myself and where I stand in relation to my world."

DISCUSSION

Tentative Conclusions

The best type of imagery for the purpose of divergent thinking appears to be that which is autonomous and which involves interaction between the self-image of a subject and the other images. This imagery is probably best applied not during an incubation period but rather at some earlier time in preparation for a creative-project.

Vividness and autonomy of imagery appear to be related to right hemispheric learning styles but amount of imagery appears to be unrelated to hemispheric learning style.

Suggestions for Future Research

While much evidence exists for the construct "right hemispheric learning style," there is little physiological evidence that various validity measures are in fact accompanied by specific brain states. Studies such as Study 2 could be extended to include measures such as EEG records of the two hemispheres of the brain and blood flow in the two halves of the brain. More variables taken from the phenomenological accounts of subjects' imagery could also be included. As Pelletier (1978) points out, a combination of physiological and phenomenological approaches is necessary in order to form a holistic understanding of human consciousness.

Clinical Implications

Cole and Sarnoff (in press) have outlined how creativity and counseling are related both in terms of process and techniques, and have described the fundamental importance of divergent thinking. Thus, results of these studies should be of interest to clinicians.

Study 3 seems to point toward encouraging clients to become more involved in interaction with their images. Watsins (1977, P. 114) lists a number of types of involvement with imagery, some of which may prove to be even more fruitful in terms of stimulating divergency.

The implication of Study 2, that autonomy is one of the central features of imagery leading to diversity, leads one to suspect that in certain clinical contexts clients should be encouraged to allow whatever images arise to flow freely through the mind rather than attempting to consciously manipulate them in some way.

The results of Study 1 may indicate that during periods of incubation clients should be encouraged to avoid imagining and become involved in some external activity. Clinicians should learn to become sensitive to the stages of creativity in order to appropriately apply imagery techniques.

REFERENCES

Assagioli, R. Psychosynthesis. New York: Viking, 1971.

Bakan, R. Imagery, raw and cooked: A hemispheric recipe. In J. E. Shorr, J. Connella, G. Sobel, and P. Robin (Eds.), Imagery: Its many dimensions and applications. New York: Plenum, 1980.

Cole, H. P., and Sarnoff, D. Creativity and counseling. Personnel and Guidance Journal (in press).

Duncan, O. D. Introduction to structural equation models. New York: Academic Press, 1975.

Durndell, A., and Wethernick, N. E. The relation of reported imagery to cognitive performance. British Journal of Psychology, 1976, 67, 501-506.

Fulgosi, A., and Guilford, J. P. Short term incubation in divergent thinking production. Assessing creative growth: Measured changes book two. Great Neck, New York: Creative Synergetic Associates, 1976.

Gordon, R. An investigation into some of the factors that favor the formation of stereotyped images. British Journal of Psychology, 1949, 39, 156-157.

Gowan, J. C. The production of creativity through right hemisphere imagery. Journal of Creative Behavior, 1979, 13, 39-51.

Guilford, J. P. The nature of human intelligence. New York: McGraw-Hill, 1967.

Haefele, J. W. Creativity and innovation. New York: Reinhold, 1962.

Hershy, M., and Kearns, P. The effect of guided fantasy on the creative thinking and writing ability of gifted students. The

Gifted Child Quarterly, 1979, 23, 71-77.

Joreskog, K., and Sorbom, D. Lisrel IV: Analysis of linear structural relationships by the method of maximum likelihood. Chicago: National Educational Resources, 1978.

Jung, C. G. Synchronicity. Princeton, New Jersey: Princeton University Press, 1973.

Khatena, J. Major directions in creativity research. The Gifted Child Quarterly, 1976, 20, 216-228. (a)

Khatena, J. Autonomy of imagery and production of original verbal images. Perceptual and Motor Skills, 1976, 43, 24-266. (b)

Khatena, J. Creative imagination imagery. Gifted Child Quarterly, 1975, 19, 149-160.

Khatena, J., and Torrance, E. P. Thinking creatively with sounds and words: Norms technical manual. Lexington, Mass.: Personnel Press, 1973.

Kubzanski, R. Creativity, imagery, and sensory deprivation. Acta Psychologia, 1961, 19, 507-508.

Kuhn, T. The Structure of scientific revolutions. Chicago: Chicago University Press, 1970.

Leonard, G., and Lindauer, M. Aesthetic participation and imagery arousal. Perceptual and Motor Skills, 1973, 36, 977-978.

May, R. The courage to create. New York: Norton, 1975.

Pelletier, K. R. Towards a science of consciousness. New York: Dell, 1978.

Perls, F. Gestalt therapy verbatim. Lafayette, California: Real People Press, 1969.

Rogers, C. On becoming a person. Boston: Houghton Mifflin, 1961.

Silveira, J. M. Incubation: the effect of interruption timing and length on problem solution and quality of problem processing. Dissertation Abstracts International, 1972, 32, 5500B.

Torrance, P. E. et. al. Your style of learning: Revised norms-technical manual. Princeton, N. J.: Personnel Press, 1966. (a)

Torrance, P. E. Torrance tests of creative thinking: directions manual and scoring guide. Princeton, N. J.: Personnel Press, 1966. (b)

Vargiu, J. A model of creative behavior. San Francisco: Psychosynthesis Institite, 1974.

Watkins, M. Waking dreams. New York: Harper Colophon, 1977.

THE INTERACTIVE EFFECTS OF IMAGERY LEARNING STRATEGY AND ORIGINALITY ON LEARNING AND LONG-TERM RETENTION

Ruey-Yun Horng

University of Georgia

Athens, Georgia

The purpose of this study was to investigate the interactive effects of imagery learning strategies and students' originality in learning and retention. Imagery learning strategies in this study were: experimenter-provided (EP), subject-generated (SG), and control group (CG). In the experimenter-provided imagery learning condition, the experimenter provided the students with linking images of the paired-associate list and were instructed to use such images to help them learn. Students in the self-generated imagery learning condition were instructed to form a linking image of their own to the stimulus and response term pairs of the paired-associate list. Students in the control group received no imagery instruction. They were simply told to study the paired-associate list for later recall.

Learning, accordingly to information-processing theory (e.g., Gagné, 1974, 1977), is a process composed of transformations of inputs to outputs. External stimuli, after being perceived by the indivudual, are transformed and stored temporarily in short-term memory. If this information is not further transformed into a proper entity and stored in the long-term memory, it will be lost in a few seconds. This information transformation, or coding process, is essential in learning acquisition and memory retrieval.

Paivio's (1971) dual-processing theory proposed two channels by which external stimuli are encoded in memory. One is a verbal, symbolic process; the other is a nonverbal, imagery process. Information could be coded in the memory into verbal or nonverbal representation. Whether it is verbal, symbolic, or nonverbal-imaginal, a representation is a meaningful transformation of the original perceptual inputs. It is often the essence and meaning of the original stimulus perceived by the organism.

Imagery is the nonverbal representation of concrete objects, predominantly visual in nature. It deals with concrete, parallel, and spatial relationships. Verbal, symbolic representation deals with abstract, sequential relationships.

Studies have shown that pictures and concrete words are better memorized than abstract words (e.g., Dilley & Paivio, 1968; Reese, 1970; Levin & Kaplan, 1972). For Paivio, this is because pictures and concrete words can be coded in memory in both imaginal and verbal representations while abstract words can only be coded in abstract, symbolic representations. Dually coded materials can be better retained in memory and more easily retrieved from memory.

It has been consistently found that an imagery learning strategy can enhance paired-associate learning (PAL) (Paivio, 1971; Reese, 1970). In PAL tasks, subjects were very often instructed to link the stimulus term and the response term with an image (e.g., Levin & Kaplan, 1972; Taylor & Joesberger, 1973; Bugelski, 1974) or they were given images (pictures or verbal depiction) of the pairs (e.g., Paivio & Yarmey, 1966; Clarkson, Haggith, Tierney, & Kobanisigawa, 1973).

For example, Clarkson et al. (1973) compared SG and EP imagery learning strategies. They found 4th and 6th graders learned better in the SG condition than in the EP condition. Kerst and Levin (1973) found children performed better in both SG and EP conditions when compared to the CG but EP and SG did not differ from each other. However, the SG group showed greater variability. Kerst and Levin suggested that there might be individual differences in producing linking images. Persons who are better at generating images could benefit more from SG imagery instruction. Their performance of those who are not natural imagers could be as good as imagers if images were provided from outer sources.

The question then was why some people are better at producing linking images. One possible answer is that they are more creative and original in thinking.

Torrance (1966, 1974) describes originality as the ability to produce ideas that are away from the obvious, commonplace, banal, or established. Mednick (1962) defines the creative thinking process as the forming of associative elements into new combinations that either meet specific requirements or are in some way useful. The more mutually remote the elements of the new combination, the more creative the process.

It seems intuitively true that in order to generate an image to mediate two unrelated terms for a PAL task, a certain degree of creativity has to be at work. For example, Brown (1973) did find that highly creative persons' PAL was not affected by the strength of association between stimulus term and response term, whereas low creative persons' was.

Inspired by previous findings, the present study was designed to test individual differences (originality) in employing imagery learning strategies (SG, EP, & CG). It was predicted that highly original persons probably are more adept at finding associative images for the PAL materials; thus, they would perform better in the SG imagery condition. However, their superiority will even off when associative images are provided by the experimenter for everyone in the EP condition. Imagery effects in facilitating learning and retention were expected to appear when comparing PAL performance (learning and retention) of imagery groups with the control group.

METHOD

Subjects

One hundred seventy-five male eighth graders were given the Torrance Test of Creative Thinking, Figural Form B (Torrance, 1974). Based on their median score on originality, the top 75 (score range: 75 to 25, $\bar{X} = 36.55$) and bottom 75 (score range: 23 to 4, $\bar{X} = 14.683$) people were selected and randomly assigned to subject-generated imagery learning strategy (SG), experimenter-provided imagery learning strategy (EP), and the control group (CG).

Design

This was a 3 (SG, EP, & CG) x 2 (high originality and low originality) factorial design. Two independent variables were imagery learning strategy and originality. The dependent variables were learning and retention.

Instruments and Materials

One hundred ninety-two Chinese compound nouns (Chuang, 1975) were rated with a 7-point scale by 21 eighth graders according to their imagery arousing capacity (Horng, 1976). Sixty high-imagery nouns (imagery value range: 6.810 to 4.952, $\bar{X} = 5.587$) were selected and randomly paired with the restriction of no obvious association within pairs and between consecutive pairs. Three lists of these thirty pairs were formed by alternating the order of pairs. Each pair was written on a 25 cm x 15 card. The lists were then tape-recorded at 6-second intervals by a male voice.

Procedure

Students in different imagery learning conditions were assigned to different rooms. They were given the written instructions first. After making sure that everyone understood the instructions, experimenters (male graduate students) started the taped PAL tasks. There were three practice PAL pairs before the real learning tasks. While the tape was reading the noun-noun pairs, the experimenter displayed the written cards to the subjects. Short sentences describing the content of imagery for the noun-noun pairs were embedded in the EP group's tape. For example, the noun-noun pairs read to the SG and CG students were as follows: "Camping-Answer, Book-Infant, Army-Animal,..."; while the noun-noun pairs read to the EP students were: "Sunshine-Blacksmith, a blacksmith was working in the sunshine; Car-Butter, a car was loaded with butter; Grain-Test, grain was the content of the test,..." (All the materials were in Chinese. The examples given here are the English translation.) Three study-test trials were given with one minute intertrials intervals. A 3-minute recall test immediately followed each learning session. Subjects were instructed to put down the response item that was paired to the stimulus item in the learning list. A posttest questionnaire was given after these three learning-testing trials. One week afterwards, a surprise test was given to measure retention. Testing time was 5 minutes.

Data Analysis

Learning scores were the sum of correct responses in three immediate recall tests. Retention scores were the number of correct responses in the surprise test. A 3 x 2 analysis of covariance with intelligence as the covariate was done on learning and retention, respectively.

RESULTS

Because students' intelligence scores differed significantly between the high originality group and the low originality group ($F(1, 114) = 8.457$, $p < .01$), it was decided that subjects' IQ scores from Mental Ability Test for Junior High School (Cheng & Lu, 1973) be used as a covariate in order to statistically control the effects of intelligence on learning and retention.

Learning

Since the test of homogeneity of regression lines was not significant ($F(5, 108) = (1.55)$, the analysis of covariance (ANOCOV) was appropriate to use. Students' adjusted means and standard deviations in learning are listed in Table 1.

Results from ANOCOV (Table 2) showed significant effects of originality ($F(1, 113) = (22.14$, $p < .001)$, imagery ($F(2, 113) = 13.14$, $p < .001$), and the imagery x originality interaction ($F(2, 113) = (4.86$, $p < .01$). Tests of simple main effects were then carried out for the interaction effects.

Table 1. Adjusted Means and Standard Deviations for Learning

Originality	Imagery EP	SG	CG	Total
Hi-Orig				
Mean	66.08	61.93	54.86	60.95
SD	8.67	12.54	15.41	13.86
Lo- Orig				
Mean	66.85	51.79	47.10	55.25
SD	10.89	16.61	17.48	17.52
Total				
Mean	66.47	56.86	50.98	
SD	9.94	16.13	17.03	

Note: Number of subjects in each cell was 20.

Table 2. Summary Table of Analysis of Covariance for Learning

Source	SS	df	MS	F	p
Imagery	4870.73	2	2435.37	13.14	< .001
Originality	4103.56	1	4103.56	22.14	< .001
IxO	1799.84	2	899.92	4.86	< .01
Error	20940.49	113	185.31		

Overall, high originality students recalled more than low originality students. But, Tukey's posteriori comparisons among means (Kirk, 1968) indicated that this superiority was significant only for the SG condition ($q(2, 113) = 3.31$, $p < .05$). There were no originality effects for either the EP or CG group ($q(2, 113) = 2.54$, $p > .05$; $q(2, 113) = (0.25$, $p > .05)$, respectively.

In terms of imagery effects, the EP condition showed highest recall. It was better than the SG group ($q(3, 113) = 4.43$, $p < .01$) and control group ($q(3, 113) = 7.14$, $p < .01$). There was no difference between the control group and the SG group ($q(3, 113) = 2.71$, $p > .05$).

For high originality students, there was no difference between SG and EP conditions ($q(2, 113) = 1.36$, $p > .05$); nor between SG and CG ($q(2, 113) = 2.31$, $p > .05$). The only difference occurred between EP and CG ($q(2, 113) = 3.67$, $p < .05$).

For low originality students, performance was best under the EP condition. Differences between EP and SG were significant ($q(2, 113) = 3.26$, $p < .05$); and differences between EP and CG were even greater ($q(2, 113) = 6.45$, $p < .01$). But, there was no difference between CG and SG ($q(2, 113) = 1.36$, $p > .05$).

These findings suggest that highly original students could use a self-generated imagery learning strategy most successfully, whereas low originality students learned more in the experimenter-provided imagery learning strategy. Although the experimenter-provided imagery learning strategy seemed to be the most effective method, highly original students performed as well in the self-generated imagery strategy. Quite contrarily, even though self-generated imagery strategy proved to be useful for high originality students, it did not produce comparable effects for low originality students. As a matter of fact, for those low in originality, effect of the self-generated imagery strategy was very close to the control group with no imagery instruction at all.

Retention

The test of homogeneity of regression lines was not significant for retention scores ($F(5, 108) = 1.03$). The adjusted means and standard deviations for all imagery x originality conditions are reported in Table 3.

A 3 x 2 ANOCOV indicated the lack of significant main effects for originality (Table 4). This might be a result of small differences of high and low originality students' performances in the EP and CG conditions ($q(2, 113) = .77$, for EP; $q(2, 113) = .84$, for CG). The only condition that was affected by students' level of originality was SG learning strategy ($q(2, 113(= 4.92$, $p < .01$). High originality students' retention was superior to that of the low

Table 3. Adjusted Means and Standard Deviations for Retention

	Imagery			
Originality	EP	SG	CG	Total
Hi-Orig				
Mean	23.77	20.99	16.98	20.58
SD	4.88	5.61	6.47	6.54
Lo-Orig				
Mean	24.81	14.35	15.85	18.33
SD	4.27	7.04	7.39	7.99
Total				
Mean	24.29	17.67	16.41	
SD	4.59	7.48	6.98	

Note: Number of subjects in each cell was 20.

Table 4. Summary Table of Analysis of Covariance for Retention

Source	SS'	df	MS'	F	p
Imagery	1392.43	2	696.22	19.20	< .001
Originality	137.91	1	137.91	3.80	< .10
IxO	311.09	2	155.55	4.29	< .025
Error	4097.77	113	36.26		

originality students.

The source of significant main effects for imagery was coming from the superiority of the EP conditions. Students in the EP condition retained more than those in the SG condition (q(3, 113) = 6.896, p < .01) and CG (q(3, 113) = 8.208, p < .01). However, CG and SG were not different in the amount of correct responses recalled (q(3, 113) = 1.313, p < .05).

The imagery x originality interaction showed that for the high originality group, SG and EP groups' retention did not differ (q(2, 113) = 2.06, p > .05); but, they both showed higher retention over the control group (SG vs. CG: q(2, 113) = 2.97, p < .05; EP vs. CG; q(2, 113) = 5.03, p < .01).

For low originality students, the EP condition proved to be better than the other two conditions (EP vs. SG; q(2, 113) = 7.75, p < .01; SG vs. CG: q(2, 113) = 6.637, p < .01). There was no difference between SG and CG (q(2, 113) = 1.111, p > .05).

Again, self-generated imagery strategy seems to work effectively only if students are high in originality. The effects of self-generated imagery was as great as experimenter-provided imagery for highly original students, while for those students who were low in originality only experimenter-provided imagery retained its efficacy after one-week's interval.

DISCUSSION

According to Mednick's associative theory of creative process, highly creative persons are better at remote associations while low creative persons are more limited by common, stereotyped associations. PAL tasks used in this study and many others resemble associative tasks in that the stimulus terms and the response terms are not obviously associated. In other words, they are low in associative value. To come up with a mediating image to link these two not-directly-related terms requires creative strength.

Inferred from this position, one might expect that the time high creativity people took to form an image for a noun-noun pair might be shorter than what low creativity students would need. Data from the posttest questionnaire tended to support this argument.

In the SG group, 45.4% of the low creativity students reported that 6 seconds were not enough for them to generate an image; only 13.1% of the high creativity students reported so. In the EP condition, 8.6% of the low creativity students and 4.3% of the high creativity students said they did not have enough time. The external source of images seems to reduce this individual difference in producing mediating images.

The results also suggest that high creativity students are able to use imagery strategy spontaneously. Lack of differences between the SG and control groups in learning suggest that highly creative persons might be able to use imagery without being told. In the posttest questionnaire, 55.6% of high creativity students in the control group reported seeing the images of the pairs; while only 27.8% of low creativity students reported so.

However, this spontaneously produced imagery might not have been deliberately used by these high originality students as a memory aid. The lack of realization that using imagery can be a learning strategy might be the reason that high originality students in the control group eventually lost their near equivalence performance to students in the self-generated imagery learning condition after a one-week interval. The other explanation would be that this spontaneously produced imagery was not very stable or not so well planted in memory. These images faded away over time. Failure of students to use imagery purposely as retrieval cues might be another explanation.

For students who were low in originality, EP imagery learning strategy produced the greatest effect. But students in the self-generated imagery condition learned and retained just about what students did in the control group. One possible explanation lies in their low ability (or lack of spontaneity in imagery production) to associate PAL tasks with appropriate images.

Imagery is a kind of ability most of us were born with. However, developmentally, imagery is gradually replaced by verbal processes in cognitive importance. Since the positive effects of imagery in cognitive functioning have been supported, it seems counter-intuitive that we should stress only verbal aspects of our internal processing capacities. As Ferguson (1977) pointed out, current education has relied predominantly on verbal, symbolic processes and nonverbal, imaginal processes are almost foreign to many people. Imagery is a resource within ourselves that could be called upon any time it is necessary. The decisions we have to make are to know when to use it, how to use it, and with whom to use it.

The results from this study suggest that at least imagery is useful in learning acquisition and long-term retention. For highly original individuals, to use imagery is not a difficult task; all they need to be told is the significance of imagery in human learning and memory, and possibly the mechanics of how imagery works in cognitive processes. Once they are introduced to and establish a mind set of imagery mnemonics, they can use it effectively without external assistance. On the other hand, for those low in originality, external assistance is necessary. Construction of learning materials with high imagery value seems more productive with low originality students. It has been found that learning materials' imagery value is an important factor in determining the ease of learning (e.g., Manning & Bruning, 1975; Van der Veur, 1975). For curriculum and instructional material designers, this is a cue to move on.

Another area in which imagery shows a great deal of potential is in teaching children with learning difficulties. In classrooms, learning difficulties are almost always accompanied (if not caused) by verbal problems. Use of high imagery materials probably is a way to get around the hindrance effects of verbal deficits in learning.

One theme that was implicit, yet untapped, in this study is the possible connection between imagery creativity. Often, creative persons have reported seeing images of a breakthrough idea at the most insightful moment (Krueger, 1976). It is likely that imagery served as a synthesized representation of previous efforts and disclosed to the individual configuratively or metaphorically a Gestalt whole of the final product. It is evident from this study that creative persons are more skilled in generating images and using them. Whether this imaginal process is a contributing factor to their creativity is an interesting question awaiting more investigation.

REFERENCES

Brown, A. S. An empirical verification of Mednick's associative theory of creativity. Bulletin of the Psychonomic Society, 1973, 216(B), 429-430.

Bugelskie, B. R. The image as a mediator in one-trial paired-associate learning: III.Sequential functions in serial lists. Journal of Experimental Psychology, 1974, 103, 298-303.

Cheng, F. B., & Lu, J. Y. Mental Ability Test for Junior High School(Form 1). Taipei, Taiwan: Society of Chinese Behavioral Study, 1973. (In Chinese)

Chuang, J. J. The effects of imagery value on paired-associate learning materials. Chinese Journal of Psychology, 1975, 17, 145-150. (In Chinese)

Clarkson, T. A., Haggith, P. A., Tierney, M. C., & Kobasigawa, A. Relative effectiveness of imagery instructions and pictorial interactions on children's paired-associate learning. Child Development, 1973, 44, 179-181.

Dilley, M. G., & Paivio, A. Pictures and words as stimulus and response items in paired-associate learning of young children. Journal of Experimental Psychology, 1968, 6, 231-240.

Ferguson, E. S. The mind's eye: Nonverbal thought in technology. Science, 1977, 197, 827-836.

Gagné, R. M. Essentials of learning for instruction. Hinsdale, Illinois: The Dryden Press, 1974.

Gagné, R. M. The conditions of learning (3rd ed.). New York: Holt, Rinehart and Winston, 1977.

Horng, R. Y. Junior high school students' imagery ratings of Chinese compound nouns. Elementary Education, 1976, 17, 34-37 (In Chinese)

Kerst, S., & Levin, J. R. A comparison of experimenter-provided and subject-generated strategies in children's paired-associate learning. Journal of Educational Psychology, 1973, 65, 300-303.

Kirk, R. E. Experimental Design: Procedures for the Behavioral Sciences, Belmont, California: Brooks/Cole Publishing Company, 1968.

Krueger, T. H. Visual imagery in problem solving and scientific creativity. Derby, Connecticut: Seal, 1976.

Levin, J. R., & Kaplan, S. A. Imaginal facilitation of paired-associate learning: A limited generalization. Journal of Educational Psychology, 1972, 63, 439-432.

Manning, B., & Brunning, R. H. Interactive effects of mnemonic techniques and word-list characteristics. Psychological Reports, 1975, 36, 727-736.

Mednick, S. A. The associative basis of the creative process. Psychological Review, 1962, 69, 220-232.

Paivio, A. Imagery and verbal processes. New York: Holt, Rinehart and Winston, Inc., 1971.

Paivio, A., & Yarmey, A. D. Pictures versus words as stimuli and responses in paired-associate learning. Psychonomic Science, 1966, 5, 235-236.

Reese, H. W. Imagery in children's learning: A symposium. Psychological Bulletin, 1970, 73, 385-421.

Taylor, A. M., & Josberger, M. Elaboration instruction and verbalization as factors facilitating retarded children's recall. Journal of Educational Psychology, 1973, 64, 341-346.

Torrance, E. P. Torrance Tests of Creative Thinking: Norms-technical manual. Bensenville, Illinois: Scholastic Testing Service, 1974.

Van der Veur, B. W. Imagery rating of 1000 frequently used words. Journal of Educational Psychology, 1975, 67, 44-56.

MENTAL IMAGERY AND CREATIVITY

Larry E. Greeson

Miami University

Middletown, OH

INTRODUCTION

Previous investigations have indicated that mental imagery facilitates learning and memory performance in both children and adults (Bower, 1970, 1972; Bugelski, 1970; Flavell, 1970; Higbee, 1979; Paivio, 1969, 1970, 1971; Pressley, 1977). Moreover, imagery processes have been found to be related to other forms of complex human behavior including creativity, intelligence, and general level of cognitive functioning (Anderson, 1978; Forisha, 1975; McKim, 1972; Piaget & Inhelder, 1971; Paivio, 1971, 1978; Shepard, 1978 a,b).

While numerous questions have been raised concerning the nature, function, and significance of mental imagery processes in human learning and cognition (Anderson, 1978; Kieras, 1978; Mandler, 1976; Shepard, 1978b), several important points seem quite clear. First, it has been demonstrated conclusively that imagery processes promote children's learning and memory performance in an often-times remarkable way (Paivio, 1970; Pressley, 1977). Second, it is generally held that imagery serves to complement verbal symbolic representation processes in learning, memory, and cognition (Anderson, 1978; Paivio, 1971; Piaget & Inhelder, 1971; Shepard, 1978b). Finally, there is

---

This paper was made possible, in part, by a William Holmes McGuffey Laboratory School Research Grant. The author would like to express appreciation to the administration and staff of McGuffey School for their support, to Professor Richard J. Hofmann for his expert assistance in data analysis, and to Debbie Bogan and Pat Flannery for their help in data collection.

evidence that mental imagery plays a critical role in the creative processes involved in many diverse fields, ranging from art and architecture to chemistry and molecular science (McKim, 1971; Paivio, 1978; Shepard, 1978a,b).

Each of these findings is of considerable significance for child development and education. While it is obvious that verbal skills are an integral part of children's learning and cognition, it is becoming increasingly apparent that imagery processes provide a potentially powerful alternative mode of symbolic representational functioning for young children, especially those purported to have difficulty in the mastery and use of written language, such as retarded children and children from culturally different backgrounds.

It has been suggested that mental imagery serves to complement verbal symbolic processes by representing, in concrete terms, the more abstract verbal, perceptual, and conceptual relationships involved in children's learning and thinking, and there is considerable evidence that this is the case (Paivio, 1970, 1971, 1974, 1978; Piaget & Inhelder, 1971; Pressley, 1977). Furthermore, the facilitative effects of imagery processes have often been found to equal and even surpass those found with verbal processes, especially with concrete learning materials (Andre & Sola, 1976; Bower & Winzenz, 1970; Levin, Davidson, Wolff & Citron, 1973; Paivio & Foth, 1970). These results are noteworthy in that verbal skills and their relationship to children's learning and thinking have been stressed for many years by educators and psychologists, while the development of imagery skills has, for the most part, been neglected or ignored (Holt, 1964; Piaget & Inhelder, 1971; Reese, 1970; Shepard, 1978a,b).

In general, the facilitative effects of mental imagery have been found to be especially strong when modeling and overt motor activity are involved in the image generation process (Kerst & Levin, 1973; Levin, McCabe, & Bender, 1975; Moynahan, 1978; Varley, Levin, & Severson, 1974; Wolff & Levin, 1972; Wolff, Levin & Longobardi, 1972, 1974). These findings are highly consistent with Piaget's theoretical views (Piaget, 1962; Piaget & Inhelder, 1967, 1969, 1971) concerning the role of observation, action, and internalized imitation in children's mental imagery development. Moreover, the results seem particularly important in light of findings concerning the facilitative effects of modeling on other forms of complex human behavior (Bandura, 1979, 1977).

In addition to improving mediated associative learning performance (Borkowski, Levers & Gruenenfelder, 1976; Brody, 1978; Greeson, Notes 1 and 2; Greeson & Jens, 1977; Simon, Ditrichs & Speckhart, 1975), modeling has been found to influence significantly a wide range of other conceptual behaviors, including concept attainment, conservation, and creativity (Arem & Zimmerman, 1975; Harris & Evans, 1973, 1974; Harris & Hassemer, 1972; Zimmerman & Rosenthal, 1974).

Furthermore, modeling-based instructional programs have proven to be especially effective in promoting the development of conceptual and linguistic skills in children with learning problems, such as retarded children and children from poverty backgrounds (Greeson & Jacobson, 1973; Jacobson, Berger, Bergman, Millham, & Greeson, 1971; Jacobson & Greeson, 1971; Jacobson, Kellogg, Greeson & Bernal, 1971; Mansdorf, 1977).

Despite the importance of such findings, most studies of children's conceptual development have ignored or underemphasized Piaget's focus on the role of social learning variables, such as modeling, observation, and imitation (Zimmerman, Note 3). Moreover, while some studies have related modeling to chilren's mental imagery development or to creativity, little evidence is available concerning the relationship between modeling, mental imagery and creativity, especially as these variables relate to associative learning, an important aspect of children's conceptual and academic development.

The purpose of the present paper is to summarize the results of two experiments that enabled an analysis of the relationships among several variables that have been found to influence children's associative learning (i.e., modeling, mediator use, item presentation mode, and mode of responding) and one index of creativity--the oriinality or uniqueness of the mediating responses generated to promote recall of the item pairs. The experiments were originally conducted in order to evaluate the effects of instructional modeling on the development and use of imagery and verbal mediation processes by children in associative learning. However, anecdotal evidence gained through an informal analysis of the children's imagery and verbal mediating responses proved intriguing in light of the originality of the responses given. The recent publication of several papers relating mental imagery to creativity (Paivio, 1978; Shepard, 1978a,b) and a rereading of Wallach and Kogan's (1965) noteworthy work on intelligence and creativity prompted a reanalysis of these data in terms of the creativeness of the mediating responses generated.

Wallach and Kogan developed an associative conception of creativity, based operationally on the statistical uniqueness or unusualness of responses given, and upon the contention that creative responding would be most likely to occur in game-like as opposed to test-like situations. The present analysis was based on the contention that a relaxed game-like associative learning situation, combined with modeling-based instruction in the use of imagery or verbal mediation processes, would provide a unique perspective concerning the relationship between associative-learning mediator use and creativity. The scoring procedure used in the present analysis was based on the technique developed by Wallach and Kogan (1965). Original or very infrequently occurring responses (those occurring two times or less) were operationally defined as creative. In addition, the mediating responses of children participating in Experiment 2 were classified also according to elaboration type, following a procedure similar to one employed by Buckhalt, Mahoney, and Paris (1976) in an analysis of associative learning mediator efficiency.

EXPERIMENT 1

Experiment 1 was based on a reanalysis and interpretation of data collected as part of an earlier study (Greeson, Note 1). The results of Experiment 1 have been presented previously (Greeson, Note 4) and are reported for present purposes in summary form.

Subjects and Procedure

Twenty-two black and ten white children attending EMR special education classes in a racially mixed, lower-middle-class junior high school participated as subjects. The children were randomly assigned to associative learning conditions that varied factorially according to instructional modeling condition (imagery or verbal mediation), item presentation mode (pictures or words), and mode response (drawn or written).

A study-recall associative-learning task was presented as a 'guessing game' in which the subjects were given modeling-based instruction in the use of mental imagery or verbal mediation responses in order to promote memory of the item pairs. Study trial performance was scored according to the number of creative mediating responses generated (i.e., unique or unusual pictures or sentences connecting the item pairs) and recall performance was evaluated in terms of correct response items given.

Results and Discussion

No significant relationship was in evidence between the subjects' ability to generate creative mediating responses and their recall performance. However, the generation of creative mediation responses was related to each experimental variable. Analyses of variance indicated that while the EMR children were capable of creative responding in both the imaginal and verbal modes of symbolic representation, they generated more creative responses under the verbally based conditions (i.e., word pairs, verbal mediation instruction, and written responses) than the conditions that were non-verbal in nature.

These unexpected findings might simply reflect the effects of age level or intelligence. However, as Greeson and Jens (1977) have suggested, the performance differences found between the imagery and verbal mediation conditions may reflect differential exposure to training and testing experiences favoring verbal learning and language development activities over mental imagery (see also Ford & Renzulli, 1976).

An informal analysis of the children's actual verbal and pictorial mediating responses yielded additional evidence concerning this issue. Table 1 indicates that there was a proliferation of sentence responses that involved similar but not identical prepositional relationships and that did not appear to be very creative in the author's view. The responses presented in Table 2 are consistent with this view. As can be seen, most of the commonly occurring mediating responses also involved prepositional relationships. An analysis of the children's picture responses provides further support for the contetion that a purely quantitative analysis may be misleading. Figures 1 and 2 suggest that, while less prevalent, the children's imagery (i.e., drawn) responses were intuitively more original or creative.

Table 1. Unique or Infrequently Occurring Sentence Responses for the Sample Pair: Fish - Lamp.

The fish jumped over the lamp.
The fish is carrying the lamp.
The lamp is the fish.
The fish is on top of the lamp.
The lamp was by the fish bowl and was fishing in it.[1]
The fish broke the lamp.
The lamp lives in the fish.
The lamp caught on fire and burned the fish.[1]
The fish hit the lamp.
The fish got hit by the lamp.
The fish hid the lamp.
The fish in the tank sees the lamp light.
The fish swallows the lamp.
The fish ate the lamp.
We fish with a lamp.[1]

[1]These responses appeared intuitively creative to the authors.

Table 2. Most Common or Frequently Occurring Responses to Pairs

The candle(is)on top of the flag.	(P=8, S=2).
The sun(is)in the wagon.	(P=24, S=4).
The cat(is)wearing the shirt.	(P=19, S=9).
The ball(is)in the house.	(P=8, S=11).
The fish(is)in the lamp.	(P=8, S=4).
The bird ate(is eating)the cake.	(P=2, S=14).
The apple(is)on the kite.	(P=12, S=14).
The tree(is)in the boat.	(P=8, S=4).
The pencil(is)in the cup.	(P=26, S=12).
The clock(is)on the umbrella.	(P=13, S=2).

Note: Most responses involve prepositional relationships. Numbers in parentheses indicate picture (P) and sentence (S) responses, respectively.

Figure 1. Selected commonly occurring, noncreative, mediating responses. These responses are presented for comparative purposes in reference to corresponding creative responses presented in Figures 2 and 3. Pairs represented are: rabbit-flower, wagon-sun, cup-pencil, and ball-house. Note that while the style and quality of the drawings differ considerably, the relationships remain the same.

While intriguing, the results of Experiment 1 must be viewed as exploratory at best. While providing only an indirect test, the findings support those of Arem and Zimmerman (1976) concerning the relationship between modeling and EMR children's creativity. Whether modeling techniques may be applied effectively to directly enhance creative responding in EMR children's mediated associative learning remains to be seen since the promotion of creativity was not the original intent of the study. Moreover, the particular conditions under which modeling is most efficacious (e.g., type of task, modeling treatment, and creativity) remain unclear.

Figure 2. Selected creative mediating responses generated by EMR junior high school children. Pairs represented: flag-candle, boat-tree, wagon-sun, fish-lamp, clock-umbrella, bird-cake.

EXPERIMENT 2

Experiment 2 was conducted in order to extend the findings concerning modeling, mental imagery, and creativity to a population of nonretarded young children, and to provide a more refined analysis of the mediating responses generated by children during associative learning. Experiment 2 was based on an analysis of associative learning data collected as part of a previous study (Greeson, Note 2).

Subjects and Procedure

The subjects were sixty middle class first and third grade children attending a racially mixed laboratory elementary school located on the campus of Miami University (Ohio). The children were assigned to modeling-based imagery or verbal-mediation instructional conditions and administered a study-recall associative-learning task identical to the one employed in Experiment 1. Item presentation mode and mode of responding were not manipulated in Experiment 2. However, a more refined analysis of the subjects' study-trial mediating responses was applied to these data, based on a classification system similar to ones used in previous studies of mediated associative learning (Buckhalt, et al., 1976). In the present analysis, the children's imagery and verbal mediation responses were assigned to categories involving action verb, locational preposition, or common feature/theme relationships between the paired items.

Results and Discussion

Table 3 presents a summary of mediating responses generated, including creative responses, as a function mediator type and instructional condition. As can be seen, the total number of different mediating responses generated by subjects in the imagery and verbal mediation conditions were almost identical. In general, the verbal mediation condition resulted in the generation of more unique and unusual responses than did the mental imagery condition. However, when the mediating responses were classified according to type, the two conditions resulted in differential levels of responding as a function of the various types of mediators generated.

The imagery-condition subjects were found to generate significantly fewer action-based mediators, and significantly more common-feature/theme-based mediators than expected by chance. By contrast the verbal-mediation condition subjects generated significantly fewer

Table 3. Frequencies of Different Mediating Responses Generated (Creative Responses in Parentheses) as a Function of Condition and Mediator Type.

Mediator Type	Condition			
	Imagery		Verbal Mediation	
Locational	56	(14)**	23**	(2)*
Action	16**	(6)**	68**	(45)**
Common feature/theme	17*	(17)*	4*	(4)*
Other (unclassifiable or inappropriate)	4	(0)	2	(0)
TOTAL:	93	(37)	97	(51)

* p< .05
** p< .01

locational and common-theme/feature mediators but significantly more action-based responses than expected. In regard to creative responding, the imagery condition subjects were found to generate a significantly greater number of creative mediating responses than expected in both the locational and common-feature/theme categories. However, the verbal mediation condition subjects generated significantly more creative responses in the action category but significantly fewer creative responses in the locational and common-feature/theme categories. Application of the large-sample approximation to the Irwin-Fisher Exact Test (Marascuilo & McSweeney, 1977) indicated that the differences between conditions were significant at the .01 level for each mediating response type.

Figure 3. Selected creative mediating responses generated by middle class first and third grade children. Pairs represented: wagon-sun, boat-tree, clock-umbrella, ball-house, bird-cake, cat-shirt, flag-candle, fish-lamp, apple-kite, cup-pencil (man throwing pencil into cup).

Figure 3 (Cont.).

Of the above mentioned differences one appears to be most noteworthy. The imagery-condition subjects generated substantially more common-feature/theme responses than did the verbal-mediation subjects, and 100% of these responses met the criterion for creativity. Most of the responses presented in Figure 3 represent this type of relationship.

It should be added that while the verbal-mediation subjects generated significantly more action-based responses that met the criterion for creativity than did the imagery-condition subjects, many of these responses were highly similar (although not identical) in nature, and did not appear to be very creative in the author's view. This finding, similar to the one involving locational preposition responses in Experiment 1, is exemplified by one subject's redundant use of verbal mediation responses (i.e., "The fish fell on the lamp. The bird fell in the cake. The kite fell on the apple. The pencil fell in the cup."). While involving an uncommon relationship among different item pairs, these sentences appear to reflect a response set that would tend to interfere with rather than facilitate learning.

CONCLUSIONS AND IMPLICATIONS

Taken in conjunction, the present findings demonstrate clearly the relationship between modeling, mental imagery, and creativity in children's associative learning. Both studies indicated that modeling-based instructional procedures, designed to enhance mediated associative learning, were effective in promoting the creative use of imagery and verbal-mediation processes even though they were not designed directly to encourage creative responding. Furthermore, while quantitative differences in mediator use were in evidence favoring verbal mediation over mental imagery, there was a clear indication that imagery processes resulted in more intuitively creative responding.

The present results take on added significance in light of the remarkable similarity in performance found with the two populations of children. Many of the most original responses occurred in both populations (e.g., the sun as wagon wheel, the candle as flag pole). These findings suggest that similar processes may have been operating despite differences in background, age, and IQ level.

Theoretically, the present findings support Wallach and Kogan's (1965) associative view of creativity. In addition, the findings provide support for Zimmerman's contention that modeling and social learning theory is a viable means of clarifying children's cognitive development (Arem & Zimmerman, 1976; Zimmerman & Rosenthal, 1974; Zimmerman, Note 3). Educationally, the present findings should provide guidelines for developing teaching methods and materials based on children's visal as well as verbal learning and thinking.

There is a need to extend the above line of investigation to other populations, tasks, and measures of creativity. However, a further analysis of these variables and processes should provide information of both theoretical and applied significance for psychologists and educators interested in mental imagery.

REFERENCE NOTES

1. Greeson, L. E. Effect of imagery instructions on free recall and associative learning performance by retarded and learning disabled children. Presented at the Gatlinburg Conference on Research in Mental Retardation, Gatlinburg, Tennessee, March, 1978.

2. Greeson, L. E. Instructional modeling and the development of mental imagery skills by grade school children. Presented at the meetings of the American Educational Research Association, Toronto, Canada, April, 1978.

3. Zimmerman, B. J. Can social learning theory live with cognitive constructivism? Paper presented at the Seventh Annual Symposium of the Jean Piaget Society. Philadelphia, Pennsylvania, May, 1977.

4. Greeson, L. E., and Vane, R. J. Mediator use as an index of creativity in EMR children's associative learning. Paper presented at the Galtlinburg Conference on Research in Mental Retardation and Developmental Disabilities, Gatlinburg, Tennessee, March, 1980.

REFERENCES

Anderson, J. R. Arguments concerning representations for mental imagery. Psychological Review, 1978, 85, 249-277.

Andre, T., and Sola, J. Imagery verbatim, and paraphrased questions, and retention of meaningful sentences. Journal of Educational Psychology, 1976, 68, 661-669.

Arem, C. A., and Zimmerman, B. J. Vicarious effects on the creative behavior of retarded and nonretarded childre. American Journal of Mental Deficiency, 1976, 81, 289-296.

Bandura, A. Principles of behavior modification. New York: Holt, Rinehart, & Winston, 1969.

Bandura, A. Social learning theory. Englewood Cliffs, New Jersey: Prentice - Hall, 1977.

Borkowski, J., Levers, S., and Gruenenfelder, T. M. Transfer of mediational strategies in children: The role of activity and awareness during strategy acquisition. Child Development, 1976, 47, 779-786.

Bower, G. H. Analysis of a mnemonic device. American Scientist, 1970, 58, 496-510.

Bower, G. H. Mental imagery and associative learning. In L. Gregg (Ed.), Cognition in learning and memory. New York: Wiley, 1972.

Bower, G. H., and Winzenz, D. Comparison of associative learning strategies. Psychonomic Science, 1970, 20, 119-120.

Brody, G. H. Imagery induction in preschool children: An examination of direct and vicarious influences. Journal of Genetic Psychology, 1978, 132, 307-311.

Buckhalt, J. A., Mahoney, G. J., and Paris, S. G. Efficiency of self-generated elaborations by EMR and nonretarded children. American Journal of Mental Deficiency, 1976, 81, 93-96.

Bugelski, B. R. Words and things and images. American Psychologist, 1970, 25, 1002-1012.

Flavell, J. H. Developmental studies of mediated memory. In H. W. Reese and L. P. Lipsitt (Eds.), Advances in child development and behavior (Volume 5). New York: Academic Press, 1970.

Ford, B. G., and Renzulli, J. S. Developing the creative potential of educable mentally retarded students. The Journal of Creative Behavior, 1976, 10, 210-218.

Forisha, B. D. Mental imagery verbal processes: A developmental study. Developmental Psychology, 1975, 11, 259-267.

Greeson, L. E., and Jacobson, L. I. A behavior modification approach to programming the language acquisition of five- and six-year-old children from poverty backgrounds. In R. D. Rubin, J. P. Brady, and J. D. Henderson (Eds.), Advances in behavior therapy. New York: Academic Press, 1973.

Greeson, L. E., and Jens, K. G. Instructional modeling and the development of visual- and verbal-mediation skills by EMR children. American Journal of Mental Deficiency, 1977, 82, 58-64.

Harris, M. B., and Evans, R. C. Models and creativity. Psychological Reports, 1973, 33, 763-769.

Harris, M. B., and Evans, R. C. The effects of modeling and instructions on creative responses. The Journal of Psychology, 1974, 86, 123-130.

Harris, M. B., and Hassemer, E. G. Some factors affecting the complexity of children's sentences: The effects of modeling, age, sex and bilingualism. Journal of Experimental Child Psychology, 1972, 13, 447-455.

Higbee, K. L. Recent research on visual mnemonics: Historical roots and educational fruits. Review of Educational Research, 1979, 49, 611-629.

Holt, R. R. Imagery: The return of the ostracized. American Psychologist, 1964, 19, 254- 264.

Jacobson, L. I., Berger, S. E., Bergman, R. L., Millham, J., and Greeson, L. E. Effects of age, sex, systematic learning, acquisition of learning sets, and programmed social interaction on the intellectual and conceptual development of preschool children from poverty backgrounds. Child Development, 1971, 42, 1399-1415.

Jacobson, L. I., and Greeson, L. E. Effects of systematic conceptual learning on the intellectual development of preschool children from poverty backgrounds: A follow-up study. Child Development, 1972, 43, 1111-1115.

Jacobson, L. I., Kellogg, R. W., Greeson, L. E., and Bernal, G. Programming the intellectual and conceptual development of retarded children with behavioral techniques. In R. D. Rubin, J. P. Brady, and J. D. Henderson (Eds.), Advances in behavior therapy. New York: Academic Press, 1973.

Kerst, S., and Levin, J. R. A comparison of experimenter-provided and subject-generated strategies in children's paired-associate learning. Journal of Educational Psychology, 1973, 65, 300-303.

Kieras, D. Beyond pictures and words: Alternative information-processing models for imagery effects in verbal memory. Psychological Bulletin, 1978, 85, 532-554.

Levin, J. R., Davidson, R. E., Wolff, P., and Citron, M. A comparison of induced imagery and sentence strategies in children's paired-associate learning. Journal of Educational Psychology, 1973, 64, 306-309.

Levin. J. R., McCabe, A. E. and Bender, B. G. A note on imagery-inducing motor activity in young children. Child Development, 1975, 46, 263-266.

Mandler, J. M. Some problems in the definition and measurement of imagery. Child Development, 1976, 47, 888-889.

Mansdorf, I. J. Learning concepts through modeling: Using different instructional procedures with institutionalized mentally retarded adults. American Journal of Mental Deficiency, 1977, 82, 287-291.

Marascuilo, L. A., and McSweeney, M. Nonparametric and distribution free methods for the social sciences. Monterey, CA: Brooks-Cole, 1977.

McKim, R. H. Experiences in visual thinking. Monterey, CA: Brooks-Cole, 1972.

Moynahan, E. D. Assessment and selection of paired-associate strategies: A developmental study. Journal of Experimental Child Psychology, 1978, 26, 266-267.

Paivio, A. Mental imagery in associative learning and memory. Psychological Review, 1969, 76, 241-263.

Paivio, A. On the functional significance of imagery. Psychological Bulletin, 1970, 73, 358-392.

Paivio, A. Imagery and verbal processes. New York: Holt, Rinehart & Winston, 1971.

Paivio, A. Language and knowledge of the world. Educational Researcher, 1974, 6, 5-12.

Paivio, A. On exploring visual knowledge. In B. S. Randhawa & W. E. Coffman (Eds.), Visual learning, thinking, and communication. New York: Academic Press, 1978.

Paivio, A., and Foth, D. Imaginal and verbal mediators and noun concreteness in paired-associate learning: The elusive interaction. Journal of Verbal Learning and Verbal Behavior, 1970, 9, 384-390.

Piaget, J. Play, dreams, and imitation in childhood. New York: Norton, 1962,

Piaget, J., and Inhelder, B. The child's conception of space. New York: Norton, 1967.

Piaget, J., and Inhelder, B. [The psychology of the child.] (H. Weaver, Trans.). New York: Basic Books, 1969.

Piaget, J., and Inhelder, B. [Mental imagery in the child.] (P. A. Chilton, Trans.). New York: Basic Books, 1971.

Pressley, M. Imagery and children's learning: Putting the picture in developmental perspective. Review of Educational Research, 1977, 47, 585-622.

Reese, H. W. (Chm) Imagery in children's learning: A symposium. Psychological Bulletin, 1970, 73, 358-392.

Shepard, R. N. Externalization of mental images and the act of creation. In B. S. Randhawa and W. E. Coffman (Eds.), Visual learning, thinking, and communication. New York: Academic Press, 1978. (a)

Shepard, R. N. The mental image. American Psychologist, 1978, 33, 125-137.

Simon, S., Ditrichs, R., and Speckhart, L. Studies in observational paired-associate learning: Informational, social, and individual difference variables. Journal of Experimental Child Psychology, 1975, 20, 81-104.

Varley, W. E., Levin, J. R., Severson, R. A., and Wolff, P. Training imagery production in young children through motor involvement. Journal of Educational Psychology, 1974, 66, 262-266.

Wallach, M. A., and Kogan, N. Modes of thinking in young children. New York: Holt, Rinehart, and Winston, 1965.

Wolff, P., and Levin, J. R. The role of overt activity in children's imagery production. Child Development, 1972, 43, 537-547.

Wolff, P., Levin, J. R., and Longobardi, E. T. Motoric mediation in children's paired-associate learning: Effects of visual and tactual contact. Journal of Experimental Child Psychology, 1972, 14, 176-183.

Wolff, P., Lemin, J. R., and Longobardi, E. T. Activity and children's learning. Child Development, 1974, 45, 221-223.

Zimmerman, B. J., and Rosenthal, T. L. Observational learning of rule-governed behavior by children. Psychological Bulletin, 1974, 81, 29-42.

SELF-CONSCIOUSNESS AS A COMPONENT AND CORRELATE OF FOCUSING ABILITY

Don Kuiken

University of Alberta

Edmonton, Canada

The hypothesis guiding this presentation is that nonevaluative self-directed attention, especially toward bodily kinesthetic events, may serve as a source of imagery that is perceived to representationally fit, intensify, and sometimes change those bodily feelings. The phenomenology of this process, called focusing, has been articulated by Gendlin (1978), who has emphasized its apparent role in psychotherapy (Gendlin, 1977; Gendlin, Beebe, Cassens, Klein, & Oberlander, 1968). Regardless of context, however, focusing is a process of imagery-guided or enhanced (Gendlin & Olson, 1970) change in self-feeling, of the conditions for which we have little concrete understanding. The role of self-directed attention in this process is the object of the present study.

Researchers studying imagery processes have often been inclined to emphasize the visual modality (e.g., Cooper & Shepard, 1973; Kosslyn, 1975; Segal & Fusella, 1969). However, Lang (1979) has articulated a model of imagery that conceives the image in its perceptual and somatic patterns and as constituting a prototype for overt behavioral expression, a position compatible with that offered by Gendlin (Note 1). Lang has reviewed evidence that during imaginal recall of a just completed task, sense organ changes and muscular adjustments occur that mimic those involved in the task (cf. Brady & Leavitt, 1966; Shaw, 1940). Similarly, instructions to form an image of an event that occurred remotely in time or to form an original image also produce patterns of sense organ and postural adjustment similar to those that might be expected were the event actually occurring (cf. Jacobson, 1930; Schwartz, Fair, Salt, Mandel & Klerman, 1976).

Although causal relations are difficult to discern in this research, one possibility is that imagery construction involves elaboration of an image with its visual, auditory, and semantic relations, and then the body responds to this imaginal product as if it were in reality present. Despite the simple appeal of this hypothesis and its consistency with the research on physiological responses to remembered and imagined events cited above, there is an alternative, although less well substantiated, possibility. Specifically, it is possible that, on some occasions at least, imagery construction involves the activation of a patterned body movement sequence that then elicits the semantic, visual, and acoustic components that complete the image. For example, one contemporary theory of dreaming (McCarley & Hobson, 1979) proposes that endogenous activation of motor sequences during sleep may produce a kinesthetic image that is then elaborated by visual, auditory, and memorial events to create the dream.

There is some indication that a similar sequence may occur during waking. In his theory of focusing, Gendlin (1978) has suggested that the bodily felt sense of an event may often precede the elaboration of its meaning in words or images. In fact, it is suggested that words or images must be allowed to "emerge" from the bodily feelings to find those that fittingly represent the bodily feeling and this may "carry forward" the affective and motor sequence that is implicit in the original bodily felt sense. This process may be analogous to the tip-of-the-tongue phenomenon (Hart, 1967) in which the feeling of knowing but being unable to say, is followed by the emergence and confident recognition of the right answer.

Hypothetically, focusing can proceed when a particular mode of attention is directed toward the felt complexity of bodily events. This mode of attention must be selective in that it should provide undistracted access to bodily feelings, perhaps especially those of the feeling-related skeletal musculature. At the same time this mode of attention must be global in that it must provide simultaneous access to the complexity of the patterns of bodily felt events as they may be manifest in facial and postural musculature especially.

There is evidence of individual differences in attentiveness to bodily events (Shields & Stern, 1979), although most of this research has largely dealt with attention to autonomic or visceral events rather than kinesthetic events. Some recent research on modes of self-directed attention has isolated a variable called private self-consciousness (Buss, 1980). Private self-consciousness appears predictive of reliance upon internal events, rather than external suggestions or expectations, when people are asked to describe themselves (Froming & Carver, in press; Gibbons, Scheier, Carver & Hormuth, 1979). This sensitivity to internal events is also suggested by research indicating the increases in private self-consciousness produce increases in reported intensity of affect in emotion-inducing situations (Scheier & Carver, 1977). Such evidence led to the hypothesis that private self-consciousness may predict focusing ability. A measure of individual differences in private self-consciousness has been developed by Fenigstein, Scheier, and Buss (1975). In addition to the relationships described above, that this variable might correlate with focusing ability was suggested by evidence of a moderate correlation between the Private Self-Consciousness Scale and a revision of the Paivio Imagery Inventory (Turner, Scheier, Carver & Ickes, 1978). This correlation suggested that not only might persons high in Private Self-Consciousness attend directly to internal bodily felt events, they might also allow that attentional mode to be a source of imagery for representing feelings during the focusing process.

The research reported above also indicates the importance of differentiating private self-consciousness from public self-consciousness (Buss, 1980). Public self-consciousness may be understood as a form of self-directed attention in which the purpose is to compare one's self-presentation with some salient standard or social expectation for what is appropriate and modifying that self-presentation accordingly. In contrast to private self-consciousness, the relationships between public self-consciousness and (1) reliance upon internal events, (2) enhanced intensity of reported affect, and (3) imagery, are not significant. On the other hand, public self-consciousness has been found related to inconsistency between self-reported attributes and actual behavior (Turner, 1978; Scheier, Note 2) and to conformity (Froming & Carver, in press). Such evidence suggests that people high in public self-consciousness might attempt to manipulate their bodily expressive activity rather than represent it in verbal or imaginal form during focusing. A useful measure of individual differences in public self-consciousness has also been developed by Fenigstein, et al (1975) and found to be factorially independent from the Private Self-Consciousness Scale. A conceptually similar measure, Snyder's (1974) Self-Monitoring Scale, was also included here because of evidence that it, too, is correlated with ability to regulate expression (Snyder, 1974) and with the use of normative information to regulate self-presentation (Snyder & Monson, 1975). A moderate correlation between Public Self-Consciousness and Self-Monitoring has been reported (Turner et al., 1978). Neither the Public Self-Consciousness Scale nor the Self-Monitoring Scale was expected to correlate with focusing ability in the present study.

In sum, the present study tested the hypothesis that individual differences in Private Self-consciousness, but not in Public Self-consciousness or Self-monitoring, would correlate positively with focusing ability.

METHOD

Subjects

One sample of 336 subjects consisted of University of Alberta students who completed the testing in the second week of an Introductory Psychology class. This sample included 190 males and 146 females.

A second sample of 67 subjects consisted of University students who completed the testing in the second week of an Introductory Social Psychology class. This sample included 27 males and 40 females.

Procedure

Both samples were given the Self-Consciousness Scale, 10 items of which constitute the Private Self-Consciousness Scale, 7 the Public Self-Consciousness Scale, and 6 a Social Anxiety Scale (Fenigstein et al., 1975). This was followed by the 25-item Self-Monitoring Scale (Snyder, 1974).

Then subjects were presented instructions guiding them through the steps that hypothetically allow the focusing process. These instructions were modifications of instructions described by Gendlin (1977) and roughly consist of the following sequence of suggestions: (1) to relax; (2) to think of a current problem or concern; (3) to attend globally to what the problem or concern feels like in one's body; (4) to find a word or phrase that seems to fit the feeling and make it more clearly stand out; (5) to let an image emerge from the feeling; (6) to let that image change until it feels just right in capturing the feeling; (7) to identify anything about the feeling that seems fresh or different.

Finally, subjects completed the Post Focusing Checklist, a 28-item self-report inventory created by Wolfe & Vanden Bos (Note 3). Persons receiving high scores on this checklist report attending to bodily events, finding words or images that fit them, feeling changes in the way they react to their problem, etc. This checklist has little clear validational data to support it, although the correlations between the checklist and the standard but more time-consuming Post Focusing Questionnaire were between .74 and .89 in the original validational study (Wolfe & Vanden Bos, Note 3) and .48 in a later effort (Platt, Note 4).

RESULTS AND DISCUSSION

As predicted, the correlations between Private Self-Consciousness and the Post Focusing Checklist were significant ($\underline{r}$ = .25, $p < .05$; $\underline{r}$ = .14, $p < .05$). These correlations are not very large and further analyses indicated that they were reliable for the males in the two populations ($\underline{r}$ = .41, $\underline{p} < .05$; $\underline{r}$ = .18, $\underline{p} < .05$) but in neither case for the females ($\underline{r}$ = .10, .09, n.s.). Despite this limited generalizability of the results, they are consistent with the notion that Private Self-consciousness is a component of the attitudes and skills that make the focusing process possible.

Also as predicted, the Post Focusing Checklist did not correlate significantly with either the Public Self-Consciousness Scale ($\underline{r}$ = .10, .11, n.s.) or the Self-Monitoring Scale (r = .09, -.06, n.s.). The hypothesis that this pattern is a function of efforts to manipulate self-expression was supported by a secondary analysis. Buss (1980) has determined that there are actually three differentiable factors on the Self-Monitoring Scale, one of which is made up of items clearly reflecting impression management (e.g., "In order to get along and be liked, I tend to be what people expect me to be rather than anything else"). In the larger sample, this subscale was found to correlate significantly and negatively with focusing ability ($r = -.11$, $p < 05$). Perhaps for subjects high on this subscale, the manipulation of bodily expressive activity precluded furtherance of the focusing process.

One factor limiting the clarity of the patterns reported here is almost certainly the Post Focusing Checklist. It is psychometrically an unknown quantity and warrants revision and validation before extensive research use. Another limitation is that classroom administration of focusing instructions does not inspire confidence that the rather subtle attentional and representational skills involved in focusing are being utilized. Nonetheless, the data reported here are generally consistent with the hypothesis that in the absence of control of expressive behaviors, attention directed toward internal bodily events may allow the emergence of the kind of imagery that furthers the focusing process.

SUMMARY

One of the prerequisites for focusing (Gendlin, 1978) is the ability to attend directly to bodily felt events and allow the elaboration of the imagery that represents and sometimes alters those feelings. In two samples studied, private self-consciousness (Fenigstein, Scheier & Buss, 1975), which has been correlated with attention to and accurate labeling of internal bodily events, correlated positively with the Post Focusing Checklist (Wolfe & Vanden Bos, Note 3), a self-report inventory completed after exposure to instructions for focusing. However, these results were largely attributable to the males in the samples ($r = .41, .18$), whereas the correlations for female participants were not statistically significant ($r = .10, .09$). Also as expected, scales for public self-consciousness (Fenigstein et al., 1975) and self-monitoring (Snyder, 1974) did not correlate significantly with the Checklist. Since these scales have been associated with control of feeling expression in accord with social expectations, the pattern of data in this study was consistent with the hypothesis that self-directed attention--without the contaminating effects of expressive self-regulation--is a component of focusing ability.

REFERENCE NOTES

1. Gendlin, E. T. Imagery is more powerful with focusing: Theory and practice. Paper presented at the American Association for the Study of Mental Imagery Conference, Los Angeles, 1979.

2. Scheier, M. The effects of public and private self-consciousness on attitude behavior consistency. Unpublished manuscript, Carnagie-Mellon University, 1978.

3. Wolfe, L., and Vanden Bos, G. Experiential focusing: New research tools. Unpublished manuscript, University of Chicago, 1970.

4. Platt, A. An experimental evaluation of three methods of focusing training. Unpublished doctoral dissertation, University of Chicago, 1971.

REFERENCES

Brady, J., and Leavitt, E. Hypnotically induced visual hallucinations. Psychosomatic Medicine, 1966, 28, 351-353.

Buss, A. H. Self-consciousness and social anxiety. San Francisco: Freeman, 1980.

Cooper, L., and Shepard, R. N. Chronometric studies of the rotation of mental images. In W. Chase (Ed,), Visual information processing. New York: Academic Press, 1973.

Fenigstein, A., Scheier, M., and Buss, A. H. Public and private self-consciousness: Assessment and theory. Journal of Consulting and Clinical Psychology, 1975, 43, 522-527.

Froming, W., and Carver, C. Divergent influences of private and public self-consciousness in a compliance paradigm. Journal of Personality and Social Psychology, in press.

Gendlin, E. T., Beebe, J., Cassens, J., Klein, M., and Oberlander, M. Focusing ability in psychotherapy, personality, and creativity. Research in Psychotherapy, 1968, 3, 217-241.

Gendlin, E. T., and Olson, L. The use of imagery in experimential focusing. Psychotherapy: Theory, Research, and Practice, 1970, 7, 221-223.

Gendlin, E. T. Experiential psychotherapy. In R. J. Corsini (Ed,), Current psychotherapies (2nd ed.). Itasca, Illinois: Peacock, 1977.

Gendlin, E. T. Focusing. New York: Everest House, 1978.

Gibbons, F., Scheier, M., Carver, C., and Hormuth, S. Self-focused attention, suggestibility and the placebo effect. Journal of Experimental Social Psychology, in press.

Hart, J. Memory and the memory monitoring process. Journal of Verbal Learning and Verbal Behavior, 1967, 6, 685-691.

Jacobson, E. Electrical measurements of neuromuscular states during mental activities. IV. Evidence of contraction of specific muscles during imagination. American Journal of Physiology, 1931, 96, 115-121.

Kosslyn, S. M. Information representation in visual images. Cognitive Psychology, 1975, 7, 341-370.

Lang, P. J. A bio-informational theory of emotional imagery. Psychophysiology, 1979, 16, 495-512.

McCarley, R., and Hobson, J. The form of dreams and the biology of sleep. In B. J. Wolman (Ed.), Handbook of dreams: Research, theories, and applications. New York: Van Nostrand, 1979.

Scheier, M., and Carver, C. Self-focused attention and the experiences of emotion: Attraction, repulsion, elation, and depression. Journal of Personality and Social Psychology, 1977, 35, 625-636.

Schwartz, G., Fair, P., Salt, P., Mandel, M., and Klerman, J. Facial muscle patterning to affective imagery in depressed and nondepressed subjects. Science, 1976, 192, 489-491.

Segal, S. J., and Fusella, V. Effects of imaging on signal to noise ratio with varying signal conditions. British Journal of Psychology, 1969, 60, 459-464.

Shaw, W. The relation of muscular action potentials to imaginal weight lifting. Archives of Psychology, 1940, 247, 1-50.

Shields, S., and Stern, R. Emotion: The perception of bodily change. In P. Pliner, K. Blankenstein, and I. Speigel (Eds.), Perception of emotion in self and others. New York: Plenum, 1979.

Snyder, M. Self-monitoring of expressive behavior. Journal of Personality and Social Psychology, 1974, 30, 526-537.

Snyder, M., and Monson, T. Persons, situations, and the control of social behavior. Journal of Personality and Social Psychology, 1975, 32, 637-644.

Turner, R., Scheier, M., Carver, C., and Ickes, W. Correlates of self-consciousness. Journal of Personality Assessment, 1978, 42, 285-289.

Turner, R. Consistency, self-consciousness, and the predictive validity of typical and maximal personality predictors. Journal of Research in Personality, 1978, 12, 117-132.

MENTAL IMAGERY: A MEMORY AID FOR THE OLDER ADULT?

Susan E. Mason

Niagara University

Niagara Univ., NY

Older adults demonstrate poor memory performance relative to young adults. This age-related difference in cognitive ability is reliably shown in most laboratory tests. Memory loss with age is also commonly reported by individuals as they reflect on developmental changes in their own behavior. Poor memory is so strongly associated with old age that is has become part of the stereotype of aging, alson with wrinkles and gray hair. It is a common belief that forgetting is one of the first signs of old age and that as we age it is natural and inevitable that we lose our memory. Further, many believe that memory loss is irreversible. The goal of researchers studying age-related changes in cognitive functioning is to determine to what extent decline with age can be prevented and to what extent memory problems associated with aging can be eliminated through mnemonic training. There is evidence that the poorer performance of the elderly may be due, in part, to age-related differences in the use of imaginal processing. Consequently, the use of mental imagery as a memory aid has become an important area of research for gerontologists.

The formation of mental images associated with to-be-learned material has been shown to be an effective mnemonic strategy. When trying to remember a word, a date, a name, or a place the information can be encoded easily is the learner forms a mental picture of it. Once an item has been associated with an image, it can later be retrieved through a decoding process. Pictures are remembered far better than words. The value of imagery as a memory aid was first recognized by the early Greek orators. They used mental pictures to help them recall long speeches. Today imagery is practiced by stage mnemonists who amaze audiences with their near perfect recall. Techniques involving imagery have been developed to help individuals deal with a variety of memory problems. Whether the problem is associating names with faces, memorizing a grocery list, or learning a foreign language vocabulary, ther is an imagery technique designed to help.

Experiments have shown that mental imagery can be used as a memory aid by young adults. Because there is a decline in memory performance with age it is important to determine whether mental imagery can be used effectively by older adults as well. Research in the area is generally designed to serve one or more of the following purposes: to assess age differences in the natural use of mental imagery, to determine what experimental conditions are optimal for imagery in the aged, and to examine possibilities for training the elderly in the effective use of mental imagery.

One way to investigate the spontaneous use of imagery by young and old adults is to test subjects in a learning task and then question them about the strategies they used in the task. With this method the elderly report using imagery less frequently than young subjects (Hulicka & Grossman, 1967; Rowe & Schnore, 1971). I wondered whether the same age difference would occur if subjects were questioned prior to the presentation of the to-be-learned material. In other words, rather than examining age differences in the reported use of imagery, the research examined age differences in the intent to use imagery.

The subjects were 26 young adults (mean age 20 years) and 26 older adults (mean age 70 years). The study included two instructional conditions: Recall Instructions (RI) and Memory Instructions (MI). One half of the subjects in each age group were assigned to each experimental condition. In the RI condition subjects were given the following instructions:

> You will be shown a list of 30 words and you will be asked to study the words. Then you will be given a test to see if you remember the words. The test will be a recall test. In a recall test you are given a blank sheet of paper and you are asked to write down as many words as you can remember. The best way to study for your recall test will be to study different words together--think of relationships between different words in the list. That way when you remember some of the words it will help you remember the words that you associated with them.

In the MI condition subjects were told to expect a memory test but did not know what type of test to expect. MI subjects were asked to think about how they might approach the task. If they had a strategy in mind they were to write a statement describing their plan. All subjects were presented with a list of 30 common, English words for 90 seconds. A free recall test was given immediately after the stimulus presentation.

Twelve of the 13 young subjects in the MI condition reported an encoding plan. Eight of those plans were considered optimal for recall (association using verbal or visual mediators). In comparison, only five of the 13 older subjects had a specific plan in mind and only two of the five were appropriate for recall. The analysis of the recall scores revealed a significant Age Group x Instructional Condition interaction. Young adults recalled a significantly greater number of words than older adults in both conditions, but the largest age difference was found in the RI condition. Young subjects benefited from knowing the nature of the memory test; older subjects did not. These results suggest that there are qualitative differences in the way young and old adults approach a memory task. Consistent with previous findings, the young subjects did report a greater tendency to use imagery than older subjects did.

Another study tested whether the finding was generalizable to situations outside of the laboratory--whether there are age differences in the use of imagery in "real life." Subjects ranging in age from 18 to 80 were asked to complete a memory complaint questionnaire. Responses to the questionnaire were used to determine what memory problems and coping strategies are relevant to the lives of young and old adults. In response to the question, "How do you deal with your memory problems?", association and imagery were mentioned more often by young adults than by older adults. The solution most often mentioned by older adults was note taking. Note taking is certainly an important strategy. I strongly suggest that my students take notes in class. I myself would be lost without a calendar or an appointment book. This strategy is extremely limited, however. We cannot always rely on notes. Consider, for example, the task of associating names with faces - a common memory problem for all ages. People are flattered when you remember their names, but the flattery turns to insult if they catch you thumbing through your note pad to find or verify the name before you can greet them.

Imagery would be a better approach in this situation. Mnemonists recommend that you form an association between an individual's name and a prominant feature of that person's face. For example, you might meet a man named Bill and notice that he has a very big nose. Picture his nose as a duck bill. The next time you see Bill you will notice his nose and immediately associate it with his name.

In order to determine what memory problems young and old experience on a day-to-day basis and whether imagery is an appropriate way to deal with those problems, I presented adults of various ages with examples of common memory problems and asked them to rate their ability to perform in each situation. Subjects were asked to consider the following memory tasks: associating names and faces, remembering telephone numbers, taking medication, remembering where you put things, remembering appointments, remembering anniversaries, remembering directions, memorizing a poem or a speech, memory for things that happened recently, and memory for things that happened years ago. For each of the ten items of the questionnaire subjects rated their own memories on a seven-point scale. Possible ratings included: very poor, poor, slightly below average, average, slightly above average, good, and very good. Older subjects had a tendency to rate their memories as average while young subjects considered their memories to be slightly above average (Mason, Note 1).

An analysis of the responses to individual items revealed that young adults and older adults suffer from different types of memory problems. The observed age-related change in memory is not simply a quantitative change but a qualitative change as well. Young subjects report difficulty remembering where objects are places, but their memories are good for events that happened recently and for appointments. In contrast, older subjects tend to forget directions but have good memories for events, recent and past. These self-report data contradict the stereotype that the elderly have good memories for past events but poor memories for recent events.

Each of the situations described in the questionnaire represents a demand on memory which could be handled with imagery. For example, the major problem for the older adults was remembering directions. One's ability to remember directions could be improved greatly with the use of imagery. One way to accomplish this would be to form an image of objects associated with the street names and numbers. Another approach would be to form a cognitive map of the route, picturing streets and their relative positions. The probability of retention would surely be highest if both approaches were used simultaneously. Perhaps older adults would benefit disproportionately from training in this area.

The research findings presented thus far indicate that older adults do not use mental imagery as often as young adults do--the young report a greater use of imagery and a greater intent to use imagery. The poor memory performance of older adults also suggests that they do not use the efficient encoding strategies adopted by younger adults. However, investigations in the laboratory and research examining daily demands on memory reveal that imagery is an important memory aid. If the elderly can be trained in the effective use of mental imagery then their memory problems could be minimized.

Researchers have manipulated instructional conditions, presentation conditions, and test conditions to determine which experimental conditions are optimal for imagery in the aged. Factors found to be important in minimizing age differences include the type of instructions given, the timing of experimental events (study and test interval), characteristics of the materials presented, the type of retention test given, and the number of practice trials.

INSTRUCTIONS

Comparisons have been made between self-generated and experimenter-provided imagery instructions (Treat & Reese, 1976). In self-generated imagery the subject is told to form a mental image of the to-be-learned item. In experimenter-provided imagery the subject is given a description of an image. Self-generated imagery is more effective for older adults than experimenter-provided imagery. One explanation for this finding is that the image a subject develops is personally more meaningful than one that is developed by someone else. Self-generated images are therefore easier to remember and this may be a critical factor for older adults. Another characteristic of self-generated imagery is that it is more demanding of the subject. It requires active processing of the items and therefore results in a stronger memory trace. Older adults may not process experimenter-suggested images to the degree that they process images in a self-generated condition.

TIMING

The timing of experimental events affects age differences in performance on most learning and memory tasks. Older adults require additonal time to study materials and additional time to respond to test items (Monge & Hultsch, 1971). Slow or self-paced conditions tend to minimize age differences. It has been demonstrated, however, that older subjects do not always make use of extra time available to them under self-paced conditions. Therefore it may be more beneficial to provide older subjects with an externally controlled slow rate of presentation and specific instructions to work slowly (Mason & Smith, 1977).

MATERIALS

The type of materials presented partially determines the ease of learning. Abstract words, numbers, and ramdom strings of unrelated words are all very difficult to learn. Concrete words, pictures, and other meaningful pieces of information are more easily committed to memory. Although the meaningfulness of the material is important to all age groups, it is of particular importance to older adults (Arenberg, 1968; Hulicka, 1967).

RETENTION TEST

Age differences in recognition performance are minimal but age differences in recall are substantial (Mason, 1979). It has been hypothesized that age differences in recall are partially due to an age-related retrieval deficit. In a recognition test the subject is presented with a set of items from which the correct response is to be selected. In recall, on the other hand, the subject must retrieve the correct information from memory. Imagery facilitates encoding and retrieval and therefore could be used by older adults to improve recall performance.

PRACTICE

Older adults often require more exposure to material to learn it as well as young adults. Once information has been learned, however, older subjects retain it as well as young subjects do (Hulicka & Weiss, 1965). To minimize age differences older individuals must be given the opportunity to review material thoroughly and they should be given extensive training in the use of imagery. Practice in forming images and decoding images will help the older individual to overcome encoding and retrieval handicaps.

In conclusion, older adults do not use imagery effectively and they demonstrate poor memory performance because of it. With the proper conditions and the proper training older individuals can use imagery as a memory aid in the laboratory and in life. In evaluating the research it appears that there are several critical elements to a successful training program for the elderly. First, the elderly should be instructed to generate their own mental images rather than work with experimenter-provided imagery. The more demanding the task, the stronger the memory trace. Second, older adults should be not only allowed but encouraged to work at a slow pace. The elderly are disadvantaged when the pacing is fast and under self-paced conditions may not take the additonal time they require. Third, materials should be meaningful. Older adults are more highly motivated to learn and remember meaningful information. Fourth, imagery should be taught as a retrieval aid. Images can serve as cues to the learned items and thereby assist the older adult in retrieving the necessary information. Finally, practice facilitates the use of imagery. The older adult should practice froming images of the items and practice decoding the images. Each of these points must be considered in the development of a mnemonic training program for older adults.

REFERENCE NOTE

1. Mason, S. E. Memory and aging: A subjective measure of performance. Paper presented at the meeting of the Gerontological Society, November 22, 1980, San Diego, California.

REFERENCES

Arenberg, D. Concept problem solving in young and old adults. Journal of Gerontology, 1968, 23, 279.

Hulicka, I. M. Age differences in retention as a function of interference. Journal of Gerontology, 1967, 22, 180.

Hulicka, I. M., and Grossman, J. L. Age-group comparisons for the use of mediators in paired-associate learning. Journal of Gerontology, 1967, 22, 46-51.

Hulicka, I. M., and Weiss, R. Age differences in retention as a function of learning. Journal of Consulting Psychology, 1965, 29, 125-129.

Mason, S. E. Effects of orienting tasks on the recall and recognition performance of subjects differing in age. Developmental Psychology, 1979, 15, 467-469.

Mason, S. E., and Smith, A. D. Imagery in the aged. Experimental Aging Research, 1977, 3, 17-32.

Rowe, E. J., and Schnore, M. M. Item concreteness and reported strategies in paired-associate learning as a function of age. Journal of Gerontology, 1971, 24, 470-475.

Treat, N., and Reese, H. W. Age, pacing, and imagery in paired-associate learning. Developmental Psychology, 1976, 12, 119-124.

TRAINING SPATIAL ABILITY

Howard M. Rhoades

Rice University

Houston, Texas 77001

The ability to create a mental image of an object and then to manipulate it mentally has significant practical application in fields such as mathematics, physics, architecture, engineering and design. It is documented that success in these fields is highly predicted by one's ability to visualize and manipulate objects (e.g. Ghiselli, 1966). Moreover, it is becoming increasingly apparent that spatial skills may reflect important intellectual capacities that cannot be measured verbally. For example, Einstein, through his own accounts, considered his primary thoughts to be visual, not verbal (Hadamard, 1945). This suggests that reasoning need not be entirely verbal in nature. If this is the case, it would be extremely useful to know if training or some other types of experience would lead to improvement of this aptitude. Although many researchers have addressed this question, available evidence does not provide an unequivocal answer. For example, two studies in 1942, one by Faubian, Cleveland, and Hassell, and the other by Churchill, Curtis, Coombs, and Hassell, showed no improvement in spatial tests (relative to a control group) after training in drafting, blueprint reading, and engineering drawing. In contrast, Blade and Watson (1955) did find evidence for the trainability of spatial ability. These investigators gathered data on male engineering students and a control group of mostly male, nonengineering students. On spatial tests, which were administered before and after one academic year, the engineering students increased their scores 37% of the distance to the ceiling whereas nonengineering students gained only 13%. However, Myers (1958) found that Naval Cadets trained in mechanical drawing scored no higher on spatial tests than those Cadets who received no training in mechanical drawing.

Studies by Ranucci (1952) and Brown (1952) found no increase in spatial ability due to having taken high school geometry courses. In contrast, a study in which 8th graders were taught geometry in a nontraditional manner found a significant increase in scores on the Space Relations subtest of the Differential Aptitude Test (Brinkman, 1966). Clearly, the evidence on the trainability of spatial visualization has not beeen clear cut.

For the purposes of this paper, studies such as the one by Blade & Watson (1955) will be placed in the category of indirect training studies. The participants did not specifically study nor practice spatial visualization techniques or problems. Rather, some other experience associated with the difference between treatment and control groups must account for the improvement. In the case of the Blade and Watson's study, the indirect training was to take place through the courses taken by the engineering students.

Another approach involves modifying one's spatial ability through direct training. That is, the treatment group receives practice on the test itself (such as McGee, 1978) or practice on non-test items that involves using those skills that the test requires. Brinkman (1966), for example, developed a programmed instruction course to teach the spatial/visual aspects of geometry and mental pattern folding. Thus, students received direct practice in spatial visualization.

In the following experiments, both indirect and direct training were further explored. First, the study by Blade and Watson was replicated and extended. No previous indirect training study reviewed looked at the effects of indirect training on females. Thus, we were interested in discovering whether the improvement found in males also occurs with females. Additionally, we wished to examine the contribution of specific course experiences to the improvement in spatial ability. In the second study, a direct training procedure was employed.

INDIRECT TRAINING STUDY

Subjects and Procedure

The Guilford-Zimmerman (G-Z) Spatial Visualization Test (1953) and the Identical Blocks Test (Stafford, 1962) were given to 285 freshman at Rice University during the early part of their first semester in college. This sample constituted 55% of the 1977 incoming class. Four semesters later, in the latter part of the 1979 spring semester, 142 students were retested on the same tests. It should be noted that the attrition rate reflects problems in scheduling retests rather than due to academic failure, which was only 3%.

At the time the students were retested, their major and list of the courses they had taken was obtained. For purposes of analysis, majors and the courses taken were categorized into the following 10 groups:

(1) Physical science (physics, chemistry, geology)

(2) Physical science laboratory

(3) Mathematics (applied mathematics & computer science)

(4) Engineering (including architecture)

(5) Engineering laboratory

(6) Biology

(7) Social science (psychology, sociology, anthropology, economics, and political science)

(8) Humanities

(9) Studio art

(10) Other (physical education, naval science, specialty courses).

Results

An analysis of the initial Identical Blocks Test showed that 56 out of 142 students made perfect scores. Thus, there was a serious ceiling effect and the Identical Blocks Test was dropped from any further consideration.

Performance on the G-Z improved over all, from a pretest mean of 22.11 to a posttest of 28.04, $F(1,141) = 179$, $p < .001$. The correlation between pre- and posttest scores was .81.

Of more concern was the hypothesis that spatial proficiency should improve as a function of spatially related curricula. In order to test this hypothesis, we divided the subjects on the basis of college major. It was felt that the different programs would involve varying amounts of spatially relevant training. An additional issue we wished to address was whether women and men benefit from academic experience differentially. Table 1 summarizes the mean pre- and posttest performances for the categories distinguished by these two variables.

Inspection of Table 1 reveals support for the hypothesis that relevant academic curricula improves performance on spatial tasks. Students majoring in social science, humanities, and "undecided"

Table 1: Mean Spatial Scores of Students in Different College Majors*

Major	n	G-Z_1	G-Z_2	G-Z (diff)
Physical Science				
Males	21	25.01	31.05	6.04
Females	7	17.29	28.75	11.46
Mathematics				
Males	8	27.84	34.13	6.28
Females	2	12.62	22.50	9.88
Engineering				
Males	38	26.54	33.14	6.61
Females	9	17.39	23.81	6.42
Biology				
Males	3	17.08	26.67	9.58
Females	5	17.25	23.05	5.80
Humanities				
Males	6	19.33	22.58	3.25
Females	12	16.19	20.79	4.60
Social Science				
Males	9	21.56	27.67	6.11
Females	12	15.77	20.19	4.42
Undeclared				
Males	7	27.07	31.04	3.96
Females	3	20.00	16.17	-3.38
All Ss				
Males	92	25.08	31.15	6.08
Females	50	16.65	22.32	5.67

(*) Maximum score = 40

programs improved less than those majoring in physical science and mathematics $F(6,128) = 3.90$, $p < .005$. There was a significant interaction between sex and major, $F(6,128) = 2.31$, $p < .04$. However, a subsequent analysis found that only in the case of physical science did the women reliably improve more than the men, $F(1,26) = 8.66$, $p < .01$. However, this should not lead one to conclude that there were no sex differences in improvement for other majors. The sample sizes for some majors were very small, resulting in severely reduced statistical power.

Since reliable differences were found among various majors, a closer look at the specific courses taken by students was undertaken. Classes were categorized at stated previously. The number of classes taken in each category was used in a multiple regression analysis to predict improvement scores. All categories were tested for the amount of variance they explained independently of all other categories. Only the number of mathematics courses taken explained a significant portion of the variance $F(1,130) = 4.01$, $p < .05$.

There were significant simple correlations between spatial improvement and (1) number of mathematics courses, $r = .21$, $p < .02$; (2) number of physical science courses, $r = .18$, $p < .04$; and (3) number of social science courses, $r = -.17$, $p < .05$. We felt that the negative correlation between social science courses and spatial improvement does not indicate that taking these courses reduces one's ability but rather is due to the negative correlation of $-.22$, $p < .01$, between the number of courses taken in social science and the number taken in mathematics.

Discussion

These results offer strong support for Blade and Watson's (1955) conclusion that proficiency on spatial visualization test is subject to improvement through relevant academic experience. The question arises: What is relevant? Blade and Watson suggested mechanical drawing as a good possibility by Myers (1958) failed to find any advantage for this type of training. The present study addressed that question empirically by observing the independent effects of specific academic courses on spatial improvement. The results obtained indicate mathematics training is relevant for spatial improvement. Not as conclusive, but also a good prospect is physical science. However, the correlation between physical science and mathematics was .38, $p < .01$, which may indicate that the critical element may be the mathematical content, which is common to both. One potential problem when doing field work and one found in this study is the correlation between the treatment (the number of courses taken in a specific area) and the subject's initial score. In the laboratory, one can control for this problem through random assignment to treatment or control groups, which was in fact done in the following study of direct training.

DIRECT TRAINING

The purpose of this study was to investigate the effects of direct and intensive training on spatial ability. A direct training procedure is one in which the subject practices and receives feedback in those skills necessary to perform adequately on the task. Direct training approaches have been used previously. For example, Sherman (1974) had subjects practice on items of the Rod and Frame Test. Connor, Serbin, and Schackman (1977) devised a way of giving children training on the Embedded Figures Test. By laminating several clear plastic sheets on which each had a portion of the complex figure, they were able to reduce the complexity of the problem by simply removing one of the sheets.

Considering training to be intensive only if subjects received more than one hour of training, of the studies referred to earlier, only the Brinkman (1966) study could be considered to be both direct and intensive.

Subjects and Procedure

Twelve Rice University undergraduates (five males and seven females, who participated for extra class credit) were randomly assigned to either treatment or control group. They were then given three pre-training tests: the Minnesota Paper Form Boards Test (MPFB), the G-Z, and the Rice Space Test (RST). The RST was developed on a Hewlett-Packard graphics terminal and was patterned after the G-Z. That is, it was a spatial visualization test the format of which was the same as the G-Z. In place of the clock, an abstract prism and pyramidal figure was substituted. The procedure for taking the test was identical to the G-Z with the exception that the initial orientation of the figure and its four possible ending orientations were displayed on the graphics terminal. The subject designated his or her answer by pressing the appropriate key on the keyboard. The first day consisted of pretesting which lasted approximately one hour. For the next three days, those in the control group participated in another non-relevant study while those in the treatment group underwent the training procedure. The training procedure consisted of mentally rotating the abstract figure about one axis on the first day, two axes on the second and three axes on the third day. Each daily session consisted of 48 trials and lasted for approximately one hour. On each trial, subjects were presented with the abstract figure in a particular orientation and asked to rotate it mentally in the direction of and in the degree to which a card for that trial indicated. When they had accomplished this, they were to press a key that displayed the abstract figure in another orientation that was either the correct final orientation for that trial or an incorrect orientation. The subject then was asked to decide if the "test" figure had been rotated correctly or incorrectly and to respond by pressing the appropriate key. If the subject was right, the next trial began. If the subject was incorrect, feedback was given as to the type of the error and the original and test figures were redrawn. If the nature of the error warranted it, the abstract figure was drawn in its correct final orientation. The subject had approximately 20 seconds to restudy that trial before the next trial began.

On the fifth day, all subjects were retested on the MPFB, the G-Z, and the RST. Alternate forms were used for the MPFB on pre- and posttesting.

Results and Discussion

The results from the pre- and posttests were analyzed using the subjects' improvement scores. As can be seen in Table 2, those subjects in the treatment group showed greater improvement on the RST than those in the control group. An unweighted means ANOVA found the main effect of treatment, $\bar{x} = 10.50$, versus control, $\bar{x} = 2.21$, to be highly significant, $F(1,8) = 27.32$, $p < .001$. This finding lends support to the hypothesis that direct training will increase one's spatial ability. Males appeared to be showing a ceiling effect on the G-Z test; thus, the females' G-Z scores were analyzed separately. That analysis resulted in the same pattern of greater improvement for the treatment group ($\bar{x} = 10.58$) than for the control group ($\bar{x} = 3.98$). However, this difference was only marginally significant, $F(1,5) = 4.57$, $p < .09$. Training had little effect on subjects' MPFB performance, the mean improvement being 4.4 and 4.22 for the treatment and control groups respectively.

At this point there seems to be support for the effectiveness of training on improving spatial visualization. However, since the sample sizes were small, it was decided that the study should be replicated. This would also allow the testing procedure for the G-Z to be changed in order to eliminate the ceiling effect shown by the men.

REPLICATION

It was felt that one reason a ceiling effect was found in the men's G-Z scores was that the test and retest were separated by only four days. Thus, the one change in the replication study was that there was no G-Z pre-test administered. This would have the effect of reducing the posttest scores, therefore raising the ceiling. In the previous study, the pre-test scores on the G-Z correlated .90 with the RST pre-test scores. Therefore, it was decided to use the pre-test scores on the RST as a covarite in an Analysis of Covariance of the post-test G-Z scores.

Table 2: Improvement scores on the Rice Space Test (group means)

	Treatment	Control
Study I		
Males	12.55	2.83
Females	8.44	1.59
Replication		
Males	12.33	7.44
Females	10.89	5.55

Method

The testing and training procedures were identical to the previous study with the exception of giving no G-Z pre-test for reasons just explained. Twelve Rice University undergraduates and graduate students (six men and six women) participated for which they were paid $5.00 per hour.

Results and Discussion

After analyzing the RST data, the pattern of results was found to be the same as that found previously (see Table 2). However, the effect of training did not reach conventional levels of significance, $F(1,8) = 2.67$, $p < .15$. A further analysis, in which replication was included as a higher-order factor showed that the main effect of training across both studies was significant, $F(1,16) = 13.85$, $p < .01$. There were no significant interactions with replication.

The Analysis of Covariance conducted on the G-Z scores showed no positive effect of training. Again, no effects of training were obtained from the MPFB data, the mean improvement scores for the treatment and control group being 5.43 and 5.60 respectively.

The results of the replication, along with those of the previous study, still lend support to the conclusion that spatial ability is trainable. However, they are equivocal on the position that the training produced any generalizable results, being rather test specific in this case. Much of this problem is felt to result from having such small sample sizes ($n = 3$ per cell), which results in one person's score weighing very heavily in the results.

GENERAL CONCLUSIONS

Overall, the present studies support the view that spatial ability can be trained. In the first study, a major influence on improvement in spatial ability was found to be the number of mathematics courses taken by a student. This finding is consistent with a body of literature attempting to understand the relationship between mathematical proficiency and spatial ability (see Maccoby & Jacklin, 1974).

The second set of experiments demonstrated that direct training does lead to improvement on a spatial visualization test (i.e., the RST). A trend towards generalization to the G-Z was discovered for women but was not replicated perhaps due to the small sample sizes involved.

The RST, a computerized spatial visualization test along with the computerized training procedure developed affords the researcher with tools to accurately measure different aspects of performance. Thus, current research is investigating learning strategies used during training sessions by measuring reaction times. The possible relationships between these strategies and the angle of rotation required can then be studied (similar to studies by Cooper & Shepard, 1973). Additionally, the link between spatial ability and visual memory would seem to be important in understanding both individual differences and the extent to which one's spatial ability can be improved.

REFERENCES

Blade, M., & Watson, W.S. Increase in spatial visualization test scores during engineering study. Psychological Monographs, 1955, 69 (12, Whole No. 397).

Brinkman, E.H. Programmed instruction as a technique for improving spatial visualization. Journal of Applied Psychology, 1966, 50, 179-184.

Brown, F.R. The effect of an experimental course in geometry on ability to visualize in three dimensions. Unpublished doctoral dissertation, Columbia University, 1954.

Connor, J.M., Serbin, L.A., & Schackman, M. Sex differences in children's response to training on a visual-spatial test. Developmental Psychology, 1977, 13, 293-296.

Cooper, L.A., & Shepard, R.N. Chronometric studies of the rotation of mental images. In W.G. Chase (Ed.), Visual information processing. New York: Academic Press, 1973.

Ghiselli, E.E. The validity of occupational aptitude tests. New York: Wiley, 1966.

Guilford, J.P., & Zimmerman, W.S. The Guilford-Zimmerman aptitude survey. IV. Spatial visualization form B. Beverly Hills, Ca.: Sheridan Supply Co., 1953.

Hadamard, J. The psychology of invention in the mathematical field. Princeton, N.J.: Princeton University Press, 1945.

Maccoby, E.E., & Jacklin, C.N. The Psychology of Sex Differences. Stanford: Stanford University Press, 1974.

McGee, M.G. Effects of training and practice on sex differences in Mental Rotation Test scores. Journal of Psychology, 1978, 100, 87-90.

Myers, C.T. Some observations of problem-solving in spatial relations test. Research Bulletin, RB-58-16, Educational Testing Service, New Jersey, 1958.

Ranucci, E.R. The effect of the study of solid geometry on certain aspects of space perception abilities. Unpublished doctoral dissertation, Columbia University, 1952.

Sherman, J. Field articulation, sex, spatial visualization, dependency, practice, laterality of the brain and birth order. Perceptual and Motor Skills, 1974, 38, 1223-1235.

Stafford, R.E. Identical Blocks, Form AA (Office of Student Affairs), University Park, P.A.: Pennsylvania State University, 1962.

VI. IMAGERY AND CLINICAL TREATMENT

A MULTIPLE COMPONENT MODEL OF CLINICAL IMAGERY

Kirk Strosahl* and James C. Ascough**

*American Lake Veterans Administration Hospital; **Purdue

*Tacoma, Washington; **West Lafayette, Indiana**

A MULTIPLE COMPONENT MODEL OF CLINICAL IMAGERY: THEORETICAL AND EMPIRICAL ISSUES

The previous decade has witnessed a rapid proliferation of imagery-based psychotherapies, ranging from psychodynamic techniques such as psycho-imagination therapy (Shorr, 1974) to more structured and focused behavior modification procedures (Cautela, 1967; Wolpe, 1958). Despite the promise of imagery as a psychotherapeutic tool, a host of issues remain about the functional and structural characteristics of this complex private process. A frank assessment of the literature indicates that theoreticians and researchers alike continue to grope for a way to conceptualize the experience of clinical images. Many theories with little consensus explain therapeutic significance of imagery, but are constrained primarily by being "technique specific" in that they describe the therapeutic impact of a single therapy or a generically related group of therapies (Singer, 1974). Conversely, limited effort has been directed toward an understanding of nonspecific imagery effects that may be related simply to the fact that imagery provides different modes for organizing personal world conceptions. Clinical experience suggests that there is something distinctive about imagery as a form of cognition that cannot be duplicated by verbal processes, but one is pressed to identify what these distinctive elements are. For example, how are images constructed and organized to form meaningful representations of aspects of the external world that, strictly speaking, are not pictorial? What are the various components of the image processing system; how are they interrelated and what functional relationship do they bear to successful imagery? Is it primarily a visual experience or is it a complex constellation of multiple representational and processing events? The purpose of this paper is to cast a critical eye on these questions, to examine influences that have hindered their resolution and to suggest a model of clinical imagery that can accommodate the enormous range of operations that occur within the sequence of clinical imagery. Hopefully, examination of these topics will illustrate their profound influence for practitioners and researchers in the upcoming decade.

THE PHOTOGRAPH METAPHOR

The deficiencies of many contemporary accounts of clinical imagery can be attributed to certain misconceptions about the structure of images. The most notable example is the photograph metaphor, which can be traced back to the work of revered scientists such as Francis Galton. This position implies that images are functional substitutes for their external referents, much in the manner that a photograph accurately maps the arrangement of persons and objects in a particular scene. Because imagery is ultimately a nonobservable event, the expediency of the photograph metaphor resides in the capacity of this approach to place images "outside" the person by equating the laws governing the structure of photographs with those underpinning the organization of images (Strosahl & Ascough, in press). One can thus infer that the same factors that moderate the efficacy of photographs will have a similar impact upon clinical imagery. In this case, photographs are least effective when they are blurred, out of focus or too vague to apprehend, while images lose impact when a like set of properties is present. This analogical relationship forms the cornerstone of the most controversial hypotheses of clinical imagery, namely, that individual differences in image vividness are somehow related to the success or failure of imagery therapies. The individual differences hypothesis is therefore analogically inextricable from the photograph metaphor and it is imperative to ascertain whether images really are mental photographs or whether they possess more complex structural and functional significance.

What can be said about the empirical validity of the photograph metaphor? Laboratory research on this subject is so vast that this presentation must be confined to a summary of the major results. Substantial information processing research indicates that images do possess spatial reproductive properties. For example, mental rotation studies demonstrate that subjects can use imagery to internally rotate one geometric figure into congruence with a second figure to complete an information processing task (Cooper, 1975; Cooper and Shepard, 1973a, 1973b). Moreover, Kosslyn (1975, 1976, 1978) has shown that images exist with reference to an internal "imagery field" and possess properties that allow "scanning" by some internal process. However, the results of perceptual comparisons studies suggest that the information presented in an image is not confined to the spatial realm, but may also include the abstract or affective properties of persons and objects (Holyoak &

Walter, 1976; Paivio, 1978). It also appears that the visual and verbal processing systems may co-represent and share processing responsibility for incoming information, with information attached to the system that is best suited for processing it (Posner & Keele, 1967; Tversky, 1969; Segal & Fusella, 1970). While one cannot reject spatial reproductive functions as integral to image processing, recent theoretical accounts emphasize that images may be but incomplete pictures or internal analogues that retain essential information but require minimal spatial input for efficient processing (Anderson, 1978; Kosslyn, 1976; Shepard, 1978). Indeed, few proponents of imagery as a functionally discrete processing system argue seriously for the photograph metaphor (Kosslyn & Pomerantz, 1977). This position is central to the critiques of imagery advanced by theorists who maintain that images are but epiphenomenon of an underlying interlingua, or a third code that processes visual and verbal input (Pylyshyn, 1973). While it is not feasible to go into the intricacies of this debate, it is interesting to note that Anderson (1978), a major propositional theorist, argued that there is a nonidentifiability between the dual system and propositional accounts. Hence, one cannot argue that one model a priori provides a more sophisticated account of human information processing. This brief review should illustrate a point of major significance for models of clinical imagery. Specifically, even at basic levels of information processing, the notion of the image as a mental photograph has a limited range of applicability. Equally likely is the proposition that imagery conveys information that cannot be rendered in pictorial form, but is "carried" via the surface image (Kosslyn, 1976).

Our argument is that the parsimony of the photograph position is too costly: the gradual elimination of imagery processes that may be critical to successful therapy. While it is unwise to reject the importance of reproductive imagery, a comprehensive clinical model must accommodate the entire array of cognitive operations extant in the clinical setting. The purpose of this section is to describe the tenets of a multiple component model of imagery that has guided our research program. Several theoretical concerns will emerge from a discussion of this model: the importance of distinguishing between functional and structural properties of imagery; the need to empirically discern the organization of the imagery system and variations in structure that occur as a function of sex; differentiating state versus trait properties of clinical imagery.

The multiple component model has two major characteristics. First, clinical images are composites of multiple representational events, ranging in complexity from reproductive molecular imagery to constructive molar imagery. These stages are analogous to Lang's (1977) stimulus and response proposition, although these terms provide only an initial distinction between two major subclasses of image processing. Molecular imagery can further be subdivided into analogue construction and juxtaposition and rudimentary sensory modality imagery. The term subjective transformation denotes the point at which subjective awareness of a whole image is present and when self-appraisal processes make the image a therapeutic event. Molar imagery includes operations that involve the completed image such as image elaboration, response clarification, mental rehearsal, internal dialogue, and self reappraisal processes. An important tenet of our model is that the visual processing system possesses a hierarchical structure in which higher order abilities subsume lower order ones. To cite an example, emotive images may contain sensory modality components but these responses do not predict the subjective impact of the whole clinical image.

The second characteristic of the multiple component model is that the visual and verbal systems co-represent and share processing responsibility for incoming information throughout the imagery sequence. An illustration will make this point clear: when you say the word "car", it is difficult to avoid creating a simultaneous visual image of a car. Similarly, when a therapist describes a scene verbally to a client, both the visual and verbal systems are activated and contribute to the imagery sequence.

The multiple component approach offers an account of individual differences in imagery ability that is not constrained by the photograph metaphor. Rather than conceptualizing imagery as a single general ability, this model emphasizes that several abilities, which act in complementary fashion, influence the integrity of clinical images. Complementary processes suggest that deficiencies in one ability may be compensated for by the increased activity of another process. Hence, individual differences can exist throughout the spectrum of imagery operations. The distinction between functional and structural properties of imagery is central to this paradigm. Structure refers to the format or organization of a covert representation; function refers to the processing of an internal representation. Essentially, the individual differences hypothesis is a functional prediction based upon suppositions about the structural nature of images, that is, images must possess a specified set of properties to promote efficient processing. The absence of vivid imagery per se does not lead to poor results in imagery therapy; rather, a poorly developed image does not lend itself to efficient processing. The traditional notion that image vividness alone is critical for successful therapy does little to represent the range of processing operations that affect the functional efficiency of clinical imagery. Equally critical in therapy may be richness of image content, emotive valence of the image and subjective responses to imagined scenes, to name but a few. Thus, it is not surprising that previous studies that assessed only sensory modality imagery have failed to isolate a significant contribution of imagery in psychotherapy (Davis, McLemore, & London, 1970; McLemore, 1972; McSweeney, 1976).

One benefit of the multiple component position is that a set of predictions can be derived about image structure that can be distinguished empirically from the predictions of competing models. We argue that various imagery abilities are arranged hierarchically according to the complexity of cognitive functioning involved. Conversely, the photograph position predicts that imagery is simply a single quasi-visual ability extant at all levels of functioning. To test these competing predictions, we asked 200 introductory psychology students to complete a battery of imagery measures, containing the Betts Questionnaire Upon Mental Imagery (Sheehan, 1967), Gordon's Scale of Image Control (Gordon, 1949) and the Individual Differences Questionnaire (Hiscock, 1978), which is comprised of two subscales measuring visual (IDQI) or verbal (IDQV) cognitive style. In addition, subjects completed several experimental measures of molar imagery ablility derived from the multiple component approach. These measures included: The Abstract Image Inventory (AI), a measure of verbal concept formation in images; Emotive Image Inventory (EI), which assesses the ability to experience emotive reactions to imagined scenes; Positive-Negative Image Differential Scale (PNIDS), which measures the respondent's capacity to imagine a series of extremely positive (VP) and negative (VN) scenes; the Image Control Scale (ICS), which assesses image control for a series of neutral (ICNEU) and negative (ICNEG) scenes. More detailed information on the experimental measures is available elsewhere (Strosahl & Ascough, Note 2). To avoid response set bias, the two sets of measures were administered on two separate days.

A principal components analysis of the correlations among imagery measures was used to illustrate the organizational relationships among the imagery processes defined by the experimental measures, each component reflecting a specific dimension of ability. Results provided strong support for the multiple component approach. Regardless of whether data were analyzed for all subjects or by sex alone, the first principle component was comprised of the AI, EI, and both subscales of the PNIDS. The variance accounted for in the first principal component was 31% for the entire subject sample, 27% for males and 35% for females. Interestingly, the visual and auditory subscales of the Betts comprised a separate component distinguishable from the molar measures. The ICS subscales constituted a second component suggesting that this measure does assess the image control dimension. Finally, the subscales of the Individual Differences Questionnaire formed a fourth component that was related weakly to the other imagery measures.

Sex differences were observed in these data. Female image structure consisted of three components, the major shift from the overall subject sample being the alignment of the visual subscale of the IDQ, the Gordon Scale and Betts subscales in the third component. Male subjects required four components that roughly paralleled the results of the entire subject sample. Some relationship

Table 1. Regression Pattern for Components Rotated to Simple Structure

Variable		Component 1	2	3	4
Loadings					
1	IDQ-VERBAL	.233	.014	-.067	.758
2	IDQI-VISUAL	.093	.329	.385	.590
3	BETTS-VIS	-.168	-.180	-.777	-.188
4	BETTS-AUD	-.184	-.042	-.805	.112
5	GORDON	.289	.395	.005	-.460
6	AI	-.689	-.015	-.354	-.068
7	EI	-.710	.005	.376	-.070
8	ICS-NEU	-.050	.905	.098	.036
9	ICS-NEG	.201	.878	.135	.052
10	PNIDS-VP	-.803	-.044	-.155	-.034
11	PNIDS-VN	-.733	-.308	.186	-.126
Eigen Values		3.464	1.956	1.210	1.101
(Total % = 67) Percentage of Variance Accounted for		31%	15%	11%	10%

between the Gordon and the IDQI was present, but sensory modality imagery was unrelated to this cognitive style dimension. The significance of this difference is unclear but the possibility that males and females differ in the structural organization of imagery raises intriguing research issues.

One major objective of this study was to determine whether imagery is a single general ability, a set of specific abilities, or some combination of the two. We contend that whatever general ability exists is defined solely by the fact that visual thought is necessary for visual imagery; any general component will thus be diffuse and cover the entire range of measures that reflect the presence of visual thought. A regression component analysis was conducted in which the first regression component was removed while remaining components were rotated to simple structure. Theoretically, the presence of a second order general ability would be reflected by minimal loadings for the rotated components, a finding not observed in the results. Values for the rotated components indicated that several specific imagery abilities remained which approximated those observed in the principal component analysis. Returning to an examination of the unrotated component, prediction of a diffuse general ability was supported by the modest loadings that all measures exhibited on this component. If this component simply reflects the fact that some form of imaginal thought is necessary to image, then one would predict that the IDQ verbal subscale would not have a significant relationship to this component. Indeed, results supported this prediction; the loading for this measure was negligible. In conclusion, one can say little about the organization of the general imagery factor; it possesses no identifiable locus in the spectrum of imagery abilities.

In addition to demonstrating that the organization of clinical imagery coincides with the multiple component approach, a second requirement for a sound model is a demonstration that these abilities can be related functionally to the processes required for effective clinical imagery. Establishing a functional relationship of this type can be accomplished in either of two ways: examine imagery tasks that are analogues of those required in the clinical setting or examine the significance of various imagery abilities directly in subjects undergoing psychotherapy. Present attention will be directed to a discussion of a recent study that involved a laboratory analogue task (Strosahl & Ascough, Note 2). We invited subjects participating in the image component study to return approximately one week later to participate in the clinical imagery exercise, which required a visualization task to parallel the requirements for effective clinical imagery. Selected scene content must evoke arousal, usually of a negative nature, and identifying scenes for all subjects is difficult and time consuming. An efficient approach is to have subjects imagine a series of written scenes, then classify and rank order their emotive valence after the task has been completed. We constructed an inventory of clinical imagery designed to allow maximum freedom for subjects while retaining degree of clinical relevance. Subjects were asked to imagine each of the 20 scenes for 30 seconds following a signal by the experimenter. Each visualization was followed by a one minute erasure period, when subjects classified scenes as negative, neutral or positive and then rated scene vividness on a 1 (perfectly clear) to 7 (no image at all) scale. Following completion of the inventory, subjects rank ordered the three most negative scenes they had imagined. Data were analyzed by a multiple regression procedure using hierarchical entrance of variables. This procedure permits a priori hypotheses to be tested by arranging the order in which sets of variables are entered into the prediction system (Cohen & Cohen, 1975). We entered sets of imagery variables on the basis of their alignment in the principal component analysis, on the assumption that the ordering of components reflected the funtional importance of these abilities in the overall imagery process. Results conformed to these predictions; on the average, molar measures predicted approximately 17% of the variance in the vividness ratings, a result that was statistically ($p < .01$). In contrast, the three remaining components failed to make a contribution to the prediction equation. We propose that that imagery abilities share a common foundation since molar functions are grounded in more rudimentary imagery processes. To test this premise, hierarchical entrance was altered so that the Betts visual and auditory scales (e.g., the third principal component) were entered at the first level of inclusion. For each negative scene, this variable set was not significant. When molar measures were then entered on the second step, the prediction system attained statistical significance for each of the three scenes, supporting the principle of hierarchical structure. This study suggests that traditional measures of imagery such as the Betts bear a limited relationship to the operations necessary for effective clinical imagery. Hence, previous clinical studies that have used such questionnaires as a sole assessment measure cannot be considered as adequate tests of the individual differences questions.

CLINICAL IMAGERY: STATE OR TRAIT?

McLemore (1976) proposed that imagery may be more a state than a trait event. While existing imagery measures encourage optimal performance, it is not certain that optimal performance is maintained across or even within therapy sessions. One reason for this argument is the effect emotive arousal has upon image integrity; furthermore, emotive states are highly unstable over time. Our attempt to determine the test-retest reliability of the experimental measures produced some intriguing results in this regard. While the reliability of the Betts scale is considered adequate for research purposes, the molar measures are more problematic. The highest reliability figure attained was .46 on the Emotive Imagery Inventory, a result that demonstrates the need for a careful reexamination of existing conceptions of imagery as a trait ability. For example, subjects who complete the PNIDS are asked to rate the emotive valence and vividness of each scene that is imagined. These scenes are extremely negative or positive in nature and should possess high reliability on the emotive valence dimension. However, this is not observed in the data; reliability for the negative scene subscale is only .20. As far as imagery research is concerned, existing trait assessment methods may have to be abandoned in favor of a more state oriented approach that, despite its reduced reliability across situations, may illuminate events that underpin the behavior/attitude change process. Indeed, Dyckmann and Cowan (1978) reported a significant relationship between state vividness ratings and the therapeutic success of subjects receiving desensitization treatment.

What about aspects of imagery ability that do possess trait consistency, such as the sensory modality assessed by the Betts Questionnaire? Are there other factors that may reduce the stability of these abilities over time? _A priori_, one can speculate that imagery therapy constitutes de facto training in imagery ability. Hence, the proposition that this ability may improve during therapy must be given consideration. We tested this hypothesis with 29 subjects undergoing systematic desensitization or covert modeling treatments (Strosahl, Ascough, & Mariotto, Note 3). Of particular concern was the possibility that poor imaging subjects exhibit improved imagery as therapy progresses. We divided subjects into groups of good and poor imagers and compared their pre-and posttreatment performance on the Betts questionnaire to a control group of relaxation training and waiting list subjects. Results supported the presence of a learning effect: poor imagers improved significantly on four of the seven sensory modality subscales, the overall result being a significant improvement in the total Betts score for this group ($p < .01$). Conversely, good imagers and control subjects did not change, decreasing confidence in the rival hypothesis that simple response set influenced scoring on all self-report measures after treatment. The results of this study illustrate a critical deficiency of previous investigations of the individual differences hypothesis, since such studies have used only a pretreatment assessment strategy. In conclusion, certain facets of mental imagery may be highly unstable due to state influences, while other imagery domains may possess greater situational stability that can by altered by extensive training.

THE ROLE OF IMAGERY IN THERAPY

The purpose of the multiple component model is to expain properties of clinical imagery and their relationship to success or failure in imagery therapy. A model is as good as the testability of its predictions. Hence, we have devoted considerable effort to examining the capacity of this approach to make specific and valid functional predictions about the role of imagery in psychotherapy.

In an examination of emotive imagery in therapy, we tested the hypothesis that molecular and molar abilities would interact to influence therapeutic outcome (Strosahl, Ascough, & Mariotto, Note 3). At pretreatment, a battery of imagery questionnaires were given to 29 test-anxious subjects (consisting of the Betts and Gordon scales and the molar measures). The Betts was administered at posttreatment to examine the learning-effects hypothesis just discussed. Posttreatment anxiety reductions were converted to residual gain scores and analyzed via a hierarchical regression procedure. Intercorrelations between gains scores and imagery measures indicated that the Emotive Image Inventory as well as the pre- and posttreatment Betts proprioceptive subscale were significantly related to treatment outcome. These measures were entered as the first set of variables in the multiple regression analysis on the assumption that they comprised the molecular and molar components of emotive imagery. Results are presented in Table 2. As a group, the scores accounted for 40% of outcome variance, a significant result ($p < .01$). In addition, protected t-test indicated that each measure contributed uniquely to predicted variance, suggestive evidence for the discon-

Table 2. Regression Analysis of Anxiety-Reduction Gain Scores and Imagery Measures

Variable	Beta	R^2	F	Protected T
Proprioceptive (PRE)	-5.99	.03		P = .004
Emotive Image	1.52	.25		p = .019
Proprioceptive (POST)	.48	.39	p = .005	p = .020

tinuity of molecular and molar imagery abilities. However, the relatively small sample size used in this analysis necessitates immediate cross-validating studies. An intriguing aspect of the results is that the pretreatment proprioceptive score was negatively related to therapy outcome, a factor that might reflect the initially deleterious effect of overly elevated responsivity to clinical images. Over treatment, the relationship is reversed; that is, better proprioceptive imagery predicts better treatment success.

An interesting finding from the standpoint of a sex differences issue was a divergence in the abilities related to treatment success for males and females in this study. Females showed a preference for concrete sensory modality assessed by the Betts, while outcome for males was strongly related to performance on the Abstract Image Inventory. Comparisons of prime order correlations revealed that only the Abstract Image Inventory difference was significant, while other comparisons showed a nonsignificant trend. For both sexes, however, the Emotive Image Inventory exhibited a sizable relationship to outcome, suggesting that sex differences in the format of imagery may produce quite similar and states.

MOLAR IMAGERY AND THERAPEUTIC CHANGE

A major distinction has been developed between molecular and molar imagery information processing. Molar imagery incorporates a variety of subjective responses that initiate the behavior/attitude change process. Subjective operations may be diverse and idiosyncratic, reflecting the unique response capabilities of each individual. A number of theories have been advanced to explain the therapeutic impact of imagery that can be integrated with reference to the multiple component approach. For example, Goldfried (1971) argued that perceptions of self control accrue over the course of imagery therapy; Mahoney (1974) stressed the importance of response elaboration, mental rehearsal, and response assimilation; Meichenbaum (1977) proposed that therapeutic change occurs when individuals learn to cope despite the presence of anxiety. Here, we are questioning why imagery therapies are effective and it is somewhat surprising that more empirical effort has not been devoted to an examination of the therapeutic impact of imagery. We contend that contemporary accounts exhibit numerous common elements, the most obvious being that persons learn to behave or think differently in threatening situations despite the presence of negative arousal. Persons entering therapy have poorly defined response options and consequently exhibit deficient coping behavior in real-life situations. Mahoney's (1974) response clarification, rehearsal, and assimilation thus become central features of the quest for self-control. The concept of perceptions of self-control emerging form a differentiation of coping responses converts to a relatively straightforward research hypothesis. Specifically, at the outset of treatment, a negative relationship will exist between the anxiety experienced in response to imagined scenes and the actual degree of coping imagery present in that scene. The course of imagery therapy should be marked by a rapid reduction of this inverse relationship since individuals learn to produce coping responses in spite of anxiety. Hence, success in therapy will be related to the development of self-control imagery and not necessarily to a reduction in scene-associated anxiety. We tested these two predictions with 39 socially anxious subjects in a study of the relative efficacy of desensitization and some variations of covert modeling (Strosahl, Chaffee, & Ascough, Note 4). Immediately following completion of the first and last active treatment sessions, subjects were given a brief questionnaire that assessed level of anxiety in response to imagined scenes and the extent to which they imagined themselves coping with those scenes. The first finding of interest was the rapid reduction of the negative relationship between anxiety and coping over the course of treatment. The initial correlation was negative and significant (-.42), but was nonsignificant at post-treatment (-.12). Second, when individual gain scores were correlated with the anxiety and coping ratings, the predicted pattern emerged. Coping imagery was unrelated (-.01) to therapeutic success as measured after Session 2 but was correlated (.30) with success in therapy after Session 5, which was the final treatment Session. This evidence suggests that the therapeutic impact of molar imagery is related to increased coping capacity, which in effect reduces the anxiety associated with imagined situations. As the individual response repertoire is expanded and differentiated over treatment, more viable response alternatives exist for any given situation and, hence, an increased perception of self-control develops. Obviously, the scope of the multiple component approach necessitates a formal program of validating research. This however, is essential for any account of clinical imagery. Our principal argument is that clinical researchers have accepted the veracity of some basic assumptions about the structure and function of imagery in the absence of a strong supporting data base. For example, our knowledge of the structural organization of the molar image system is woefully deficient. Without a firm conception of the structural characteristics of clinical images, studies of image function are unlikely to produce meaningful or reliable results. We thus believe that a major task facing researchers in this decade will be determining key facets of image structure and their relationship to efficient image processing. Moreover, this task will require a wide-spectrum effort to standardize imagery assessment procedures, so that replications and cross-validations can be consummated. Most importantly, theoreticians and researchers should approach the topic of clinical imagery not as something that only other people possess but as something that a substantial part of one's everyday experience. Artificially to separate imagery as a target for laboratory study from imagery as personal experience may be acceptable for information processing research but is inconsistent with our intuitive knowledge of events that precede the behavior/attitude change process in imagery therapy.

SUMMARY

Imagery is a promising psychotherapeutic tool that nevertheless remains a complex and poorly understood phenomenon. Deficiencies in current theoretical accounts are attributed to the restictive influence of the "photograph" metaphor of imagery, which information processing research shows to have only a limited range of applicability. Equally critical facets of image construction and processing are examined with reference to a multiple component model, which proposes that the sequence of clinical imagery is comprised of several representational events of a reproductive and constructive nature. Data are cited to support the proposal that imagery abilities are hierarchically organized according to the complexity of cognitive functioning involved. Research is described that suggests that measures of constructive imagery ability can be related funtionally to both clinical analogue visualization tasks and to success or failure in imagery based behavior therapies. Important theoretical issues are also examined: sex differences in image structure, state and trait components of imagery ability and imagery as an ability that is learned over the course of therapy. The therapeutic impact of imagery is related to the increasing capacity to cope with anxiety-producing situations. Empirical results that demonstrate that the presence of coping imagery can be related empirically to therapeutic success. Existing theoretical accounts of therapeutic change are integrated within the context of the multiple component approach in order to demonstrate their numerous common assumptions.

REFERENCE NOTES

1. Strosahl, K. Relative efficacy of covert modeling, desensitization and relaxation training in the reduction of test anxiety. Unpublished manuscript. Purdue University.

2. Strosahl, K. and Ascough, J. Relating the structure and function of imagery: An empirical analysis. Manuscript submitted

for publication. Purdue University, May, 1980.

3. Strosahl, K., Ascough, J., and Mariotto, M. Imagery integrity and its relationship to analogue behavior therapy outcome. Manuscript submitted for publication. Purdue University.

4. Strosahl, K., Chaffee, R. and Ascough, J. A process and outcome investigation of covert modeling variations in the treatment of social anxiety. Manuscript submitted for publication. Purdue University.

REFERENCES

Anderson, J. Arguments concerning representations for mental imagery. Psychological Review, 1978, 85, 249-277.

Cautela, J. Covert sensitization. Psychological Reports, 1967, 20, 459-468.

Cohen, J. and Cohen, P. Applied multiple regression analysis for the behavioral sciences. New York: Wiley, 1975.

Cooper, L. Mental rotation of random two dimensional shapes. Cognitive Psychology, 1975, 7, 20-43.

Cooper, L. and Shepard, R. The time required to prepare for a rotated stimulus. Memory and Cognition, 1973, 1, 246-250. (a)

Cooper, L. and Shepard, R. Chronometric studies of the rotation of mental images. In W. Chase (Ed.), Visual information processing. New York: Academic Press, 1973. (b)

Davis, D., McLemore, C. and London, P. The role of visual imagery in desensitization. Behavior Research and Therapy, 1970, 8, 11-13.

Dyckman, J. and Cowan, P. Imaging vividness and the outcome of in vivo and imagined scene desensitization. Journal of Consulting and Clinical Psychology, 1978, 46, 1155-1156.

Goldfried, M. Systematic desensitization as training in self-control. Journal of Consuting and Clinical Psychology, 1971, 37, 228-234.

Gordon, R. An investigation into some of the factors that favour the formation of stereotyped images. British Journal of Psychology, 1949, 39, 156-157.

Hiscock, M. Imagery assessment through self-report: What do imagery questionnaires measure? Journal of Consulting and

Clinical Psychology, 1978, 46, 223-230.

Holyoak, K. and Walker, J. Subjective magnitude information in semantic ordering. Journal of Verbal Learning and Verbal Behavior, 1976, 15, 287-299.

Kosslyn, S. Information representation in visual images. Cognitive Psychology, 1975, 7, 341-370.

Kosslyn, S. Can imagery be distinguished from other forms of internal representation? Evidence from studies of information retrieval time. Memory and Cognition, 1976, 4, 291-297.

Kosslyn, S. and Pomarantz, J. Imagery, propositions and the form of internal representations. Cognitive Psychology, 1977, 9, 52-76.

Kosslyn, S. Measuring the visual angle of the mind's eye. Cognitive Psychology, 1978, 10, 356-389.

Lang, P. Imagery in therapy: An information processing analysis of fear. Behavior Therapy, 1977, 8, 862-886.

Mahoney, M. Cognition and behavior modification. Cambridge: Ballinger Publishing Co., 1974.

McLemore, C. Imagery in desensitization. Behavior Research and Therapy, 1972, 10, 51-57.

McLemore, C. Factorial validity of imagery measures. Behavior Research and Therapy, 1976, 14, 399-408.

McSweeney, A. Imagery as a variable in the efficacy of systematic desensitization. Dissertation Abstracts International, 1976, 36, (10-B), 5271.

Meichenbaum, D. Cognitive behavior modification: An integrative approach. New York: Plenum Press, 1977.

Paivio, A. Mental comparisons involving abstract attributes. Memory and Cognition, 1978, 6, 199-208.

Posner, M. and Keele, S. Decay of visual information from a single letter. Science, 1967, 158, 137-139.

Pylyshyn, Z. What the mind's eye tells the mind's brain: A critique of mental imagery. Psychological Bulletin, 1973, 80, 1-24.

Segal, S. and Fusella, V. Influence of imaged pictures and sounds on detection of visual and auditory signals. Journal of Experimental Psychology, 1970, 83, 458-464.

Sheehan, P. A shortened form of the Betts Questionnaire Upon Mental Imagery. Journal of Clinical Psychology. 1967, 23, 386-389.

Shepard, R. The mental image. American Psychologist, 1978, 33, 125-127.

Shorr, J. Psychotherapy through imagery. New York: Intercontinental Medical Book Corporation, 1974.

Singer, J. Imagery and daydream methods in psychotherapy and behavior modification. New York: Academic Press, 1974.

Strosahl, K., and Ascough, J. Clinical uses of imagery: Experimental foundations, theoretical misconceptions and research issues. Psychological Bulletin, 1980, in press.

Tversky, B. Pictorial and verbal encoding in a short term memory task. Perception and Psychophysics, 1969, 6, 225-233.

Wolpe, J. Psychotherapy by reciprocal inhibition. Stanford: Stanford University Press, 1958.

THE ROLE OF MENTAL EVENTS IN BEHAVIOR THERAPY

Alvin Enis House and Martha B. Campbell

Illinois State University

Mackinow, IL

THE ROLE OF MENTAL EVENTS IN BEHAVIOR THERAPY

The human ability "to see in the mind's eye" has been of interest to those who ponder human behavior throughout recorded history. Systematic philosophical speculation within western civilization regarding mental imagery is often traced to Hume's distinctions in the 18th century between the impressions arising from externally produced sensations and the faint images of these experiences that formed thought (Hume, 1912). Hume saw the primary distinction between these two types of mental experiences to be the greater force and vividness of the sensations. The question of how mental images are distinct from percepts has remained a key issue in philosophical inquiries on the topic.

Empirical investigations of imagery began with the pioneering work of Fechner (1860) on the nature of mental imagery, followed in two decades by the work of Galton on individual differences in mental imagery ability (Galton, 1880, 1883/1973). Most work on the measurement of mental imagery can be traced to Galton's early questionnaire studies.

Despite this long history, fundamental questions regarding the utility of mental imagery as a variable remain. This is especially evident in the two disciplines that have most seriously considered the pictures of the mind's eye: philosophy and cognitive psychology. Within philosophy a number of writers have questioned whether mental images should be considered "images" and whether or not they occur in the mind (Dennett, 1969; Ryle, 1949; Sartre, 1948, 1962; Shorter, 1952). Images also have their defenders--who clearly believe that there are mental images, that they are seen, and are in the mind (Hannay, 1971; Warnock, 1976).

Within cognitive psychology a similar distinction can be made between investigators who assign some usefulness ot the concept of mental imagery in accounting for mental processes (Bower, 1972; Kosslyn, 1978a, 1978b, 1978c; Kosslyn & Pomerantz, 1977; Neisser, 1967, 1970, 1972; Paivio, 1971; Shepard, 1978) and those who claim that all functional internal representations consist of propositional networks (Anderson & Bower, 1973; Pylyshyn 1973; Simon, 1972). At issue is whether images should be considered as functional representations or as epiphenomena within a cognitive processing model. Paivio's Imagery and Verbal Process (1971) is a documented argument for the greater recognition of the role played by imagery in cognitive processing. The emphasis within cognitive psychology during most of the 20th century has been almost exclusively on verbal processes. The explanation for this deemphasis of imagery is almost universally the same: behaviorism (Bower, 1972; Holt, 1964; Klinger, 1971; Simon, 1972; Singer, 1966).

> "In its early day when psychology was considered the science of mental life, investigators paid serious attention to human responses such as imagery, daydreams, and the stream of consciousness. But during the past half century, with Watson's behaviorism and operationalism as the dominant American Zeitgeist, there has been relatively little systematic study of spontaneous imagery or conscious fantasy. Only psychoanalysis as a discipline has collected information about patterns of consciousness, dreams, daydreams, and marginal states of awareness" (Singer, 1966, P. XIV).

> "Our relative ignorance of fantasy arises out of an historical moratorium on the investigation of inner experience, especially in the United States, approximately from 1920-1960. The behavioristic and neobehavioristic tide that swept academic departments of psychology during these 40 years transformed psychological science.... One of the costs was the relative neglect of some classical psychological problems, not the least of which was the description of inner experience" (Klinger, 1971, P. 10).

The emphasis on verbal processes as the basis for cognitive functioning did arise fairly directly from behaviorism and Watson's conclusion that images were ghosts with no functional significance. Paivio points out, however, that the negative emphasis on mentalistic concepts (imagery and meaning in particular) was not restricted to behaviorism--the rote learning tradition established by Ebbinghaus in 1885 had also contributed to this development.

Clearly, however, the most significant force shaping the early behavioristic philosophy regarding images was the ideology of John

B. Watson. Although initially couched in terms of methodological behaviorism--restricting the domain of psychology to those topics that could be studied objectively--Watson's major thrust was much more significant: to eliminate states of consciousness as proper objects of investigation (Watson, 1913, 1924). Mackenzie (1977) has argued that the critical feature of early behaviorism's concern with objectivity was the rejection in principle of any concern with mental events: "'objective psychologists' rejected introspection because they were anti-mentalistic; they did not become anti-mentalistic on the basis of having had to reject introspection" (P. 13). The rejection of mentalistic concepts was taken up by other voices (Kantor, 1947; Kuo, 1976). The position of radical behaviorism was that all human behavior could be explained without the use of mentalistic concepts such as awareness, imagery, belief, and expectancy. Essential concepts were translated into behavioral terms (Tolman, 1932; Watson, 1913, 1914) and the others were discarded as epiphenomena. Among the discards was imagery, Watson's "ghosts" of sensation. Watson was willing to retain thinking but not imagining. Thinking for Watson became a special type of subvocal verbal behavior, and verbal behavior could be studied. His fundamental argument was with the images essential to the structural and functional schools. Watson's choice of propositional representation as the only type of cognitive processing has had a fundamental impact on the development of behavioristic thought. Although some current behavioral theorists are beginning to recognize the necessity of utilizing variables such as imagery and meaning for a complete account of human behavior (Erwin, 1978), this utilization is often to continue the radical behavioristic tradition of translating cognitive events into behavioral terms. For instance, Skinner (1974) speaks of imagery as seeing in the absence of the thing seen and believes this results from the reinforcement of perceptual behavior.

In contrast to the philosophy of behaviorism expounded by Watson and his followers, the early behavior therapists tended to exclude much consideration of deliberate thought but clearly retained the notion of mental images. In the early 1950's, Wolpe had begun to experiment with the use of imaginary situations for desensitization (Wolpe & Lazarus, 1966). By the time Wolpe's seminal work was published in 1958, imaginal presentation had become a standard aspect of systematic desensitization. Other early uses of imagery by behavior therapists included Gold and Neufeld (1965), Kolvin (1967), Lazarus (1958), Lazarus and Abramovity (1962), McGuire and Valence (1964), and Stampfl (1967). Bell (1976) has pointed out that the application of behavior therapy techniques such as systematic desensitization has made respectable the discussion of topics such as mental imagery, imagination, and other cognitive functions.

The retention of mental imagery as a working concept by the early behavior therapists represented a very pragmatic decision: it was simply practical and possible to do things with imagery that would not be practical or possible in vivo. In keeping with their behavioral traditions the "mental" aspects of mental imagery were minimized, and a loose physiological model often advanced (Hebb, 1968; Wolpe, 1958). Speaking of images, Wolpe wrote:

> "Just as light rays from a pencil may initiate in my nervous system a series of changes leading to the specific neural events that are correlated with my seeing a pencil, so may other antecedents (such as the word 'pencil') also have among their consequences these particular neural events, and I then have an imagined image of a pencil. Of course, there are also differences between what is seen and what is imagined, because the afferent neurons activated by a real pencil have other neural connections that are not shared by the neurons activated by the word 'pencil'" (Wolpe, 1958, P. 16).

Images were thus conceptualized as basically analogous to external stimuli with the only important difference being that they were subjective or private events. The implicit view of imagery in most behavioral presentations seems to be one of relatively static pictures that the client passively experiences on command of the therapist--a picture seen in the mind's eye; for instance, a cat imagined by an ailurophobic. This view of images allowed a selective inattention by behavior therapists to the fact that they were dealing with mental processes, and it is this largely unexamined conception of imagery that continues in the behavioral tradition today despite suggestions of its inadequacy (Neisser, 1972).

One consequence of equating mental imagery with external stimulus presentations has been an almost total focus on the vividness and clarity of imagery as the only relevant variable. The fact that there is little explicit discussion in the behavioral literature of image quality is interesting in view of the central role played by imagery in so many behavioral techniques. Desensitization manuals, however, do often include in their troubleshooting section problems in visualizing--indicating that the image of the client may be vague or unclear (Marquis & Morgan, 1968; Wenrich, Dawley, & General, 1976). Practice in visualizing scenes and verbally describing the scene aloud is often prescribed as a remediation if vagueness occurs. Alternative methods such as in vivo desensitization may be suggested. The use of hypnosis or relaxation training to increase the vividness of imagery is also used.

Unfortunately, Neisser (1970) has pointed out that the vividness of images as measured by ratings is a poor indicator of the functional usefulness of the images, showing little correlation with performance in visual memory, artistic ability, or with anything else. Although other investigators would dispute this strong position on vividness of images (Marks, 1972; Richardson, 1972; Sheehan, 1972) it does seem clear that there are relevant variables other than vividness that influence the effectiveness of imagery. Neisser (1970) reviews evidence that "visualization" or "spatial relations," defined as the mental manipulation of visual form, does relate to memory and other indications of information content. Neisser and Kerr (1973) for instance found that images of concealed objects were less "vivid" or "good" in the introspective reports of subjects, but were just as effective mediators of memory as other images. Neisser (1967) has also argued that the "realness" of an image does not depend on its vividness. He uses as an example that psychotic hallucinations may be very real for the person and at the same time apparently very vague and indistinct. Neisser (1970) asserts that while subjects differ in the reality status they assign to their images, these differences are not necessarily related to performance on visual memory tasks. Although there clearly is individual variation in the quality of imagery that affects progress in behavioral procedures such as desensitization, it is by no means clear that vividness is the relevant variable. Richardson (1969) distinguishes between "habitual visualizers" or those who have fairly vivid concrete imagery, and "habitual verbalizers" who have relatively weak concrete imagery, little visual imagery, and who show a preponderance of kinaesthetic (from the larynx and tongue) verbal auditory imagery. Considering the necessity of a clearly imagined scene for successful desensitization, there is a question as to whether verbalizers could be treated with desensitization as well as visualizers.

Gordon (1949, 1950) distinguished between controlled imagery that is deliberate and could be easily influenced by the conscious wishes of the imager, and autonomous (uncontrolled) imagery that might be deliberate or spontaneous but could not be easily influenced by the person experiencing the imagery. Richardson (1969) reviewed evidence on control and vividness, and indicated that for some tasks, such as the mental practice of a sport, vividness might lead to impairment if imagery was not controllable. Likewise, Richardson (1972) has suggested that the possession of vivid imagery without a corresponding ability to control it could result in a failure to benefit from desensitization therapy.

There is some recognition by behavior therapists that other sorts of problems occur. Marquis, Morgan, and Piaget (1973) discuss problems of inability to hold a scene, perseveration of a scene, and early or late onset of a scene in desensitization. They also discuss the client disassociating him- or herself in the image (seeing him- or herself as an object rather than the subject of a scene). Although some attribute lack of arousal to theoretically anxiety arousing scenes as always due to poor visualization (Wenrich, Dawley, & General, 1976), Wolpe has recognized that this can occur in between 5% and 15% of clients, even though they can clearly visualize a scene (Wolpe, 1958, 1976; Wolpe & Lazarus, 1966). Of related interest is a statement in Bernstein and Borkovec's

(1973) relaxation manual that one of the most disruptive influences on a client's progress can be the presence of distracting, intrusive thoughts.

As a hypothesis requiring empirical investigation it would seem that four aspects of imagery might affect its clinical utility: vividness (the subject's ability to form mental pictures clearly and in rich detail), reality quality or "realness" (the subject's) investment in experiencing the images as if experiencing the actual stimulus), control (the subject's ability to initiate, manipulate, and terminate desired images while suppressing undesired images), and information storage (the subject's spatial-relations ability). It could be speculated, for example, that clients who dissociate or imagine scenes without experiencing anxiety are displaying a deficiency not of vividness but of reality quality (investment). In this regard it is interesting to note that Wolpe believed hypnosis (which Neisser sees as influencing investment) accelerated progress in desensitization. Difficulties with intrusive images would involve the control factor. It is not clear if individual differences in spatial relations ability significantly affect response to systematic desensitization.

A second consequence of the unexamined view of imagery apparent in the behavioral literature has been the continued inattention to the potential integrative value of mental imagery. The symbolic value of mental images, visions, dreams, and fantasies has, of course, long been of interest to psychoanalytic investigators. Anthropologists, often influenced by analytic theories, have also recognized the integrative function of images--the ability of images to serve as symbols for an idea, a philosophy, a world view. However, it does not require uncritical acceptance of concepts such as the collective unconscious to recognize that an image can serve as a concrete prompt (or discriminative stimulus) for carrying out an extensive range of new behavior that may be based on previous abstract (verbal) development. The potential facilitative role imagery can play in behavior change is apparent in several European-based psychotherapies (Singer, 1974). To consider this issue further it is useful to consider the range of application of imagery procedures in behavior therapy.

A wide range of behavioral techniques has utilized imaginal presentation of stimuli. Cautela has summarized the advantages of using imagery in behavioral procedures (1970a, 1970b, 1971). A partial list of the techniques using mental imagery would include: systematic desensitization, thought stopping, the use of positive images in relaxation, emotive imagery, covert sensitization, covert reinforcement, covert negative reinforcement, covert extinction, covert punishment, cognitive rehearsal, cognitive modeling, implosion, coping imagery, orgasmic reconditioning, and hypnosis. There are also other techniques originally developed by other therapeutic schools and sometimes used by behavior therapists such as fixed role therapy (Kelly, 1955), guided affective imagery (Leuner,1969), and various Gestalt therapy techniques.

One manner of attempting to bring some order to this confusing mass of procedure is to classify imagery techniques by their intended function as seen in Table 1. For instance, many behavioral techniques use imagery basically to expose the client to a stimulus situation, essentially a stimulus input function. Desensitization, for instance, uses imagery to present stimuli because this is more convenient or more possible than presenting the stimuli _in vivo_. Images may also be used because they allow a rehearsal function--mental practice of new behavior. This may be the express purpose of the procedure, such as cognitive rehearsal, or it may be an indirect result of a more primary function such as exposure. Desensitization, for instance, as well as exposing clients to stimuli also gives imaginal practice in dealing with these stimuli in a nonfearful manner. Finally, it is possible to conceive of imagery serving an integrative function--helping to give the client an altered cognitive view of his situation. Again this may be the direct intent of a procedure as in fixed role therapy, or it may be an indirect consequence. Coping imagery employed in desensitization gives the client mental practice in dealing successfully with difficult situations, but also provides an image of oneself as someone who can deal with the situation. The new mental image of a competent self subtly forces a reconsideration by the client of his or her ability to deal with the world.

Kelly's fixed role therapy, for example, not only gives clients imaginal and real practice in carrying out new behaviors, it also gives them the experience of thinking about themselves and other persons' reactions to him in a different way. Often the mental image of the person whose role the client is taking will come to serve as a cue or discriminative stimulus to carry out the new behavior. In a case treated by the first author with fixed role therapy the assumed role was that of Captain Kirk form the television series Star Trek. The client had a long history of ineffective and dysfunctional social relations. He appeared to lack social skills, was nonassertive, and often dealt with people in an indirect and passive-aggressive manner. Desensitization of his social anxieties and assertive training led to a rapid improvement of his social skills within the therapy session but did not generalize to his other social encounters. The client reported he simply could not bring himself to begin acting differently. In a maneuver inspired mostly by desperation, fixed role therapy was initiated after it was learned that the client was a great admirer of the character from the television series. After a series of ups and downs the intervention ultimately proved very successful. When the client was asked in retrospect what was most helpful he gave a very interesting answer: The first occasion that he was to have

Table 1. Classification of Imagery Techniques by Function

I. Exposure function
   A. Respondent model
      1. Systematic desensitization
      2. Emotive imagery
      3. Covert sensitization
      4. Implosion
      5. Orgasmic reconditioning
   B. Operant model
      1. Covert reinforcement
      2. Covert negative reinforcement
      3. Covert punishment
      4. Covert extinction
   C. Observational learning: Covert modeling
   D. Hypnosis
   E. Interference
      1. Thought stopping
      2. Positive imagery

II. Rehearsal function
   A. Direct result
      1. Cognitive rehearsal
      2. Coping imagery
      3. Hypnosis
      4. Fixed role therapy
   B. Indirect result
      1. Systematic desensitization
      2. Emotive imagery
      3. Orgasmic reconditioning
      4. Covert reinforcement
      5. Covert negative reinforcement
      6. Covert punishment
      7. Covert extinction

III. Integrative function
   A. Direct result
      1. Hypnosis
      2. Fixed role therapy
      3. Guided affective imagery
   B. Indirect result
      1. Coping imagery
      2. Covert modeling
      3. Cognitive rehearsal

put the new role into effect involved a dinner meeting with a social and professional group important to the client. As he walked into the dining hall he experienced an image of Captain Kirk walking into the same room. This initial image was spontaneous but did prompt the client to adjust his posture, gait, and eye contact with others. These were behaviors we had worked on in therapy in the past. Thereafter, throughout the evening and on subsequent occasions, whenever the client felt at a loss to cope effectively he would deliberately visualize for a second his hero in his situation and use the new skills learned in therapy to respond accordingly.

What is significant in this case and others where the procedure was used deliberately is that mental images can serve as cues to cognitive restructuring of thoughts, feelings, and attitudes about a situation. Images can serve a symbolic function in concretely representing a great number of abstract ideas. Cognitive behavior modification, building on the conceptions of investigators such as Rotter (1954) and Bandura (1969), has focused on the demonstration that changes in client's ideas, attitudes, and feelings can precipitate as well as follow behavior change. However, most formulations of cognitive behavior modification are almost entirely verbal or prepositional in nature (Beck, 1976; Ellis, 1971; Meichenbaum, 1977). As Meichenbaum (1979) has pointed out, cognitive behavior modification evolved out of a merger of the technical methodology of behavior therapy with the clinical methods of cognitive-semantic therapists. To date there has been little systematic work on the possible use of imagery for an integrative or symbolic function. There appears to be significant clinical and research potential in this direction, which would extend previous syntheses of behavior therapies and imagery procedures (e.g., Kroger & Geyler, 1976; Tugender & Ferinden, 1972).

A final point that may require constant repetition in the area of imagery concerns the need for continued research and conceptual rigor if progress is to be made. To recognize that it may be necessary to talk about imagery, meaning, and other cognitive variables to give an adequate account of human behavior is not to say that introducing these concepts will automatically lead to advance. In the absence of public referents, discussion of mental processes can easily become endless metaphysical speculation. Kendall and Korgeski (1979) have discussed this issue in reference to the need for methods of assessing cognitions in the use of cognitive behavior therapies. Conceptual insights will serve no purpose if not followed up with empirical demonstrations.

SUMMARY

This paper examines the role played by mental events, particularly images, in behavior therapy. Mental imagery was dismissed by behaviorism as an epiphenomenon and radical behaviorists restricted their explanation of private events as observables to propositional processes. Early behavior therapists, in contrast, retained mental imagery as a useful procedure but accepted a very narrow view of this activity. Although recent years have seen an increase in behavioral discussion of cognitive variables, the view of mental imagery continues to be a rather limited one. The consequences of these historical decisions are discussed in the context of practical difficulties in the current behavioral use of images and possible uses of imagery that could be developed within behavior therapy. A classification of behavioral procedures that use imagery is proposed based on the primary function served by the imagery.

REFERENCES

Anderson, J. R., & Bower, G. H. Human associative memory. New

York: Wiley, 1973.

Bandura, A. Principles of behavior modification. New York: Holt, Rinehart & Winston, 1969.

Beck, A. T. Cognitive therapy and the emotional disorders. New York: International Universities Press, 1976.

Bell, G. K. Clinical hypnosis: Warp and woof of psychotherapies. In E. Dengrove (Ed.), Hypnosis and behavior therapy. Springfield, Illinois: Thomas, 1976, 271-277.

Bernstein, D. A., and Borkovec, T. D. Progressive relaxation training. Champaign, Illinois: Research Press, 1973.

Bower, G. H. Mental imagery and associative learning. In L. W. Gregg (Ed.), Cognition in learning and memory. New York: Wiley, 1972.

Cautela, J. Covert reinforcement. Behavior Therapy, 1970, 1, 33-50.

Cautela, J. R. Covert negative reinforcement. Journal of Behavior Therapy and Experimental Psychiatry, 1970, 1, 273-278.

Cautela, J. R. Covert conditioning. In A. Jacobs and L. B. Sachs (Eds.), The psychology of private events. New York: Academic Press, 1971, 109-130.

Dennett, D. C. Content and consciousness. London: Routledge & Kegan Paul, 1969.

Ellis, A. Reason and emotion in psychotherapy. New York: Lyle Stuart, 1971.

Erwin, E. Behavior therapy. New York: Cambridge University Press, 1978.

Fechner, G. T. Elemente der psychophysik. Leipzig: Breitkopf & Härtel, 1860.

Galton, F. Statistics of mental imagery. Mind, 1880, 5, 301-318.

Galton, F. Inquiries into human faculty and its development. New York: AMS Press, 1973. (Originally published, 1883.)

Gold, S., and Neufeld, I. L. A learning approach to the treatment of homosexuality. Behavior Research and Therapy, 1965, 2, 201-204.

Gordon, R. An investigation into some of the factors that favour the formation of stereotyped images. British Journal of Psychology, 1949, 39, 156-167.

Gordon, R. An experiment correlating the nature of imagery with performance on a test of reversal of perspective. British Journal of Psychology, 1950, 41, 63-67.

Hannay, A. Mental images--a defense. New York: Humanities Press, 1971.

Hebb, D. O. Concerning imagery. Psychological Review, 1968, 75, 466-477.

Holt, R. Imagery: The return of the ostracized. American Psychologist, 1964, 19, 254-264.

Hume, D. An inquiry concerning human understanding. Chicago: Open Court, 1912.

Kantor, J. R. Problems of physiological psychology. Bloomington, Indiana: Principia Press, 1947.

Kelly, G. A. The psychology of personal constructs. Vol. I. A Theory of Personality. New York: Norton, 1955.

Kendall, P. C., and Korgeski, G. P. Assessment and cognitive-behavioral interventions. Cognitive Therapy and Research, 1979, 3, 1-21.

Klinger, E. Structure and functions of fantasy. New York: Wiley, 1971.

Kolvin, I. "Aversive imagery" treatment in adolescents. Behavior Research and Therapy, 1967, 5, 245-248.

Kosslyn, S. M. The representational-development hypothesis. In P. A. Ornstein (Ed.), Memory development in children. Hillsdale, New Jersey: Erlbaum, 1978.(a)

Kosslyn, S. M. Imagery and internal representation. In E. Rosch & B. Lloyd (Eds.), Cognition and categorization. Hillsdale, New Jersey: Erlbaum, 1978.(b)

Kosslyn, S. M. Imagery and cognitive development: A teleological approach. In R. S. Siegler (Ed.), Children's thinking: What develops? Hillsdale, New Jersey: Erlbaum, 1978, 291-323.(c)

Kosslyn, S. M., and Pomerantz, J. R. Imagery, propositions, and the form of internal representations. Cognitive Science, 1977, 1, 265-296.

Kroger, W. S., & Feyler, W. D. Hypnosis and behavior modification: Imagery conditioning. Philadelphia: J. B. Lippincott Co., 1976.

Kuo, Z. Y. The dynamics of behavior development (Enlarged Ed.). New York: Plenum, 1976.

Lazarus, A. A. New methods in psychotherapy: A case study. South African Medical Journal, 1958, 33, 660-663.

Lazarus, A. A., and Abramovity, A. The use of "emotive imagery" in the treatment of children's phobias. Journal of Mental Science, 1962, 108, 191-195.

Leuner, H. Guided affective imagery (GAI): A method of intensive psychotherapy. American Journal of Psychotherapy, 1969, 23, 4-22.

Mackenzie, B. D. Behaviorism and the limits of scientific method. Atlantic Highlands, New Jersey: Humanities Press, 1977.

Marks, D. F. Individual differences in the vividness of visual imagery and their effect on function. In P. W. Sheehan (Ed.), The function and nature of imagery. New York: Academic Press, 1972, 83-108.

Marquis, J. N., and Morgan, W. G. A guidebook for systematic desensitization. Palo Alto, California: Veterans' Workshop, Veterans Administration Hospital, 1968.

Marquis, J. N., Morgan, W. G., and Piaget, G. W. A guidebook for systematic desensitization (3rd Ed.). Palo Alto, California: Veterans' Workshop, Veterans Administration Hospital, 1973.

McGuire, N. J., & Valence, M. Aversion therapy by electric shock: A simple technique. British Medical Journal, 1964, 1, 151-153.

Meichenbaum, D. Cognitive-behavior modification. New York: Plenum, 1977.

Meichenbaum, D. Cognitive-behavior modification: Future directions. In P. O. Sjöden, S. Bates, & W. S. Dockens, III (Eds.), Trends in behavior therapy. New York: Academic Press, 1979.

Neisser, U. Cognitive psychology. New York: Appleton-Century-Crofts, 1967.

Neisser, U. Visual imagery as process and as experience. In J. S. Antrobus (Ed.), Cognition and affect. Boston: Little, Brown, 1970.

Neisser, U. Changing conceptions of imagery. In P. Sheehan (Ed.), The function and nature of imagery. New York: Academic Press, 1972.

Neisser, U., and Kerr, N. Spatial and mnemonic properties of visual images. Cognitive Psychology, 1973, 5, 138-150.

Paivio, A. Imagery and verbal process. New York: Holt, Rinehart & Winston, 1971.

Pylyshyn, Z. W. What the mind's eye tells the mind's brain: A critique of mental imagery. Psychological Bulletin, 1973, 80, 1-24.

Richardson, A. Mental imagery. New York: Springer, 1969.

Richardson, A. Voluntary control of the memory image. In P. W. Sheehan, (Ed.), The function and nature of imagery. New York: Academic Press, 1972.

Rotter, J. B. Social learning and clinical psychology. Englewood Cliffs, New Jersey: Prentice-Hall, 1954.

Ryle, G. The concept of mind. New York: Barnes & Nobel, 1949.

Sartre, J. P. The psychology of imagination. New York: Philosophical Library, 1948.

Sartre, J. P. Imagination. Ann Arbor: The University of Michigan Press, 1962.

Sheehan, P. W. A functional analysis of the role of visual imagery in unexpected recall. In P. W. Sheehan (Ed.), The function and nature of imagery. New York: Academic Press, 1972, 149-174.

Shepard, R. N. The mental image. American Psychologist, 1978, 33, 125-137.

Shorter, J. M. Imagination. Mind, 1952, 61, 528-542.

Simon, H. A. What is visual imagery? An information-processing interpretation. In L. W. Gregg (Ed.), Cognition in learning and memory. New York: Wiley, 1972.

Singer, J. L. Daydreaming. New York: Random House, 1966.

Singer, J. L. Imagery and daydream methods in psychotherapy and behavior modification. New York: Academic Press, 1974.

Skinner, B. F. About behaviorism. New York: Knopf, 1974.

Stampfl, T. G. Implosive therapy, Part 1: The theory. In S. G. Armitage (Ed.), Behavior modification techniques and the treatment of emotional disorders. Battle Creek, Michigan: U.S. Publications, 1967.

Tolman, E. Purposive behavior in animals and men. New York: Century, 1932.

Tugender, H. S., and Ferinden, W. E. An introduction to hypno-operant therapy. Orange, New Jersey: Power, 1972.

Watson, J. B. Psychology as the behaviorist views it. The Psychological Review, 1913, 20, 158-177.

Watson, J. B. Image and affection in behavior. Journal of Philosophy, Psychology, and Scientific Method, 1913, 10, 421-428.

Watson, J. B. Behavior: An introduction to comparative psychology. New York: Holt, 1914.

Watson, J. B. Behaviorism. New York: The People's Institute, 1924.

Warnock, M. Imagination. Berkeley: University of California Press, 1976.

Wenrich, W. W., Dawley, H. H., and General, D. A. Self-directed systematic desensitization. Kalamazoo, Michigan: Behaviordelia, 1976.

Wolpe, J. Psychotherapy by reciprocal inhibition. Stanford, California: Stanford University Press, 1958.

Wolpe, J. Theme and variations. New York: Pergamon, 1976.

Wolpe, J., and Lazarus, A. A. Behavior therapy techniques. New York: Pergamon, 1966.

THE PSYCHOLOGIST'S IMAGINATION AND SEXUAL IMAGERY

Joseph E. Shorr

Institute for Psycho-Imagination Therapy

Los Angeles, California

Does the stream of consciousness belong solely to literary figures such as Franz Kafka, James Joyce, Virginia Wolf, etc., or can the psychologist's imagination be used to capture this stream and make it eligible for scientific investigation? The Watsonian denial is a thing of the past, yet still most cognitive psychologists regard consciousness as if it were merely short-term storage or a central processing unit.

Dr. Ulric Neisser (1979) says, "Such a notion does not make contact with personal continuity, the control of feelings, the contrast between 'inner' experience and external reality...New ideas about consciousness now seem to come from non-psychological sources: from neuroscientists like Sperry, sociologists like Goffman, and young people on mind-expanding trips" (p. 99-100)

To this I must add several other non-psychological sources of imagination. One example of this is the book _A Perfect Vacuum. Perfect Reviews of Non-Existent Books_, by Stanislaw Lem, a book of fiction in the form of literary criticism of imaginary books by imaginary authors.

What extraordinary imaginative gifts this author surely has! How many of us with our degrees and publications would be capable of this capacity to create something out of such a perfect vacuum?

The _New Yorker_ cartoonist, Weber, shows a man seated, looking very intelligent, away from a group of people at a gathering. As he is approached by the hostess he says, "I'm sorry, but I can't carry on an intelligent conversation. I'm visual."

Consider the imagination of Muriel Spark (1975), the author who in her short story "The First Year of my Life" makes the fictional claim that "Babies in their first year of life, in their waking hours, know everything that is going on everywhere in the world; they can tune into any conversation they choose, switch on to any scene" In her tongue-in-cheek manner, she says scientific proof is shortly on the way. "Perhaps the final touches are being put to the new manifesto in some cell at Harvard University," she writes.

It's the year 1918, and Spark engages in ESP conversation with the Czar of Russia, Marshall Foch, and D. H. Lawrence. What extraordinary use of imagination!

Woody Allen, when he was a stand-up comic, told a story about his departure to Italy to do a film. While there he meets this beautiful Italian woman who falls madly in love with him. In typical Woody Allen fashion he says, "I showed her no mercy." And as time went on and Woody Allen had to return to America, this woman became so sad that she became a streetwalker, moved to Venice, and drowned.

What kind of imaginative ingenuity does Woody Allen possess? Are we, as psychologists, able to utilize such imaginative capacity in our work?

I confess I do not know the answer. What I will attempt in this paper is to show that to study the waking imagery of humans is really an inquiry into consciousness itself. I will also show some of the workings of the imagination from certain observations of sexual imagery.

My first point is that imagery in human beings may be the integrative force that helps us comprehend perception, motivation, subjective meaning, realistic abstract thought, memory, and affect. I say "may be" because imagery in humans is evidently instantaneous, effortless and ubiquitous, and further complicated by the need of reportability by the individual to ensure verification.

A clear example of this phenomenon is amply demonstrated when one is asked <u>not</u> to imagine a red giraffe. Despite the fact that we are asked not to, most persons get an image of a red giraffe that is spontaneous, effortless and ubiquitous.

Arieti and a nonpsychological theorist named Albert Einstein (in his Gedanken experiments) claim that image formation is actually the basis for all higher mental processes. It can not only re-evoke what is not present, but it can retain the memory of the feeling for the absent object. (Example: the image of your mother.) It is common, acceptable knowledge that goal imagery can motivate us positively and aversion imagery can motivate us negatively.

All knowledge of the past in one's development allows us the possibility of the transmission of this knowledge for us to be better able to cope with the future events. The images of life experience need to be remembered and transmitted if life is to exist, as John Dewey long ago suggested. Without memory images we would at best vegetate, and probably die.

My second point is that we use the concept of "waking imagery" rather than daydreaming, reminiscing, ruminating and fantasizing. While I am certain that all of us at certain times daydream, reminisce and fantasize, we must make the distinction between the images of sleep and dreams and those images that occur to us while awake. It is my contention that some sort of imagery goes on constantly in our heads whether we are thinking, problem solving, or reasoning, as well as when we are daydreaming and fantasizing. To my way of thinking, this constant flow should be more clearly defined as waking imagery. Daydreaming, visual hallucinations, and fantasizing are all part of the waking imagery.

My contention is that to study daydreaming may yield one set of data for analysis, to study fantasy may yield another set of data for analysis and comprehension. The same could be said for early recollections and types of reminiscences. To study the flow of images that are neither daydreaming nor fantasy may yield another set of information for understanding not only cognitive processes but personality factors as well.

This is based on my clinical experience with directed imagery and its ability to bypass censorship through projection to yield more deeply, heretofore unanalyzable data about the individual's personality.

I will attempt to demonstrate this point by explaining the use of certain directed sexual imageries that are offered to the person who is asked to close his eyes and relax and then to trust his imagination.

Psycho-Imagination Therapy has developed categories of directed (and spontaneous) imagery such as Dual Imagery, Body Imagery, Sexual Imagery, Task Imagery, Self-Image Imagery, Couples Imagery, General Imagery, Special Imagery, Parental Imagery and Group Therapy Imagery. I will confine my remarks in this paper to directed sexual imagery and couples imagery.

The sexual imagination of men and women perhaps represents the most fertile avenue of the mind going in unbelievable directions and most often in the privacy of the self. Since we are dealing with the most vulnerable and sensitive areas of human existence, revealing and exposing the sexual imagination should be done in an atmosphere free of judgment and with warm feelings of acceptance.

Individuals can fantasize or imagine sexual happenings from memory images nearly congruous in feelings to their past actual occurrence. Empirical exidence indicates that sexual imagery can be so vivid that the physiological response can cause increased heartbeat rate, a rise in temperature, rapid breathing, vaso-congestion, and even orgasm. Of course, other imageries besides sexual ones can be near-re-creations, but sexual images are certainly the example par excellence.

In fact, my experience indicates that when persons say they cannot have images, they will respond when I ask them if they can imagine sexual scenes or recall sexual memories. So far this has resulted in no failures.

Sexual themes are a fertile area for the imagination to play upon. They have power because of their importance in our lives. Images of sexuality we have during intercourse or in place of it, as in masturbation, are as common as rain. Then there are other images related to the strategies of interaction between men and women that anticipate sexual outcomes, acceptance, or rejection.

Sadistic or masochistic images may emerge, as well as images of dominance, rejection, jealousy, unfavorable comparisons, feelings of heartbreak, joy, sin, being dirty, etc. Whatever our use of sexual imagination, its content can provide more graphic and immediate psychological self-knowledge than perhaps any other kind of mental activity.

Since sexual conflicts deal with the most vulnerable, the most tender, the most shame-inducing and the most guilty feelings, they are the most difficult to disclose to oneself and others. In order to get at these conflicts, I start with general imagery situations that have no obvious sexual overtones, but that have, through clinical use, proved to be sexually revealing.

Sexuality is what we conceive it to be: a valued or worthless commodity; a means of procreation; a defense against loneliness; a form of communication; a tool of aggression, control, power, punishment, submission; a sport; an act of love; an art; beauty; an ideal state; evil; good; luxury; recreation; reward; escape; a source of self esteem; a means of expressing affection--maternal, paternal, fraternal, or simply human; a way of rebellion; a source of freedom; a duty; a pleasure; a communion with the universal; a mystical ecstasy; a death-related wish or experience; a road to peace; a cause; a mode of pioneering and exploring; a skill; a biological function; a manifestation of psychic health or disease; a simple sensory experience; a product of what we have learned in relationships with others.

Since, as you can see, it is impossible to be encyclopedic

about sex in one chapter, I am directing my remarks to the general application of Psycho-Imagination Therapy to sexual matters.

I will start with those imaginary situations that seem to bypass the censorship of that person insofar as sexuality is concerned in nearly all cases.

One of the most unusual phenomena is the response that persons give to the directed imaginary situation, "Imagine you are in a room with a hole in the center of the floor. Imagine looking through the hole and tell me what you see, do and feel." Now, after having thousands of persons responding to this imaginary situation we are finding that 98% of the respondents are revealing some aspect of their sexuality and/or relationships. The projective qualities of this imaginary situation are such that I have yet to find one single respondent who in advance of this directed imagery knew what subjective meaning would result.

Additionally, when a person is asked to imagine going down into the hole and then asked how he feels, what he does and what he sees, a great deal of additional sexual material can be elicited. By using sentence completions such as "I feel ________," "I wish ________," "I must ________," "I will ________," "I secretly ________," "I fear ________," "I need ________," "Never refer to me as ________," etc., subjects' answers are quantitatively scorable with an interscorer reliability of experienced scorers at the 1% level of confidence. Of course, their qualitative interpretive value is extrememly great for the dialogical processes of therapy or for diagnostic test purposes. Nondirective dialogue about the imagery is the method used to deduce meaning of the image, leading to consensual validation.

Here is an actual response from a 30-year-old woman. I will not attempt interpretation or patient-therapist dialogue.

> The room is dark; it's very hard to find the hole. When I look through I see a crocodile. Wow! I just can't go down--but I'll try. Whoo! My dress flies up. I'm an easy target. (Laughs) Roger the crocodile will do me in--I don't belong down there.

The imagery responses and flow in this imaginary situation give us valuable information about motivation, subjective meaning, affect and, very often, conflict about aspects of sexuality.

The 2% of the thousands of respondents who did not show projective aspects of sexuality were two categories of persons: those persons who were terminally ill and saw the hole as relating to death, and those male prisoners at Chino State Prison for Men who saw the hole in the floor more as an escape route than as sexual responses. There were 27 male prisoners in this study.

But, since 98% of respondents did see this imaginary situation as sexually related, would other similar kinds of imagery situations reveal the same phenomenon? Putting on my imaginative hat, I tried the following:

(IS) Imagine you take an elevator to the basement. There you see a painting with a cover on it. Remove the cover. What do you see, feel and do?

When dialogue is made between the subject and what is in the picture, valuable sexual information may emerge. Also, if one asks subjects to feel as if they are the painting and to speak as the painting in "I feel ________," "The adjective that best describes me is ________," "I wish ________," "I must ________," etc., sexual and/or relationship material can be gleaned.

The paintings may range from peaceful scenes to nudes, terror-stricken paintings, daggers, blood, mothers, fathers, and siblings.

Again, experience with over 500 respondents shows this imaginary situation to yield sexual information such as sexual attitudes, feelings and conflict. Again, nondirective dialogue is the method used leading to consensual validation.

Another imaginary situation, when offered to subjects, yields sexual information in the following manner. Several thousand persons have taken the following imagination situation:

(IS) Imagine three doors, one at the left, one in the center, and one at the right. Imagine opening each door and tell me what you see.

In each case the person is asked to imagine what he or she sees and then, imagining he or she <u>is</u> what he or she sees, the person is asked to finish the following sentences:

I feel ____
The adjective that best describes me is ______________
I wish ____
I must ____
I need ____
I secretly _____________________________________
I will ____
I fear ____
Never refer to me as ____________________________

I will only discuss what we are finding occurs in about 95% of the respondents in the center, or middle, door. Again through consensual validation we find that this center door invariably reveals sexual information and attitudes combined with many aspects of relationships.

Again, so far no respondents in advance of doing this imagery situation have been able to predict that it may have subjective meaning of a sexual nature or aspects of relationships.

Another imaginary situation that seems to have an extremely high frequency of sexual orientation and/or relationship is the following:

(IS) Imagine lying on your stomach looking down. What do you see, do and feel?

Again, consensual validation of a dialogical, nondirective manner appears to gather subjective meaning about sexual matters and related subjects from about 95% of the 1,000 respondents.

Again, we ask the subject to finish the following sentences listed above while he or she is doing this imaginary situation.

In these four imaginary situations just presented--which, by the way, are items on the Shorr Imagery Test, the Supplementary Shorr Imagery Test and the Shorr Couples Imagery Test--certain test constructs appear evident. From clinical observation, human beings tend to "see" sexual elements of personality in cellars, basements, in the earth, in holes in the floor, and in the center of certain things--oftentimes lower parts of the centers of images. This appears in over 90% of persons who are asked to imagine these situations.

What is remarkable is that no sex differences have been found with thousands of respondents, in that both men and women offer sexual information to these imaginary situations.

These observations are mine and those of other workers in Psycho-Imagination Therapy, and have been explored with thousands of persons. At this point, these constructs are in need of experimental designs to help us produce further valid studies.

In another category within sexual imagery are the more direct sexual imaginary situations that are presented "out in front," as it were. From these we would expect to get sexual information, and before the person begins imagining he or she will probably know that it must contain some sexual content. Nevertheless, the patients are asked, as always, to close their eyes, relax, and, trusting their images, respond to the imaginary situation.

Here are a few of them:

(IS) Imagine an animal that comes out of a penis and an animal that comes out of a vagina. (And after a few minutes, the subject is asked to have both animals walk down a road together.)

Although it is obvious that these are sexual items, persons image animals readily and call on their productions for analysis and feelings. For example, one person gave a crocodile for the animal out of the penis and a little white rabbit coming out of the vagina. When the subject was asked to imagine them walking down a road together, the crocodile was being constantly foiled by the white rabbit so that no matter how hard he tried, he could not capture and devour the rabbit. This turned out to be, by the patient's own report, that she feared men sexually and played a very calculating game of sexually defeating men from having her.

The unusual point of this example is that only when she did the imaginary situation did she begin to understand her behvior--since accompanying the imagery production were powerful feelings and physical symptoms of sweating. Thus, despite prior knowledge that the imaginary situation was sexual, she trusted her imagery and it then served to bypass certain conscious censorship into greater awareness.

A second sexual imaginary situation in this "out in front" category is:

(IS) Imagine a man on a six-foot-high mound of earth, and you are below. (Or, this can be reversed to have the subject imagine a woman on a six-foot mound of earth and with you below.)

Again, we are getting at attitudes, feelings and conflicts relating to relationships between men and men, men and women, or women and women. Sexual power plays of dominance and submission often are revealed by this imaginary situation. Again, results with over a thousand persons indicate that despite what appears obvious, people, in trusting their imagery, are often surprised by where their imagery productions lead them and the awareness they receive as a result.

Starting with imaginary situations that seemed to be totally projective of sexuality and/or relationships, without subjects realizing in advance that they were revealing such information and attitudes, I proceeded to those imaginary situations that were obviously sexual to the subject, and found that they also provided valuable clinical material.

The fact that persons could function revealingly in this manner made me again put on my psychologist's imagination hat. I began to see that perhaps it was possible to ask an individual to imagine that he or she was in various intimate relationships with the person that he or she was, indeed, intimate with.

For example, it seemed to me that I could take a couple who were on intimate terms and, having them imagine each other in self-other combinations, perhaps uncover interpersonal dynamics heretofore unrevealed.

Psycho-Imagination Therapy's theoretical orientation is based on the interpersonal concepts of Harry Stack Sullivan. If one is to use such concepts with the additional aid of imagery--that is, projective images of self-other relationships--it is possible to add dimension and clarity to our knowledge.

After nearly two decades of therapeutic work with patients using imagery, my knowledge of imagery productions, especially relating to sexuality and relationships, made it possible recently to develop the Shorr Couples Imagery Test. In addition to most of the preceding imaginary situations, certain self-other intimate imagery was used.

Here are several examples:

The first imaginary situation of this kind is the one in which the individual is asked to:

(IS) Imagine that you are tiny, and that you are on the face of your spouse (partner). What do you see, feel and do? What does your spouse (partner) see, feel and do?

The subject, of course, is asked to relax and trust his or her images.

One person said:

I find myself tiny, real small. I am on the cheek of my wife. She doesn't know I'm there. I feel like a voyeur. I climb up the nose and peek into her eyes. I see a coldness there. There doesn't seem to be any feelings. The longer I stay there, the more I know she will not notice me. I am hoping against hope she will be tender to me. Is it hopeless for me to ever believe I will get a response?

The same person is then asked to reverse the imagery sequence in self-other style, as follows:

(IS) Imagine that your spouse (or partner) is tiny, and that he or she is on your face. What do you see, do and feel? What does your spouse (or partner) see, do and feel?

The same person responded as follows;

I see my wife tiny on my face. Funny how she looks into my mouth and then shuts my mouth. Is she afraid of my mouth? She then looks into my nose with her foot and peeks up at my eyes. She seems frightened as hell--I sure don't know why. She seems to be terrified. Wow! I can't believe it.

Clinical experience with this man and his wife showed her to be a detached, schizoid person who was terrorized at close relationships. He wanted response and tenderness from her and was constantly rebuffed by her protective detachment.

Of course, of particular interest was to hear the response of the wife to the same imaginary situation. When she was asked to imagine herself as tiny on the face of her husband, this is what she said:

> I go right to his moustache and hide. I am surprised by all the skin roughness and little bumps. Skin can be quite ugly--I never realized how much. And the hair from his nose bothers me. Why can't he trim it? I go back into the moustache and hide.

Then, when she was asked to imagine her husband tiny on her face, she gave the following reaction:

> He comes on strong--right onto my cheek. He looks into my eyes and begs me to have sex with him. I'm annoyed but I won't show it. But he won't go away. Why doesn't he go away? Enough of this image.

As you can see, this self-other couples imagery is loaded with interpersonal dynamics that could lead to many therapeutic possibilities.

Still another self-other couples imaginary situation is as follows:

> (IS) Imagine staring at your spouse's (partner's) naked back. What do you see, do and feel?

Then the same person is asked the second part of this self-other question:

> (IS) Imagine your spouse (partner) staring at your naked back. What do you see, do and feel? What does your partner (spouse) see, feel and do?

As you can see, self-other attitudes about each to the other can be revealed from the imagery responses. Then, when we have the spouse's (or partner's) response to the same two-part self-other question, we have a great deal of information about attitudes, feelings, and conflicts from both persons in an interpersonal dialogical and imagery manner.

Yet another self-other imaginary situation that I find useful among many is:

(IS) Imagine your spouse (partner) whispering something into your ear. What does she/he whisper? What do you see, do and feel? What does your spouse (partner) see, do and feel?

Here is one man's answer:

It's gossip. She's feeling the need to make herself more by making someone else less, and I would be somewhat irritated by that.

When that man was asked to imagine himself whispering something into the ear of his spouse (partner) and asked what he saw, felt, and did, this is what he said:

'I love you.' I am saying it because I want her to feel good about it; give her reassurance. I'm feeling tender. I see her smiling.

Without attempting any interpretation, one can readily see a fertile field for dialogue and, of course, interpersonal dynamics of personality at play.

Another category of sexual imagery that involves parental imagery as well is those imaginary situations that involve imagined intimacy with one or both parents and the individual. Since an enormous amount of influence is exerted by the mother and father in the formative years of development on the sexual attitudes of the growing child, we must be especially interested in how much of that influence is still in operation in the individual's present sexual dynamics.

This is especially true in relation to the so-called perversions, extreme sadomasochistic behavior, and sexual denial, since nearly all available writing on these subjects emphasizes the role of the mother and father in the early life of the individual.

One of the imaginary situations involving parents, which strongly reflects an individual's sexual dynamics, is the following:

(IS) Imagine taking a shower with your mother.

Here is one man's response:

Yuck! Horrible. She's horrible looking. I'd be afraid I'd have an erection or she'd attack me sexually. And (pause) what about my father finding out? Yuck!

A woman gave the following response to the same imaginary situation:

My mother giggles a lot. She would giggle a lot. It would be more like I am the parent and she is the child, and she would react and behave as a child.

"Taking a shower" with one's father in imagery can also be fruitful as to sexual attitudes and conflicts.

I will mention two other parental imageries that seem to relate to intimacy, sexuality, closeness, as well as to possible conflicts. These are:

(IS) Imagine whispering something into the ear of your mother or father. Then reverse it and have them whisper something into your ear.

(IS) Imagine dancing with your mother or father.

(IS) Imagine holding the face of your mother or father in your hands, then have each of them hold your face in their hands.

I would like to add that many of the imaginary situations outlined above can be utilized in group therapy interactions in which all of the group members imagine themselves in such situations with one of the group members, and having reported their feelings and images, have that individual react in turn to the individual members of the group. I will have more to say about the use of sexual imagery in group therapy in depth at another time.

In summary, I have tried to show that the stream of consciousness is not the sole property of literary figures. Through imagery-the mental function that integrates perception, motivation, subjective meaning and realistic abstract thought--psychologists may get at the stream of consciousness and make it eligible for scientific investigation.

Using the sexual imagery of patients through Psycho-Imagination Therapy mentods as a window into consciousness--into the working of the imagination.

REFERENCES

Allen, W. Getting Even. New York: Vintage, 1978.

Aquilar, I., and Wood, V. N. Therapy through death ritual. Social Work, 1976, 21, 48-54.

Arieti, S. Cognition in psychoanalysis. Journal of the American Academy of Psychoanalysis, 1980, 8, 8.

Bower, G. Mental imagery and associative learning. In L.W. Gregg (Ed.), Cognition in learning and memory. New York: Wiley, 1972.

Deleuze, J. P. F. Animal magnetism. Translated with an appendix of notes and letters added by T. Hartshorn. New York: Wells, 1879. (Originally published, 1825).

Gur, R., and Gur, R. Correlates of conjugate lateral eye movements in man. In S. Harnard et. al (Eds.), Lateralization in the nervous system. New York: Academic Press, 1977.

Lem, S. A perfect vacuum. Perfect reviews of non-existent books. New York: Harcourt, Brace, Javonovich, 1971.

Neisser, U. Contemporary Psychology, 1979, 24, 99-100.

Offit, A. The sexual self. New York: Ballantine, 1977.

Piaget, J., and Inhelder, . Verbal imagery in the child. London: Routledge and Kegan, 1971.

Shorr, J. E. Clinical categories in therapeutic imagery, in J. L. Singer and K. S. Pope (Eds.), The power of human imagination: Scientific investigations into the flow of human experience. New York: Plenum, 1979.

Shorr, J. Psycho-imagination therapy. New York: Thieme-Stratton Intercontinental Medical Book Corporation, 1972.

Shorr, J. Psychotherapy through imagery. New York: Thieme-Stratton Intercontinental Medical Book Corporation, 1974.

Shorr, J. E. Shorr imagery test. Los Angeles, California: Institute for Psycho-Imagination Therapy, 1974.

Spark, M. The first year of my life. New Yorker Magazine, 1975.

Tauber, E. S. Reflections on sexual perversions. Contemporary Psychoanalysis, 1975, 11, 1-14.

USING DEATH IMAGERY TO INDUCE PROPER GRIEVING: AN EMOTIVE-RECONSTRUCTIVE APPROACH

James K. Morrison

Albany Medical College

Albany, NY

Despite the recent surge of interest by psychotherapists in mental imagery (Sheikh, 1977), the use of imagery techniques to help psychotherapy clients complete the grieving process has, with few exceptions (e.g., Aguilar & Wood, 1976; Ahsen, 1968; Morrison, 1978), gone generally unreported. Perhaps this apparent neglect of the grieving process in psychotherapy generally reflects how our society protects the bereaved from facing the reality of death by restricting them to the role of passive observer. Such roles make it very difficult for the grief-stricken to come to grips with the death of a loved one (Nichols & Nichols, 1975).

Death imagery has many uses. Recently, the use of the fantasizing process in private exercises to deal with one's <u>own</u> death has been encouraged within the humanistic movement (e.g., Koestenbaum, 1976). Some clinicians (e.g., Sheikh, Twente, & Turner, 1979) have begun to use death imagery as a way of promoting personal growth among psychotherapy clients who wish to fantasize their own death. However, in this article the use of the term "death imagery" is restricted to those clinical attempts to use imagery techniques to induce the proper grieving of another, i.e., a loved one. It is the purpose of this article to briefly delineate a theoretical and operational approach to the grieving process in such a way as to illustrate how imagery can be used as a supplemental technique by those therapists who judge that their clients need to work out unresolved feelings about a deceased loved one.

Requests for reprints should be sent to James K. Morrison, Ph.D., P.C., 678 Troy-Schenectady Rd., Latham, NY 12110.

A Theoretical Approach to Grieving

The personal construct theory of George Kelly (1955) lends itself very nicely to an interpretation of the need for proper grieving. A person who has lost a friend or relative through death has a need to properly understand his or her thoughts and feelings about that person. When, for example, grieving persons cannot understand their feelings (e.g., anger, guilt) about the deceased, they often become depressed and/or anxious. If, as Kelly asserts, persons are like scientists trying to understand the world around them, one can grasp why, in trying to grieve, unexpected feelings tend to disconfirm long-cherished constructs persons have of themselves and the deceased. Since a person's cognitive processes are psychologically channelized by the ways in which they anticipate events, the sudden shock of unpredicted emotional reactions (e.g., anger about someone they really loved) can throw the cognitive system into great disarray.

Working within the view that people often perpetuate dysfunctional life patterns by employing a rigid, unworkable set of constructs, it follows that the degree to which a person alters his or her interpretation of past, present, and future hinges, in part, on the quantity and quality of information that can be brought into focus. Thus, on the occasion of a loved one's death, improper grieving may restrict the type of data used, leading to depression (or some other psychological problem); proper grieving may provide data that can lead to a sometimes painful but more satisfying interpretation of oneself and one's life events. The constructs that often emerge from proper grieving tend to disrupt dysfunctional behavior patterns when the folly of those patterns is brought into clear focus. Thus, a husband who finally understands how angry he always was at his now deceased mother may cease displacing much of this anger on his wife.

Imagery techniques can help immensely to elicit new information about self and others. Often one's constructs of self and others are too vague and partially formed to be useful in constructive ways. When imagery techniques are used properly, the evocation of information stored imaginally enables a client to focus upon the inadequacy of those constructs in that they really do not enable one to properly anticipate life's events. Thus, people who have a tendency to intellectualize about themselves will often be unable to interpret unexpected strong feelings that erupt on the occasion of a parent's death. For example, a client of mine could not understand the apparent contradiction between his construct of his mother as a "loving mother" and his feelings, provided by her death, of anger, until I elicited childhood-related imagery of his mother as angry, aloof, and cold. Until her death, the client had selected out the negative data about his mother.

Emotive-Reconstructive Psychotherapy

The techniques I use in inducing proper grieving are derived from emotive-reconstructive therapy (Morrison, 1979; Morrison & Cometa, 1977; Morrison, in press; Morrison & Cometa, in press). This therapeutic modality is theoretically based on the personal construct theory of Kelly (1955) and Piaget (1972) and incorporates the use of mental imagery as its primary technique. Guided mental imagery is used to elicit imagery associated with early developmental periods and traumatic events (e.g., the death of a loved one at any age).

Role-playing and deep breathing are often combined in the attempt to elicit clear feelings. However, the elicitation of feelings that do not lead to clear, constructive insights is considered to be of little or no value.

This type of therapy is also rooted in a consumer-oriented approach to the client (Morrison, 1979), wherein the rights of the client are protected. Considering the potential impact of imagery on feelings, the client needs to very carefully consider such a therapeutic process. The use of contracts, consumer advisory boards and specified goal-setting are helpful in this regard.

The Clinical Use of Imagery: Practical Applications

The induction of the grieving process is often performed with appropriate clients who present problems of depression. During the first contact it is often apparent that some depressed clients have not made the connection between their depression and a death of someone close to them.

The grieving process can take place at almost any point during therapy. However, due to its potential for eliciting a deeply emotional experience, the grieving process is usually introduced after a client has built up some initial trust in the therapist. Frequently, the client has several other more immediate problems to discuss before the process of grieving would make sense to the client. In cases where the client is very reluctant to discuss a death, the therapist can usually quite safely conclude that this client does need to do some grief work whenever the client's resistance to grieving has decreased. A client who cannot discuss a loved one's death without strong expressions of uncontrollable feeling is also a good candidate for the grieving process in therapy.

The case of a 48-year old, married executive will help to illustrate the strong effect of even one session of grieving on the way a client construes his or her world. John came to me complaining of "deep, deep depression". His responses on the Psychotherapy Problem Checklist (Morrison & Teta, 1979) indicated excessive anxiety (e.g., tight chest, stomach tied up in knots, feeling anxious a great deal, restless sleep, excessive worries, etc.) accompanying his depression. A relatively high score on the A-Trait Scale of the State-Trait Anxiety Inventory (Spielberger, Gorsuch & Lushene, 1970) further confirmed the client's high level of anxiety. The client was convinced he was having a "nervous breakdown".

In the one introductory history-taking session, the client cried profusely while talking of his mother's death when he was four. Shortly after this death, his father placed him in a foster home. Because of the severity of the client's symptoms, I asked the client if he would be willing to begin emotive-reconstructive therapy immediately. He agreed and, after a full description of the therapy, we began to use imagery in our next meeting.

After two imagery sessions I decided that many of the client's problems were caused by poorly elaborated constructs of his family. I felt that some of these constructs may have been formed in the client's attempt to cope with his mother's death. In the client's third imagery session (our fourth meeting), I used imagery to reconstruct his mother's death. The following is an uninterrupted transcript of the more dramatic part of that third session (T = therapist; C = client):

T: I want you to close your eyes and recall to mind clearly all the possible images associated with your mother's death, wake, funeral and burial. Let's begin with her actual death.

C: I remember mom lying in the front bedroom...an open area. I was conscious of mom being very ill. I remember the doctor. He attended my mother. I was in a back bedroom. I can remember a new baby. (Client begins to cry loudly.) That's my kid brother. He was 2 weeks old. I also remember my sister being in the house. I remember my grandmother standing by mom's bed. I pushed through all the people and jumped on mom's bed. Oh, oh boy (client gasps and appears to be in psychic pain)! I pulled the sheet off mom. My grandmother took me off the bed. I squirmed away from her. (Client begins to cry again.) I jumped back on the bed. Then they took me out of there. Oh! Oh! Oh! Why did she have to die so young?! I think of all the people who had moms year after year. They were lucky. Oh, boy! I remember going downstairs. They brought mom back in a casket. Flowers were all around. My father was in a chair in the corner. I climbed up on his lap. Dad was trying to hold back his tears. Then I ran over and climbed into the casket before anyone could catch me. I guess I knew they'd take her away. Oh! Oh! Oh! (Client appears to be in emotional pain.)

T: I want you to talk to your mother. Tell her all the things you never got a chance to say to her.

C: Mom, I hope I'll see you again. I'm not really afraid to die. Mom, I've got to see you one more time. You were so beautiful. I wish I could reach out and and hold you. Oh! I never had a chance to talk to you.

T: Talk to her as if she were alive now.
C: Oh Mom! If I could just take you home with me...and take care of you. Ma, maybe I could have changed things if I could have taken you home. Oh, I didn't want you to leave. I missed you. Oh, it hurts. Oh, boy...oh...oh...if I could just pick you up and carry you home. I'm not afraid of dying. Just to see you. Oh, boy, I see bright lights...real bright lights...all lit up. My arms are numb. My hands are numb. Oh, God! I wish I could do something to bring you back. Oh! Oh boy!
T: What else do you need to say to her?
C: If you were here you'd never have to worry about anything. I'd make sure you'd have anything you wanted. You'd not want for anything. You'd be able to smile all the time. Ma, you'd smile if I took care of you. Even though dad was gone, you'd be happy. I just wish I had that chance.
T: Tell her about your life since she died.
C: I don't know if you'd be proud of me running away and joining the service at 15. I had to protect our country. You'd have been proud. I was a good soldier. I did my job well. I went to school under the G.I. Bill. Got my high school diploma. Did college work. I know you'd be happy about that. Then I became a state trooper. I got the job on my own. I was a good trooper. You'd laugh seeing me as a judge in later years. I was such a wild man as a kid. I sat as a judge in the same building in which you worked. Oh, mom, you'd never work in one of those sweat shops again! I did a lot of dumb things but overall...I can see her lying in the casket...I didn't do so bad. You'd be proud. Oh, oh! (Agony shows on his face.) I gave it my best shot. I wish you could have been around to see some of the things I did. I tried hard because I had a lot of you in me. I tried hard. Yeah, I tried hard. Always tried to treat people well. Always been a gentleman. I made a lot of political speeches. Did a real good job. Never let you down. I'm proud of the way I worked.
T: Can you say goodbye to your mother now?
C: Oh, mom. I guess I got to leave you. I'm going to see you again. I'll be there. I'm sure of that. Yeah, you'll smile just like you're smiling now. I'll hug you. (Now he speaks to the therapist.) She's smiling.
T: I think you know she would have been proud of you. All right, I want you to relax for a while before opening your eyes.

From this transcript the reader can see the powerful emotional effect of vivid imagery associated with a loved one's death on the client. The psychic pain caused by never having had his mother during most of his life created such an incredible need in the client for a mother that at the age of 19 he married a woman five years older who reminded him of his mother. This relationship was extremely problematic because, of course, no woman could live up to the idealized image he had created of his mother. The client searched and searched for this perfect woman in many brief affairs, but for nought.

In probing the depths of his pain related to his mother's death, the client began to realize how he had repressed the memory of the events surrounding her death in order to escape the pain associated with those memories. But in blocking the pain he had formed simplistic constructs about his mother that proved to be unworkable in relating to other women. Later in therapy the client also remembered that he had also formed an idealized image of his father. As he put more and more pieces of the puzzle together, a more realistic view of his family and himself began to emerge. He began to relate much more easily with his wife and children, and he reported a significant reduction of depression and anxiety after that third session.

The client was able to elaborate clearly the meaning of that third session when asked to do so two months later. He saw that session as a breakthrough after which his whole construct system seemed to change. He also began to report a dramatically improved sex life and more ease in handling negotiations connected with his work.

This case illustration demonstrates how the evocation of painful feelings through imagery, little understood or able to be coped with in childhood, can lead a client to change his constructs of a deceased parent to such an extent that his perceptions of the living are also different and more consonant with constructive living. The use of imagery techniques are often useful in facilitating the grieving process. To die within oneself through immense pain can often be a rebirth in living.

The author would caution other psychotherapists not to use image ry techniques to induce the grieving process until they have first used such techniques related to less emotion-inducing events. Furthermore, therapists should first deal with any need on their own to grieve more properly before attempting to assist others in grieving. Such cautions aside, the use of imagery to assist the grieving process can be a valuable clinical tool for most therapists.

SUMMARY

A psychotherapeutic approach to properly grieving the loss of a loved one is outlined in theory and technique. Based primarily on the personal construct theory of George Kelly, this approach emphasized the emotive-reconstructive use of imagery techniques. Imagery is used to elicit previously poorly-defined feelings about the deceased and these feelings, under the guidance of the therapist, are in turn used to induce a change in the client's poorly elaborated system of constructs. A detailed case study is used to illustrate the use of these techniques.

REFERENCES

Aguilar, I., and Wood, V. N. Therapy through death ritual. Social Work, 1976, 49-54.

Ahsen, A. Basic concepts in eidetic psychotherapy. New York: Brandon House, 1968.

Kelly, G. The psychology of personal constructs (2 Vols.). New York: Norton, 1955.

Koestenbaum, P. Is there an answer to death? Englewood Cliffs, NJ: Prentice-Hall, 1976.

Morrison, J. K. Successful grieving: Changing personal constructs through mental imagery. Journal of Mental Imagery, 1978, 2, 63-68.

Morrison, J. K. Emotive-reconstructive therapy: Changing constructs by means of mental imagery. In A. A. Sheikh and J. T. Shaffer (Eds.), The potential of fantasy and imagination. New York: Brandon House, 1979.

Morrison, J. K. A consumer-oriented approach to psychotherapy. Psychotherapy: Theory, Research and Practice, 1979, 16, 381-384.

Morrison, J. K. Emotive-reconstructive therapy: A short-term use of mental imagery. In J. E. Shorr, J. Connella, G. Sobel, and T. Robin, (Eds.), Imagery: Its many dimensions and applications. New York: Plenum, 1980.

Morrison, J. K., and Cometa, M. C. Emotive-reconstructive approach to the psychotherapeutic use of imagery. Journal of Mental Imagery, in press.

Morrison, J. K. and Teta, D. C. Simplified use of the Semantic Differential to measure psychotherapy outcome. Journal of Clinical Psychology, 1978, 34, 751-753.

Nichols, R., and Nichols, J. Funerals: A time for grief and growth. In E. Kubler-Ross (Ed.), Death: The final stage of growth. Englewood Cliffs, NJ: Prentice-Hall, 1975.

Piaget, J. Judgement and reasoning in the child. Totowa, NJ: Littlefield, Adams, 1972.

Sheikh, A. A. Mental images: Ghosts of sensations? Journal of Mental Imagery, 1977, 1, 1-4.

Sheikh, A. A., Twente, G. E., and Turner, D. Death imagery: Therapeutic uses. In A. A. Sheikh, and J. J. Shaffer (Eds.), The potential of fantasy and imagination. New York: Brandon House, 1979.

Spielberger, C. D., Gorsuch, R. L., and Lushene, R. E. Manual for the State-Trait Anxiety Inventory. Palo Alto, CA: Consulting Psychologists Press, 1970.

INTERPERSONAL CONFLICT AND MENTAL IMAGERY

Thomas Mallouk

Community Mental Health Center

Chester, Pennsylvania

"People who have a faith or a philosophy will gain unintentional self-illumination in conjunction with their actual performance, they are led on by everything that befalls them, by ideas, by truth itself and by God. Self-reflection may serve them on the way but it is never a primary force, it only becomes effective through actual being, which in turn lays hold of its help. But once self-reflection in the form of psychological study of the self becomes the whole atmosphere in which a person lives, there is no end to it since the person's psychic life is not yet being itself but only a place where being is envisaged. There is a dangerous tendency in psychotherapy to convert the psychic actuality of an individual into an end in itself. The person who turns his psyche into a god because he has lost both world and god finds himself standing finally in a void" (Karl Jaspers, 1964, P. 33).

If consciousness, as Csikszentmihalyi (1978) suggests, must be understood in a holistic context, then there should be evidence in the products of consciousness of the integration of the person in his or her world that the notion of holism suggest. If contents of consciousness are to be considered an essential and critical area of study in psychology, they must have explanatory value for understanding the behavior of people at the level of human action and experience. Up until now, the study of consciousness *per se* has done little to address the criticisms by behaviorism that consciousness is an epiphenomena that contributes little if anything to the control, prediction or understanding of behavior. The recent work of Mischel (1973) and Meichenbaum (1977) among others has begun to consider the role of consciousness in the form of expectencies, values, inner speech, etc. in the behavior of people. Consciousness, then, has finally been accorded a place in the thinking of behaviorally-oriented psychologists; however, the question of meaning, which has been proposed from the psychoanalytic tradition, is left for the most part unaddressed, even by these more holistically-oriented behaviorists. While behaviorism has foresaken the question of meaning in people's lives, psychoanalysis has attempted to get to the roots of the individual's meaning by examining the content of consciousness of the person out of context. Psychoanalytic thought has to create a context within the psyche because it does not recognize the context of action and experience in the world of the person. Meaning is always grounded in context. The complexity of the psychic structure postulated by psychoanalysis is a reflection of the inability of the theory to make use of the forces operating in the context of the person to help explain behavior and meaning.

If we assume that a person is holistically integrated into the world of his or her experience, then there should be evidence in the conscious contents to help explain behavior. If a person is motivated to express and defend core meanings of the psyche, there should be evidence of this in the content of consciousness. While consciousness itself may have certain properties that reflect the laws of consciousness, as Klinger (1971) has suggested, the content of consciousness can only be adequately understood in the context in which it has emerged. Just as the psychophysical laws of the early introspectionists are the outcomes of the most rigorous control of context, the most fruitful exploration of consciousness at the level of human action and experience will be accomplished when we can study it in naturalistic settings.

The question of how to study consciousness in naturalistic settings and still maintain a modicum of scientific and experimental rigor is not easily addressed. At this point, the bulk of the work in the study of consciouness has turned towards the study of the free flow of consciousness (Singer, 1974; Hope & Singer, 1978; and others). The problem with this approach is that consciousness in day-to-day activities does not flow freely, but rather shifts and changes depending on context. Without considering context, theories of consciousness will inevitably develop theoretical constructs residing within the skin of the individual to account for the shifts that take place in the conscious flow. While this is something of an overstatement, the point should be made that without systematically considering context, theories of consciousness will inevitably attribute to the organism constructs that might better be explained when the nature of the experiential context is considered.

Traditionally, the assumptions of holism have been carried by the phenomenological school of psychology. Unfortunately, the direction of phenomenological inquiry has for the most part preoccupied itself with methodological and theoretical issues in such a way as to isolate the individual and misinterpret Heidegger's (1962) notion of Dasein or Being in the world. In this connection

I am in agreement with Joseph Shorr (1972) when he criticizes the lack of task orientation of existential phenomenological psychology.

The systems perspective that has recently developed and gained so much popularity in the family research area lends itself very readily to the assumptions of holism. Unfortunately, this point of view, perhaps in reaction to individually-oriented theories and especially psychoanalysis, has foresaken the study of consciousness and the questions of meaning in favor of issues related to structure of interactional patterns. The exceptions to this have been those theoreticians and practitioners whose roots are essentially psychoanalytic. Because this point of view has developed within clinical contexts, there is very little experimental research in this area. There have, however, been ambitious attempts at naturalistic study of the family. The work of Kantor and Lehr (1975) is an attempt to develop an integrated system of categories for describing the behavior of families in natural settings.

The most fundamental strategy of all psychotherapy, although it is rarely if ever recognized, is what might be thought of as naturalistic observation and guided introspection. Without any systematic knowledge of what naturalistic observation has to offer us, we are left with the jumble of theoretical assumptions and private observations that are the stock and trade of most psychotherapists.

Kantor (1980) has recently articulated the outcome of his systematic application of his theory of family process to clinical work with couples in conflict. His technique has been naturalistic observation and guided introspection. But in this case, the observation has been of the person in context. Out of this clinical research has come a phenomenon he calls the critical identity image, which bears upon the important issues relating to the study of consciousness, imagery, and questions of meaning, identity, motivation and values.

THE CRITICAL IDENTITY IMAGE

A brief description of Kantor's ideas is in order. Since the language of the original work is somewhat complex, I will attempt to describe in as nontechnical a manner as I can, the basic observations and concepts. The interested reader is referred to the original paper (Kantor, 1980). What Kantor has observed and what couples readily attest to (Mallouk, Note 1) is that in their day-to-day activity and in the processes of interaction couples have certain conflicts that are repetitive. Furthermore, these conflicts have a ritual quality in that each of the people in the conflict behave in highly stereotypic ways in response to the stereotypic behavior of the other. The conflict may begin innocently enough but before long the couple escalates their demands on the other into what Kantor calls the ritual impasse. Kantor calls the fight, itself, an identity struggle. Having observed these repetitive fights in his naturalistic observation of families (Kantor, 1975), Kantor decided to explore the internal experience of the participants in clinical work.

His technique has been to work with the couple to persuade them to enact their conflicts in the consulting room. When the couple is engaged in the throes of a ritual impasse, Kantor intervenes and asks each of the individuals to scan their memory for a visual image of the first time they experienced the feelings they are having in the fight. The images that people generate with this procedure invariably have dramatic explanatory value in terms of the meaning and behavior of the participants. The images themselves link the individuals to their current context and to their past. They are called "critical identity images."

The structure of the critical identity image consists of a foundation image and a positive identity claim.

> During their identity struggles, people confront each other not with the competing critical identity images themselves (for these are beneath the surface of awareness, and usually remain there unless they spontaneously surface or are clinically elicited...) but rather with competing claims about reality: About how things are or how they ought to be. Such claims are always specific and contextual. For example, a man's failure tc phone his wife as he promised may raise in his wife a sense of abondonment in need. "For me, fidelity is unerring reliability," she argues. "For me, fidelity is authenticity," her husband counters. These competing identity claims tend to be active assertions of positive values. The foundation image, the memory picture from which the positive identity claim is constructed, may be either a positive or negative experience. Negative images of pain, suffering and/or disappointments are transformed into positive claims. Assertions intimate partners use in their ritual struggles are based on positive representations of identity. Most people, however, enter adult relationships with incomplete transformations. Their intimate relationships, then, become both context and occasion for completion. Where this fails, the job may be passed on to the therapist. (Kantor, 1980, Pp. 150).

The most important point to be recognized in relation to this phenomenon is that the situations that elicit the repetitive behavior and the image bear a structural similarity to the original foundation experience. While the image is derived from the past, it influences behavior (indeed it instructs the person to behave in certain ways) in the present. According to Kantor, it is primarily visual and spatial although in my clinical work I have observed that auditory aspects are often important. The images are action oriented and include at least one other person. Finally, they have unneutralized energy connected with them that Kantor maintains cannot be neutralized.

An example is in order. In generating an image of this kind the first task is to prepare the way by mapping the person's presenting complaints in the context in which they occur. A twenty-five year old male client who originally came to therapy for alcoholism was working on control of his aggression, which has become more of a concern now that he has stopped drinking. By inquiring about situations in which he gets angry, he found that it is usually when he is with his girlfriend and she spends inordinate amounts of time talking with others when he is waiting for her. As he described a particular situation, he became affectively engaged and this was intensified by my interventions to help him reexperience the situation he was referring to. (The use of conventional imagery techniques is very effective in this regard.) Once he affirmed that he was experiencing the same arousal as in the situation with his girlfriend, I asked him to scan his life experience for a memory picture of the first time he had experienced these emotions.

> I sorta have a really vivid image. I don't know whether it relates or not. I was in third grade. There were a lot of people in my class that were maybe as much as a year or two older than I was. They used to pick on me and stuff. Well, they were organizing a kickball game for our recess, or something, on the playground, the kid that was sitting next to me was the one that was organizing it -- getting everybody together. I sorta let him know, somehow, that I wanted to play too; but he just ignored me and it didn't seem like they wanted me to participate. I ended up getting really pissed off at this one kid, and I left a nasty little note on his desk. He had gone off somewhere organizing, or whatever, and he came back to his desk and found this little note, and he looked at the note, and he looked at me, and he took it up to the teacher. The teacher got real mad at me, and pulled my desk out in the hall and left me sitting out there in the hallway. After that I can just remember being on the playground at recess time and I was bawling my eyes out because nobody wanted to play with me and stuff and the teacher didn't seem to care. Just standing out there watching all the kids play. It didn't seem like she gave a damn!

Subsequent work with this image and the current life situation which stimulated it, revealed that the stage was set for conflict with his girlfriend when she asked him to take her to visit her friends on an evening when he was very tired and wanted to just stay home. He was unable to say "no" to her because as he said, "It just would not be right--why should she be left out of all the fun?".

Here, we can see that the client is identifying either with the teacher in his image or with the boy who was organizing the game and with himself in the earlier situation. To say "no" to his girlfriend would be tantamount to endorsing the behavior of the teacher and his peer. His girlfriend's request for help in joining her peer context (and her unwillingness to take his gentle indications of being tired and unwilling to help) invokes the image and the psychic pain associated with it and enjoins him to do the right thing; namely to help her participate with her peers. The unintended consequence of his agreement to help the girlfriend is that he feels isolated in that he has not attended to his own current needs.

A variety of other interpretations and connections might be drawn. His weak protest to his girlfriend about being tired resembles his report of the way in which he indicated to his peer that he wanted to be included in the kickball game. His being left out in the hall bears a resemblance to his being kept waiting for his girlfriend while she talked to her friends. All of the interpretations require a minimum of speculation because the self-report and affirmation, the current behavior, and the relevant past experience of the client are readily available to the clinician once the image has been elicited.

THE CRITICAL IDENTITY IMAGE AND ITS RELATION AND INTERFACE WITH OTHER CONCEPTS

This type of image is not entirely new to therapists and researchers in the field, although to my knowledge no one has ever identified these images or articulated their unique character. Singer and Pope's (1978) excellent collection on the use of imagination and imagery touches on this phenomenon from different points of view. Reyher (1978) reports a case of a client with whom he uses emergent uncovering psychotherapy. In this example, the therapist persistently enjoins the client to lie down, close his or her eyes, and report with complete honesty everything that comes to mind. Throughout the transcript the therapist points out nonverbal behavior and the client's failure to keep his or her eyes closed. Finally, the client succeeds in keeping his or her eyes closed and says "'That's funny; I just thought of my father giving me a swat at the dinner table when I was a kid.' (This blatant transference reaction, or parataxic distortion, opens up a new direction for the proceedings.)" (P. 72)

The concept of parataxic distortion dismisses the relationship between the current context and the image. When understood from a contextual point of view, it becomes clear that the image of being threatened by the more powerful male figure is not only a distortion, but also an illumination and a commentary on the context the person is experiencing. This is by no means criticism of the methods of eliciting the image, but rather an illustration of the maxim that the products of consciousness, and especially visual images, cannot be adequately understood or explained except in terms of the context in which they emerge. The priority attributed to certain types of images is a function of the aims of the psychotherapies from which they emerge. The analytic system is the product of the analytic context.

In this connection, Reyher's (1978) assumption that "spontaneous visual imagery is unpredictable, and, therefore, irrelevant to the purposes of most interpersonal relations" is contradicted by the empirical evidence and by his own case illustrations when examined from a different point of view.

The work of Ahsen (1968) is consistent with the implications of Kantor's discovery of critical identity images. Indeed some of his case examples bear a strong resemblance to the critical identity images. His case of a woman with menstrual pain (P. 341) includes all the elements of the critical identity image including the therapeutic prescription to convert negative foundation experience into a positive identity claim. Ahsen, however, does not make distinctions among different classes of eidetic images based on their function or their relation to contextual events, except as they bear upon a particular case.

The critical identity image differs from eidetic imagery in that it is primarily elicited in an interpersonal context and relates to behavior of an interpersonal nature. There are those (Minuchin, Rosman, & Baker, 1978) who would argue that all behavior, including somatic symptoms, is interpersonal. In this connection, the distinction made by Minuchin between the context in which the symptom develops and the context that sustains the symptom is a useful one. In any case, while the critical identity image relates to interpersonal behavior, somatic complaints might be understood as behavior in relation to the self that is guided by an eidetic image. It should be noted that in the images that underlie somatic complaints, the behavior in relation to the self is often an attempt at an adaptive response to interpersonal events. The critical identity image and eidetic images are related in that they share a common ground in terms of the foundation experience. They represent themselves differently in the current situation of the client based on the differing responses to foundation experience. In the case of the critical identity image, the person decides to be in a positive way, while in the case of somatic disturbance, the client attacks the body in response to psychic pain. This attack on the body is adaptive in that it spares the person attack on the source of their pain (often a powerful parental figure) or a direct attack on their self-esteem ("I feel bad, therefore I am bad").

The reason that the critical identity image has not been isolated as a unique phenomenon until now has to do with a focus on individuals, even when behavior in context has been considered. The use of mental imagery in psychotherapy has made use of the image as a symbolic representation of a behavioral pattern. While there is often no formal attempt to specify the behavior being represented, the manipulation of the image has as its consequence the implicit suggestion of behavior change. On another level the ability to have an image and to change an image is an experience that helps the client to recognize that change is possible and that the client is an agent for change (Meichenbaum, 1978). Crampton's (1969) paper on the use of mental imagery illustrates the point I am trying to make. In elaborating the images of an individual client, the connection between the image and the behavioral pattern it represents is tacitly recognized and utilized to effectuate change in the image and by implication change in the person's actual behavior outside the therapeutic encounter.

It is important to recognize that I am referring in this connection to behavior in a different way than it is ordinarily conceived in behavioristic psychology. As long as we do not make use of the image, the behavior that is represented by the image can be conceived in the atomistic way that classical behaviorism espouses. Once it is represented in the image, however, the behavior is part of a pattern, inextricably linked to a system of meaning. To suggest a change within the context of the image is to anticipate a change in the meaning system of the client. This point cannot be stressed too strongly for it offers the link between a strictly behavioral psychology with its admirable practicality and a humanistic psychology, concerned with issues of human meaning.

The patterns of behavior that characterize human life usually involve other people and the formation of meaning invariably has consequences for those with whom we are intimately involved. In contrast to Shorr's (1972) concept that "In any dyadic relationship there is always one person who defines the relationship" (P. 7), my position is that both people define the relationship. In the process of forming a relationship the rules for how to behave and resolve conflicts are negotiated (Jackson, 1965). The differences between people have their roots in what Rokeach (1968) has called "beliefs about self identity." His studies of children who are misidentified by a parent shed light on the implicit dangers and threat to identity of intimate relations. If the process of intimate relations is one in which an individual allows the other to define the self or have impact on how one sees oneself, then the potential for conflict is twofold. There is, first of all, the inevitable vulnerability that is experienced when people make themselves available to another in this way. Secondly, there are the real differences among people and the implicit threat of these differences to the people who are allowing the differences between them to matter.

The critical image represents a thoroughly analyzed phenomenon at the depth level of processing (Craik & Lockhart, 1972). The person in the foundation experience has taken in information through a variety of channels (visual, auditory, kinesthetic) and has made decisions about the self and how to behave that express the meaning this experience has for the person. For this reason, the image is extremely well retained in memory. It is usually not held in consciousness because it is uneconomical to do so (Bateson, 1972). It is highly accessible to consciousness because the decision in relation to the experience is continually expressed in day-to-day life in the form of the positive identity claims and the behaviors that underlie them.

The positive identity claim seems to be a case in point of Klinger's (1977) notion of current concern and cues. As Sullivan (1953) has observed, attention illuminates cues relating to self-esteem. In the interactions between intimates the recognition and acceptance of one's positive identity claims is of fundamental concern. When events take place that are structurally similar to the foundation experience, specific cues relating to the original experience draw the attention of the individual and motivate him or her to act in ways prescribed by the critical image.

Singer (1973) has speculated on the role of imagination and imagery in the formation of identity. He suggests, "It is likely that as we store new material, we label it as more or less relevant to particular urgent issues of our lives. In a sense, we "'ticket' it for replay as part of a more general plan" (P. 195). This point of view is shared by Craik and Lockhart (1972) in the area of memory research and dovetails nicely with the critical image. The foundation experience can be thought of as a specially coded experience in terms of which later experiences will be judges. If a current situation is structurally similar to the foundation experience, the person acts in a specified way in an attempt to change the situation and fend off the implicit attack on the self. (It is important to mention that in this scenario I am assuming a negative foundation experience. Kantor (1980) makes it clear that his conception of the critical identtiy image includes both negative and positive foundation experiences.) If the action the image bearer takes changes the structure of the situation (see Miller, Galanter & Pribram (1960) for a more formal discussion of behavior that relates to this description), the person moves on to other experiences. However, if the action the person takes has the paradoxical effect of reinforcing or reintroducing the structurally similar situation, the person will again act in a specified way to correct the similarity and assert the positive identity claim. If each successive action has the paradoxical effect of reintroducing the threatening experience, or if it does not change it, the person will act in the specified way in a positive feedback loop. This positive feedback loop has differential cutoff points depending on the nature of the context in which it occurs, but has the potential to escalate into a crisis in situations that are regarded as central to the identity of the image bearer. In light of the profound stakes in terms of self-esteem, of failure in intimate relations, and of the considerable evidence (Gilbert, 1969; Ryan & Watson, 1968) that in the face of frustration the natural response is to repeat the behavior intended to gain a target, it is not surprising that couples engage in processes of mutual frustration and escalated struggle.

The persistence of unresolved conflicts in couples--i.e., the ritual impasse--can be conceived of as a failure or breakdown of the incentive disengagement cycle identified by Klinger (1977). The positive identity claim is an incentive in intimate relations. In the example of the young man mentioned earlier, his positive claim is that he brings people together and does not allow them to remain isolated. His critical identity image enjoins him to act in certain ways that are often highly adaptive and gratifying for him. In a disagreement with his partner he cannot afford to lose the incentive of the positive identity claim. In the type of conflicts Kantor has isolated, each person has a similar stake and so neither can afford to give up what they believe the demands of the other imply: namely, some aspect of their positive sense of self.

Kantor's work with couples has shed light on the intuitively appealing notion that otherwise apparently healthy people act in what appear to be pathological ways in the context of their intimate struggles with their partners. This is not because people are good at hiding their latent pathology, but rather because it is only or primarily in a context as compelling as the intimate encounter of spouses that permission to leave the field is so hard to come by.

Rather than some perversity on the part of individuals in continually exposing themselves to "experiences which are poisonous and growth inhibiting" (Crampton, 1972), the people in the ritual impasse are attempting to gain access to a part of the world and experience that is inaccessible to them because of the necessarily constraining aspects of their behavior and imagery. In helping people who are troubled by repetitive and unresolved conflicts it is not enough to help them to stop fighting, for people need to find meaning in their struggles. Without finding some positive value in their trouble, they will inevitably come to see themselves or each other in a negative light.

When people are in the throes of a ritual impasse, they experience a sense of no choice because the interplay of their image and their behavior and the responses this elicits in the context exercise a strangle-hold on their perception of reality. Their view is so constricted that they see no choice but to act in a highly stereotypic way. The attention of each person is intensely focused to pick up cues in the behavior of the other that resonate with his or her to behave in the stereotypic way. This helps account for the observation that repetitive fights in couples often involve character attribution.

The inverse of Csikszentmihalyi's (1978) contention that "the ability to focus attention (voluntarily) is the most basic way of reducing onto-logical anxiety, the fear of impotence or non-existence" (P. 341) is that being forced to attend to the demands of the ritual impasse is inherently anxiety-provoking. As ritual struggles escalate the potential for psychic pain or schism increases. The choice to end a relationship is often experienced as the only alternative to psychological disintegration. It is suggested that functional psychosis may in some cases be the unfortunate outcome of uncontained ritualized identity struggle in which people are bound by their image structure to act in a certain way and bound to stay in the transactional field; i.e., double bound (Bateson, Jackson, Haley & Weakland, 1956). Psychosis may be the sad parody of the rewarding (Klinger, 1971; Singer, 1966, 1973) and adaptive (Csikszentmihalyi, 1975) aspects of fantasy, daydreaming, and imagination.

What each person in an intimate context represents is a potential challenge to the individual's "world image" (Watzlawick, 1978), which is based on specific learning experiences in the past. The ritual impasse holds the promise for each individual of expanding their world by the inclusion of what cannot be seen within the constraints of their imagery. Crisis can be thought of as a situation or set of circumstances that threatens a person's basic assumptions about his or her world and evokes the key experiences in the past that have influenced the assumptions. The response to crisis is critical to future development. If the challenging information is excluded, the vision of the person narrows and behavior becomes more stereotypic. The consequence of this narrowing of vision is that more situations in the person's world become potentially threatening. In addition the failure to successfully resolve a crisis has the potential to become a negative foundation experience with the psychological burden of being transformed into a positive identity claim.

CLINICAL CONCERNS AND CONCLUSION

In closing, I would like to take some time to address issues relating to clinical conserns and theories of therapy. The question might legitimately be asked as to the importance of utilizing the images of clients in helping them with their unresolved conflicts. Why, if behavior, affects, and cognitions are inextricably linked, is it necessary or important to access the images on which these are based?

On the level of clinical efficacy, when people are engaged in their ritual fights they are confronting each other with propositions and assertions about the world based on their identity claims. These propositions and assertions are examples of digital forms of information processing (Watzlawick, 1978) and are subject to the constraints of this highly analytical, abstract and logical mode of thinking. The person in the ritual impasse is affectively engaged by the challenges that the other person presents while attempting to process information digitally. Because the affective engagement (the unneutralized energy of the critical image) is rooted in the past, digital forms of communication are at a loss to process this level of arousal without access to the past experience. How often have you heard one member of a couple in their fight say, "What are you so mad about?" and the other try to account for their arousal in terms of some detail of the current situation. If a therapist attempts through the logical processes of conventional therapy to persuade the couple to give up their self-destructive behavior, he or she will be handicapped by constraints of this form of communication that is already problematic for the couple.

In eliciting the critical identity images, the therapist is helping the couple to shift from a digital mode of information processing to an analogic mode. It should be pointed out that the elicitation of the image is quite easily accomplished once the couple or client is engaged in the ritualized sequence of behavior. This can be explained by the observation that in a ritual impasse there is a redundancy in the digital aspects of information processing. This aspect of the total information processing system is at the limits of its capacity and all new information is kept out by the repeated sequence. In this state of affairs the parts of the brain that control digital processing (Bakan, 1978) are highly activated. This high level of activation is generalized to the parts of the brain that control analogic forms of cognitive processing. In this way the visual imagery is rendered more accessible to consciousness by a simple instruction on the part of the therapist to shift attention to the analogic forms. The shift to the analogic mode has many fortunate consequences for the conduct of psycho-therapy, as Watzlawick (1978) has pointed out.

The drawing out of the critical identity image brings the person from the center of the phenomenal field to a position at the periphery and introduces the founded nature of their experience at that moment. In the throes of a ritual impasse, the person indulges in character attributions and globalizations that are a consequence of the failure of logical processes to attenuate the differences being expressed. Once the image is elicited, there is a movement from the global to the specific in such a way that the person's experience is made more meaningful by its immediate and unmistakeable connection to the past. At the same time the symbolic aspects of current behavior is represented side by side with the real situation. With immediate comparison available, whatever differences exist between the real situation and its symbolic analogue can be examined and utilized to help the person have a new experience, rather than a repetition of the old.

Another advantage of using the critical identity image with couples is that it provides a neutral, shared territory or medium for communication in the form of a visual schema. Futhermore, this schema is outside the direct interactional field of the couple. In order to view their images they are forced to move (metaphorically, and sometimes literally) from a position facing each other in an antagonistic fashion to being side by side watching the symbolic elements of their struggle.

Klinger (1978) reports that the detail reported in the imagery of experimental subjects is highly correlated to the visualness of the imagery. This sheds light on the importance for clinical purposes of rendering the critical images of the client more visual. It is in the specific detail of the images that the idiosyncratic meaning for the client is embedded. In pursuing the elaboration of the image the client will often "see" something that initially was not apparent. This detail may well relate in a significant way to current context in which the instructions from the image are carried out.

Meichenbaum (1978) has accurately pinpointed the problem of focusing on imagery without considering the meaning system of the client in which the image is embedded. Part of the reason for the false distinction between "imagery" and "verbal" therapies, however, is that we have not yet developed sufficient specificity with respect to images to isolate those that are inherently meaningful for the client. By taking conflict in context as our starting point and allowing this to guide the client's exploration, the client will generate images of an inherently meaningful nature.

In this respect I must disagree with Meichenbaum (1977) when he maintains that the labeling and coding, which is part and parcel of all psychotherapies, holds the key for elaborating the meaning of the experience for the client. These procedures function to create a safe context in which clients can experience the contradictions inherent in their images and the ways they express them in specific contexts. It is the images themselves that are the key to the meanings of the client. The context of shared beliefs that is elaborated in the therapeutic dialogue functions as a transitional system of meaning to anchor the person through the inevitable disorganization that change implies.

Klinger (1971) has stated, "Since imagery of some sort occupies most of an individual's conscious moments, an inquiry concerning the function of imagery may be tantamount to an inquiry concerning the function of consciousness" (P. 140). This paper is presented in the hope of stimulating interest in the questions relating to the use and function of imagery. The value of Kantor's ideas, coming as they do from a different realm of inquiry will, I hope, encourage others to consider the value of naturalistic observation and behavior in context for research and theorizing in this area.

REFERENCE NOTES

1. Mallouk, T. A survey of the self reports of couples in terms of interpersonal conflict. Unpublished manuscript, 1979.

REFERENCES

Ahsen, A. Basic concepts in eidetic psychotherapy. New York: Brandon House, 1968.

Bakan, P. Two streams of consciousness: A typological approach. In K. S. Pope and J. L. Singer (Eds.), The stream of consciousness: Scientific investigations into the flow of human experience. New York: Plenum, 1978.

Bateson, G. Steps to an ecology of mind. New York: Random House, 1972.

Bateson, G., Jackson, D., Haley J., and Weakland, J. Toward a theory of schizophrenia. Behavioral Science, 1956, 1, 251-264.

Craik, F., and Lockhart, R. Levels of processing: A framework for memory research. Journal of Verbal Learning and Verbal Behavior, 1972, 11, 671-684.

Crampton, M. The use of mental imagery in psychosynthesis. Journal of Humanistic Psychology, 1969, 9, 139-153.

Crampton, M. Toward a psychosynthetic approach to the group. New York: Psychosynthesis Research Foundation, 1972.

Csikszentmihalyi, M. Beyond boredom and anxiety. San Francisco: Jossey-Bass, 1975.

Csikszentmihalyi, M. Attention and holistic approach to behavior. In K. S. Pope and J. L. Singer (Eds.), The stream of consciousness: Scientific investigations into the flow of human experience. New York: Plenum, 1978.

Dicks, H. Marital tensions. New York: Basic Books, 1967.

Fairbairn, W. An object relations theory of personality. New York: Basic Books, 1952.

Framo, J. Symptoms from a family transactional viewpoint. In N. Ackerman (Ed.), Family therapy in transition. Boston: Little, Brown, 1970.

Gilbert, D. Reward expectancy strength as related to the magnitude of frustration in children. Unpublished Ph.D. dissertation, University of Southern California, 1969.

Heidegger, M. Being and time. New York: Harper and Row, 1962.

Izard, C., and Tomkins, S. Affect and behavior: Anxiety as a negative affect. In C. Spielberger (Ed.), Anxiety and behavior. New York: Academic Press, 1966.

Jackson, D. Family rules: Marital quid pro quo. Archives of General Psychiatry, 1965, 12, 589-595.

Jaspers, K. The nature of psychotherapy. Manchester: Manchester University Press, 1964.

Kantor, D., and Lehr, W. Inside the family. San Francisco: Jossey-Bass, 1975.

Kantor, D. Critical identity image: A concept linking individual, couple and systems perspectives. In J. Pierce and L. Friedman (Eds.), Family Therapy: Combining psychodynamic and family systems perspectives. New York: Grune and Stratton, 1980.

Klinger, E. Structure and functions of fantasy. New York: Wiley, 1971.

Klinger, E. Meaning and void: Inner experience and the incentives in people's lives. Minneapolis: University of Minnesota Press, 1977.

Klinger, E. Modes of normal conscious flow. In K. S. Pope and J. L. Singer (Eds.), The stream of consciousness: Scientific investigations into the flow of human experience. New York: Plenum, 1978.

Meichenbaum, D. Cognitive behavior modification: An integrative approach. New York: Plenum, 1977.

Meichenbaum, D. Why does imagery in psychotherapy lead to change? In J. L. Singer and K. S. Pope (Eds.), The power of human imagination: New methods in psychotherapy. New York: Plenum, 1978.

Miller, G., Galanter, E., and Pribram, K. Plans and the structure of behavior. New York: Holt, Rinehart and Winston, 1960.

Minuchin, S., Rosman, B., and Baker, L. Psychosomatic families. Cambridge: Harvard University Press, 1978.

Mischel, W. Toward a cognitive social learning theory of personality. Psychological Review, 1973, 30, 252-283.

Pope, K. S. and Singer, J. L. (Eds.), The stream of consciousness: Scientific investigations into the flow of human experience. New York: Plenum, 1978.

Reyher, J. Emergent uncovering psychotherapy: The use of imagoic and linguistic vehicles in objectifying psychodynamic processes. In J. L. Singer and K. S. Pope (Eds.), The power of human imagination: New methods in psychotherapy. New York: Plenum, 1978.

Rokeach, M. Beliefs, attitudes and values. San Francisco: Jossey-Bass, 1968.

Ryan, T. and Watson, P. Frustrative nonreward theory applied to children's behavior. Psychological Bulletin, 1968, 69, 111-125.

Shorr, J. E. Psycho-imagination therapy: The integration of phenomenology and imagination. New York: Intercontinental Medical Book Corporation, 1972.

Singer, J. L. Daydreaming: An introduction to the experimental study of inner experience. New York: Random House, 1966.

Singer, J. L. The child's world of make-believe. New York: Academic Press, 1973.

Singer, J. L., and Pope, K. S. (Eds.), The power of human imagination: New methods in psychotherapy. New York: Plenum, 1978.

Sullivan, H. The interpersonal theory of psychiatry. New York: W. W. Norton, 1953.

Tomkins, S. Affect, imagery, consciousness. New York: Springer, 1962.

Watzlawick, P. Language of change: Elements of therapeutic communication. New York: Basic Books, 1978.

THE APPLICATION OF HUMOROUS IMAGERY SITUATIONS IN PSYCHOTHERAPY: CASE ILLUSTRATIONS

Frank J. Prerost

Western Illinois University

Macomb, IL

The Humorous Imagery Situation is a diagnostic and therapeutic device developed by the author for use in psychotherapy sessions. This newly created therapeutic imagery technique is an integration of the directed daydream with the therapeutic and diagnostic properties of humor. Through this integration the potentials of the directed daydream and humor allow for a safe confrontation and healthy resolution of personal conflicts and sources of stress.

In the directed daydream as used by such individuals as Hammer (1967) and Scheidler (1972) the conflicted individual confronts personal inadequacies and sources of anxiety in the guided mental images experienced by the client. In these images a reconstruction of the origins underlying psychic conflicts occur allowing the client to develop new patterns of adjustment and cope with the conflicts faced. Confronting the sources of stress and anxiety at the level of the daydream allows for quicker resolution as the emotional climate for exploring problems in behavior and attitudes is theoretically not threatening to the client. If these personal difficulties were faced at a directly conscious level, anxiety and fears could impede the therapeutic process. Symbols within the daydream can be more directly faced and conflicts more readily conquered.

In considering methods to promote resolution of personal conflicts while removing any vestiges of personal threat in imagery situations, the Humorous Imagery Situation technique was conceived. The value of humor to assist in an individual's ability to cope with conflict and stress has been documented by numerous investigations. Wolfenstein (1954) noted the importance of the "joke facade" to disguise sexual and aggressive conflicts while alleviating anxiety and stress. Using humor to cope with problems in interpersonal relationships has been reported by Yorukoglu (1974). The effort to come to grips with a stressful situation through the medium of humor appears to signal better adjustment than strategies of withdrawal or aggression.

The mechanism by which humor assists to facilitate mental adjustment includes the substitution of a frame of mind incompatible with anxiety or distress. The playful mood can prohibit a truly angry, frightened or depressed one. Levine (1977) pointed to the role of mastery as a coping function of humor. Laughing in the face of distress is an attempt to prevent being overcome by the fearfulness of a situation and overcome by anxiety. Used in the diagnostic sphere, the degree of humor appreciation present in a person has been found to relate positively with healthy psychological adjustment (O'Connell, 1960), negatively to more repressive life styles (O'Connell, 1970), and negatively with degree of depression (Nussbaum and Michaux, 1955). Harrelson and Stroud (1967) showed humor to be a good indicator of mental-health-related progress over time.

The direct use of humor in psychotherapy has been reported by a number of authors including Levine (1977), Greenwald (1975), and Orfandis (1972). But the employment of humor occurs in a nonsystematic fashion, resulting in typically anecdotal evidence for its effectiveness. The Humorous Imagery Situation technique attempts to incorporate the therapeutic benefits of humor appreciation in a systematic fashion within the use of mental imagery during psychotherapy sessions.

METHOD

In the Humorous Imagery Situation (HIS) technique, imagery situations are developed following consultation with the client in the initial interview sessions. Scenes are developed that reflect areas of greatest personal concern and hold the greatest potentials for eliciting stress or anxiety for the client in real life. With assessment of central stressful themes centered in real life situations, imagery situations that will be used during HIS are developed by the therapist for use in subsequent treatment sessions. These situations can be events actually experienced by the client or those potentially stressful to encounter. Thus the actual situations used in HIS vary from client to client depending upon the personal life situation and psychic adjustment.

During the HIS technique, the client is seated in a chair conducive to relaxation and comfort. After a period in which a state of relaxation is induced through different mental exercises, the imagery situation is introduced. The client is directed to picture a particular scene described in detail, including such factors as: the people present, activities going on, appearance of the surroundings, and feelings of the imagined participants. In the sessions the client is provided with information in sufficient detail concerning the image used to allow for development of the mental image to an adequate degree.

Once the client is involved in the image situation one of two procedures is used by the therapist. The first procedure is to introduce humor into the image by directing the client to see people laughing in the situation including him- or herself. This is followed by questions designed to elaborate on the mental image concerning the humor going on in the situation. Questions used include: "Who is laughing most in the situation?" "How can you participate in the laughter more fully?" "What is causing the laughter?" "What do you see to be most funny in the situation?" "How can the situation become funnier for you? For others?" "Are you enjoying the laughter?" "Do something or say something that is funny for the situation." "Are you laughing with others in the situation?" The goal of the questions and directions is to encourage involvement of the client with the ongoing scene of laughter and eventually to be adept at creating humor in the situation.

The second procedure that is used is to interject humor directly into the daydreams. Suggestions are made that direct the fantasy toward humorous outcomes and events. Comments are made introducing incongruences and absurdities into the imagery situations. The client is directed to imagine scenes and events that point to the absurd restraints and inhibitions a client may be placing on him- or herself in everyday functioning. Skill of the therapist is important in this procedure to be able to translate the clients' areas of conflict into humorous situations. It should be pointed out that there is less chance of insulting or ridiculing the client when humor is employed in the HIS technique than if it is directly used in the treatment sessions. Thus the HIS technique involves two equally important processes. First, the development of humor by the client with practice for understanding the humor appreciation in situations; and second, humor provided by the therapist's direction and interventions in the imagery situation.

In utilization of the HIS technique a balance is struck between these two processes. It is important therapeutically for the client to participate in both humor events: those suggested externally by therapist and the client's personally designed humor. The latter humor appears to reflect on personal concerns and conflicts that enable expression or examination of these conflicts through imagery experience and symbols. The former humor provided by the therapist allows for the development of more constructive coping patterns through guidance it provides.

RESULTS

The HIS technique has been used effectively with numerous male and female clients in the age range of 18 to 33 years of age. The clients involved in the HIS method can be classified into two general categories. The first category was of individuals who were experiencing neurotic-like symptom patterns with anxiety, low self-esteem, and depression. This group of clients were unable to identify any particular source to their psychic discomfort and all had consist histories of adjustment difficulties. The remaining clients receiving HIS were experiencing stress reactions with anxiety to particular life change situations, e.g., divorce, away from home for the first time, romantic break-up. None of the clients evidenced severe psychological pathology and all clients possessed at least average cognitive abilities.

With the group of clients experiencing situational adjustment reactions, the images used in the HIS were designed to focus around the life changes and were not as varied or numerous as the HIS used among the clients with histories of adjustment difficulties.

In reviewing the content during the HIS, a pattern emerged in terms of the humor types occurring during the course of treatment. A three stage pattern was discovered in which the clients' humor changed in a consistent fashion. In the early sessions during HIS, humor within the images was interpreted by the clients in a self-critical, self-blaming fashion. Thus, a Stage 1 period evolved in which clients saw personal ineptness and inadequacies as the source of imagined humor. During this initial stage the clients resisted attempts to direct attention toward other sources of humor and focused on personally conceived shortcomings. All clients went through this Stage 1 during HIS in which they were the target of humorous situations.

As treatment continued in further sessions, Stage 2 humor content becomes apparent. In this period, humor during HIS takes on sexual and aggressive qualities and overtones. No longer are the clients targets of the humor but humor is directed toward others in the images. Within the HIS, the client views hostile attacking humor or ridicule of others as being humorous and the cause of laughter in the HIS. The individuals involved in scenes usually include parents, spouses, or childhood friends as well as acquaintances in positions of authority. These individuals most frequently become the targets of the sexual and aggressive humor produced by the client. Usually an increase in overt laughter occurs as the client enters this Stage of the HIS.

The sexual/aggressive humor dissipated as HIS continued in therapy and began to be replaced with participative types of humor responses with social overtones. This Stage 3 humor imagery found clients able to laugh at personal shortcomings in a confident nonthreatened fashion. Clients during Stage 3 found themselves initiators of humor in social settings without relying on sexual/aggressive attacks on others. The HIS during this stage, became more vivid and elaborate in the detail described by the client. The client at this stage was able to perceive the incongruencies of social situations and appreciate the humor within them. Clients who reflected Stage 3 content consistently in HIS soon terminated treatment and reported effective control over their lives.

DISCUSSION

The initial experiences with the use of the HIS technique have been gratifying. Client change toward effective coping skills and resolution of personal conflicts have been evident. The integration of the directed daydream with humor has proved to be a beneficial marriage. Progress in the HIS procedure has produced an unexpected finding, that of the stages of humor content found. Examination of the humor content during HIS formed the three stages described, which appear to reflect the clients' effective use of imagery to deal with personal conflicts and develop efficient patterns of coping behavior. Further study is being made of the usefulness of the humor content for its diagnostic properties in signaling appropriate timing of treatment termination.

To date the HIS has appeared most effective with clients facing situational stresses emanating from significant life changes, and among those individuals experiencing depression and/or inhibitions connected with low levels of self-esteem. The HIS provides a medium conducive for the expression, examination, and resolution of personal difficulties and inadequacies. Its effectiveness is shown in the stages found. Stage 1 content mirrors directly and symbolically the conflict areas and deficiencies of the client. Following expression of the distress, the clients examine perceived problems in the development of the imagery. Stage 2, with its sexual/aggressive content, provides an outlet for the client to probe his or her emotions. As the feelings are understood Stage 3 content comes into predominance. At this stage humor is confidently suggested and appreciated, strengthening the clients' ego structure and coping behavior repertoire.

CASE ILLUSTRATION

The HIS technique and the three stage phenomena of humor during therapy were demonstrated in the case of Linda. This client was seen twice weekly for a total of sixteen sessions. She was a twenty-five-year-old female who entered treatment because of fluctuating moods of depression and intense anxiety, the latter symptom evidencing itself in near immobilizing fear when she would become apprehensive about her future.

In the initial interview Linda appeared highly anxious and uncertain of herself. She complained of difficulty in sleep patterns and difficulty in concentration. Although attractive and of average stature, she evinced many characteristics of a low self-esteem level with self-doubt apparent in many areas of functioning. Review of her psychological and developmental history produced no well-defined history of psychic difficulties and no previous experience with psychological treatment. The current anxiety was judged related to her current life situation and the stress created by a failing marriage and a desire for a divorce. She had been in an unhappy marriage for the previous three years and at the time of entering therapy the home atmosphere was unpredictable and uncertain.

The imagery situations used in HIS with Linda were designed to exhibit familiar locales in which Linda could deal with the sources of her anxiety. One of the central locations used during HIS was a community restaurant-bar which was a center of social and family activity in her community. The HIS technique necessitated that Linda imagine the bar, people, and activities there. As therapy commenced Linda demonstrated a series of Stage 1 images. In this stage of HIS, content revolved around such issues as Linda being ridiculed and laughed at while in the bar. Issues of concern that were developed included attitudes of the neighbors, who viewed Linda as inept in housework and being a mother; criticism by parents who thought of their daughter as just another "divorcee" interested in sexual relations with many men; interactions with the husband showing his disdain for her sexual abilities; and male peers seeing Linda as physically unattractive and unintelligent. In the HIS these themes continually reappeared in the Stage 1 period. Linda's laughter during HIS would dissolve into tears as she examined these themes. Linda's laughter in the image situations was always interpreted as being directed at her as a victim or due to her social naivete. Directions from the therapist interjecting humor into the HIS helped to alleviate some of the psychological pain experienced by the client.

Linda later began to show hostile/sexual humor during HIS. In this, and to an example of movement to Stage 2, the hostility was turned primarily to her husband. Linda laughed as she imagined her husband failing at such behavior as trying to pick up attractive women, performing sexually, and controlling his liquor intake. Humor began to be found by attacking critically neighbors and friends who frequented the bar. The shortcomings and frailties of others become the source of humor appreciation in this Stage 2. Absurd caricatures were formed of significant others in her life as the client extended and amplified the weaknesses of others. Linda during this Stage of HIS needed less direction for humor situations from the therapist than in the previous stage. She preferred to develop the imagery situations with less direction than before. Coincidentally in this period of treatment, Linda began to take steps to obtain a divorce from her husband and make plans for her future.

In the final stages of therapy, Linda's HIS focused on socially acceptable humor and participative types of humor. This Stage 3 type of content was seen as the client now saw herself as capable of initiating humor laughing at her own frailties as well as those of others. Images became centered around meeting old friends and making new ones. The interactions seen were constructive ones in which she began to develop new relationships and interests. In these scenes Linda now saw herself as possessing valued traits and characteristics and did not need to feel awkward and the target of being made fun of by others. Laughter occurred in conjunction with enjoyable pursuits; e.g., dancing and social interactions. As her HIS content continually reflected these conditions, the client reported greater confidence in herself and began to look forward to being single again. The marriage failure was no longer interpreted as a sign of her inadequacies. Linda focused away from past mistakes and self-doubts toward the potentials of the future.

SUMMARY

The Humorous Imagery Situation technique is a method used in therapy that entails the integration of the directed daydream technique with the psychologically beneficial effects of humor appreciation. Although humor has been reported effective in psychotherapy as a means to deal with conflicts and create more adaptive coping skills, the systematic utilization of humor in the therapeutic setting has been limited. Developed by the author, the Humorous Imagery Situation technique focuses on two processes during therapy: the patient's ability to develop humorous outcomes to imagery situations and theinterjection of humor into imagery situations by the therapist. Results with the Humorous Imagery Situation technique have demonstrated its usefulness with a number of anxiety reactions and life crises. It has been found that images during Humorous Imagery Situations develop into a pattern of three stages. These stages can be defined in terms of the humor content found in the imagery situations. The therapeutic and diagnostic properties of the images are discussed.

REFERENCES

Greenwald, H. Humor in psychotherapy. Journal of Contemporary Psychotherapy, 1975, 7, 113-116.

Hammer, M. The directed daydream technique. Psychotherapy: Theory, Research, and Practice, 1967, 4, 173-181.

Harrelson, R., and Stroud, P. Observations of humor in chronic schizophrenics. Mental Hygiene, 1967, 51, 458-461.

Levine, J. Humour as a form of therapy. In A. J. Chapman and H. C. Foot (Eds.), It's a funny thing, humour. Oxford: Pergamon, 1977.

Nussbaum, K., and Michaux, W. Response to humor indepression: A predictor and evaluator of patient change? Psychiatric Quarterly, 1955, 24, 560-572.

O'Connell, W. E. The adaptive functions of wit and humor. Journal of Abnormal Psychology, 1960, 61, 263-270.

O'Connell, W. E. Wit, humor and defensiveness. Newsletter for Research in Psychology, 1970, 12, 32-33.

Orfandid, M. M. Children's use of humor in psychotherapy. Social Casework, 1972, 53, 147-155.

Scheidler, T. Use of fantasy as a therapeutic agent in latency-age groups. Psychotherapy: Theory, Research and Practice, 1972, 9, 299-302.

Wolfenstein, M. Children's humor. Glencoe, IL: Free Press, 1954.

Yorukoglu, A. Favourite jokes of children and their dynamic relation to intrafamilial conflicts. In A. J. Chapman and H. C. Foot (Eds.), It's a funny thing, humour. Oxford: Pergamon, 1977.

COVERT MODELING IN THE CONTEXT OF STORYTELLING:

OBSERVATIONAL LEARNING IN THERAPY WITH CHILDREN

Paul E. Van Wyke

William S. Hall Psychiatric Institute

Columbia, SC

Communication theorists (e.g., Bandler and Grinder, 1976; Watzlawick, 1978) have emphasized that a core element in successful psychotherapy is the generation of choice regarding alternative patterns of affect, behavior, and cognition. People who do not feel at ease do not have choices available to them; conversely, those who feel masterful in new and difficult situations are those who can easily entertain possible alternative avenues of action. Similarly, descriptive psychologists (Ossario, 1976) define psychotherapy as an expansion of the person's behavioral potential.

More than two decades ago Kelly (1958) specifically addressed the importance of cognitive flexibility in the psychotherapy experience. He formulated psychotherapy as a joint venture where the therapist and client engage in an experimental effort designed to discover and change the client's constructions of reality, including the beliefs and affective experiences that are responsible for the perpetuation of a narrow range of choices.

This experimental or observational stance on the part of the client that underlies the generation of alternatives is accepted as an essential component in psychotherapy from diverse theoretical orientations. For example, analytic theorists speak of the observing ego; gestalt and experiential therapists talk of the reflective self; and behavioral theorists emphasize the role of vicarious learning. In psychotherapy, then, there is a recognized need for a shift from personal self-absorption, which results in immobilization, to gaining appropriate distance from one's situation, resulting in a perspective that incorporates flexibility and potential for change.

APPLICATION OF MODELING IN PSYCHOTHERAPY

Modeling (Bandura, 1969) is an explicit and potent vehicle for generating new choices or learning new responses in everyday experience and in psychotherapy. A significant part of modeling occurs with conscious effort on the part of the modeler (e.g., teacher) or on the part of the observer (e.g., apprentice, student). In the world of everyday experience children have an active interest in the activities, thoughts, and feelings of other children; children learn by keenly watching other children and adults who possess desired skills or qualities. Children have the same fascination for ideas and experiences of others as they do for the acquisition of skills.

Likewise, the learning experience called psychotherapy involves deliberate modeling of the therapist's manner, dress, and ideas. Within the context of therapy it is also common for the therapist to be asked specific questions regarding his or her childhood or current family life. Frequent questions implying specific comparisons are also asked regarding other children who come to therapy sessions, especially if they were observed in the waiting area.

On a more private, personal level modeling also occurs via unconscious absorption akin to the process of identification as discussed by dynamic theorists (e.g., Schafer, 1968). It is well accepted that attitudes regarding self/others (e.g., competence, hate) and constructs about the world (e.g., justice, hope, fear) reflect the basic orientation of significant others in the child's life. With regard to psychotherapy, the impact of the modeling on patterns of thinking and language in addition to overt behavior and style is frequently apparent, even for those who eschew the importance of the therapist's personal characteristics. Thus, modeling essentially provides a complex vicarious experience involving affect, cognition, imagery, and interpersonal elements in addition to overt behavioral rehearsal. Neither parents nor psychotherapists can avoid their modeling influence.

Reinforcement theorists (e.g., Mowrer, 1966) have contributed to the understanding of the conditions under which modeling occurs. An essential component is the similarity or match between the model and observer in terms of desired goals and personal characteristics. Awareness of these variables allows the modeler/therapist to arrange conditions that foster identificatory outcomes.

Since therapists themselves can be simiar to the client in only a limited number of ways the range of influence via direct modeling is limited. Group therapy expands the range of potential modeling behavior, and this factor contributes significantly to the effectiveness of the group process (Yalom, 1975). Individuals in a group are frequently at various stages in terms of personal change, which instills the recognition and hope that alternatives do exist. Since the alternatives need to be accepted as such by the observer, it is also important that a desired similarity exists between the model and observer. This vicarious experience provides the spectator with specific, tested alternatives, reducing the anxiety associated with change.

THE USE OF METAPHOR IN PSYCHOTHERAPY

The challenge in psychotherapy is usually not in the generation of particular alternatives but in the process of presenting the alternatives. "Advice" is frequently perceived as intrusive and not applicable in the specific situation of the client. Successful interventions need to address the defensive posture associated with change.

One particularly useful approach to resistance that promotes psychological distance involves metaphoric language patterns. For analytic therapists (e.g., Alexsandrowicz, 1962) the metaphor generally leads to more direct communication regarding problems. However, some communications theorists (e.g., Watzlawick, 1978) contend that the most efficacious therapy avoids or blocks logical, explanatory language patterns and operates instead within the realm of symbol, imagery, and analogy.

Storytelling represents a specific use of metaphor. Regarding the application of storytelling in psychotherapy, Fox (1980) states, "Virtually any sorrow can be endured if it can be made into a meaningful story. Conversely, joys are magnified once one is able to tell the story to another" (P. 40). Stories essentially establish a different, less personalized framework within which to explore alternatives.

The Mutual Storytelling Technique (Gardner, 1971), which is used in psychotherapy with children, is organized around specific metaphors based on a make-believe television production. After the child provides the initial story, the therapist provides an alternative story in order to open up new avenues of behavior, affect, and thought. The direction of the story, then, is determined by the content of the child's story and the therapist's thematic understanding.

COVERT MODELING IN PSYCHOTHERAPY

Metaphoric communication of the type cited above can be very helpful if coupled with appropriate imagery. However, the stories are frequently quite symbolic and removed from actual experience. In addition, they lack many of the elements incorporated in modeling procedures since the focus is on the content rather than the process of learning. An approach that to some extent bridges the gap between the modeling process and the use of metaphor is covert modeling, which was specifically introduced by Cautela (1971). The procedure was developed for clients who claimed that they could not imagine themselves performing certain behavior. They indicated that even though it was not possible for them to visualize themselves performing the behavior they could clearly imagine someone else doing the same thing. The client is instructued to imagine him- or herself watching movie scenes of the character performing the behavior that the individual wants to perform; specific outcomes (i.e., positive or negative) are also introduced. Although there is predominantly a visual focus in this technique, Cautela does instruct the individual in the use of all the senses. Covert modeling (Kazdin, 1974, 1976) has been used most extensively in therapy aimed at the reduction of avoidance patterns and development of assertiveness. Similarity of the observer to the covert model in terms of personal characteristics and internal (coping) experience have been underscored.

COVERT MODELING IN THE CONTEXT OF STORYTELLING

The psychotherapy technique presented in this paper primarily represents an extension of the covert modeling technique. However, it incorporates the flexibility and potency of communication via metaphor, and is particularly adapted for working with children.

Children enjoy stories about other people and are frequently able to discuss issues of personal concern when they are presented as other children's problems since psychological distance is preserved. From a developmental standpoint children are restricted in their metacognitive ability or ability to think about the characteristics of their own thinking and experience (Flavell, 1979). Thinking about another, similar individual in an actual situation can generate the experience of thinking about oneself.

The covert modeling in this approach is cast in the context of everyday experience of children who are appropriately similar to the identified client. The model is introduced into the natural flow of the therapeutic interaction at any point where the therapist judges that the child would benefit from an observational learning experience that demonstrates alternative patterns of affect, behavior, and/or cognition.

One key element relating to the effectiveness of this approach is the extent to which the therapist is able to capture the essential affective experience of the child and represent it meaningfully, via modeling, using appropriate visual, auditory, and kinesthetic imagery. Kinesthetic imagery focused on the inner response of the model is particularly important for establishing a connection with the affective experience of the child. Therefore, when making reference to the matching experience of another individual, it is clinically beneficial to report the model's description of bodily sensation and body imagery. For example, the therapist may say that another child starting school reported that his or her feelings were bumping each other inside, or that a child whose parents had divorced said he wished he were made of rubber so he wouldn't feel like he was going to be torn apart.

Establishing a context for the model's experience that is similar to that of the child without promoting a personal loss of distance is also an important element in this extension of covert modeling. Any successful therapeutic metaphor preserves the essence of the actual problem situation of the individual and it is consistent with the goals and overall value orientation of the client (Gorden, 1979). Auditory and visual imagery especially help to create a setting with sufficient richness and detail. For example, if a child has lost a sibling through a drowning accident the therapist may present a story about a boy who had recently reported, with tears in his eyes, how he had lost a brother in an auto accident. Seemingly irrelevant detail such as the kind of cars involved, the specific location of the accident and the sounds (e.g., the screech of tires) may enhance the meaningfulness of the experience for the client. (Omission of this detail frequently brings questions regarding what actually happened and where it occurred.)

Specific characteristics of the model are also important to consider in establishing the appropriate context for the story. Typically the individuals who are introduced as models are slightly older and slightly ahead in the therapeutic process. In addition, the difficulties of the models are generally constructed as more extreme and the situations more severe than the client's counterparts. The models are individually based on the subjective experience of the client, including attitudes, values, and expectancies. For example, the popularity of the model may be a significant positive factor for one client whereas it may diminish the effectiveness of the model for another individual. Even though the model characteristics may vary from client to client, the model presented is successful in the therapeutic enterprise in areas where the client is having difficulty.

Incomplete sentences, vague or non-referring pronoun usage, and asking questions such as "Guess what happened next?" can be used to elicit the participation of the client in the construction of the story if the therapist is not certain of the appropriate content. For example, the therapist might comment that a young boy had said, "This place makes me...," or the therapist could say that a youngster reported that his or her parents' fighting made him or her feel a certain way; or the therapist may nod knowingly when asking the client, "And guess what the boy's dad did when he got drunk?" The information provided by the child is based on his or her own imagery. This approach using covert modeling does not involve the high level of cooperation and specific willingness to engage in visual imagery exercises as is required in the more formally structured covert modeling procedure.

EXAMPLES OF COVERT MODELING IN THE CONTEXT OF STORIES

The above covert modeling approach has been used successfully in a wide variety of clinical situations, including dealing with resistance in psychotherapy, eliciting and labeling confusing feelings, promoting specific behavioral change, and changing cognitions regarding past or current events. Although the modeling component is common to all the examples presented below, other covert conditioning procedures are frequently included, i.e., in the context of the stories the children vicariously experience specific positive and negative consequences of certain behavior, affect, and cognition.

Reducing Resistance

Children and adolescents are frequently unwilling participants in the process of psychotherapy, at least initially. They either refuse or find it difficult to engage in specific visual imagery procedures. However, presentation of a report about another child can automatically trigger the imagery that the child does not voluntarily produce.

As an illustration, this therapist was meeting with a thirteen-year-old boy who refused to talk about his recent trouble involving theft and drug use. His lack of investment in changing bothered his parents a great deal. When we were alone I said to him that I didn't think his parents understood how difficult this experience was for him. He stared blankly out of the window. I further commented, "It's been awfully hard for other people your age to talk here too. I met several months ago with a fifteen-year-old boy who had gotten into some serious trouble, but he said nothing was wrong with him. He sat on the couch for 12 sessions without saying a word. Now and then he glared at me and once he spit on the floor. After meeting weekly for three months I commented that it must be very, very hard to come here every week when there is nothing to change. At that point his eyes got a little watery and he said, "Sometimes I think I'm really going crazy.' Well, we met only three times after that because that was the hardest part."

In response to that vignette the younster asked several questions regarding the nature of the other boy's difficulties. He also asked what I did when the boy spit on my floor. His involvement in the therapy process increased substantially.

Emotional Labeling

A nine-year-old child whose father was away on a military duty assignment was referred for evaluation of excessive fear and academic under-achievement. In the playroom he stood motionless, glancing periodically at me with obvious fear and apprehension. As I crouched down next to him I commented, "I can see you're not so sure about this place and about me. I remember a boy who was so scared that he would not look at me at all. When I looked at his chest I could see that he was taking very deep breaths. Soon he went and sat in the corner over there with his back toward me. When I put my hand on his shoulder, like this, I said 'It takes a long time to learn to trust somebody.' Right then, tears came into his eyes, and he said, 'I don't like to be scared.'"

At the point when the boy in the story began to cry, the eyes of the youngster in the playroom filled up with tears. The session was very moving and quite profitable in terms of his disclosure that he was consistently beaten by his new stepmother while his father was away.

Pacing Behavioral Change

In several instances therapy over the course of many weeks or even months has revolved around the model who provides the pacing and direction for change. For example, a seven-year-old boy was referred because of concerns about his gender identity. He was a slightly over-weight and effeminate boy who frequently expressed the desire to be a girl. When we first entered the playroom he noticed a doll bed and dolls in the corner of the room, and he quickly announced--and continued to exclaim--that he was not going to play with the dolls. I then told him about another boy who protested about the dolls, but who had secretly told me that he really wanted to play with them. The client developed an extreme curiosity about this other boy, and each of our sessions began with his question, "Well, have you seen Salvadore?" Although the client never talked directly about his own concerns he continued to ask numerous questions about Salvadore, i.e., why he felt the way he did or whether he was changing. As Salvadore, in the stories, reached a healthy resolution regarding his gender and became involved in activities appropriate to his age and gender, e.g., Little Leagues baseball, the other youngster began changing in the same direction.

Changing Cognition

The "insights" of adults, conveyed through interpretations, are often disregarded by children as "silly" or patently false. However, more serious consideration is given to the newfound understanding of a child in a similar situation. These "discoveries" of other children provide a means to promote an alternative way of thinking about a current or past situation. As an illustration, I was meeting with an eight-year-old girl whose parents were vying for her custody during their divorce proceedings. Each parent was directly conveying to the child that his or her love was more substantial than that of the other parent. During our therapy sessions I commented to her that "Another girl whose parents were getting a divorce told me that it felt like her mother was pulling on one arm and her dad was pulling on the other arm, and she imagined that she was going to rip apart. She said she wished she were made of rubber." In response the child patient remarked, "That's just how I feel!"

While the patient was playing later in the sandbox, the model was again introduced, this time to reveal her discovery--through her sand play invoving a conservation experiment--about the essence of love. I reported, "All of a sudden she looked at me with a smile and said 'I know how it is! Love doesn't come in different amounts; it comes in different shapes!' She said it made her understand what was really happening with the divorce."

This story about another child's discovery allowed the patient to begin thinking about the love of her parents in a very different light. Although insecurities obviously persisted, she began sleeping better at night and playing more appropriately with peers.

FACTORS INVOLVED IN COVERT MODELING

What does the observational stance, established through the use of covert modeling, accomplish, and why does it appear to be such a significant component in successful psychotherapy? This approach promotes a clear difference between the person and his or her behavior. The parallels or similarities between the model and client establish a personal identification although the proposed alternatives are still a matter of choice. These alternatives can be offered explicitly without being perceived as a demand couched in the context of advice. This approach minimizes the experience of a prescription that requires acceptance or rejection.

The expansion of behavioral potentials is related to an understanding of self-concept (Ossario, 1976). Individuals who feel stymied typically have a way of viewing themselves that precludes certain options even though they are well within their capacity to perform. Where therapists can see potential for change the clients cannot. The change occurs when the client is able to expand his or her self-concept to include the new options. In the covert modeling approach the options are directly tested by individuals who are like the client in fundamental ways. The model essentially demonstrates that change is possible rather than simply argues, however convincingly, that the options are real.

Therapy, then, is explicitly a learning experience where specific options get generated and tested. Covert modeling as presented facilitates this process. Because of the diminished sense of self-absorption, the client experiences him- or herself as an actor rather than as a reactor to external situations or internal states. Actually, the therapy experience promotes a perspective that even goes beyond seeing oneself as an actor; the individual is simultaneously an observer and evaluator/critic of one's own behavior (Littmann, 1980). What was heretofore unthinkable or unimaginable--or imagined in a way that prevented change--is observed and appraised as a viable alternative to the way things are for that person. The observational stance facilitates change to the extent that the client projects him- or herself into the situation and concludes that "it fits."

SUMMARY

The present article presents a psychotherapy technique developed primarily for use with children and adolescents that is based on the idea that effective therapy establishes balance between emotional experience and an observational stance. With regard to establishing the individual as a spectator, the importance of modeling in everyday experience and therapy is discussed. Metaphorical communication via storytelling is also emphasized as a way to reduce the defensive posture of clients and establish a connection with significant elements of emotional experience. Covert modeling, introduced by Cautela, promotes psychological distance but it lacks flexibility and assumes a more clearly established alliance than is frequently the case in working with children and adolescents. The modeling in the present approach is introduced into the natural flow of therapy via storytelling, and it incorporates significant elements of visual, auditory, and kinesthetic imagery. Case examples are presented to show the application in overcoming resistance, labeling emotions, changing cognitions, and pacing behavioral change. Factors underlying the efficacy of the procedure are discussed.

REFERENCE NOTES

1. Cautela, J. R. Covert modeling. Paper presented at Fifth Annual Meeting of the Association for Advancement of Behavior Therapy, Washington, D. C., 1971.

2. Littmann, J. Personal communications. July, 1980.

REFERENCES

Aleksandrowicz, D. The meaning of metaphor. Bulletin of the Menninger Clinic, 1962, 26, 92-101.

Bandler, R. and Grinder, J. The Structure of Magic. Vol. II Palo Alto, CA: Science and Behavior Books, Inc., 1976.

Bandura, A. Principles of Behavior Modification. New York: Holt, Rinehart, and Winston, Inc., 1969.

Bandura, A. Psychotherapy based upon modeling principles. In A. E. Bergin and S. L. Garfield (Eds.) Handbook of Psychotherapy and Behavior Change. New York: Wiley, 1971, Pp. 653-708.

Berger, S. M. Conditioning through vicarious instigation. Psychological Review, 1962, 69, 450-466.

Cautela, J. R. and Bacon, M. G. Covert conditioning: A theoretical analysis. Behavior Modification, 1977, 1, 351-365.

Cautela, J. R., Flannery, R. B., and Henley, S. Covert Modeling: An experimental test. Behavior Therapy, 1974, 5, 494-502.

Chertock, S. L., and Bornstein, R. H. Covert modeling treatment of children's dental fears. Child Behavior Therapy, 1979, 3, 249-255.

Flavel, J. H. Metacognition and cognitive monitoring: A new area of cognitive-developmental inquiry. American Psychologist, 1979, 34, 906-911.

Fox, R. E. The joy of inventing stories. Voices, 1980, 39-45.

Gardener, R. A. Therapeutic communication with children. New York: Science House, 1971.

Gordon, D. Therapeutic Metaphors. Cupertino, CA: Meta Publications, 1978.

Grinder, J. and Bandler, R. The Structure of Magic. Vol. I. Palo Alto, CA: Science and Behavioral Books, Inc., 1976.

Kazdin, A. E. Covert modeling, model similarity, and reduction of avoidance behavior. Behavior Therapy, 1974, 5, 325-340.

Kazdin, A. E. The effect of model identity and fear-relevant similarity on covert modeling, Behavior Therapy, 1974, 5, 624-635.

Kazdin, A. E. Assessment of imagery during covert modeling of assertive behavior, Journal of Behavior Therapy and Exper. Psychiatry, 1976, 7, 213-219.

Kelly, G. Man's construction of his alternatives. In G. Lindsay (Ed.) The Assessment of Human Motives. New York: Holt, Rinehart, and Winston, 1958.

Mowrer, O. H. The behavior therapies, with special reference to modeling and imitation. American Journal of Psychotherapy, 1966, 20, 439-461.

Ossario, R. G. Clinical Topics: A Seminar in Descriptive Psychology, LRI Report No. 11. Boulder, CO: Linguistic Research Institute, 1976.

Schafer, R. Aspects of Internalization. New York: International Universities Press, Inc., 1968.

Watzlawick, P. The Language of Change. New York: Basic Books, 1978.

Yalom, I. D. The Theory and Practice of Group Psychotherapy. New York: Basic Books, Inc., 1975.

KINETIC IMAGERY IN MOVEMENT PSYCHOTHERAPY

Erma Dosamantes-Alperson

University of California

Los Angeles, CA

INTRODUCTION

In 1974 I coined the term "movement psychotherapy" to refer to a form of therapy that integrates movement, imagery, and verbalization through a single unified process and where the practitioner is formally trained as a dance-movement therapist as well as a psychotherapist (Dosamantes-Alperson, 1974, 1976, 1980a). Because the type of movement psychotherapy I practice is closely related to Gendlin's experiential philosophy and theory, it is referred to as "Experiential Movement Psychotherapy" (Gendlin, 1973).

Distinctive features that characterize the experiential approach to movement psychotherapy are: (a) the emphasis given to the use of movement as a medium of experience, expression, and communication; (b) the importance assigned to the client's derivation of personal meanings from nonverbal experiencing; (c) the acceptance of a somatopsychic view of client resistance that encompasses both blocks in the expression of overt body movement as well as breaks in the flow of the client's own subjective experiencing; and (d) the consideration given by the therapist to the evolving psychodynamics engendered by the movement process itself as well as to the nature of the ongoing therapeutic relationship (Dosamantes-Alperson, 1980a).

This paper was presented at the American Association for the Study of Mental Imagery Conference, Minneapolis, June, 1980. Requests for reprints should be addressed to Erma Dosamantes-Alperson, Ph.D., D.T.R., Director, Movement Therapy Program, Department of Dance, University of California, Los Angeles, 405 Hilgard Avenue, Los Angeles, California 90024.

In this presentation I will describe and illustrate several procedures I have evolved to facilitate my clients' derivation of personal meaning from the step-by-step tracking of their bodily-felt experiencing and its transformation into kinetic images and verbal associations. The term "kinetic image" will be used in this presentation to denote images that are produced from body movement experiences or that occur simultaneously with body movement.

FOCUSING ON BODILY-FELT EXPERIENCE

Knowledge of how one is feeling at any given moment in time can only be obtained from actual contact with and experience of one's body-self. The term "body-self" refers to the totality of what is experienced kinesthetically, emotionally, and cognitively when one attends to the sense of one's physical self (Dosamantes-Alperson, 1980b).

According to Jourard (1974) a reduction in our somatic perception results in our inability to detect physically and psychologically devitalizing situations and relationships that eventually cause us to sicken. A consistent finding of outcome psychotherapy research, supportive of Jourard's contention, is that clients who are able to tune in to bodily-felt experiencing at the outset of therapy are also most likely to benefit from psychotherapy (Gendlin et al., 1968). It appears, therefore, that a high degree of somatic perception is important for the accurate appraisal of the effects of our environment upon us.

I have developed a procedure, "body-focusing", that helps to increase a person's body-self awareness and feeling reactivity (Dosamantes-Alperson & Merrill, 1980). Body-focusing involves a process of inward-attending to emergent sensations, incipient body movements, and images. It entails: (a) scanning (relaxed attention is paid to all sensations); (b) discriminate sensing (sensations are labeled and assessed in terms of their physical as well as their affective intensity); (c) affective selecting (the most predominantly affective percepts are singled out for more focused attention); and (d) transforming (images are generated from these affectively-charged stimuli).

In body-focusing clients are first taught to relax through a modified version of Jacobson's (1970) self-operations control method. This type of relaxation is of value because it is not dependent on external biofeedback machines for its tension reducing effects and because it seems to induce in clients a greater receptivity to sensory and kinesthetic cues.

Subsequent to this relaxation procedure and while clients are still lying down with their eyes shut, their attention is drawn to the total sense of their bodies along a comfort-discomfort continuum. Following this global assessment, their attention is drawn to distinctive parts of their bodies, one at a time. As clients begin to focus on individual body parts, they are asked to assess each experientially along a number of bipolar physical continua (e.g., tight-limp, light-heavy, hot-cold, etc.) and then in terms of bipolar affective continua (e.g., openness-closedness, softness-toughness, etc.) The therapist suggests to clients that they "zero in" on the feeling quality that best describes their experience of each body part without censoring whatever feelings emerge.

Following this discriminate sensing of their body-selves, clients are encouraged to select the most affectively-charged bodily sensation or sensed incipient body movement and to allow visual images to be formed from this sensory-motor experience.

Body-focusing appears to facilitate clients' ability to tune in to "where and what hurts today" that is, clients learn to sense as well as to locate the source of pain in their bodies (e.g., "the tight shoulder," "the contracted gut," or "the tightened lower back"). Images that emerge from pained body parts enable clients to place the sensation of pain within the past social context to which the pain belongs. The following clinical case excerpt will illustrate this point.

> In the course of a movement psychotherapy session, Elaine experienced an extreme throbbing pain as coming from one of her ovaries. The kinetic image she developed from this bodily experience was that of a young infant stomping about. This kinetic image, in turn, gave rise to a memory association of a hysterectomy operation she had undergone some time prior, and then to the current painful realization that she would not now be able to give birth to a child of her own.

It has now been impirically demonstrated that clients who participate in experiential movement psychotherapy groups (where the transformational process from one mode to another is encouraged) show an increase in feeling reactivity, spontaneity, self-acceptance and capacity for intimate contact with others in comparison to control groups drawn from the same client population (Dosamantes-Alperson & Merrill, 1980).

EXPERIENCING PERSONAL AND INTERACTIONAL WORLDS THROUGH KINETIC IMAGES

The term "personal space" refers to the immediate space surrounding a person's body that s/he experiences as his or her private experiential domain. The space outside of a person's personal space is generally perceived as more public and more accessible to others (Hall, 1966; Sommer, 1969).

The size of a person's personal space and the perceived permeability of its boundaries appear to vary with the person's emotional experience of a given situation. Horowitz et al. (1969) found that "schizophrenics" required larger buffer zones from others than did "normals." Kinzel (1970) found similar results with prisoner populations; violent prisoners required larger body-buffer zones than did nonviolent prisoners.

In my own movement psychotherapy practice, I have observed that depressed clients tend to narrow their personal space and to make it less available to others while angry or assertive clients tend to enlarge their personal space and even to extend it intrusively into others' personal space.

I have found an experiential exploration by clients of their personal and interactional spaces to be clinically useful because it appears to acquaint them with the personal meanings they attach to these phenomenologically significant spaces as well as to facilitate their perception of the continuity between their internal (private and primarily nonverbal) and their external (public and more verbal) phenomenological worlds.

In order to facilitate my clients' actual physical contact with their personal space, I have found it necessary to familiarize them with movements I call "internal-intrapsychic movements." These are subtle incipient body movements which are experienced by clients when they close their eyes and attend inward in a receptive manner to emergent internal sensations, kinesthetic impulses and images (Dosamantes-Alperson, 1979).

While in a receptive state (a relaxed and inward-attending state), clients are verbally cued to experience themselves as "being in the center of their personal space" and "to get in touch with how far this space extends away from their bodies." They are then encouraged to visualize the boundaries of this space and to discover the texture and height of these boundaries by approaching these through touch and movement. Once they have established the boundaries of their personal space, they are invited to explore through movement "the inside" of this space, to attend to spontaneously emerging images, and finally to interact with those elements encountered in these images that trigger the strongest affective reactions.

When clients stop moving, the therapist suggests to them that they sense whether it is possible for them "to move through the boundaries of their personal space" and, if it is, "to explore the space outside" through movement. Clients who cannot do so are encouraged to get in touch with the sense of what is difficult about such a task and to discover "what the resistance they experience is about" by allowing kinetic images to evolve in relation to this sense of no-movement. I use the term "physical resistance" to refer to the clients' inability to move and to instances where the flow of their experiencing becomes temporarily blocked (Dosamantes-Alperson, 1974, 1979).

Clients who are able to move to the space outside are encouraged "to sense the transition they experience as they move from" inside to outside and to stay focused on their affective reactions as they move in relation to objects or persons actually encountered in the outside space. When clients move in an exploratory fashion in space they begin to use what I call "external-interactional movements." These are obvious, explicit movements that occur when clients move with their eyes open and assume an exploratory attitude toward their environment and others (Dosamantes-Alperson, 1979).

The following description of a movement psychotherapy session will illustrate how a client moved to explore her internal (personal) and her external (interactional) spaces, the spontaneous images she derived from this body movement exploration, and the subsequent verbal meanings she ascribed to her nonverbal experience.

> As Pat began to explore her personal space through movement, one could observe her movements becoming increasingly constricted. The spontaneous image she evolved from this body movement experience was that of a "broken heart." As she physically identified through movement with this image, she became aware of an internal split. Her awareness of this split became enhanced by her discovery of two opposing or bipolar qualities in her right and left hands. She proceeded to explore the meaning of this body split through a movement interaction between her hands.
>
> She found that her right hand was rigid and upright while her left hand was limp and curled inward toward her body. The feeling qualities she associated to her right hand were "strength," "power" and "anger" while those she associated to her left hand were "softness," "seductiveness" and "manipulativeness." As the interaction developed, she discovered that when her left hand attempted to control her right one through a passive and seductive sort of manipulation, her right hand became increasingly taut and rigid.
>
> As the interaction continued, she found a way to establish what to her would be a more acceptable relationship between her hands. She discovered that if she approached her right hand with her left hand in a more direct and less beguiling manner, her right hand became more responsive and yielding.
>
> In the verbal commentary that followed her nonverbal experience, Pat stated that she related the image of a "broken heart" to her recent separation from her husband. She mentioned experiencing anger when she encountered her manipulativeness because it underscored her own powerlessness and deceptive behavior in her marital relationship. She commented that as her "feminine" left hand became more direct and less manipulative, she experienced herself as stronger and able to stand on her own two feet. She claimed to experience herself as "more whole." This in turn,

permitted her to move through her personal space boundaries with ease and to be open to the outside environment.

A focused phenomenological exploration of their personal space, its boundaries, and the interactional space outside can provide clients and therapist with the following kinds of information:

1. Affective state of the moment. Clients associate their affect to their sensed degree of expansiveness or constrictiveness while inside their personal space.

2. Degree of privacy or social interaction preferred at the moment. Clients can assess how accessible they are to interactions with others by the manner in which they move past the boundaries of their personal space and through the physical resistances they encounter while attempting to do so.

3. Personal meanings ascribed to nonverbal experience. The individual personal meanings clients derive from their nonverbal (less conscious) experiencing are revealed to them though the content themes that emerge from their kinetic images.

4. Preferred style of interacting with self and others. Through the phenomenological experience of moving from "inside to outside" clients have an opportunity to observe how they react to internalized self-attributions and to perceive how these self-attitudes become reflected in the manner with which they interact with others in the external world of here-and-now social relationships.

5. Therapy process changes occurring in intrapsychic and interpersonal life spaces. The client's phenomenological exploration of personal and interactional life spaces allows the therapist an opportunity to track changes over the course of the therapeutic process in these two spheres of clients' lives.

EXPLORING BODY-INTROJECTS RELATED TO SELF AND OTHERS

Past unfinished situations that are either embedded in relationships with significant others or relate to polarized attitudes one holds towards one's self can continue to have power over one's life without one's awareness. These situations may be brought to consciousness and be worked through by clients by having them locate the problem within their bodies--discovering in what part of their bodies the conflict lies.

Shorr (1972) has found that conflicts about the self and others may be worked through from the spontaneous images developed by clients out of different parts of their bodies. The content themes revealed in these conflicts appear to relate in a meaningful way to the particular body part selected by the client. Thus, the head will tend to trigger associations related to the individual's cognitive and intellectual concerns while attending to the heart will give rise to associations that pertain to the feeling side of the person. Conflict resolution involves the client's experiential integration or synthesis of the polarized emotional elements encountered within the imaginary situation.

As a movement psychotherapist I have found a way to facilitate my clients' conflict resolution generated from body-introjects in the following way: (a) their attention is drawn to that part of their bodies in which the problem is felt to exist; (b) they are encouraged to develop kinetic images from that particular body part; (c) they are asked to identify through bodily-felt movement with those elements from their kinetic images that they experience as most emotionally charged. [By identifying gesturally, posturally and through felt-movement with abstract and concrete aspects of images, clients ferret out the essential feeling qualities they associate with each symbol (Langer, 1953; Lamb and Watson, 1979)]; (d) finally, clients are invited to develop movement interactions or dialogues between symbols they select as most emotionally-charged.

The procedure outlined above appears to facilitate a synthesis or merging of the bipolar affective attitudes that characterize the experience of conflict. This primarily nonverval synthesis can be subsequently symbolized at a verbal level. Gendlin (1973) refers to the step by step effects produced by the moving of one's experience in this manner, as "experiential shifts."

The following (videotaped) movement psychotherapy excerpt will illustrate how a client worked through a conflict by focusing on the body part in which she perceived the problem to reside.

> Anita tuned into the body part she expreienced as problematic for her at the present time, her vagina. The images that emerged from this part of her body was that of an egg that eventually hatched into a chick. As Anita became identified with the chick and began to explore her environment through movement, she became aware that her footing was wobbly and her movements were uncertain and indirect. She experienced herself as "still needing a Mommy rather than a Daddy."
>
> The verbal exchange that followed her nonverbal experience helped her to clarify and make explicit the meaning of this experience for her within the context of her current life. She realized that she felt herself to be sexually inexperienced and as needing to learn a great deal more about her own sensuality.

SUMMARY

In this presentation I have attempted to describe several body-movement concepts and procedures I have developed in my practice as an experiential movement psychotherapist.

The first procedure described was "body-focusing," which teaches clients to discriminate bodily sensations and kinesthetic reactions in terms of physical and emotional experiential dimensions. This procedure provides clients with an internal gauge for assessing their own emotional reactions. By having ready access to these reactions, clients can then evaluate the vitalizing and devitalizing aspects of any given situation in which they find themselves.

The second procedure presented was "the phenomenological exploration of internal (personal) and external (interactional) life spaces." Such a procedure seems to help clients to perceive the personal meanings they attach to these life spaces as well as see how these two realms interact and affect one another.

The final procedure discussed was a "body-introject" procedure that encourages clients to locate a problematic situation within their own bodies. Such a procedure provides clients with an opportunity to work through less conscious and less verbal aspects of conflicts that relate to "self" and "other" issues.

REFERENCES

Dosamantes-Alperson, E. Carrying experiencing forward through authentic body movement. Psychotherapy: Theory, Research and Practice, 1974, 11, 211-214.

Dosamantes-Alperson, E. Experiential movement psychotherapy. Art Psychotherapy, 1976, 3, 1-5.

Dosamantes-Alperson, E. The intrapsychic and the interpersonal in movement psychotherapy. American Journal of Dance Therapy, 1979, 3, 20-31.

Dosamantes-Alperson, E. Dance-movement therapy: An emerging profession. Journal of Energy Medicine, 1980, 1, 114-119. (a)

Dosamantes-Alperson, E. Contacting bodily-felt experiencing in psychotherapy. In J. E. Shorr, G. E. Sobel, P. Robin, and J. A. Connella (Eds.), Imagery: Its Many Dimensions and Applications New York: Plenum 1980. (b)

Dosamantes-Alperson, E., and Merrill, N. Growth effects of experiential movement psychotherapy. Psychotherapy: Theory, Research and Practice, 1980, 17, 63-68.

Gendlin, E. T., Beebe, J., Cassens, J., Klein, M., and Oberlander, M. Focusing ability in psychotherapy, personality and creativity. In J. Shlien (Ed.), Research in psychotherapy (Vol.III). Washington, D.C.: American Psychological Association, 1968.

Gendlin, E. T. Experiential psychotherapy. In R. Corsini (Ed.), Current psychotherapies. Itasca, IL: F. E. Peacock, 1973.

Hall, E. T. The Hidden dimension. New York: Doubleday, 1966.

Horowitz, M. J., Duff, D. F., and Stratton, L. O. Body-buffer zone. Archives of General Psychiatry, 1969, 11, 651-656.

Jacobson, E. Modern treatment of tense patients. Springfield, IL: Charles C. Thomas, 1970.

Jourard, S. M. Healthy personality. New York: Macmillan, 1974.

Kinzel, A. F. Body-buffer zones in violent prisoners. American Journal of Psychiatry, 1970, 127, 59-64.

Lamb, W., and Watson, E. Body Code. London: Routledge and Kegan Paul, 1979.

Langer, S. K. Feeling and form. New York: Charles Scribner's Sons, 1953.

Shorr, J. E. Psycho-imagination therapy. New York: Intercontinental Medical Book Co., 1972.

Sommer, R. Personal space. Englewood Cliffs, NJ: Prentice-Hall, 1969.

BRIDGING THROUGH IMAGERY: AN INTEGRATION OF THE SELVES THROUGH ART THERAPY, A VISUAL DIALOGUE

Dee Spring

The Woman's Centre

Placentia, California 92670

Art therapy is an isthmus of the conscious and unconscious, intertwined with the mystery of the entanglement of our inner selves. It is the expulsion of the garbage into energy of rebirth which flows through the inner conflicts of the primitive and the symbolic; the eccentric and the ordinary; the perfect and the imperfect. It is the bringing forth of the known and unknown.

Most of us fantasize about how it would be if we could someway magically possess all the tools to create exactly the kind of life we want. Yet most of us do not use the tools within our grasp or give ourselves the chance to pursue that which we want the most. We continue to push our aspirations, hopes and dreams further into our fantasy area and deny our potential by saying "I'm not important," "everything gets in my way," or "it's too much trouble." In denying our potential, we also deny our individuality. We cease to be important to ourselves and feel cut off, stagnated, unfulfilled. It is easier to run with the tide, let others make decisions for us, choose another's philosophy and copy the most popular life style of the day. This is our way of identification with something, someone. Yet we're not satisfied with what we are; we feel there must be more. But how do we get there, how do we start, where do we stop, or do we stop; what's out there, who am I? It is as though each of us has many parts that dangle. We desire to pull those parts together because it seems logical that there would be more strength and potential if all the parts were going in the same direction. We could then stop being entangled in our own tentacles, or being teased by the many loose ends floating around. Perhaps we should go on a "part hunt". This would be a way to investigate our parts and see how they fit together, or if they fit together. We need to learn what can be integrated, what can be discarded, what needs to be oiled or repaired and what new parts are needed. Then we can go about the task of putting us all together into one integrated whole. Tools are needed for working on the parts, a supplier is needed for the new parts, a receptable for the discards and since we're unfamiliar with the process of fitting these parts together, we need an instructor or guide.

The first tool we need is a willingness to accept ourselves as we are, our world as it is and a knowledge that we can only begin from where we are right now. Another tool is exploration. We need to explore in order to learn how we are put together, how we got here, influences on and in our lives, what we want out of life, our comfort zones, how all the parts fit together. Perhaps the most important tool we have at our disposal is the communication of the unconscious. The unconscious serves as a guide, a friend, and an advisor to the conscious. This tool and part is like a two-way radio, both a receiver and sender. We know the unconscious and communicate with it. The unconscious used as a tool to integrate the whole is extremely valuable in defining the complexity of our problems and possibilities. These are but a few of the tools that we can incorporate. All those mentioned, as well as those not mentioned, some of which must be discovered for each individual, can be used in many ways. These tools combined with different philosophies and attitudes or exchanged with other more adaptable integration processes provide an enviroment for therapeutic change. The search for the proper tools may be lengthy since none of our parts are standardized.

Once the proper tools are accumulated, the search begins for the supplier of the new parts. We, the storehouse of ourselves, are the supplier of the new parts. It is our ability to use the inventory we have on hand to manufacture the new parts. This process may be painful and time consuming. If there is a shortage of materials, the scrap parts may have to be recycled. If, however, the supplier can find a new part that will just slip right in place of the old one, the process is much simpler. By using the right tools and perseverance and letting ourselves be honest with ourselves in the diagnosis of the damaged or worn out part, we may speed up the process. However, if we continue to stumble over the dangling parts because we continue to deny our potential as a repairman, then the supplier gets tired of our indecision and decides that the new part wasn't really important and ceases to pursue the search. If, on the other hand, the new part is supplied, the proper tool is used, the process of integration can continue uninterrupted until such time as another problem of assembly is encountered.

As the assembly of the whole continues, we find a need for a receptacle for the parts we choose to discard. How do we decide what to discard and how, since all parts, whether new, damaged, worn out or functional are in some way appurtenant to the whole we want to achieve? When we accept ourselves as we are and our world as it is and begin from where we are right now, we find that we can let go of old parts such as feelings, ideas, attitudes, conditioning and comfort zones. These go into the receptacle that is ourselves. The discards are put into our experience bank and recycled to reinvent the new parts we are fond of and very much attached to. Therefore, the receptacle sits empty for a long time. Once we overcome the fear and insecurity of handling the new part and assure ourselves that the new part does fit and really works, it becomes easier to make the entries into the ominous repository. When we've gone through the process once, it becomes easier to diagnose the inoperability and discard the part. Each time we pursue the process, we come closer to the potential of a complete configuration of ourselves. We become increasingly aware of how good it feels to unload the garbage. However, it becomes abundantly clear that over a period of time our machine is in constant need of maintenance and repair.

Since the process of fitting the parts into our own configuration and giving the configuration a rhythm is unfamiliar at the beginning, we must find an instructor or a guide. Perhaps at a point in time we will not need further instruction or guidance, but support as well.

Art can be the instructor in the process of developing a configuration of the parts. The vehicle of art is a personal experience with one's self in using the tools we all possess and in actuality is a way of being one's own instructor as well as supplier, tool maker, and receptacle. Art provides a visual blueprint or diagram from which we can begin to bind the parts together. Art gives us the freedom and guidance in employing philosophies, attitudes, and feelings in a way that is acceptable. Art is a highly personal, humanistic approach that affords each of us the actuality of developing our full potential through our inner resources. It affords us the experience of seeing us through our own eyes. If we pursue feedback from others, it also gives us the experience of seeing us through other's eyes. Through art, we possess the capability to integrate the inner and outer self, conscious and unconscious. We can develop our own special isthmus of philosophy through an integration of our parts.

I believe the analogy just drawn comments on my basic philosophy of what I feel is valuable in accomplishing an integrated personality and is the basic approach to helping others reach their full potential. Even more involved than this is the philosophy of unconscious and conscious which I feel is a joining together of feelings to make a genuine self. It is in the dark pools of the unconscious that we remember how to be ourselves. We can be ourselves there, for no one can gain entry to see us or hear us. We don't have to wear our mask, worry about acceptance or approval.

In our conscious, however, we are concerned about all of the things which get in our way such as conditioning, acceptance, approval, ego, pride, etc. These are some of our dangling parts. Our unconscious could be called the "real me"; the conscious, "the cultivated me". Through the processes of art, these two "me's" can be integrated by a communication between the two forces. We sometimes push away our unconscious because it gets too close or someone laughs or judges what we have said or done about our feelings, thoughts or visions. We become entangled in what we should be, rather than what we are. In essence, the blending of our inner and outer selves is the most natural human way; children do it constantly, but then they are themselves--at least for awhile! They do all the things we adults would like to be free to do.

It hasn't been too many years since I began to learn who I was and accept me for what I was. It was only after my own personal therapy that I could understand that I was a person who did not have to be identified by a husband, family, friends or neighborhood. I was O.K. without any identification other than my own. Before I could get there, I had to accept me as I am, my world as it is and that I could only begin from where I am right now. I learned very quickly that my unconscious held a showcase of history, advice for the present and a guide for the future. After a period of time, I realized that I was forming a new philosophy, one with which I was comfortable, but which also wasn't accepted by some of my old friends. I decided to get rid of the old friends! When I finally put those worn out parts in the repository, I felt a newness in my life, an excitement that pushed me to find other misused or damaged parts and discard those also. Through a process of learning, I discovered that my unconscious also had special powers to understand people, to pick up things about people without them telling me. As I became me, I found I could pick up incidents, feelings, happenings and all sorts of wonderful things. I went through alot of tumultuous years before I began to learn how to integrate this inner self with the outer self and accept it. Once I began to realize harmony of these two forces, I found I was actually living a new philosophy--a philosophy of my own making. I realized quite unexpectedly that this had been accomplished through my work as an artist. I had learned about who I was. I could work out my emotions and inner turmoil with a paint brush, clay, plaster, collage or hot wax and dye on a cloth.

The philosophy that developed very naturally for me (not always pleasant) is one that I feel is beneficial to the process of art therapy. We, as people, are many times bewildered by the complexity of our problems, our daily lives and the possibilities we encounter. We have many resources within ourselves. We are our own supplier of new parts, as well as the receptacle for old parts; we have parts that dangle and loose ends that flap in the breeze. We are all human and, as such, have basic needs, emotions, feelings and a desire to belong, to be a part of. We also have the tools to disassemble, repair, add or subtract and then put all the parts together to form a workable whole, to create homogeneity. We have a constant guide, friend and advisor to our conscious. It is our unconscious. We consistently have an instructor for expanding our knowledge about parts. Our instructor is the art media whether we be artist or those who always say, "I can't draw a straight line." We have within our grasp the opportunity, through the art media, to see ourselves visually both inside and out, creating a visual dialogue. And even though we feel we have two philosophies, we also have the capacity through a dedicated process to unite those philosophies. Each of us is unique in having that unprecedented ability to make our own isthmus of philosophy and live it.

The foregoing idea of integration through waking imagery followed by visual projection onto art media served as the basis for an 18-week guided art therapy workshop. The workshop successfully showed that:

> The psychological forces and mechanisms involved in artistic creation are closely akin to those that underlie the development of human personality; they are no less complex, no easier to describe...(art activity gains) its motive power...from within the personality; it is a way of bringing order out of chaos--chaotic feelings and impulses within, the bewildering mass of impressions from without. It is a means to discover both the self and the world and to establish a relationship between the two. In the complete creative process, inner and outer realities are fused into a new entity (Ulman, 1975, P. 13).

The purpose of the workshop was to guide individuals to design and complete visually what they felt was their total configuration and how they realted to their environment. The idea of the project was to ascertain how individuals would relate feelings of their inner and outer worlds to very abstract ideas. The anticipated outcome of the project was to have individuals realize that there would always be intersections or impasses that Perls (1969) describes as "being stuck or lost," that when intersections are encountered, one must be willing to go through the pain in order to achieve the next level of self-awareness or adult maturation. Through this process there would be new ways to grow, new plateaus to reach and new space to fill. It was hoped that through the process of the designed activities, each individual would acknowledge that change occurs, a new energy level is reached, there is a leveling off, sometimes a backward slide, another growth period and another leveling off. This may occur in a regular pattern as individuals continue their integration process. The ultimate result of the group process was for each individual to come to the conclusion that personal growth is internal. With the growth, various energy levels and awareness levels are visible through the therapeutic use of art.

The thought of the project had occurred while working with clients who were of the opinion that if they involved themselves in some type of therapy for a short while, their problem would be solved and they would "live happily ever after". I found clients to have difficulty in realizing that integration is a continuing process; it begins when the individual is dissatisfied with where he is right now and discovers that to get off the merry-go-round of his own therapy, someone else must throw the switch to stop the machine. The individual must take a look at the obvious through the eyes of someone else, a guide; to become aware of the self as "a whole and genuine person..." (Fagan, 1970, P. 34). This is the difficulty. Individuals are phobic and avoid suffering. They stay immature and continue to manipulate the world rather than suffering the pains of growing up (Perls, 1969). One is comfortable in immaturity, for being adult means being alone and taking responsibility for one's feelings and actions. I found these ideas to be very prominent in the 18-week workshop series. I also found that as individuals accepted the challenge of self to work through pain of maturation, energy levels never experienced before became realities and that the process of encounter with self, through the therapeutic use of art, provided rapid awareness. Clients felt addicted to the process. The more the process, the more the involvement, the more they wanted; the more they became involved with the creative process, the more their depth of awareness. The deeper the awareness, the more they responded to abstract and primitive analogies and personal symbolism, the more they realted in terms of nonverbal communication and sensing, the more they worked on abstract activities, the more they realted to their everyday world, bringing forth feeling and thinking states which had not surfaced. The more this occurred, the more understanding of personal processes occurred. The acceptance of self and others was definitely in the feeling state rather than the verbal state and the vibrations and rhythms experienced many times reached an energy level that was phenomenal. The accelerated growth from this in-tune-ness with self was the addiction expressed by so many clients.

The workshop began with very subjective activities and from the beginning sparked creativity and abstract thinking as well as real struggles in visually relating the activities. Frustration was very obvious, but little resistance was encountered. Group members discovered, by visual mean, many parts of themselves that they would like to get rid of such as anger, resentment, sadness and hurt. They discovered other parts that needed repair such as critical attitudes, self-consciousness, and lack of decision making. Interestingly enough, they also discovered new parts they wanted to add such as assertiveness, less game playing, goal setting, sensitivity, and better image of self. Many clients related that they had not thought about making real changes since they felt this was obtainable. Until they began to become aware of the feeling and thinking states, they felt "stuck and lost," no way out of the dilemma.

By drawing out thinking and feeling states, individuals became aware of alternative approaches to dilemmas. As individuals manufactured their personal visual dialogue, encountering themselves, they realized they could not deny authorship of their own work. They realized that activities served as cues, that creative endeavors bypassed personal censorship. These creative endeavors provided proof that

> Creativity is one of the major means by which the human being liberates himself from the fetters, not only of his conditioned responses but also of his usual choices (Arieti, 1976, P. 4).

As one creative endeavor followed the other, individuals became excited about the discovery of self. The use of imagination and the production of art in a nonthreatening environment produced enjoyment, relief from conflict, and feelings of accomplishment. It was interesting to note that Ernst Kris' theories expressed in "Psychoanalysis and the Study of Creative Imagination" were being realized and well supported by the changes taking place in the participants. My ideas had basically followed his and had been the premise on which the activities were designed, relative to the addiction of freedom to create and the ability in each person to get in touch with feelings through creative endeavors, especially those activities that are guided to produce a state of awareness in the here and now. Kris (1952) states the following:

> Common to all manifestations of creative imagination, the first place is subjective experience. This tends to be infinitely differentiated in intensity and duration and to appear as an ingredient or accessory in many moods. Three characteristics of this experience seem outstanding:
>
>> First, subjects are aware of the limitation of conscious effort. Second, they are aware of a specific feeling. It is never a neutral one. There is always some frequently a very high, emotional charge involved. Third, even if excitement rises, the mind tends to work with high precision and problems are easily solved. If we adopt a broad meaning to the term "problem solving" we can say that some "problem solving" is always going on, even in art (P. 334).

The guided activities proved to be highly personalized experiences that continued for months following the initial impact. Individuals became acutely aware of their incompleteness and began the task of integration as a result of visual imagery and creative spontaneity within a framework of guidance, support and a nonthreatening environment. Arieti (1976) supports the development of this process in his statement:

> Creative work seems to have a dual role; it enriches and expands man who will be able to experience new dimensions inwardly (P. 5).

The following experience of a highly creative male participant in this workshop supports and documents the inward growth discussed by Arieti and what I observed as a manifestation of concentrated guided imagery and art therapy.

The participant was a 36-year-old male borderline sociopath with a history of unhappy and short-term female relationships, few male relationships after his teenage years, inability to hold a job for any length of time; a Viet Nam veteran; unable to read and write above the fourth grade level; and unsuccessful in his daily life relative to personal accomplishment. He was extremely angry and rebellious, paranoid and hostile, and he was a pathological liar. In his early years, he had skirmishes with law enforcement and most relationships were sadomasochistic. At the time he entered treatment, he was extremely depressed, defeated, and had low self-esteem (bathing once weekly). He could see no way out of his dilemma and his financial distress not solutions to his conflicts. He had no offers of employment, no security, and no support system.

The first two workshop activities produced some amazing results and awareness for this individual. The first activity, entitled "Goin' on a Part Hunt," produced a drawing of a computer blowing out fire and clouds of smoke. There were no doors for entry to the internal parts. There was no way to repair the computer should it break down. He stated the following:

> I was astonished at what I learned about myself. I suspected a lot about not letting others see inside, but didn't want to admit that I was a completely closed person. I thought I shared, but realized when I saw the computer that I shared with no one. I kept everything inside. I programmed myself not to feel, to have perfect control, to act and interact in prescribed ways. I take everything in, but give nothing out. Information could be put in, but nothin' came out. My energy came from within, but it was anger and ready to explode. I am perfectly contained; I need nothing and nobody--people always hurt me.

The computer was exactly how this client was perceived by others and was a visual dialogue of how he felt. He didn't like what he saw when he finished the art product. He also stated:

> After seeing that monster, I want to change--get rid of it. I don't like myself that way. I can't figure a way out of that computer.

Later in the series, he redesigned the computer and solved his problem of getting out. His way out was making doors where the front panels were. His biggest difficulty came in making a decision about what kind of door knobs to use. His self-esteem improved as he accepted the challenge of redesigning his computer to get his feelings outside. The redesigning of this computer took 10 weeks because of the internal conflict and struggle.

During the second activity, entitled, "Parts I want to Replace, Repair or Discard," the participant, who had drawn the computer, drew his anger. He was angry at himself because he wouldn't let himself out of the computer. Over the years he had trapped himself, programmed himself and tortured himself, sharing with no one. He refused to change or seek education for which he had an insatiable appetite he would not admit. Working through this in the group, he smashed the drawing, squashed it, tore it, grunted at it, and finally, after a great deal of struggle, threw it across the room. His whole body relaxed and he said, "Oh, I feel so much better, I've wanted to do that for years." He was extremely fatigued afterwards. Watching this participant was exciting because of his own breakthrough. From past experience, I knew he would reach a new energy level in a week or less. He was no exception. At the next group meeting, he was very excited about self and stated, "I feel so good, I can hardly sit still." This was quite a change from his usual passive and programmed behavior.

From relieving some of his anger, this individual had a particularly high energy level through the third activity and it was during this session that he unconsciously began to use his left hand instead of the right hand, which he had used all of his life. He used the left hand as though he had always used this hand. He was totally unaware of the switch until the group called his attention to it. I had suspected, from his past history, that he had been left-handed at an early age and I felt this was a part of the suspected dyslexic condition. His first reaction was to deny the usage of the left hand, but it was observed by group members. He could not play his routine game of denying the reality of himself. This particular incident intrigued me to work with him more and get some testing done to ascertain if there was a learning disability that had gone undetected all of these years. I suspected dyslexia from his behavioral patterns and past history.

Through some extensive testing, it was ascertained that this individual did indeed have both dyslexia and dysgraphia. Once this diagnosis was confirmed and the individual understood the reasons for his lack of success, he began to make plans for a future. The possibility of a healthy future erupted out of his involvement with the creative process. He discovered he had a talent and could conceivably expand from this foundation. He had discovered a springboard from which he could explore and discover the realities of himself. Before the workshop concluded, he had enrolled in a junior college to pursue a degree in art.

Today this individual is close to graduation with an A.A. degree and has enrolled in a university to complete his B.A. in art. He has participated in many art shows and has gained acclaim as a producing artist in three-dimensional art. He is working at the university as a peer counselor with persons who are handicapped or have learning differences. He has recently received an award as "Distinguished Man On Campus," for his dedication to projects involving handicapped students.

His recent success, probably his first from his presented history, is a direct result of 18 weeks of concentrated imagery and art therapy. Personal tools, methodologies, and conflicts came together for this individual as he designed and completed his visual dialogue. He could not deny the authorship of his own images and art work. He was unable to censor his normal patterns denying the reality of self. The continual process made each activity more vivid and dynamic, connecting his inner and outer worlds. The connections made from the eruption of buried material enabled him to build a bridge from which he could survey his unique rhythmic life flow and correct the run-off by utilizing the wasted energy. Putting images into a form that could be seen and touched added a powerful dimension to self-confrontation and healing. I call this "Integrative Art Therapy".

> The way we perceive visually is directly related to how we think and feel; the correlation becomes apparent when we represent our perceptions with art materials. The central figures we depict emerge from a diffuse background and give us clues to what is central in our lives. The way we use lines, shapes, and colors in relationship to each other and to the space we put them in indicates something about how we pattern our lives. The structure or the lack of it in our forms is related to our behavior in living situations.
>
> Realizing how we use our visual perception in creating art forms can give us new insights into how we can use our perceptiveness to create more integrated lives (Rhyne, 1973, P. 9).

WORKSHOP SUMMARY AND WORKSHOP ACTIVITIES

The materials and activities (Table 1) not only provided a sensual experience, but evoked feelings within the participants of moving out of old comfort zones and changing patterns. The group related that the discovery of discarding feelings that they were attached to was painful, but necessary and important. Discoveries of such ideas as "much had to be discarded before potentials could be reached" and that it was "all right to be uncomfortable" were important. Another discovery by the group came when the discarded parts were passed around for all to feel. It was also nice to be able to let others touch discards. When others understood and cared, the garbage was just another part of humanness. The other relevant discovery was: by passing the art objects around, vibrations from others were picked up and this brought about an intuneness that was a very beautiful experience. The closeness among the participants was a new awareness level seldom experienced, but extremely vital and meaningful to personal awareness of self and others. Out of the negative connotation of discards or garbage had come positive feelings that replaced the negative feelings about the "ugly" side of us all. Fitz Hugh Dodson (1976) supports this theory by stating:

> ...drop into a trash can those parts of yourself which were not adequate or which you did not like. Now use your imagination to endow yourself with positive traits to replace the negative parts you have consigned to the junk heap. Imagine yourself being treated differently by your friends, your parents, your family...(P. 120).

At this point in the workshop, I had confirmed my own theory of how tremendously important mental imagery and creativity is to the mental health of all persons. I, through the visual arts, had confirmed my belief that the combination is extremely important as tools in treatment of people regardless of what the problems are. Certainly the same program design is not applicable in all cases, but the design concept is one that can be used for the benefit of personal growth for many types of individuals. Over the past five years of experience with a variety of clients, I have seen this concept work rapidly with lasting results. Especially in this workshop has the concept been confirmed that guided art therapy combined with spontaneity, imagery, and creativity produces rapid personal growth. I've found participants to find the support they need in such an environment, the necessary frustration to discover for themselves, the necessary structure and freedom to produce, spontaneity that reduces the pitfall of being caught up in detail, imagery for exploration, and a sufficient encounter with self to produce immediate results. I have found that regardless of the activity, the participant involves self in dealing with those things that are personally important in the here and now.

Table 1. Group and Individual Activities

PART A: Exploration and Discovery	8 weeks
1. Goin' on a Part Hunt	Oil Pastel
2. What Parts Will I Replace, Repair or Discard?	Oil Pastel
3. My Journey to Find Tools and Parts (Fantasy Trip)	Felt Tip
4. My Tools and My Tool Box	Collage
5. How Will I Replace and Repair my Parts?	Oil Pastel
6. My Discards	3-Dimensional Fibers
7. Waste Receptacle	3-Dimensional Fibers
8. My New Parts Are...	Oil Pastel
PART B: My Configuration	5 weeks
1. Needs and Wants (Fantasy Trip)	Paint
2. The Two Me's	Clay
3. My Integration	Paint
4. My Instructors, Advisors, Suppliers & Manufacturers are...	Collage
5. My Configuration (Shape and Color)	Any Media
PART C: Integration	5 weeks
1. My External Environment vs My Internal Environment	Clay
2. My Relationship to Things and People in My Physical Environment	Collage
3. Dreams and Schemes - Goals and Souls Fantasy Trip	Paint

Table 1 (continued)

4. The Real Me vs the Cultivated Me	Any Media
5. The New Me	A Costume made to wear - any media

REFERENCES

Arieti, S. Creativity: The magic synthesis. New York: Basic Books, 1976.

Dodson, F. The you that could be. Chicago: Follett, 1976.

Fagan, J., and Shepherd, I. Life techniques in Gestalt therapy. New York: Harper and Row, 1970.

Kris, E. Psychoanalysis and the study of creative imagination. In The Bulletin of the New York Psychoanalysis Society and Institution. New York: New York Academy of Medicine, 1952.

Perls, F. Gestalt therapy verbatim. Moah, Utah: Real People Press, 1969.

Rhyne, J. Gestalt art experience. Monterrey, California: Brooks-Cole, 1973.

Ulman, E., and Dachinger, P. Art therapy in theory and practice. New York: Schocken, 1975.

AN ART THERAPY APPROACH TO THE DRUG ABUSER, CORRELATING BEHAVIORAL, NARCISSISTIC, AND LATERALITY THEORY

Evelyn Virshup* and Bernard Virshup

*Private Practice; **Univ. of So. Calif. School of Medicine

*Woodland Hills, California; **Los Angeles, California

Drug addicts form a complex, heterogeneous group; it is probably not possible to speak of the treatment of "the drug addict." In leading a group of drug addicts using art as therapy, it appeared that there was a subset whose traits of spontaneity, of timelessness, and of nonlinear, nonlogical, appositional thinking, showed a remarkable similarity to the functions of the right brain that have been elucidated in numerous clinical and experimental studies.

We have also noted that these traits derive from very early, narcissistic conflicts which are difficult to treat verbally because of their origin in the nonverbal oral stage. The addition of art therapy allows a controlled regression to the stage of fixation, permitting the individual to explore the conflicts nonverbally.

If the addict is, in this process, using right brain functions, then we have a physiological basis for the use of art therapy and other nonverbal therapies. It also adds a new physiological basis for present psychoanalytic theories. Of even more importance, it gives direction to a field looking for more effective tools. The purpose of therapy then is to evolve from a state of right brain dominance, with its nonverbal regressions and fixations, to one of balance with the left brain functions of sequential verbal insight, purposefulness, logic, and propositional thinking.

In this theoretical context, the essential process of art therapy is:

1. Regression to the right brain nonverbal conflicts through the use of art materials.
2. Elucidation of the conflict nonverbally through art.
3. Transition from nonverbal to verbal expression of the conflict

by writing a myth or fantasy about the art.
4. Improving verbal insight by encouraging the patient to relate the story to him or herself.
5. Gradually increasing verbal skills, and thus the use of the left brain functions, while keeping the focus on insight, and on resolution of conflicts.

What does art therapy add to the therapy process? How exactly does it work with drug abusers and why should it work any better than any of the many other therapies currently employed in drug abuse treatment?

The two major therapies today are those analytically based and those behaviorally based. Art is compatible with, and adds something to, each.

ANALYTIC ORIENTATION

From the analytic viewpoint, drug addiction is an attempt on the part of the addict to compensate for developmental and structural defects (Krystal, 1970). "During early childhood and prior to the resolution of the Oedipus complex and the formation of the superego, the still incomplete psychic structure requires an ongoing object relationship to maintain psychic homeostasis. The object compensates for the immaturity of the ego until its functions have developed; the adult borderline and psychotic personalities remain to a large extent dependent on their objects to supplement ego and superego functions" (Karland, 1978, P. 93).

"Psychoanalysts, in reconstructing the narcissistic line of development, find evidence that those who abuse drugs have experienced a sudden loss (separation, death, divorce, hospitalization), severe frustration, or traumatic disappointment in their relationship with their parents. . . at an early age when the idealized objects were not yet distinct from the person' own self-feelings" (Kurland, 1978, P. 158).

According to Kohut (1977), "the afflicted individual suffers from the weakness, from a weakness in the core of his personality. He suffers from the consequences of a defect in the self. The symptoms...arise secondarily as an out-growth of a defect in the self... They are all attempts, unsuccessful attempts, it must be stressed, to remedy the central defect in the personality.

"The narcissistically disturbed individual yearns for praise and approval or for a merger with an idealized supportive other because he cannot sufficiently supply himself with self-approval or with a sense of strength through his own inner resources. . .The addict. . .craves the drug because the drug seems to him to be capable of curing the central defect in his self. It becomes for him the substitute for a self-object which failed him traumatically at a time when he could still have had the feeling of omnipotently controlling its responses in accordance with his needs as if it were a part of himself...The ingestion of the drug provides him with the self-esteem which he does not possess. Through the incorporation of the drug he supplies for himself the feeling of being accepted and thus of being self confident; or he creates the experience of being merged with a source of power that gives him the feeling of being strong and worthwhile. And all these effects of the drug tend to increase his feeling of being alive, tend to increase his certainty that he exists in this world.

"...Whatever the chemical nature of the substance that is employed, however frequently repeated its consumption, however cleverly rationalized or mythologized its ingėstion with the support from others who are similarly afflicted...no psychic structure is built, the defect in the self remains" (Kohut, 1977, P. vii-viii).

Kohut emphasizes that it is important to ascertain the adequacy or inadequacy of the parents as self-objects of the child, in terms of providing self-esteem regulation which the child should later be able to perform on his own: "...it will be of crucial importance to ascertain the fact that a child could find neither confirmation of his own worthwhileness nor a target for a merger with the idealized strength of the parent and that he, therefore, remained deprived of the opportunity for the gradual transformation of these external sources of narcissistic sustenance into endopsychic resources, i.e., specifically into sustaining self-esteem and into a sustaining relationship to internal ideals" (P. ix).

It is significant in the art therapy process that such experiences occurred during a time before the child had developed speech. Because they occurred during the oral stage primarily, they are nonverbal and relatively inaccessible to verbal techniques. They are much more accessible through nonverbal techniques, especially those using art materials in a spontaneous and unstructured way, which encourages regression, Gazzaniga pointed out that developmentally the imagery-processing system precedes the language system. Therefore early memories prior to the development of the language system are accessible in the visual or imagery system but are inaccessible through the verbal system.

Psychoanalytic therapy techniques explore the unconscious mechanisms by free association and by dreams, relying heavily on transference and interpretation. The patient must come to his own insights as the "dream belongs to the patient" (Adams, 1978) That is, ultimately the patient must say for himself what the symbolism represents.

In art therapy, the spontaneous drawing produces material

comparable to a dream. In the somewhat altered state of consciousness typical of creative endeavor, the critical faculty of the individual is blocked, allowing access to the nonverbal. Art, like dreams, is a "royal road to the unconscious." In addition, the production is permanent; it can be looked at and described. The artist can, in the manner of Gestalt therapy, identify with and "be" the object drawn. Although the interpretation is up to the individual, the material, being on paper, cannot be suppressed or forgotten, and is available for review (Rhyne, 1974).

Analytic psychotherapies involve regression, insight, cognitive reevaluation, affective discharge, integration, and maturation. Art therapy accelerates these processes, because the arts are inherently integrative. As Ulman (1977) states: "Art has the power to unite opposing forces within the personality and to help reconcile the needs of the individual with the demands of the outside world" (P. 14). In other words, art has inherent restorative and therapeutic possibilities apart from insight.

BEHAVIORAL ORIENTATION

The second major therapy is that of behaviorism, which sees drug addiction as the result of reinforcement, both by the addictive properties of the drug itself, mediated through intracerebral neurotransmitters, and by the reinforcing effect of anxiety reduction. One powerful tool the psychotherapist has for controlling drug use is to increase the probability of behavior incompatible with drug use (Kurland, 1977).

Greenspan (1977) discusses an integrative approach, the "psychoanalytic learning model." This model emphasizes understanding that environmental determinants have specific effects, depending on the structure of the personality, on the formulation and maintenance of maladaptive behavior patterns. In this model, external experiences are defined in terms "of classes of discriminative stimuli and reinforcers which are derived from stage-specific organizations of the ego and drives."

The art therapist provides a setting in which both psychic and interpersonal behaviors can be safely tried out. The art therapist allows these perceptions and behaviors to occur within the group, but primarily on paper, where trial of new behaviors is without risk. Clients commonly move along a continuum toward healthy behaviors in a series of small steps. Wurmser (1977) has listed a number of minimum and necessary requirements for safe group process in order to establish a basis for effective therapy. How art therapy group rules are structured to meet these criteria are presented in Table 1.

Table 1. Summary of Wurmser's (1977) Criteria for Safe Group Process and Description of How Art Therapy Group Rules Meet These Criteria

Wurmser's Criteria for Minimum and Necessary Requirements for Safe Group Process	Art Therapy Group Rules Meeting These Criteria
Provide nurturing support.	Approval is for trying; whatever the client does on paper is appreciated.
Avoid engulfment.	The art therapist does not get involved with meeting the needs of the patient personally...only by supplying the art materials.
Avoid intrusiveness.	The client is invited to share, but is never pressured.
Maintain distance.	Contact is limited to supplying art materials and direction, and to listening to the meaning of the work.
Avoid supporting the sense of abandonment and despair.	The invitation to share feelings is an open one, often repeated and often accepted. Negative feelings are only acknowledged, never given reinforcement.
Allow symbiotic conflicts to be expressed and to become interpretable.	The drawings are full of such conflicts, expressed in a form that allows the client to see them and to interpret them for himself.
The patient must not feel exploited and treated as a nonhuman object.	The art therapist is not authoritative but is facilitative. In addition, she or he can share her own drawings and identify with those of clients, if appropriate.

Table 1 (continued).

Wurmer's Criteria for Mimimum and Necessary Requirements for Safe Group Process	Art Therapy Group Rules Meeting These Criteria
Clients who are claustrophobic and fear engulfment need more space and time in which to develop trust.	No demands are made; the clients draw and share at their own rate.
Clients who fear isolation and loneliness need more direct support.	The group situation produces expressions of approval and support whenever the client shows his or her work, filling the need for contact, and reinforcing the production of meaningful art.
Limit setting and external structure without moralistic implication.	Acting out happens on paper. When acting out disrupts group activity, group (not therapist) sanctions occur.
Avoid countertransference, punishment, or indulgence.	A skillful leader used the group to deal with deviations from group norms, and non-confrontation to extinguish sociopathic behavior.
Handle demands for giving and indulgence.	In the art therapy setting each client is responsible for his or her own art product and behavior.
Tolerate a therapeutic moratorium until thrust is built up.	What the client does is entirely up to the client; the therapist gives an open-ended invitation.
Show respect for the client.	Art therapists give respect and admiration to the client for willingness to draw and to share, and appreciation for the creativity and imagination shown by the drug addict.

Table 1 (continued).

Wurmer's Criteria for Mimimun and Necessary Requirements for Safe Group Process	Art Therapy Group Rules Meeting These Criteria
Hope	Hope is realistic, based on observation by clients of perceptible progress in achieving goals.
A working alliance: encouraging the cooperation of that part of the client willing to experience pain in order to improve. ("In most instances these patients are too sick, too self-destructive, too demanding to leave much room for such rational cooperation" [Wurmser, 1977, P. 69].)	Art therapy encourages that part of the client that becomes fascinated by the process of transforming feelings into art. This occurs easily and commonly in art therapy with drug addicts.

Behaviors thought to be conducive to avoiding drug dependency are positively reinforced. The reinforcements used are therapist approval, group approval, and self approval. Behaviors leading to drug dependency are extinguished by nonreinforcement. Wurmser has described some important defense mechanisms and defensive behaviors characteristic of drug abusers, which he contends represent the addict's search for effective defenses against unmanageable affects and intense destructive wishes. These defensive behaviors, or operants, with therapeutic goals and the art therapy approach are presented in Table 2.

ART THERAPY OF DRUG ABUSERS

Such defensive maneuvers and the use of drugs are the client's attempts to ameliorate the painful affects associated with the psychopathology. Psychotherapy attempts to help the client work through conflicts and improve coping abilities in order to reduce the affect to a point where the use of drugs is not as compelling. The following summarizes some of the more important psychodynamic concepts of the psychopathology of drug abusers, with therapy goals and the specific contributions that can be made by art therapy. The following interpretations are summarized from Adams, Krystal and Raskin, Kurland, Kohut, Khantzian, and Wurmser.

Most analysts seem to agree that the major problem of many drug abusers is that of fixations at a pre-oedipal stage, with a narcissistic conflict over the inability to incorporate a perception of a good mother; the mother object is instead external, and because of exper-

Table 2. The Art Therapy Approach in Attaining Therapeutic Goals in Treatment of Drug Abusers in Terms of Wurmser's (1977) Operants and Therapeutic Goals

Operants	Therapeutic Goals	The Art Therapy Approach
Avoidance mechanisms, especially denial and rationalization.	To allow the use of these and other defenses listed, and even to have them appreciated; however, they are clarified so that they come under the client's control, to be used as necessary, rather than reflexively.	Even with his or her art production before him or her, the client can still choose not to "see" the manifest or symbolic content; yet it is there when he or she is ready to look at it. The client is in charge of the timing.
Averting of attention.	Learning to focus attention in one place for prolonged periods of time.	Art can, and does, become totally engrossing.
Dissociation, breaking of connections, splitting, fragmentation.	To make manifest and to integrate the various sequestered and compartmentalized parts of the self gradually.	The visual perception of the graphic representation of these various parts (e.g., on different or same piece of paper, on different or same day) leads to a strong force to pull the various parts together. A typical exercise is to have the clients draw different animals (different parts of the self) walking down a road together talking. This also occurs with spontaneous drawings.
Externalizing, projecting.	To take responsibility for owning one's own psychodynamic mechanisms, in order to gain control over them.	The client is invited and encouraged to project onto paper. This is done easily because

Table 2 (continued).

Operants	Therapeutic Goals	The Art Therapy Approach
		it makes use of the client's need to disown and project. But then he or she is required as an integral part of the process to write a description of the art product "as though he were that object." In this way, he or she takes it back into himself.
Provoking, inviting retaliation, risking, transgressing. Testing limits of permission and caring of the world to prove to oneself that it doesn't care.	To be able to accept the limits of the world, and to set one's own limits realistically, without having to act out one's own aggressive-guilt-masochistic needs.	Art therapy allows full expression of these behaviors and feelings...on paper, which never gets provoked, never retaliates, rarely gets injured. If the therapist can avoid an open confrontation prematurely, the group can generally, with peer pressure, deal with the situation.
Using drugs to deal with the intense negative feelings induced by stress.	To find another, better way of handling stress.	Art is a traditional way of discharging affect harmlessly, and can itself help resolve the conflicts that precede the affect. An art journal used regularly to record feelings about stressful events can become a substitute harmless addiction.

iences in the oral stage, seen as withholding. Freud did not find therapy useful in narcissism, and, indeed, therapy of drug addicts has not been overwhelmingly successful; but perhaps art therapy has something significant of offer.

Once difficulty in therapy is that of affect regression. Feelings become suddenly and irresistibly overwhelming and out of control (Wurmser, 1977). Drug abusers have poor control over feelings and difficulty controlling impulses (Kurland, 1977). The therapeutic goal is to develop the ability to express, channel, and control these feelings without being frightened by them.

In art therapy, these feelings are recognized by the use of colors, and by deficient line containment of the more disturbing colors; by the manifest cognitive content and by the symbolic meaning; by the behavior of the client as he or she draws, or as he or she describes the content; and, in a negative way, by the extent to which he or she avoids appropriate interpretations.

The art therapist encourages the expression of these feelings in pictures, in which the appropriate materials and colors encourage control by superimposing line drawings over and around unconfined colors; by verbalization about the emotion-laden drawings by the client at a rate compatible with control by the client. The skilled art therapist can encourage or decrease the expression of feelings as appropriate, i.e., as the client can gain control over them.

Because these narcissistic needs depend on outside objects for fulfillment, there are repeated episodes of failure to get needs met. This results in despair, depression, disappointment, disillusionment, and low self-esteem. The drug abuser needs to experience success, and to feel confidence.

In art therapy, every picture is a success because the client can always express something on paper; it is a fail-proof situation. On paper, also he or she can get whatever he or she wants, symbolically, and can experience the same good feelings he or she would have in actuality.

Narcissistic dependence on outside objects leads to manipulative behavior to achieve control, which is often expressed socially as charm and as lack of respect for those so conned.

The drug abuser can learn to relate more authentically through art therapy. Superficial charming pictures with little or no emotional content are, by comparison with others in the group, obviously inauthentic. Group and therapist approval is for authentic expression of real feelings. This becomes the group norm within several sessions.

Fear of loss of control of the object relationship can lead to excessive control over others. This is manifested in compulsive attempts to direct the behaviors of others, and valuing objective symbols of being given to, as with material possessions. Coupled with an introjected bad mother image, and with superego accusations, this fear may be turned inward toward compulsive control and evaluation of one's own behavior.

In the art therapy experience, this is manifested by an excessive attention to the value of the art product, which is then tight, rigid, controlled. The art therapist then will emphasize the process and deemphasize the drawing itself as object, and will allow less controllable media, such as water colors and clay.

Actual loss of control, coupled with reduced satisfaction of needs often causes depression in drug abusers, sometimes intense, with a feeling of going downhill, helplessness, and giving up. There are overt suicide attempts. In the narcissistic drug abuser, the loss that is central to the depression was that of a relationship with a parent during the oral stage.

The issue of loss is best raised in art therapy by having the clients draw pictures of parents, and dealing with the feelings aroused nonverbally through the art. Verbal expressions are also encouraged. The entire question of family relationships is also approached by drawings of families...and these are usually evocative of much feeling (Kwiatkowska, 1978; Rubin, 1978; Wadeson, 1980).

The drug abuser has an unrealistic fantasy for total caretaking by the mother object to meet his or her infantile needs. In some, this is expressed as a desire for warmth, union and protection. In others, failure to have these needs met results in psychological distancing, alienation, and impairment in the capacity for establishing close relationships.

The art therapy group supplies a group in which each client can find out what he needs for her- or himself. It has a caring atmosphere, without demand, and without a mechanism for manipulation, since the focus is on the art process. The client therefore can relate closely with others and accept the available caring (which is never excessive because of the preoccupation with drawing), or can work only on the drawing without relating, if that is his or her need at the time.

Since others are only objects for filling one's own needs, drug abusers are isolated from emotional contact with others. They often have a sense of loneliness, of not being in touch with their feelings, of distance from reality.

Art therapy allows a remarkable avenue of establishing contact with others because of the similarity of concepts and feelings expressed in the art work of drug abusers. By identifying with the products of others, and by having them identify with one's own, a communication of feelings begins.

"The major conflicts of the sociopathic, narcissistic drug-abusing patient are around aggression and guilt" (Adams, 1978, P. 295). "The sociopath is tormented by (unconscious) guilt precisely because of a superego that is overly severe and punishing" (Adams, 1978, P. 291). "The patient does not feel he is worthy of love and 'loving' him increases his guilt and his propensity to act out. The sense of guilt and subsequent seeking of condemnation and punishment constitutes the sociopath's 'masochistic search' as reflected in his battle with authority" (Adams, 1978, P. 295). The goal of therapy is to match feelings and thoughts with the words that describe them; to discharge impounded frustration--aggression" safely; and to "externalize the punishing superego," with reintrojection of a healthier superego (Adams, 1978, P. 295).

When pictures are produces that have content of guilt, shame, and aggression (which is frequent), they are verbally described by the client, and then reproduced with as much color and content as the client is comfortable with, until he or she becomes comfortable with and even bored by them. The affect, in this way, extinguishes. When good figures are produced, they also are discussed and admired. The good feelings are taken in as the client identifies with them in the Gestalt manner. In the art therapy situation, all such emotions can be expressed freely on paper, safely; or at least, the client can in time grow to feel safe, and can allow the expression of these feelings at a rate and in a manner with which he or she feels safe. Instead of aversive consequences, disclosures are met with appreciation and respect.

The drug addict is usually confused about hir or her psychodynamic mechanisms and own personal identity. This identification is likely to be totally that of an "addict," "parolee," "ward of the court," "sick," or experimental subject.

Through their artwork, drug abusers gradually gain a visual sense of identity since they have learned to demonstrate to themselves through experience with the art materials that "what you draw is who you are." They come to identify themselves as a "right brain person in a left brain world" (Virshup) which then can live with comfortably, since it is descriptive without being condemnatory.

Drug abusers usually have low self esteem. In addition to confusion about their personal identity, they have a tendency to devalue what they do know. They are crushed by the slightest disappointment concerning self concept. Although preoccupied with material accomplishments, they have few, if any. By virtue of being in a rehabilitation unit, they have even failed in being good drug addicts. They therefore need to acquire some sense of identity for which they can feel pride.

Drug abusers are often imaginative and creative, qualities they haven't used constructively. When they come to value their art products, they are valuing themselves in a very real sense and their self-image begins to improve. Since a good self-image is necessary to be constructive and productive out in the world, they are likely to enter a gradually improving spiral.

The drug abuser is often regressed to or fixated at a pregenital stage of development. Sexual ambiguity, homosexuality, fear of homosexuality are not uncommon. Marital difficulties and estrangement are frequently found. Sex is seen as something to receive rather than to give. Women often become prostitutes and there are some who, like their own mothers, become child abusers.

Many client pictures attest to the progressively improved sexuality of the clients.

Many drug abusers are relatively nonverbal. They complain of an inability to communicate internal distress through meaningful verbalization. They feel a need to be heard, understood, and paid attention to, but are without the means for expressing the need. It may be that the drug abuser is often an introvert. Certainly morphine given to drug abusers made them more introverted while at the same time making them feel more normal.

Much artwork is a cry of distress and for help that can be easily read by those familiar with the language. It is a language that drug abusers seem to learn easily. It may be for them the optimum medium for communication. Many drug abusers either have interests in the arts, or avidly acquire them when exposed.

Anxiety, often without affective awareness, and often accompanied by depersonalization, is common in drug abusers. They daily relive dreams of terror over helplessness and worthlessness of the self. It may be related to undischarged drives and to danger of psychic disorganization. There may be an element of fear of expressing or acting out uncontrollable anger or of sexual excitement. There may be anxiety about the failure to meet real needs or narcissistic needs (Krystal & Raskin, 1970). Such fears and anxieties may persist until there is self-awareness, self-understanding, emotional reeducation, and personality integration (Adams, 1978). However, having regular dependable relationships with commitment and altering the cognitive and emotional expectation of loss or desertion were effective in an outcome study (Pickens and Heston, 1979).

In addition to the trust and security of the commitment by the art therapist, anxiety can be reduced by reexperiencing the anxiety-producing situation in imagery, allowing extinction of the anxiety response in an atmosphere of safety and caring. Often it seems that it is enough to bring out into the open the behaviors or blocked feelings that have interfered with their emotional growth process. They then become more integrated, more responsible, happier, and better able to cope with the many frustrations of growing up in their worlds.

Narcotics are not just ways of reducing psychic pain. They also induce euphoria. Experimental animals will choose, and work for, euphoria-producing drugs. The rush of intravenous heroin has been described as a sensation different from and better than sexual orgasm. Abstinence programs that do not include some substitute gratification do not keep the clients in therapy; the number that complete treatment is dismally small. When a substitute gratification is included, the number finishing therapy increases markedly.

"In the course of his art work...(he) may have a stirring experience, at once physical, rational, and emotional. Physically, the experience will produce a quickened or slowed heartbeat, a rush of sweat; a lump or dryness in the throat; tears, blush or pallor; a sensation in the area between the heart and the stomach; a weakness in the knees, changes in the pupils, or changes in speech and tone of voice. Emotionally, the experience will touch the person's inner core." (Betensky, 1973, P. 333)

Art itself can be an addiction, but it is a safe substitute for narcotics, and leads to growth and increased self esteem.

REFERENCES

Adams, J. W. Psychoanalysis of drug dependence. New York: Grune & Stratton, 1978.

Betensky, M. Self-discovery through self-expression. Springfield, Illinois: Thomas, 1973.

Gazzaniga, M., and LeDoux, J. The Integrated mind. New York: Plenum, 1978.

Greenspan, S. Substance abuse: An understanding from psychoanalytic, developmental, and learning perspectives. In J. D. Blaine and D. A. Julius (Eds.), Psychodynamics of drug dependence (National Institute of Drug Abuse Research Monograph No. 12). Washington, D.C.: Department of Health, Education, and Welfare, 1977.

Khantzian, E., and Treece, C. Psychodynamics of Drug Dependence: An Overview. In J. D. Blaine and D. A. Julius (Eds.),

Psychodynamics of drug dependence (National Institute of Drug Abuse Research Monograph No. 12). Washington, D.C.: Department of Health, Education, and Welfare, 1977.

Kohut, H. Preface. In J. D. Blaine and D. A. Julius (Eds.), Psychodynamics of drug dependence (National Institute of Drug Abuse Research Monograph No. 12). Washington, D.C.: Department of Health, Education, and Welfare, 1977.

Krystal, H., and Raskin, H. Drug dependence. Detroit: Wayne State University Press, 1970.

Kurland, A. A. Psychiatric aspects of opiate dependence. West Palm Beach, Florida: CRC Press, 1978.

Kwiatkowska, H. Family therapy and evaluation through art. Springfield, Illinois: Thomas, 1978.

Pickens, R. W., and Heston, L. L. Psychiatric factors in drug abuse. New York: Grune and Stratton, 1979.

Rhyne, J. The Gestalt art experience. Stockton, California: Brooks/Cole, 1974.

Rubin, J. Child art therapy. New York: Van Nostrand Reinhold, 1978.

Ulman, E. Art education for the emotionally disturbed. American Journal of Art Therapy, 1977, 17, 13-16.

Virshup, E. Right brain people in a left brain world. Los Angeles, California: Guild of Tutors Press, 1978.

Wadeson, H. Art psychotherapy. New York: Wiley, 1980.

Wurmser, L. Mr. Pecksniff's Horse? (Psychodynamics in Compulsive Drug Use.) In J. D. Blaine and D. A. Julius (Eds.), Psychodynamics of drug dependence (National Institute of Drug Abuse Research Monograph No. 12). Washington, D.C.: Department of Health, Education, and Welfare, 1977.

CONTRIBUTORS

Merrill Anderson
Houston Cardiovascular
Rehabilitation Center
6418 Fannin Street
Houston, Texas 77030

James C. Ascough
Psychological Service
American Lake Veterans
Administration Hospital
Tacoma, Washington 98493

Paul Bakan
Psychology Department
Simon Fraser University
Burnaby, British Columbia
Canada V5A 1S6

Theodore X. Barber
Cushing Hospital
P. O. Box 190
Framingham, Massachusetts 01701

Martha Campbell
Route #1, Box 230
Mackinow, Illinois 61755

Erma Dosamantes-Alperson
Department of Dance
University of California at
Los Angeles
Los Angeles, California 90024

Albert R. Gilgen
University of Northern Iowa
Department of Psychology
Cedar Falls, IA 50613

William Glackman
Psychology Department
Simon Fraser University
Burnaby, British Columbia
Canada V5A 1S6

Larry Greeson
Department of Educational
Psychology
Miami University
Oxford, Ohio 45056

Ruey-Yun Horng
University of Georgia
Department of Educational
Psychology
Athens, Georgia 30602

Alvin Enis House
Psychology Department
Illinois State University
Normal, Illinois 61761

Eric Klinger
Division of Social Sciences
University of Minnesota, Morris
Morris, Minnesota 56267

Don Kuiken
Department of Psychology
University of Alberta
Edmonton
Canada T6G 2E9

Audrey M. Kuna
1113 Draper's Meadow W.
Blacksburg, Virginia 24060

Charles J. List
Department of Philosophy
State University of New York
College at Plattsburgh
Plattsburgh, New York 12901

Thomas Mallouk
Crozer-Chester Medical Center
Community Mental Health Center
Chester, Pennsylvania

Susan Mason
Psychology Department
Niagara University
Niagara University, New York
14109

James K. Morrison
678 Troy-Schenectady Road
Latham, New York 12110

Donald J. Polzella
Department of Psychology
University of Dayton
Dayton, Ohio 45469

Frank J. Prerost
Department of Psychology
Western Illinois University
Macomb, Illinois 61455

Charles M. Rader
Arnold Vinson & Associates
163 North Lexington Parkway
St. Paul, Minnesota 55104

Howard M. Rhoades
Department of Psychology
Rice University
Houston, Texas 77001

David Sarnoff
Department of Educational
Pyschology and Counseling
University of Kentucky
Lexington, Kentucky 40506

Dennis M. Senchuk
School of Education
Indiana University
Bloomington, Indiana 47405

Joseph E. Shorr
Institute for Psycho-Imagination
Therapy
580 S. San Vicente Boulevard
Los Angeles, California 90048

Jerome L. Singer
Department of Psychology, Box 11A
Yale University
New Haven, Connecticut 06520

Nicholas P. Spanos
Department of Psychology
Carleton University
Colonel By Drive
Ottawa
Canada K1S 5B6

Dee Spring
The Woman's Center
516 North Placentia Avenue
Placentia, California 92670

Kirk Strohsahl
Department of Psychological Sciences
Purdue University
West Lafayette, Indiana 47907

Auke Tellegen
Department of Psychology
University of Minnesota
75 East River Road
Minneapolis, Minnesota 55455

Dan Tomasulo
Brookdale Community College
Newman Springs Road
Lincroft, New Jersey 07738

Roni Beth Tower
Department of Psychology
Yale University
New Haven, Connecticut 06520

Paul E. VanWyke
William S. Hall Psychiatric Institute
University of South Carolina
Columbia, South Carolina 29202

Bernard Virshup
4900 Dunman Avenue
Woodland Hills, California 91364

Evelyn Virshup
4900 Dunman Avenue
Woodland Hills, California 91364

Sheryl C. Wilson
Cushing Hospital
Box 190
Framingham, Massachusetts 01701

INDEX

MIX
Papier aus verantwortungsvollen Quellen
Paper from responsible sources
FSC® C105338

If you have any concerns about our products,
you can contact us on
ProductSafety@springernature.com

In case Publisher is established outside the EU,
the EU authorized representative is:
Springer Nature Customer Service Center GmbH
Europaplatz 3, 69115 Heidelberg, Germany

Printed by Libri Plureos GmbH
in Hamburg, Germany